HEARD MELODIES ARE SWEET

HEARD MELODIES ARE SWEET

A History of the London Philharmonic Orchestra

Edmund Pirouet

Heard melodies are sweet, but those unheard
Are sweeter; therefore ye soft pipes play on.
                    Keats, *Ode on a Grecian Urn*

The Book Guild Ltd
Sussex, England

This book is sold subject to the condition that it shall not, by way of trade or otherwise, be lent, re-sold, hired out, photocopied or held in any retrieval system or otherwise circulated without the publisher's prior consent in any form of binding or cover other than that in which this is published and without a similar condition including this condition being imposed on the subsequent purchaser.

The Book Guild Ltd,
25 High Street,
Lewes, Sussex

First published 1998
© Edmund Pirouet, 1998

Set in Times
Typesetting by Poole Typesetting (Wessex) Ltd, Bournemouth

Printed in Great Britain by
Bookcraft (Bath) Ltd, Avon

A catalogue record for this book is
available from the British Library

ISBN 1 85776 381 5

CONTENTS

Foreword		vii
Introduction and Acknowledgements		ix
1	Birth Pangs	1
2	Pre-War 1932–39	9
3	The Phoney War 1939–40	23
4	Blitzkrieg, Priestley and Hylton 1940	32
5	Tours and Tribulations 1940–42	40
6	The King Returns 1942–44	51
7	Competition 1945	61
8	Guests 1945–49	68
9	Eduard van Beinum 1949–50	80
10	Sir Adrian Boult 1950–57	91
11	Interregnum and William Steinberg 1957–60	117
12	John Pritchard – A Changing Scene 1960–66	127
13	Bernard Haitink – Years of Achievement 1967–72	138
14	Haitink – The Later Years 1972–79	152
15	Sir George Solti and the Fiftieth Anniversary 1979–83	168
16	Klaus Tennstedt 1983–87	179
17	From Rumour to Residency 1988–90	195
18	Homecoming? 1990–93	205

19	Hoffmann and After 1993–96	217
20	Towards the Millennium 1996–98	227
	Appendix A Principal Conductors and Leaders	238
	Appendix B Out-of-Town Concerts 1947–48 to 1951–52	239
	Appendix C Education	240
	Appendix D Selected Concert Programmes	243
	Bibliography	255
	Index	257

FOREWORD

From the time of its formation by Sir Thomas Beecham, the London Philharmonic has always played a central role in the orchestral life of London. As this book shows, it is a story that has not been without its ups and downs. The last chapter quotes some words written in 1952 by the then Chairman and Managing Director, Thomas Russell:

> 'It can be shown that we are spending too much or too little on music; too much for those who think concert-goers should pay for their own pleasures; too little for those who believe in cultural values and who want to see our standards of performance and listening raised to the highest international level. Our national mind has never been made up on whether the symphony orchestra is a necessity or a luxury. We keep our orchestras barely in existence, with no reserves to call upon and at the mercy of adverse happenings. Artistic policy is always hampered and continuity threatened. If symphony orchestras are to be finally regarded as a luxury, then it is evident that, in our straitened circumstances, it is one we cannot afford. If, on the other hand they are a cultural necessity to a civilised nation, then we must ensure the survival of their finest qualities, in spite of heavy national expenditure in other directions.'

These prophetic words show that despite attempts by successive governments to deal responsibly with the Arts, very little has changed over the years. Yet despite the numerous problems faced by the orchestra, some of which seem no nearer a solution than they were half a century ago, one of the themes which runs throughout the book is the determination shown by successive generations of musicians who, from the time, shortly after the outbreak of the Second World War, when the orchestra of the day took the courageous step of assuming responsibility for running their own affairs, have always striven to maintain the highest standard of excellence.

As a member of the London Philharmonic for the past twenty-three years, I am proud to be part of this great tradition, to have the privilege of working with such a highly dedicated group of professional musicians, and to have been so closely associated with many of the great conductors and artists of the day.

Undoubtedly we face a challenging future. I am however confident that as we approach the dawn of a new century it will be our privilege to continue offering the London public music making that is vital, exciting and stimulating.

Bob St. John Wright
Chairman of The London Philharmonic Orchestra

INTRODUCTION AND ACKNOWLEDGEMENTS

Thomas Russell's book, *Philharmonic Decade*, published during the Second World War, told the story of the early years of the London Philharmonic, though Russell dealt with the formation of the orchestra in somewhat sketchy fashion, being more concerned with developments from the time when, shortly after the start of the war, the players assumed responsibility for the LPO's affairs. Subsequently the fiftieth anniversary was marked by a photographic record, edited by Jerrold Northrop Moore, but inevitably the format limited the linking narrative to a brief outline of events. This book sets out to try and tell the story in greater detail, unravelling the long train of events leading up to its formation, and delving into the unhappy chapter of events arising from the London County Council's decision not to appoint the London Philharmonic as resident orchestra at the time of the Royal Festival Hall's opening in 1951.

A book such as this could not have been written without the willing co-operation of many people, including members of the orchestra past and present, and its administrative staff. I am grateful to Bob St. J. Wright, the Chairman, and his fellow Directors, for allowing this intrusion into the orchestra's affairs, for giving me access to their files and permission to quote from the orchestra's house magazine, *Philharmonic Post*, and other publications. Of those working at 35 Doughty Street, I owe special thanks to Frances Cook, who introduced me to the archives, press cuttings, and other historical documents: to James Grigor and David Laughton for advice on financial matters, and Elaine Steabler in the press office for background information about current events. Others who assisted in ways great and small include Dawn Day, Donald Keys, Louise Mitchell, Melinda Morley, Fiona Putnam, Meredith Schilling and Elizabeth Soussi. John Amis and Felix Aprahamian, who worked for the LPO during the war, talked freely about those days; Philip Stuart provided details of the LPO's first recording sessions; Glyndebourne's Head of Press and Public Relations, Helen O'Neill, responded to my enquiries about the design of the new opera house and construction of its orchestra pit. Rosalie Cody, for many years the Concerts Director, produced some vintage wartime programmes, and Michael Goold, a fount of knowledge about the wartime activities of Britain's orchestras, provided a schedule of the concerts given by the LPO between 1939 and 1945, together with much background information. Paul Collins of the Royal College of Music allowed me access to their archive of concert programmes. Franz Welser-Möst reviewed the residency as seen from the rostrum, and many past and present players gave willingly of their time, notably Nicholas Busch, Simon Channing, Celia Chambers, Michael Boyle, Bill Cody, Wrayburn Glasspool, Josephine St Leon and Bob St. J. Wright. The manuscript was read in whole or in part by Celia Chambers, Nicholas Busch, Bob St. J. Wright and Laurence Watt, all of whom offered valuable advice and numerous insights. I am also indebted to my wife, for coping with my absorption with the subject and for her practical suggestions on ways of clarifying the parts of the narrative. A list of sources is given in the bibliography. Readers can speculate on the relevance of *Wisden's Cricketers Almanacs* for 1941 and 1947.

Like many of my generation I first heard the LPO in the early post-war years, when they performed throughout the suburbs of London and in many provincial towns and cities, retaining from those days a special regard for this orchestra. This book is therefore dedicated, with gratitude, to the spirit of London Philharmonic past, the members of London Philharmonic present, and the prospect of London Philharmonic yet to come.

1

Birth Pangs

The London Philharmonic Orchestra made its public debut on 7 October 1932, at the opening concert of the Royal Philharmonic Society's 121st season. The complex chain of events leading up to its birth was, however, a long-drawn-out process, whose roots lay in the chaotic orchestral scene which existed in London.

Despite the longevity of many of our musical institutions – the Royal Philharmonic Society was founded in March 1813 – until 1930 this country had no fully permanent symphony orchestra. The nearest equivalent was the Queen's Hall Orchestra, conducted by Sir Henry Wood. However, even after Wood's manager, Robert Newman, outlawed the deputy system, which allowed players who found a more lucrative engagement to send someone else to take their place, this orchestra fell short of providing its members with full-time employment. Though abolition of the deputy system gave Wood and Newman first call on their services, the musicians were only paid for rehearsals and concerts at which they performed, and with many blank days and weeks in the calendar, they had to supplement their income from other sources.

Nor was the London Symphony Orchestra (the LSO), formed in 1904, in any sense full-time. Formed by members of the Queen's Hall Orchestra who objected to the restrictions imposed by Newman's refusal to allow continuation of the deputy system, the LSO performed under many distinguished musicians, but the nature of its formation, based on the players' desire to retain freedom of action, meant its members were to be found in the ranks of other orchestras which performed on an irregular basis, including the orchestra of the Royal Philharmonic Society, the Royal Albert Hall Orchestra, and the orchestra of the Royal Opera House.

Outside London there were orchestras in Birmingham, Glasgow and Manchester, and in several seaside resorts and spa towns. Of these, the Bournemouth Municipal Orchestra, formed in 1893, was employed all the year round, but until the late 1930s, when the band was enlarged to symphonic proportions, it numbered less than fifty players, forcing its conductor Sir Dan Godfrey to compromise, redistributing parts written for some instruments to other sections of the orchestra, or omitting them altogether. In any event the weekly symphony concerts were only part of the orchestra's workload: much of its time was spent playing music of a lighter nature: Godfrey's orchestra can hardly be rated a symphony orchestra.

The activities of the other provincial orchestras were limited to the winter months. Sir Charles Hallé and his successors may not have been afflicted by the deputy system, but suffered from the fact that the orchestra came together for less than half the year. Manchester's season lasted from part-way through October until late March and, like the Queen's Hall Orchestra, the players were only paid performance by performance. They too had to find other ways of boosting their income. The Birmingham orchestra, founded in 1920, was also employed seasonally, as was the Scottish Orchestra, with the season in Scotland even shorter, from November until February, a situation unchanged until the Second World War when, in the face of a boom in the demand for concerts, it was extended from three to six months. During the summer the musicians dispersed around the country, many playing in the municipal orchestras employed by, among others, Eastbourne, Hastings, Scarborough, and Torquay. When autumn came and the provincial orchestras re-assembled, it could take time before they again played as disciplined ensembles.

The impetus for creation of a full-time orchestra in London began with the advent of broadcasting, music playing an important part in the output of the newly formed British Broadcasting Company. Initially many musicians and managements were hostile, fearful that broadcasting would adversely affect public concerts, among them William Boosey of Chappell's, the leaseholders of Queen's Hall, who would not allow the BBC to broadcast from that venue. In March 1927, shortly after the BBC became a Corporation, Chappell's, who spent heavily on the Proms and the winter activities of Wood's orchestra, announced that they could no longer afford to do so. Faced with the prospect of an empty hall, Boosey, who had been in the forefront of those opposed to broadcast music, smartly changed his position. Under an agreement between Boosey and the BBC, the Corporation assumed responsibility for the Proms, and was given the right to promote concerts in Queen's Hall during the winter. Wood, whose contract with Chappell's prevented him from broadcasting, was given the luxury of daily rehearsals – until then three rehearsals sufficed for each week's concerts – but Chappell's would not release the orchestra's title, and for three years the Proms were given by 'Sir Henry Wood and his Symphony Orchestra'.

The BBC first gave public concerts in 1924, using the Central Hall, Westminster and the Royal Opera House. The playing of the 'National Orchestra' recruited for these concerts fell short of the adventurous programming, its shortcomings underlined by the Hallé Orchestra, under Sir Hamilton Harty, who on their periodic visits to Queen's Hall 'played the pants off' their London rivals. There were also external comparisons at work. Walter Damrosch and the New York Symphony Orchestra visited London in 1924, demonstrating playing of a higher calibre than anything being achieved in the capital, as did Wilhelm Fürtwangler and the Berlin Philharmonic three years later. These comparisons were disheartening. Measured against the Berlin and New York orchestras, none of those in London were in the second rank, let alone the first, and the BBC in particular came in for much hostile criticism. The weight of criticism directed at the BBC was a powerful stimulus to the management of the infant Corporation. Sir John Reith, the Director-General, Roger Eckersley, the Director of Programmes, and Percy Pitt, the Director of Music, determined to rid themselves of this slur on its reputation, with the formation of a new orchestra seen as the solution to their problems.

At much the same time Sir Thomas Beecham concluded that a new orchestra was necessary to the realisation of his ambitions, envisaging himself as Musical Director and Principal Conductor. Some of the finest playing heard in London came from his pre-war Beecham Symphony Orchestra, which made its debut in 1909 and was in the pit for opera seasons promoted by Beecham and financed by his father, seasons of considerable brilliance, introducing a string of works by contemporary composers, including *Electra, Der Rosenkavalier* and *Salome*. If the last-named shocked the sensibilities of some, it was not at the expense of the box office.

Though the First World War put paid to Beecham's orchestra, he did much to ensure that the Hallé Orchestra, the LSO and the Royal Philharmonic Society stayed afloat. However, from 1919 until 1923 he was fully occupied in dealing with a complicated settlement of his father's estate. In the meantime the Hallé Concert Society appointed Sir Hamilton Harty their conductor, and even after Beecham's return to musical activity, the Royal Philharmonic Society, mindful of the terms imposed on them in 1916 in return for saving them from closure, were disinclined to engage him. In addition to being appointed a Director, Beecham insisted on chairing every meeting he attended, that his secretary Donald Baylis should fill the vacant post of honorary secretary, and that he and Baylis should be responsible for the choice of programmes and recruitment of the orchestra. If the Society were grateful for his rescue act, it must have been a relief to them to regain control of their affairs. It was 1928 before Beecham again conducted one of their concerts.

Of all the conductors appearing before the public Beecham's name almost certainly carried more weight than any other, and in March 1928 Sir Landon Ronald, Principal of the Guildhall School of Music and Drama, approached the BBC on his behalf, suggesting they co-operate in the formation of a new orchestra. It would have been a feather in the BBC's cap to have given London an orchestra with Beecham at its head, and though Beecham had from time to time expressed himself forcibly on the subject of broadcasting, from past experience his public utterances were to be taken with a pinch of salt. The BBC therefore felt justified in opening negotiations with him.

From the outset the BBC found these fraught with difficulty. There was always a gulf between the optimistic estimates prepared by Beecham and his associates and the BBC's own figures, while it was impossible to keep the details confidential. There was no way of stopping Beecham talking, as he saw fit, to other interested parties and to the press. Apart from difficulties arising from the lack of confidentiality, the BBC found Beecham constantly changing his tune, depending on his audience at the time. Often the first the management knew of his latest proposal came from reading their newspapers.

Beecham was anxious to involve the Royal Philharmonic Society in his plans, discussions with the Society on their involvement in the scheme running in parallel with his discussions with the BBC. Using the columns of the *Daily Mail* in which to parade some of his ideas, including the terms on which he proposed the players would be employed, Beecham put forward a wide-ranging scheme to the Royal Philharmonic Society, embracing the Society's own annual series of concerts, which would be much expanded and guaranteed against loss; Sunday afternoon concerts in the Royal Albert Hall; concerts in London's suburbs; provincial concerts, on the lines of tours organised by the London concert agent Lionel Powell; recording sessions for Columbia; and concerts with leading soloists. Quite where the BBC fitted in was far from clear, especially when Beecham subsequently suggested to the Society that all the orchestra's London concerts should be given in their name. There were further uncertainties surrounding the orchestra's title. At first he spoke of it as the London Philharmonic, a little later the *Daily Mail* informed its readers that it was to be the Royal Philharmonic, and at other times it was referred to as the London Orchestra. The title might not have been of great significance, but these twists and turns were indicative of the way Beecham changed his tune as the whim or fancy took him.

Another problem lurking in the background was the figure of Sir Henry Wood who, from long experience, had strong views on the quality of individual London musicians. If the BBC went into partnership with Beecham, using the orchestra for the Proms, there was a possibility of quibbles from Wood as to its make-up. Moreover, since it was widely known that Beecham's ambitions embraced opera as well as concerts, this opened up another area of uncertainty, with the prospect of conflicting demands for the services of the orchestra. The BBC hoped to form the orchestra in time for the 1929 Proms, but it was impossible to tie Beecham down. By midsummer the BBC's patience had run out, and though it was again necessary to resort to the title 'Sir Henry Wood and his Symphony Orchestra' for the 1929 Proms, the BBC began setting its own plans in motion, offering terms to a nucleus of players and booking Queen's Hall for the winter of 1930–31.

The orchestra which now appeared was the BBC Symphony Orchestra. Percy Pitt stepped down from the BBC as Director of Music, to be succeeded by Adrian Boult, whose conducting of the orchestra earned high praise and an invitation from Sir John Reith to add the post of Chief Conductor to that of Director of Music: Beecham appeared to have been pipped at the post by a rank outsider. For nearly two years his wider plans remained in abeyance and, at least in public, there was no further talk of a new orchestra.

Among those with whom Beecham had discussed his plans were the LSO, suggesting that he would want to employ a sizeable proportion of the orchestra which played for the opera season at Covent Garden, and because that body was largely composed of members of the LSO, this posed a serious threat to the orchestra's independence. Through Beecham gave an assurance that he would do everything possible to allow the LSO to continue its own annual series of concerts, the LSO responded by producing and implementing its own plan, one remarkably similar to the proposals put by Beecham to the Royal Philharmonic Society, including concerts in London and the provinces, opera and recording. The result of these negotiations, carried out quite separately from those between Beecham and the BBC, and involving the London concert agent, Lionel Powell, who was in the Beecham camp during his negotiations with the BBC, enabled the orchestra to draw up a contract providing a nucleus of work for the next three years, with doubts about the LSO's future apparently resolved.

The LSO was fully aware that the advent of the BBC's orchestra would provide what were likely to be unpalatable comparisons. To improve playing standards, the Dutch conductor, Willem Mengelberg, whose concert with the LSO in October 1929 stood out in a season of which the best that could otherwise be said was that the quality of the orchestra's performance was variable, was invited to take charge during 1930–31. He accepted, on condition that the deputy system, already under attack, was finally abolished. It was a timely invitation, for the opening concerts of the BBC Symphony Orchestra were an outstanding success. Nevertheless, despite competition from that source, 1930-31 was artistically and financially successful.

Mengelberg's services were only available for one season, and the following year much of the work was undertaken by Beecham, with equally satisfactory results. There were, however, problems ahead. From set fair the barometer rapidly turned to unsettled. In the knowledge that Beecham had never abandoned his intention of forming a new orchestra, and in view of the number of concerts he was to conduct, the LSO invited him to become a Member, an invitation he accepted, suggesting he should also act as their musical adviser. In November 1931 Beecham outlined new proposals, explaining that he had 'been asked' to form a new orchestra, expressing his wish that this should be the LSO, and asking whether the Board would consider changes in the ranks of the orchestra 'should this be necessary'.

At this point it would appear, at least on the surface, that Beecham was acting in good faith, for it was largely his efforts that averted a serious crisis arising from the death of the orchestra's agent Lionel Powell, whose solicitors were compelled to notify the LSO that his estate could not fulfil any further responsibilities under his contract with them. With the prospect of cancellation of a provincial tour and all the London concerts arranged by Powell, this could have involved players and orchestra in serious financial loss. They were therefore indebted to Beecham, who provided the railway tickets to enable the tour to go ahead, and obtained financial support from the Gramophone Company, as well as from among his own circle of friends. In addition, several of those appearing with the orchestra reduced their fees, or performed for no fee at all, their generosity enabling the LSO to survive without serious damage to its finances.

The LSO was also bending its attention to the problems arising from the necessity of reorganising and strengthening the orchestra's personnel. The Directors and Beecham drew up and exchanged two lists, the first of players whose services should be retained, the second those whose performance was considered unsatisfactory. The lists prepared by each side were not an exact match, but there was a considerable degree of unanimity, although adoption of either, or any compromise, would have led to substantial changes. But, unknown to them, steps were being taken which were to frustrate their ambitions, for behind the scenes Beecham and his cohorts were drawing up plans for a new orchestra, securing many engagements the LSO must have believed were their prerogative. By May 1932 it was possible to inform the Royal Philharmonic Society that the Courtauld-Sargent Concerts, a provincial tour organised by Harold Holt, Powell's partner, who headed the successor firm of Harold Holt Limited, and gramophone sessions had been secured or promised to the new orchestra, and the Society decided to abandon its long-established practice of recruiting its own, opting instead to engage Beecham's, a further fillip for Beecham and his backers.

The LSO learned of what might be afoot when Malcolm Sargent, who was closely involved with Beecham, informed two of the Directors, John Alexandra and Anthony Collins, that Beecham's backers considered the Board of the LSO to be unnecessary. They were briefly reassured when, at a meeting instigated by Harold Holt, they were told no firm decisions had been reached, but this reassurance was short-lived. Almost immediately a letter was received from Holt, stating there would be no further negotiations with the LSO, which 'had lost most of its former prestige, and no longer commanded the confidence of the public'. Collins went to see Beecham, who admitted dictating the letter sent by Holt, telling Collins it was his view that the LSO should be involved in the new scheme, but his Board did not share his opinion. Doubts as to Beecham's intentions were intensified when Sargent tried to cancel the LSO's engagement for the Patrons' Fund Rehearsal of the Royal College of Music, proposing that the new orchestra should be engaged in the LSO's stead. Lingering hopes that the LSO would feature in Beecham's plans were all but extinguished, and negotiations with him petered out.

It is impossible to determine with certainty the real cause of the breakdown between Beecham and the LSO, especially when they were apparently in broad agreement on the vexed issue of personnel, and the LSO was willing to enter into a scheme involving a considerable loss of independence. Neither history of the LSO, that of Herbert Foss and Noël Goodwin published in 1954, or Maurice Pearton's, written twenty years later, provides a satisfactory answer. At the time the LSO laid much of the blame on Sargent. Others have attributed the blame to Beecham's backers, and it has even been claimed that Harold Holt was the prime mover. So far as Sargent is concerned, it would have been out of character for Beecham to allow a henchman to take independent action, especially of so fundamental a nature, nor, for much the same reason, does the suggestion that Holt was responsible ring true. It seems equally unlikely that Beecham abandoned the LSO because his backers refused to finance that orchestra, one of them, Lord Howard de Walden, protesting that his support had always been conditional on a reconstructed LSO being the vehicle for Beecham's plans and refusing to transfer his allegiance. Nor does the Royal Philharmonic Society's claim to have been the driving force stand up to examination. The Society, whose concerts were looking decidedly lacklustre compared with those of the BBC and the revitalised LSO, lacked the resources to do so. It was, however, to Beecham's advantage to secure their concerts, providing him with justification for using the name London Philharmonic. To achieve his ends he naturally kept them informed of progress.

Beecham, moreover, was not one to be subject to the dictates of others. His actions during the war, in virtually taking over of the affairs of the Royal Philharmonic Society; his conduct during negotiations with the BBC; his abandonment of the LSO, when matters were apparently proceeding smoothly and, many years later, his desertion of the LPO to form his last orchestra, the Royal Philharmonic, lend support to the belief that he was always playing a devious game, using the LSO as a stepping stone to bring his plans to fruition. The exchange of lists of acceptable and unacceptable players may have shown both parties in reasonably close agreement on a troublesome issue. It would also have enabled Beecham to identify players willing to listen to his overtures when the time came to recruit his own orchestra, the invitation extended to him to become a Member of the LSO presenting him with a golden opportunity of gaining inside knowledge of their plans. What then of his actions in helping the LSO overcome the crisis arising from the death of Lionel Powell? At that stage a stricken LSO would have been no help. Far better to keep the LSO afloat, and in the dark as to his real intentions, stringing them along until his plans were further advanced. Indeed for a time there was an alternative plan, proposed by Sir Landon Ronald, for an amalgamation of the LSO, the orchestra of the Royal Philharmonic Society and Ronald's own Royal Albert Hall Orchestra. Many leading players appeared in all three. Such a scheme, had it got off the ground, would have been a threat to Beecham's plans.

With the support of Lord Howard de Walden and others who remained loyal, and thanks to finding several new outlets, notably in the film studios and at Glyndebourne, where players from the LSO made up the orchestra for John Christie's new venture, the LSO survived to lead a robust, independent, and distinguished life of its own.

2

Pre-war 1932–39

From its first concert the LPO, as the orchestra quickly became known, jumped straight into the front rank. There were upwards of a dozen rehearsals and the programme, an amalgam of music close to Beecham's heart, was designed to show players and conductor to advantage:

Berlioz: Overture, Le Carnaval Romain; Mozart: Symphony No. 38 in D – *'The Prague'*; Delius: An English Rhapsody, Brigg Fair; Strauss: Symphonic Poem, Ein Heldenleben

At the conclusion of the overture part of the audience was roused to such a pitch that people stood on their seats to applaud, unprecedented behaviour for the supposedly reserved British, and when Beecham reappeared after the interval the applause was so great it was two or three minutes before he could launch his players into *Ein Heldenleben*. The press were enthusiastic. Neville Cardus, in a long review for the *Manchester Guardian*, commented, 'At present the orchestra is like a new machine – a little too crisp and polished. In a few weeks the mellowing will begin. A Continental saying is that there are no good and bad orchestras, only good and bad conductors. By this argument the London Philharmonic Orchestra ought soon to rank with the best in the world', and Ernest Newman, never one to give praise lightly, was moved to write 'nothing so electrifying has been heard in a London concert room for years', rightly pointing out that because the orchestra made its debut at a concert of the Royal Philharmonic Society, its title 'will inevitably set up confusions with the old Royal Philharmonic'. Though the two were wholly independent, the similarity of title continued to be a source of confusion.

For all the artistic success attending the LPO's opening concert, one problem was immediately apparent. The hall was not full, and this continued to be the case. With three orchestras competing for the same audience, there were too many concerts and too few people able to afford Queen's Hall prices. Even for the middle classes the higher priced seats represented an expensive night out, not to be undertaken with any great regularity. Problems arose from the proliferation of concerts and clashes in programming, and in an attempt to make concert planning more effective, a meeting took place between representatives of the BBC, the LPO, the LSO and the principal concert agents. One result was the *London Orchestral Concerts Guide*, a bi-monthly brochure listing the concerts given by each, and inserted in every concert programme.

In addition to the concerts of the Royal Philharmonic Society, a substantial list of engagements included the Courtauld-Sargent Concerts, the Robert Mayer Children's Concerts and those of the Royal Choral Society. A contract had been negotiated with the Gramophone Company Limited, and even before appearing in public a section of the orchestra went into the recording studio where, conducted by Sargent, they accompanied the Royal Choral Society in four choruses from *The Messiah* and two from *The Creation*. During the summer the orchestra was employed for the International Opera Season at the Royal Opera House Covent Garden, and performed for Colonel de Basil's *Ballet Russe de Monte Carlo*, popularly known as the Russian Ballet. There were provincial tours and a series of Sunday Orchestral Concerts, given in conjunction with Harold Holt, later re-titled 'The Beecham Sunday Concerts'. The Sunday concerts and the opera seasons were to prove a financial achilles heel.

The task of recruiting players was completed quickly and without difficulty. The LPO was led by Paul Beard, plucked from the ranks of the Birmingham Orchestra. Despite the fact that he had been leading orchestras for nearly ten years, the BBC had considered him too young to appoint as leader of the BBC Symphony Orchestra; Beecham had no such qualms. The second violins were led by George Stratton, recruited from the LSO; the violas by Frank Howard; the cello section by Anthony Pini, and the basses by Victor Watson. The woodwind principals were outstanding: flute, Gerald Jackson; oboe, Leon Goossens: clarinet, Reginald Kell, and bassoon, John Alexandra. The first horn was Francis Bradley; the principal trumpet John Cozens; the trombone section was led by Edward Garvin; James Bradshaw played the timpani, and the harpist was Marie Goossens. The LPO was a judicious blend of youth and experience, and according to Frank Howes: 'was new not merely as an organisation, but in personnel. There had been in London some half a dozen different orchestras, but many of the same players turned up in them all, and their faces were familiar to each other and to the concert-goer. It is said that on the morning of the first rehearsal of the LPO the players eyed each other cautiously like a lot of new boys at school. Sir Thomas had picked his instrumentalists here, there, and everywhere.'

The qualities of the section principals were demonstrated when, as frequently happened, they were given an opportunity to step out in front of the orchestra to play solo parts. The taxing violin solo in *Ein Heldenleben* presented Paul Beard with an early opportunity of justifying Beecham's decision to appoint him leader, Cardus describing his performance as 'the most poetic I have heard'. Beard also played the solo part in Harty's Violin

Concerto, with the composer conducting, and joined forces with Anthony Pini in the Concerto for Violin and Cello by Delius. Undoubtedly, however, the Crown Prince among the orchestral soloists was Leon Goossens, who performed the Oboe Concerto by his brother Eugene, as well as concertos by Bach, Handel, Marcello and Ticciati, several of them arrangements by Beecham of music by these composers.

Of the work undertaken by the LPO, the concerts of the Royal Philharmonic Society occupied a position of special importance. Until now the Society had employed an orchestra hand-picked from the best musicians in London, and because those invited did their best to avoid engagements which clashed with the Society's concerts, the Society suffered less than other organisations from the deputy system. It was, however, never an ideal orchestra. Wagner got to the root of the problem, describing it as 'magnificent, as far as the principal players go. Superb tone – but no sense of style'. Meeting six or eight times a year, under a stream of guest conductors, there was never any likelihood that it could develop a real identity. Competition from the BBC Symphony Orchestra, and improvements in the playing standards of the LSO, posed a threat, but with the engagement of the LPO the concerts regained their former prestige; indeed, the years leading up to the war can be seen as a highpoint in the Society's history.

In 1932–33 the Society increased the number of concerts from eight to ten; the following year there were eighteen, and thereafter they usually numbered twelve. Between 1932–33 and 1938–39 the Society promoted ninety concerts, all but one given by the LPO, the exception a concert by the Dresden State Orchestra, who took LPO's place while they were touring Germany. Of these Beecham conducted more than half, the programmes showing how wide Beecham's sympathies lay, and if his principal loyalties to the music of his own lifetime remained with composers whose cause he promoted prior to the First World War, Delius, Sibelius and Strauss, nevertheless he conducted works by Bartok, Holst, John Ireland, Gordon Jacob, Vaughan Williams and Walton, gave the first performance of *The Tale the Pine Trees Knew* by Bax, the first European performance of Bloch's Violin Concerto, and the first London performances of Pfitzner's Piano Concerto and Rachmaninov's *Rhapsody on a Theme of Paganini*. The most notable omission was music of the second Viennese school, who were in any case being championed by the BBC.

The Society played host to many distinguished foreign conductors, giving the orchestra an opportunity of playing under musicians such as Willem Mengelberg, Pierre Monteux, Bruno Walter and Felix Weingartner. Weingartner, then in his seventies, first appeared with the LPO in January 1935. He had conducted the music of Brahms in the presence of the composer, his reputation in the 1920s and 1930s as an interpreter of the great German classics on a par with that afforded to Otto Klemperer a quarter of a century later. Cardus wrote of him that 'He was famous in the legendary age of Berlin and Vienna. He knew Brahms. He belongs to the cultured epoch of music, the epoch of good taste – and sound scholarship'. Many years later, during an interval at the Royal Albert Hall, a discussion between two players on the merits of the previous evening's performance of the *Symphonie Fantastique*, was terminated by the remark 'Ah! But you should have played it under Weingartner. Then you really knew the work.' If Weingartner's programmes were drawn from a narrow range of music, much Beethoven and Brahms, filled out by works from the pens of Haydn, Mozart, Schubert and Schumann, with only an occasional departure from the German repertoire, his concerts were notable events.

Weingartner was held in high esteem by the orchestra, but Mengelberg's rehearsal methods were less appreciated. Bernard Shore, sometime principal viola of the BBC Symphony Orchestra, put his finger on the problem when he explained how 'He will talk for ten minutes on end... he does not rehearse for rehearsing's sake, though he may talk for talking's sake.' Berta Geissmar, Beecham's personal assistant, recalled a rehearsal of the *Prelude and Liebestod* from *Tristan*, during which 'he treated the orchestra as if they had never heard or played this music before', prompting one player to remark 'If he goes on like this, there will be a hell of a row'. Experienced in the ways of conductors, she defused the situation by tactfully mentioning that the LPO had performed the opera many times under Beecham and Fürtwangler.

The range of engagements indicated how much Sargent's involvement was central to Beecham's plans. As a result of work with which he was associated, he brought with him two wealthy backers, Samuel Courtauld and Robert Mayer, both of whom were appointed Directors, as were the Rt Hon. the Viscount Esher, well known as the Trustee of many an artistic or educational enterprise, and Baron Frederick d'Erlanger, a minor composer of no great talent, who had in the past given generously to the LSO. It may be assumed that Beecham was more interested in d'Erlanger's money than his music, prompting d'Erlanger's early resignation.

Because the Robert Mayer Children's Concerts required only a small orchestra, and were given minimal rehearsal, Mayer's financial backing was of greater importance than the modest amount of work provided by the concerts. The Courtauld-Sargent Concerts, on the other hand, occupied a significant place in the calendar. Based on a scheme operating in Germany, enabling people of modest means to obtain tickets at much reduced prices, they were the brainchild of Mrs Samuel Courtauld. Backed by her husband's money, Mrs Courtauld approached a wide range of large employers, the Civil Service, banks, department stores, and the London Teacher's Association among others, inviting them to send representatives to an exploratory meeting, where she outlined her plan for an annual series of concerts in Queen's Hall, with tickets sold on a subscription basis. These could only be obtained by groups of not less than six people and offered substantial discounts on the normal price of tickets.

The immediate response so far exceeded Mrs Courtauld's expectations that nine hundred seats were guaranteed that evening, nearly twice the number she hoped for. Some seats in the grand circle and the stalls were held back for the general public, and sold at full price, so that when the inaugural season commenced, in October 1929, all one thousand nine hundred seats available on subscription had been taken up and several hundred would-be applicants turned away. Subsequently, to meet growing demand, every concert was repeated, and in 1932–33 each programme was given three times. The Proms were not the only concerts given with minimal rehearsal, but with the certainty that Samuel Courtauld would meet any deficit, every Courtauld-Sargent concert received at least three rehearsals, the series representing a valuable block of work.

The Courtauld-Sargent Concerts took their name from the appointment of Sargent as Musical Director, Mrs Courtauld deciding to link his name to that of her husband. In 1929 Sargent was still on the threshold of a career and his appointment aroused some hostility, mainly on the grounds of youth and inexperience. His supporters pointed out that many distinguished continental conductors received major appointments at an even younger age – Mengelberg became conductor of the Concertgebouw Orchestra at the age of 24 – and there were few enough openings in Britain for the younger generation of conductors. How were Sargent and his contemporaries to gain experience if they were not given opportunities to conduct? The Courtaulds turned a deaf ear, and by the time the LPO appeared on the scene most of the critics had fallen silent.

The Courtauld-Sargent Concerts could, with the exception of the Proms, lay claim to be the most successful promoted in London. Not only were they sold out in advance, they were sold out for programmes which were, by any standards, adventurous. During their first three years, with the LSO on the platform, Otto Klemperer gave the first London performance of Bruckner's Eighth Symphony; Bruno Walter conducted *Das Lied von der Erde* and the *Resurrection* Symphony of Mahler; Hindemith appeared as soloist in the first British performance of his Viola Concerto, and Stravinsky, as performer in his *Capriccio* for piano and orchestra, and conductor, of the *Firebird* Suite and the *Symphony of Psalms*. When the LPO took over in the autumn of 1932 the year's opening programme included the first performance in this country of Martinů's Concerto for String Quartet and Orchestra, and later in the season they gave the first performance of the Fourth Symphony of Bax. The following year brought another Bax symphony, Beecham, in Sargent's absence, conducting the premiere of the Fifth, and year by year the repertoire ranged far and wide, from Michael Haydn's *Turkish Suite* and items from Thomas Arne's *The Masque of Alfred* to the first public performance in Britain of

Hindemith's *Mathis der Maler* Symphony; from Palestrina's *Stabat Mater* to Busoni's Violin Concerto. Though the programming was adventurous the Courtaulds ensured the public were offered a well-balanced diet, and Sargent being Sargent, most seasons included at least one choral work. *Belshazzar's Feast* was given in January 1933, less than eighteen months after its first performance, other major choral works including the *Missa Solemnis*, Berlioz' *Childhood of Christ* and Verdi's *Requiem*.

Except in 1933–34, when Sargent was convalescing after a serious illness, his concerts taken over by Beecham, Julius Harrison and Leslie Heward, he conducted three or four programmes a year, guest conductors including Fritz Busch, Robert Heger, Erich Kleiber, Carl Schuricht, Fritz Stiedry, George Szell and Bruno Walter. In addition to his work for the Courtauld-Sargent Concerts and the Robert Mayer Children's Concerts, Sargent also conducted those of the Royal Choral Society, for which the LPO was employed, and, after Beecham, was the conductor most often seen on the rostrum when the LPO performed in the concert hall.

Mrs Courtauld died in December 1932, but though her husband's main interests lay elsewhere, notably in the world of art, he remained loyal to his wife's devotion to music, taking an active part in planning each season and underwriting the concerts until they were discontinued after the first winter of the war. The firm of Courtauld's was much involved with London's orchestras during the 1930s, Samuel Courtauld's support for the LPO matched by another of the firm's Directors, Mr F.J. Nettlefold, who gave substantial backing to the LSO.

The Beecham Sunday Concerts provided an outlet for some of the artists managed by Harold Holt, and for a year or two these offered wide-ranging programmes, Beecham conducting the Oboe Concerto by Eugene Goossens, Lalo's Symphony and Poulenc's Concerto for Two Pianos, the piquancy of the composer's orchestration probably commending the last piece to him. In the following winter Delius was represented by his Piano Concerto and two performances of *Paris*; Robert Heger conducted Mahler's Fourth Symphony; another Beecham programme included *Kindertotenlieder*, strange territory for him, and the final concert of the year the *Serenade* by the obscure German composer Clemens von Frankenstein. Thereafter the dictates of finance restricted the range of music, much Beethoven, Brahms, Dvorak, Mozart, Sibelius and Wagner, but offering only the occasional tit-bit, such as Méhul's Overture '*Les deux aveugles de Tolède*'. Even Beecham's beloved Delius was all but relegated to the sidelines, but despite conservative programmes Beecham and Holt continued to lose heavily on these concerts.

During spring and summer the LPO's activities were carried on within the walls of the Royal Opera House. For the International Season of Opera, performances of as many operas as possible were crammed into a period of eight to ten weeks, running from late April to June and, with the Russian Ballet following hard on the heels of the opera season, there was little or no respite for the players. Paul Beard, who resigned as leader in 1936, to join the BBC Symphony Orchestra, reputedly told Sir Adrian Boult that one more day of rehearsing and performing Wagner, starting at ten in the morning and finishing at midnight, would have finished him.

The 1933 season involved thirty performances, including two cycles of *The Ring* and nine other operas. In these circumstances there were few excursions into unfamiliar territory. Every season included *The Ring*, with *Bohème, Otello, Parsifal, Rosenkavalier, Tosca* and *Tristan and Isolde* among the most frequently performed operas, but despite Beecham's advocacy of his music there was little Mozart, with *Figaro* a notable absentee. Among lesser-known works, *Arabella* was judged by Ernest Newman to be 'like a third brewing of *Rosenkavalier* tea-leaves', a view not entirely shared by posterity, and the Coronation Season of 1937 included two operas by Gluck, *Alceste*, a production of the Paris Opera, who provided the principal singers, the chorus and *corps de ballet*, and *Orfeo*. It was thought that by itself the latter would provide too short an evening's entertainment, the Russian Ballet contributing a somewhat odd bedfellow in the shape of Massine's choreography for *The Blue Danube*. The only native work to be performed was *Don Juan de Mañara* by Eugene Goossens, which received its first, and to date its last, performances in 1937. Goossens' opera had a mixed reception. Ernest Newman, never lavish with his praise, was among the small band of enthusiasts, but majority opinion was that the composer suffered from a badly constructed libretto – the work of Arnold Bennett, based on his own play of the same name – with the singers too subordinate to the orchestra.

Beecham occasionally conducted for the ballet, but most performances were in the hands of younger men, including Antal Dorati, Anatole Fistoulari and Efrem Kurtz. One other name requires special mention, that of Georg Solti, who paid his first visit to this country in 1938, conducting a number of ballet performances. Many years later, recalling what was one of his earliest experiences as a conductor, Solti was to recount the frustration he felt because rather than directing the music at what he believed to be the correct tempi, of necessity he had to adjust his conducting to suit the needs of the dancers. For the orchestra, accompanying the ballet was generally unrewarding work, and long before the season was over the playing standard declined, Edwin Evans' enthusiastic review of the first night of the 1934 ballet season, 'Never, either in pre-war days nor in ours has the Russian Ballet had such orchestral playing as it had last night from the LPO', giving way to Ernest Newman's end-of-term report that 'According to the programme the orchestra was the same LPO that had done such brilliant work during the opera season. Without this assurance I should never have believed it; a worse performance of the Tchaikovsky it would be difficult to imagine.'

In addition to provincial tours the LPO performed at several of the triennial Music Festivals held in early autumn. For most provincial cities visiting orchestras were a rarity, and as though to make up for the fact, the festivals packed as much music as possible into the shortest possible time. Lasting from three to five days, with a strong choral element, often involving two concerts a day, they must have been as mentally exhausting for the audience as they were physically demanding for the players. It was customary to commission one or more new choral works, of which by far the most celebrated was *Belshazzar's Feast*, which burst on the world at Leeds in 1931. It was hardly to be expected that the pieces commissioned from George Dyson and Cyril Scott for the 1934 Festival could match the sensation created by Walton, and neither has survived. The Norwich Festival of 1936 involved music of greater significance, including an early work by Britten, the cantata *Our Hunting Fathers*, and the first performance of Vaughan Williams' *Five Tudor Portraits*. Vaughan Williams had taken some racy verses by the 16th-century poet John Skelton, which would hardly raise an eyebrow today, but prompted the elderly Countess of Albermarle, sitting in the front row of the audience, to get up and depart in protest, whereupon Vaughan Williams, who was conducting, congratulated the chorus on their diction.

The Sheffield Festival of the same year gave rise to a highly publicised dispute between Beecham and Sir Henry Wood, making one of his few appearances with the pre-war LPO. There was considerable rivalry between the two men, and Wood, who in accordance with his customary practice asked for an orchestra list, raised objections to the departure of Paul Beard as leader and his replacement by David McCallum, recently recruited from the Scottish Orchestra. Wood tried to insist that Beard should lead the orchestra, maintaining that it was unreasonable to expect him to appear with a leader of whose capabilities he had no knowledge. Though Wood's position was untenable he gave way with a singular lack of grace, giving Beecham an unmissable opportunity of enjoying himself hugely at Wood's expense. Why Wood chose to engage in a public dispute he had no hope of winning is far from clear, but it was hardly the best background for a week of music making. Those taking part remembered it as an unpleasant experience, conductor and orchestra resentful of each other's attitude. The gargantuan programmes would have done nothing to lighten the atmosphere; Verdi's *Requiem* occupied the first half of one evening, followed after the interval by Mozart's *Haffner* Symphony and Liszt's First Piano Concerto as the orchestral filling to a choral sandwich that concluded with *Belshazzar's Feast*.

Paul Beard's departure was one of many changes in the orchestral ranks. After a year as principal second violin, George Stratton resigned, returning to the LSO as leader, the Directors of that orchestra taking the practical view that whatever their feelings about players who joined the LPO, their first duty was to appoint the man they considered best suited to the job, in this case Stratton.

Another who left was Bernard Andrews, one of the original members of the first violin section; like Beard, he joined the BBC Symphony Orchestra. Among the woodwind Gerald Jackson left after a year, to be succeeded as principal flute by Leonard Hopkinson, and then by another fine player, Geoffrey Gilbert, and after serving as principal clarinet for five years Reginald Kell gave way to Bernard Walton. The list of players serving in the ranks of the LPO during these years reads like a roll-call of the best known orchestral musicians of the immediate pre-war and post-war periods.

The LPO first went abroad in 1935, giving two concerts in Brussels in connection with an International Exhibition. The programmes included a high proportion of British music, including works by Bax, Lord Berners, Delius, Elgar, Holst, Dame Ethel Smythe, Sullivan, Walton and Vaughan Williams, but despite careful planning the first concert narrowly escaped disaster, both the orchestral parts and Beecham's batons going astray. The Librarian of the Brussels Philharmonic Society produced parts for the Overture to *The Mastersingers* and Mozart's Symphony No. 40, which formed part of the programme, enabling Beecham to at least start the concert, though at a much later hour than the advertised time. Meanwhile a frantic search went on for the missing parts, which were finally unearthed in the luggage department at the station, and rushed to the hall, allowing the orchestra to perform most of the remaining items, with *Beni Mora* by Holst the only casualty: Beecham's batons were discovered in his hotel bedroom! These concerts took place over a weekend in the middle of the ballet season, with another orchestra deputising for the LPO on Saturday. Returning home on Monday, the orchestra went straight from the train into the pit at Covent Garden for that evening's performance.

A more extended tour took place a year later, with concerts in eight German cities: Berlin, Dresden, Leipzig, Munich, Stuttgart, Ludwigshafen, Frankfurt and Cologne. Beecham had recently appointed a new personal assistant, Dr Berta Geissmar, Fürtwangler's former manager and secretary, and manager of the foreign tours undertaken by the Berlin Philharmonic Orchestra. Dr Geissmar was a Jew, and when the Nazis came to power her connections with Fürtwangler afforded her some protection, but as time went by she came under increasing pressure from the regime, who wanted Fürtwangler and the orchestra to replace her. After making her way to America, she came to Britain, where Beecham took her under his wing, commencing work with him just before the start of the 1936 International Opera Season.

Despite the fact that before leaving Germany Dr Geissmar had been threatened that if she ever returned she would be arrested, one of the first tasks given her by Beecham was to complete arrangements for the LPO's tour. The arts in Germany were deeply entangled in the machinations of the Nazi Party leaders, who regarded the tour as politically prestigious, and were anxious to ensure everything proceeded smoothly, an approach by Beecham to Ribbontrop, his country's Plenipotentiary Extraordinary, securing cast-iron assurances that Dr Geissmar could return to Germany as often and for as long as she liked. In complete contrast to the treatment given to her before leaving, she found that as Beecham's emissary she was welcomed by the regime. For Beecham the tour provided a golden opportunity for enhancing the orchestra's reputation, and while it was not without its difficult moments, he successfully avoided the political pitfalls.

The tour opened in Berlin on 13 November 1936, in the presence of Hitler and members of his entourage. It would have been normal practice, at a concert attended by the Head of State, to play the respective National Anthems, but many of the players would have objected to playing the *Horst Wessel Hymn*, and to avoid embarrassment anthems were dispensed with. The diplomatic importance given to the concert by the Nazi authorities was evidenced by the fact that although Beecham remained backstage in the conductor's room, they found it necessary to fake a photograph showing him in Hitler's box during the interval. The programme given in Berlin consisted of:

Dvorak: Slavonic Rhapsody No. 3 in A flat major; Haydn: Symphony No. 5 in D; Berlioz: Overture, Le Carnaval Romain; Handel, arr. Beecham: Suite. The Gods Go a-Begging; Elgar: Enigma Variations

The numbering given to the Haydn symphony is curious. No copy of the programme is extant, and though both Dr Geissmar and Russell refer to it as No. 5, it seems more likely that the symphony in question was No. 93 in D, which like several other works taken on tour had been played in London before the orchestra's departure. The opening concert was broadcast and after the first item, which Hitler applauded warmly, Beecham, disregarding the presence of the microphone, remarked to the orchestra, 'the old bloke seems to like it': other versions carry rather stronger wording. Next day one English paper carried the headline 'Mysterious voice on the wireless during Sir Thomas Beecham's concert'. The concert was followed by a party hosted by the Berlin Philharmonic Orchestra, an occasion of much conviviality, the Berliners variously amazed, delighted, surprised and mystified by Beecham, who climbed onto a table to conduct his musicians in two rousing verses of 'The more we are together'.

Other works performed in Germany included two Mozart symphonies, Nos 31 in D (*The Paris*) and 39 in E Flat, Sibelius' Second and what was known in the old numbering as Dvorak's Fourth. In addition to the *Enigma Variations*, British music was represented by Lord Berners' Suite, *The Triumph of Neptune*, two short pieces by Delius and Vaughan Williams' Overture, *The Wasps*. Every concert was sold out, and artistically the tour was a considerable success. Towards its end embarrassment arose over a growing sum in unspent marks entrusted to the care of Dr Geissmar, which under German currency regulations could not be taken out of the country. Individuals holding currency on behalf of non-residents could run up against stiff penalties, and if the money was banked it could only be released by means of a complicated bureaucratic procedure. Beecham was prepared to gamble that because he was a guest of the government, the German Customs would not examine his luggage, and took charge of the marks. His assumption proved correct. Rumour had it that not long afterwards he paid a return visit to Germany, successfully disposing of the marks in a remarkably short space of time.

In March of the following year the LPO performed in another European capital, Paris. The visit was marred only by the fact that whereas for their visit to Brussels the sea had been kind to them, on this occasion the weather was atrocious, many players suffering badly from sea-sickness. Like the tour of Germany the concert in Paris was given at the invitation of the government, who underwrote the cost. During the interval Beecham was decorated by the French President as a Commander of the Legion of Honour, protocol requiring that he should wear this for the second half of the concert, despite his obvious unease at having to do so. Negotiations also took place for a visit to Italy. Beecham insisted that, having been invited to Germany by the government of that country, the Italian government should follow suit. The Italians were unable to make up their minds, and in the summer of 1938 the tour was postponed for a year, the passage of which saw the Munich crisis come and go, and against a darkening international background the time was no longer ripe for such a venture.

Despite the success of the LPO's backers in securing work for the orchestra, these engagements were insufficient to keep it fully employed. Initially the players were paid engagement by engagement and, though Beecham had first call on their services, were free to undertake other work, providing this did not interfere with their obligations to the LPO. In 1935 there was a change in the terms of employment and it was decided to pay them weekly, placing an additional strain on financial resources which were already stretched to the limit: funds were not always available to meet the pay-bill, and it was said that at one point some players were owed up to £300 in arrears of overtime, the equivalent of several months' earnings. Beecham consistently opposed public or municipal subsidy, looking to his wealthy backers to foot the bill, but by 1936 Courtauld and Mayer had resigned, unwilling to continue bailing the organisation out, though they continued to support the concerts bearing their respective names. Courtauld and Mayer had both dug deep into their pockets in support of the LPO. From now on there was to be a limit on the extent of their liabilities.

Following the resignation of Courtauld and Mayer a new company, The London Philharmonic Concert Society Limited, was formed, with Beecham and his solicitor as sole Directors, and an unsuccessful attempt made to secure new capital. Possibly Beecham was not addressing the right audience. In the absence of public money many musical organisations were sustained by guarantors who, if receipts failed to balance the costs, undertook to foot all or part of the bill. Guarantors were usually drawn from the wealthier ranks of the community, but in 1933 the Hallé Concert Society, faced with increasing losses, and a declining number of guarantors, extended the scope of their scheme, reducing their minimum guarantee from £100 to £10, of which only 20 per cent would be called upon in any one year. The Hallé's scheme attracted over four hundred new guarantors, and despite the fact that the majority only provided support at the minimum level of £10, gave the Society financial backing of over £1000 a year.

The experience of the Hallé suggests that a more widely based appeal might have met with greater success. It was not, however, Beecham's nature to act in such a way. The natural constituency to which he looked was a limited section of society for many of whom, with some notable exceptions, music formed a social rather than an artistic function, the hand-to-mouth funding of the LPO by private patrons failing to provide any kind of stability. Long before the outbreak of war in September 1939 put paid to the existing arrangements, there were doubts about the LPO's ability to survive, even under peacetime conditions.

The last pre-war season took place against a background of political crisis. It opened with the LPO accompanying the Russian Ballet, and throughout the winter the players were kept extremely busy. In addition to concerts for the Royal Philharmonic Society, the Courtauld-Sargent concerts and those of the Royal Choral Society, Beecham mounted a Sibelius Festival, conducting all seven symphonies, most of the major tone poems and, in two concerts given in the Aeolian Hall rather than Queen's Hall, much of the music written for a small orchestra. Beecham also undertook a long series of recorded concerts for Radio Luxemburg, for each of which he also gave a verbal introduction. These broadcasts, lasting about half an hour, were low in artistic merit, being primarily devoted to what Beecham usually described as 'lollipops', including isolated movements from symphonies, but the revenue was valuable in helping to keep the most pressing creditors at bay.

The LPO's last concert appearances before the outbreak of war formed part of the London Musical Festival of 1939, of which Sir Walford Davies wrote in his foreword to the Festival handbook, 'never has a musical event of such scope and comprehensive importance been planned for London'. With programmes treading well-worn paths, this was hard on Sir Henry Wood and the Proms, nevertheless the range of musical activity undoubtedly justified the title. The centrepiece was a cycle of nine Beethoven concerts by the BBC Symphony Orchestra, two conducted by Boult, the others by Toscanini. Other attractions included the LSO under Bruno Walter; Reginald Jacques and the Bach Choir performed the *St John Passion*, and *The Dream of Gerontius* was given at the Albert Hall; chamber music took place in a wide variety of locations including, in a foretaste of wartime music making, the National Gallery; and open-air entertainment included performances in Regents Park and a brass band concert, with fireworks, at Kenwood. The LPO gave two concerts under the auspices of the Royal Philharmonic Society, the first conducted by Beecham, the second by Wood, performed at a celebrity concert for which the soloist was Fritz Kreisler and, conducted by Sargent, gave a programme of English music at a Robert Mayer Children's Concert.

The London Music Festival also embraced the International Opera Season, but whether because of the international situation, or the fact that too many operas had been repeated year in, year out, attendances fell away. There were also rumours of backstage difficulties between some of the visiting singers from Germany and exiled Jewish singers. Beecham conducted *The Ring*, *Aïda*, *Don Giovanni, Tristan* and *The Bartered Bride*, though when illness forced him to withdraw, the last performances of *Aïda* and *Don Giovanni* were entrusted to Wynn Reeves, whose normal position was at the second desk of the first violins, and who, from all accounts, obtained thoroughly satisfactory performances. Basil Cameron was also called in to conduct a performance of *Tristan*, a considerable undertaking in circumstances which prevented him from rehearsing with either singers or orchestra.

The opera season ended with *Tristan* under Beecham, the last performance given by the LPO before the outbreak of war. Beecham's tongue-in-cheek utterances, and what to the unobservant might have seemed a deceptively casual attitude to rehearsal, disguised a capacity for hard work. As well as conducting the LPO he was involved in the activities of the Hallé and the Liverpool Philharmonic, and off the rostrum carried the burden of planning each season, with added worries arising over the parlous state of the LPO's finances. Weighed down by the struggle to keep the orchestra afloat, the constant round of concerts, opera and recordings, and troubled by his back and his feet, Beecham had been ordered by his doctor to take a year's sabbatical. Though this was to include a visit to Australia, in response to an invitation from the Australian Broadcasting Commission, his schedule there would be far less intense than that which he habitually carried out in England.

The autumn was to have opened with performances for the Russian Ballet and a provincial tour under Weingartner; the usual round of concerts for the Royal Philharmonic Society and other bodies had been arranged, while for the longer term Dr Geissmar was engaged with the first stages of planning a visit to Canada and the United States. It can only be a matter of conjecture whether or not the organisation had the resources to carry these through. The decision to pay the players weekly cost the management dear, and poor support for the 1939 International Opera Season put an immense strain on its resources. Moreover, for all the artistic success enjoyed by the LPO over the past seven years, the players' dependence on Beecham meant there was little sense of corporate identity. The orchestra remained a collection of individuals, bound together only by their work on the concert platform, while however high their regard for Beecham as a musician, the loyalties of many were stretched to the limit by the fact that considerable amounts were owed to them. With the LPO's finances fragile in the extreme it must have been open to question whether, in Beecham's absence, it would have been possible to raise sufficient funds to keep the orchestra afloat. In the event, Britain's declaration of war on Sunday 3 September put all of these plans, and a great deal else, in abeyance.

3

The Phoney War 1939–40

It wasn't phoney for the people of Poland; the passengers and crew of the *Athenia*, which sailed from Liverpool before the declaration of war and was sunk on the evening of 3 September, 112 of the passengers on board losing their lives; the RAF airmen killed next day, in an attack on Wilhelmshaven; the crews of the aircraft carrier HMS *Courageous*, sunk on 8 September off the coast of Ireland, and the battleship HMS *Royal Oak*, sunk at her moorings by a U-boat that penetrated the defences of Scapa Flow. It was phoney only because expectations, possibly fuelled by the images of Alexander Korda's film of H.G. Wells' *The Shape of Things to Come*, that the start of a new war would be accompanied by devastating air raids did not immediately come to pass; because Hitler, after conquering Poland, did not immediately attack in the West.

Two days before the declaration of war the Prom season was brought to an abrupt end, the government, fearing the worst, ordering an immediate shutdown of cinemas, concert-halls, theatres and other places of entertainment, the BBC Symphony Orchestra departing for an undisclosed location, later revealed as Bristol. The BBC had also secretly recruited a number of musicians for a BBC Salon Orchestra, a group of sixteen players, who were supposedly to play good-quality light music. Several were drawn from the ranks of the LPO, including Leon Goossens, Anthony Pini, Frederick Riddle, and Victor Watson. The way the BBC went about their recruitment, and the fact that their talents were largely wasted on music of moderate quality, added to the annoyance caused when the LPO found themselves without several key players.

What nobody could have foreseen was that the war would produce a boom in the demand for orchestral music, some of the most dramatic effects of which were seen in the provinces. At the outbreak of war Liverpool had a brand new hall, the Philharmonic Hall, opened only a few months earlier, and owned by the Liverpool Philharmonic Society. In 1942 Liverpool Corporation put itself in the front rank of those supporting the Arts by purchasing the hall, undertaking to let the Society use it rent-free, with an additional grant of £4000 a year, providing the Society placed the orchestra on a full-time basis. By that time the BBC had disbanded its Salon Orchestra, enabling Liverpool to recruit a number of leading players, and amid all his other activities Sargent accepted an invitation to become principal conductor of the newly formed Liverpool Philharmonic Orchestra, a post he occupied for the next six years.

The Hallé, after a tentative start, steadily expanded its activities, and by 1941–42 was promoting many more concerts than before the war. In 1943, in the face of the example set by Liverpool, the Society placed its orchestra on an all-the-year round basis, inviting John Barbirolli, then in America, to return home as Chief Conductor. In Birmingham, despite initial fears that it would have to disband – the Town Hall was requisitioned and their conductor, Leslie Heward, incapacitated by tuberculosis – the orchestra survived, and by the war's end it too had been placed on a permanent footing. Sadly Heward himself, an enormously talented musician who must otherwise have been destined for greater things, did not live to see the seeds planted in Birmingham come to flower. After making a partial recovery, his health again broke down, and he died in May 1943. The Scottish Orchestra also extended its season from three months to six, though it was not until after the war that this orchestra was employed all the year round.

For the LPO and the LSO the war years were to involve travelling the length and breadth of the country, giving concerts in out-of-the-way places, many of which had never before played host to a symphony orchestra. But this lay in the future. For the musicians, like most of the population, early September was a time of much anxiety and great uncertainty. A meeting of creditors took place a fortnight after the declaration of war. The message was plain; the company had no assets, there were no wealthy benefactors to bail them out, there was nothing for anyone. The meeting took the only possible course, approving the voluntary liquidation of the company. And that could well have been that.

That it was not the end of the LPO, that the orchestra survived was due to a small group of players, notably Charles Gregory, the principal horn, who succeeded Francis Bradley when Bradley resigned after the first year of the orchestra's life. Bradley later rejoined as third horn, and he and Gregory spent part of the summer on holiday together, using some of their time to discuss ways in which if, as seemed likely, the worst came to the worst, the LPO could be kept alive. Back home they involved Francis Stead, the principal trombone, in their discussions and were ready, when the creditors' meeting took place, to offer constructive ideas about the future. Many players had at one time or another been members of the LSO. Mindful of their experience with that orchestra, and that it operated as a self-governing organisation, once the business of liquidating the existing company had been concluded, and the other creditors had departed, the players, with Beecham's approval, elected an orchestral Committee. Gregory, Bradley and Stead were automatic choices, with Reginald Morley, the orchestra's sub-leader, John Alexandra, the principal bassoon, and finally Thomas Russell, a rank-and-file member of the viola section, the other members. Russell was later appointed Secretary and Business Manager, a post he held for over a decade, playing a major role in shaping the orchestra's destiny. In the early days, however, it was the Committee's Chairman, Gregory, who took the leading role in guiding the orchestra through a minefield of unforeseeable difficulties.

The varied musical experience of members of the Committee was representative of the orchestra as a whole. Charles Gregory, like many brass players, learned his trade in the services, playing in the RAF Band. Returning to civilian life he played with the LSO as fourth horn, graduating to principal, joining the LPO in the same position in 1933, a year after the orchestra's formation. Francis Bradley, noted as one of the orchestra's raconteurs, also honed his skills in the armed services, in his case the band of the Scots Guards, and after military service played in the LSO and the orchestra of the British National Opera Company before joining the LPO. After a year as principal horn, he left to join the BBC Symphony Orchestra, where he played under Toscanini, returning to the LPO in 1938.

Francis Stead, a Yorkshireman of few words, first played in a brass band at the age of eight. For some years his professional career was divided between the Scottish Orchestra and, during the summer months, the Municipal Orchestras of Harrogate or Hastings. He too joined the LPO in 1932, and was later promoted to principal. Reginald Morley, the sub-leader, studied under two distinguished teachers, Carl Flesch and Max Rostal, and by the age of fifteen was playing in an opera orchestra. He was another founder member of the LPO, playing among the first violins, and as an experienced copyist was responsible for marking up orchestral parts. After a year's absence, spent leading the Jacques Orchestra, Morley returned to the LPO in 1938 to share the front desk with David McCallum.

As a Director of the LSO John Alexandra, whose earlier experience had been with the Scottish Orchestra and the Queen's Hall Orchestra, was involved in that orchestra's negotiations with Beecham, joining the LPO when Beecham offered him the position of principal bassoon. Thomas Russell, the sixth and final member, was elected to the committee because, according to his own report of the proceedings, the rank-and-file string players wanted a representative from among their numbers. Before joining the LPO in 1935, Russell spent several years playing for the BBC in their Cardiff Studios.

It took courage to think of planning ahead, for in those first days of its new existence the LPO had nothing it could claim as its own: no assets, no bank account or cheque book, no music library, no premises, no legal status and no engagements. Beecham, whose planned departure for America was now delayed, undertook to meet the expenses of forming a new company, and for a time the Committee was able to meet in the Royal Opera House. It quickly became clear that their presence was unwelcome, after which meetings took place in Lyons teashops or pubs. Many plans were discussed and rejected, but with fears about imminent attack from the air allayed, at least for the time being, the restrictions on public entertainment were slowly being lifted, and they set about resuscitating a tour of the provinces. With little or no likelihood of any other business in prospect, it was not too difficult to persuade hall managers to reconfirm the bookings already made. Nevertheless it was a considerable achievement on the part of those concerned that, within a fortnight of the creditors' meeting on 18 September, the LPO was travelling to Cardiff for its first concert since the outbreak of war. Before making the journey there was one vital problem to overcome, the fact that they had no cash to purchase the railway tickets. That problem was solved by Sidney Beer, a wealthy amateur musician, who had conducted an occasional concert in the past, the price for his assistance an undertaking to offer him a share of the conducting when the orchestra resumed its activities at Queen's Hall.

The LPO was now a much smaller orchestra. Several players departed, doubtful that the orchestra had a future, and others were called up, reducing the playing strength from the pre-war figure of ninety-six to around seventy. The biggest reduction was in the string band which, compared with the former complement of sixteen first violins, fourteen seconds, twelve violas, ten cellos and eight basses, numbered twelve firsts, ten seconds, eight violas, six cellos and six basses. The loss of leading players to the BBC's Salon Orchestra was resolved by promotion of the deputy principals, Maurice Ward leading the violas, Edward Robinson the cellos, John Silvester taking over the double bass section from Victor Watson, and Horace Halstead sitting in the chair vacated by Leon Goossens. Another player who left soon after the outbreak of war was David McCallum, his position as leader filled by Thomas Matthews. A native of Liverpool, Matthews studied under Carl Flesch and Albert Sammons, joining the Hallé Orchestra at the age of eighteen. As well as embarking on a solo career, the summer of 1939 saw him installed as Director of Music at Buxton Spa. Matthews had also been appointed leader of the orchestra which performed for the Liverpool Philharmonic Society. Liverpool's orchestra was still operating on a part-time basis, and with the LPO's engagement book far from full during the winter of 1939–40 he found little difficulty in fulfilling responsibilities to both orchestras. With the LPO's playing strength much reduced there was little immediate need for recruitment, with most positions filled by players recruited by Beecham, who were willing to take the risk of transferring their loyalties to the new management.

The LPO was now registered under a new name, Musical Culture Limited, and, thanks to help from William Hawkes, found temporary premises in Empire House, before moving to an address in Regent Street. Dr Geissmar provided invaluable experience, but before many weeks had passed it became clear that something had to be done to strengthen the management side of their affairs, the Committee having been given a considerable spur in the shape of a document dictated by Beecham, highly critical of the way affairs had been handled since passing out of his hands. It was decided to dispense with the services of the Company Secretary and, casting around for someone to replace him, Russell was asked to take on this role, as he put it, 'on the slender foundation that I had spent some time in the office of an insurance company, and that before the war had contributed articles on musical subjects to various journals'. In this he was doing himself considerably less than justice, proving the ideal man to take charge of the orchestra's business affairs. For a time he somehow managed to carry out his new duties while taking his place in the ranks of the orchestra, but this was an impossible task, and from henceforth his work lay behind the scenes. Because Russell was required to spend much of his time travelling with the orchestra, he recruited a pre-war journalist, Felix Aprahamian, to take charge of matters at the London end, where in addition to Berta Geissmar, who threw in her lot with the new management, working without remuneration, another young man cutting his first musical teeth in the office was John Amis. Throughout the war years the administrative machine continued to operate on the tightest of shoestrings, and time and again proved itself capable of great elasticity and resource.

The credit for giving London its first orchestral concert of the war goes to the LSO, who appeared in Queen's Hall on Sunday 8 October, the day after the 1939 Prom season should have ended. The LPO's Cardiff concert took place a week earlier, and appears to have been the first given in the provinces, but the palm for resuming musical activity must go to Sadler's Wells Opera who, before the end of September, initiated a series of matinée performances at the theatre in Rosebery Avenue. Shortly afterwards Dame Myra Hess began her lunchtime concerts at the National Gallery, which had been stripped of its treasures, and though for a time, when the bombing of London was at its height, the concerts had to be given in the basement, they continued throughout the war years. Taking place every day from Monday to Friday, the National Gallery concerts were a considerable source of solace to many Londoners.

The LPO returned to the platform of Queen's Hall at the end of October, where a regular Sunday series was instituted, and as well as these performances, concerts were arranged both in and around London, their work outside central London assuming greater importance than the tours undertaken before the war. By the end of the winter concerts had been given in twenty or more towns and cities, many relatively close to London, but others as far afield as Blackpool, Grimsby, Huddersfield and Liverpool. Some provincial concerts were arranged with the help of Harold Fielding, yet to make his name as a theatrical impresario, and there was modest but welcome support from the Pilgrim Trust, who underwrote the cost of four provincial concerts, one of which, before a packed hall at Rugby School, was given with the help of a donation from the school itself. One Sunday in December provided a foretaste of the future, with an afternoon concert conducted by Beecham in the Davis Theatre, Croydon, and an evening performance of the same programme at the Coliseum. Some experimental lunchtime concerts were given in the Central Hall, Westminster, but these proved financially disastrous and were quickly discontinued.

The early months of the war were not the time for taking risks, and programmes were almost exclusively confined to standard classics, but while Beecham's Queen's Hall concerts were well supported, this was not the case for those entrusted to Sidney Beer. As a matter of policy ticket prices were reduced, and empty seats, of which there were all too many at Beer's concerts, were a matter of grave concern. Because musicians employed as extras were paid in full, with whatever was left, after payment of the other expenses, divided among the members of the orchestra, empty seats could mean empty pockets. Fortunately it was possible to limit the number of concerts entrusted to Beer, and for a time at least he dropped out of the picture. In addition to conducting the LPO Beecham was also active in the provinces, conducting the Hallé when that orchestra resumed its activities in October. When he was away Sir Adrian Boult, Basil Cameron, Malcolm Sargent and Sir Henry Wood accepted invitations to conduct.

Though Beecham remained in Britain for the time being, it was still his intention to leave for America in the not-too-distant future, leading to work in the recording studio, a number of records being made which the company intended to issue gradually during the period of his absence. Work of this kind was welcome, but the financial position was a constant source of concern, and by the start of 1940 it was evident that if the future of the LPO was to be secured, outside help was necessary. There was little or no hope of assistance from the sources which had supported the orchestra in the past. The era of Courtauld, Mayer and Nettlefold and their like was all but at an end. Instead it was decided to appeal to the audience by means of an insert in the programme at a Queen's Hall Sunday concert, and Beecham, approached by Russell, agreed that this would have greater impact if he were to support it with a speech from the platform. His blend of cajolery, common sense, flattery and wit produced a generous response, sufficient to keep the LPO afloat for the immediate future.

A month or two later, as a gesture of thanks to those who contributed, a small magazine, *Philharmonic Post*, made its first appearance. This had an immediate welcome and was quickly sold out. One result of reducing seat prices was that the orchestra's concerts were attracting a younger clientele than would normally have been seen at Queen's Hall in pre-war days, bearing more resemblance to the audience which attended the Proms or the Courtauld-Sargent Concerts, than the fashionable members of society who had formed the core of Beecham's supporters. A sizeable proportion appeared to be interested in the activities and workings of a symphony orchestra, and for the next decade and a half *Philharmonic Post* provided a forum for the orchestra's ideas, chronicled developments as they occurred, featured many orchestral personalities and gave its readership an introduction to some of the less familiar music to be performed. At its peak, circulation reached over ten thousand. There were many supporters of the orchestra who regretted the magazine's demise.

Russell's energy was phenomenal. He was responsible for preparing programme notes, wrote much of the editorial material for *Philharmonic Post*, contributed to a number of other publications, and in 1942 brought out a slim volume entitled *Philharmonic* which, taking some of his articles as a basis, set out to explain what was involved in the business of running an orchestra. Two years later he produced a second book, *Philharmonic Decade*. In addition to encapsulating the history of the LPO up to that point, this enlarged on the problems of running an orchestra under wartime conditions and argued the case for financial support from the state.

With the LPO granted a new lease of life, both Courtauld-Sargent and the Royal Philharmonic Society announced that they would give concerts during the winter of 1939–40. This was the last season of Courtauld-Sargent Concerts, and they remained adventurous to the end, the programmes including two works new to this country, Prokofiev's Symphonic Poem *Nuits d'Egypte*, and Honegger's *Nocturne*; the horn section earned prominence in Schumann's *Concertstück*, and a choral concert comprised *Fauré's Requiem* and rarities by Elgar, Mozart and Stanford. The Royal Philharmonic Society's concerts took place on Thursday afternoons, a move designed to enable the audience to arrive home without enduring the worst rigours of the black-out, but which considerably restricted the ranks of those who could attend. Beecham conducted twice; Sir Hamilton Harty's programme included the first concert performance of his *John Field Suite*; Sir Henry Wood was in charge of a concert in aid of the Benevolent Fund of the Incorporated Society of Musicians, at which the *Serenade for Music*, composed by Vaughan Williams for Wood's seventieth birthday, was performed; and the final concert of the regular series was given under Sargent. To assist the Society overcome serious financial difficulties, the LPO promoted an additional concert on their behalf, the players generously forgoing their fees for performing. The difficulties of travelling across Europe reduced the number of visiting musicians from the Continent of Europe to a trickle, but the concert was notable for the last appearance in Britain of Felix Weingartner. Once Hitler's forces overran the rest of Europe his activities were confined to Switzerland, where he died in 1942.

The new date for Beecham's departure was set for April 1940, his last concert with the LPO before leaving taking place at the beginning of that month. As the war progressed an increasing number of concerts were organised supporting a variety of charitable causes. The winter months had seen the Finnish people engaged in a courageous defence of their country after being attacked by Soviet Russia. Though the fighting did not form part of the major European conflict, the spirited resistance of the Finns attracted much sympathy in Britain, and Beecham's concert, made up of the music of Sibelius, was given in support of the Finland Fund. The concert attracted a full house, and afterwards Gregory hosted a post-concert dinner for Beecham, conductor and orchestra parting on terms indicating mutual regard for each other, Gregory leaving no room for doubt that, however much the orchestra regretted Beecham's departure, they still regarded him as their chief.

Yet whatever the tributes offered to Beecham on his departure, what can one make of his protracted absence from this country? Including an initial visit to Australia, he spent four and a half years away from home, mostly in America, with excursions to Canada and Mexico, conducting a sequence of mostly inferior orchestras, and indulging himself verbally at the expense of his hosts and his countrymen. It was not a war effort to be proud of, bearing no comparison with that of other British musicians. Sir Adrian Boult, who conducted the Hallé, the LPO and the LSO whenever his BBC duties allowed, often without taking a fee or charging expenses, Basil Cameron and, until his last illness and death, Sir Henry Wood, all worked tirelessly, as did Albert Coates, Constant Lambert and many others. Malcolm Sargent, conducting in Australia when the war broke out, pleaded with the Australian Broadcasting Commission to be released from his contract, in order that he could return home immediately, and though this was refused, did everything possible to expedite his return, arriving in England before the year was out. Throughout the war Sargent took on a colossal workload, and on his own estimate during 1942 conducted an average of a concert a day. John Barbirolli was also abroad in September 1939. Under contract to the New York Philharmonic, he had no immediate hope of returning, but in 1942, with the Battle of the Atlantic at its height, he persuaded Mr A.V. Alexander, the First Lord of the Admiralty, to allow him to take passage to England in order that he might use part of his vacation conducting the LPO and the LSO, spending a month crisscrossing the country and giving over thirty concerts before embarking on the equally perilous return journey to the USA. In 1943, no longer conductor of the New York Philharmonic, he was invited to become Principal Conductor of the Hallé Orchestra. Barbirolli and his wife reached Lisbon in a Portuguese freighter, where briefly their lives were in the balance. Booked to fly from Lisbon to Dublin, at the last minute they obtained seats on an earlier plane to London. Normally the Allies and the Germans left commercial flights alone, but as a result of a rumour that Churchill would be on the later flight, the aircraft was shot down and all on board were killed, including the actor Leslie Howard. There was no contractual reason for Beecham to prolong his stay in America, delaying his return until the autumn of 1944, by which time the Battle of the Atlantic had long tilted in the Allies' favour, and his biographers offer no satisfactory explanation as to why he did so. In response to an enquiry from an admirer as to why he had postponed his planned sabbatical, Beecham replied, 'the country was in a state of emergency, and so I emerged'. This quip cannot hide the fact that, for much of the war, Beecham turned his back on his countrymen.

4

Blitzkreig, Priestley and Hylton 1940

In the immediate aftermath of Beecham's departure three Beethoven concerts were given in Queen's Hall, conducted by Basil Cameron, Charles Hambourg and Malcolm Sargent. Attendances were encouraging, leading to a short series of music by Bach, under Sargent, Sir Adrian Boult and Sir Henry Wood. But the war was entering a new phase. The German invasion of Denmark and Norway took place on the day of the first Beethoven concert. Hopes that the Norwegians, supported by Allied troops, would be able to repel the invaders soon faded, and by early May Norway was being evacuated. Worse was in store, and on 10 May, two days after the first Bach concert, Hitler attacked Holland and Belgium. With the events of the next few weeks an uninterrupted chapter of disasters, audiences at the Bach concerts were disappointing, while the impossibility of bringing other plans to fruition again brought the LPO close to collapse.

One avenue being explored by Russell was an approach from an Italian conductor, Fausto Magnani, who wanted to conduct in Britain. Formerly principal cello of the Orchestra of La Scala, Magnani was an unknown quantity as a conductor. Nevertheless, with the engagement book unsatisfactorily empty, it seemed worth arranging a meeting in Paris, where the would-be débutante was living. Quite what Magnani's qualifications were is uncertain. According to Russell, he possessed 'enormous faith in his own talents and in the originality of his approach to the orchestra'. The upshot of their meeting was a plan for Magnani to conduct a gala concert in London, for which Magnani undertook to foot the bill, and Queen's Hall was booked for the end of May. Just how well the orchestra would have responded to 'the originality of his approach' must be open to doubt, the German assault in the West putting paid to this venture and Magnani abandoned plans to make his reputation in Britain, departing instead for New York, where he failed to make any great impact on the musical life of America.

Of more importance were plans for an Anglo-French Festival. The Society of British Musicians had a similar project in train, and it was agreed to make the Festival a co-operative event, with the organisation undertaken by Russell in partnership with Edward Clark. An approach to the French Ministry of Fine Arts produced a favourable response, and though there were only limited facilities for travelling to France, official circles in Britain placed enough importance on the Festival to justify granting Russell and Clark permission to visit Paris. The background to their visit was sombre. By the time they arrived German troops were less than seventy miles away, and an air raid led to one meeting with their French opposite numbers taking place underground. During their brief stay the city was declared a military zone, and it was only with difficulty that they obtained the approval of the French military authorities to their departure. In the days leading up to the Festival the news from the continent became steadily worse. The Germans entered Paris on 14 June and three days later, twenty four hours before the first concert was due to take place, the new French leader, Marshal Pétain, broadcast to the French people, informing them that negotiations for an armistice were under way. The impossibility of any of the French musicians who were to take part travelling to Britain had been apparent for some time, but the opening concert went ahead, conducted by Basil Cameron instead of Phillipe Gaubert, with Clifford Curzon replacing Marguerite Long as soloist, and John Ireland's Piano Concerto substituted for that of Ravel. One other event took place, a concert of chamber music, the collapse of France putting paid to the rest of the Festival.

These were not the only concerts to be cancelled. As the orchestra reported in its magazine, 'all the phases of wartime life conspire to deal serious blows to the welfare of the orchestra. A concert is arranged and advertised, a large proportion of the seats sold – and the hall is suddenly commandeered by a military authority. Or, an air raid scare takes place in a provincial town immediately before a concert, with disastrous results.' This last may have referred to a mini-festival, which Herbert Menges, who had a long association with Brighton, suggested promoting in the town. Three concerts were arranged over one weekend, Menges conducting the last, which the BBC arranged to broadcast, with the others entrusted to Cameron and Sargent. The timing could not have been worse. On the opening night German bombers visited the town for the first time, and though all three concerts took place, the effect on attendances was disastrous.

The flow of funds generated by Beecham's appeal had never completely dried up, and from time to time further sums continued to arrive. But these funds were quickly eaten up by the cost of railway tickets and a decision to begin purchasing music rather than hiring it. The provision of music was an area where they were already indebted to Sir Adrian Boult, who placed his collection of scores and parts at their disposal, as did a resident of Huddersfield, Mr Kay, who owned a sizeable collection, and the decision to purchase additional parts, though costly in the short term, was designed to have long-term benefits. With the failure of the Brighton concerts the LPO's reserves were all but exhausted, and once again the orchestra's existence was in jeopardy. Yet from this low point the fortunes of the LPO were about to change dramatically.

Behind the scenes Berta Geissmar was making considerable efforts to find ways in which more significant funds could be raised. As a result of her pre-war experience of working with Beecham at Covent Garden she was able to approach a wide range of people whose influence might be brought to bear, leading to an invitation for Russell to visit the author and broadcaster J.B. Priestley, who expressed interest in the orchestra's problems and wanted to know more. Russell found Priestley sympathetic, anxious to know if his skills could be used to the orchestra's advantage, and particularly interested in Russell's description of the response to the appeal made by Beecham earlier in the year. That appeal was limited in nature, with little in the way of publicity, and their discussion led to a plan for a new appeal, to be launched by a concert in Queen's Hall. The concert was to involve not one but three conductors, and Priestley would take part, speaking about the orchestra from the platform. Priestley was one of the most popular broadcasters of the day, with a wide following, many listeners finding his Yorkshire accent a welcome variation from standard BBC English. Enrolling his support helped to ensure the widest possible publicity.

Russell found Priestley's enthusiasm infectious, to the extent of being won over by the suggestion that, despite the difficulty of working to what would normally have been an impossible time-table, the concert should take place the following week. To ensure concert and appeal made the maximum impact, Priestley and Russell hit on the idea of calling the event a 'Musical Manifesto'. Hurried telephoning found a willing response from conductors and soloist, Queen's Hall was booked and the following programme advertised:

Elgar: Overture, Cockaigne (**Sir Adrian Boult**); Grieg: Piano Concerto in A minor (**Eileen Joyce and Basil Cameron**); Sibelius: Symphony No 2. in D (**Dr Malcolm Sargent**)

The timing of the concert, which took place on 18 July, was fortunate. Though France had fallen, and some air attacks were taking place, mainly on shipping and towns along the south coast, London itself was still relatively quiet. It would be mid-August before the Battle of Britain started in earnest and German planes were seen over the capital in any numbers. The combination of conductors and soloist, and the support of Priestley's name, ensured that despite the short notice, the first objective was achieved without difficulty: the hall was sold out.

The subsequent response exceeded all expectations. Priestley's involvement ensured that, in addition to advance publicity, the concert and appeal were widely covered afterwards, and the office was inundated by donations, ranging from substantial cheques – an anonymous Scottish donor gave £1000, and a cheque for the same amount was received from the Hon. James Smith, a Director of the Royal Opera House, now in the armed services – down to shilling and half-crown postal orders. They came from people in all walks of life: adults, children, members of the armed forces, the wealthy, the middle classes, and those of modest means. One donation came from California. When everything had been banked and every donation acknowledged, financial disaster had been averted and the LPO could look to the future with more confidence than at any time since the outbreak of war.

There was also help from some unexpected sources, the bandleader Joe Loss donating the proceeds of an evening's entertainment by his orchestra. Richard Tauber was another musician to offer practical help, suggesting that he should give a concert in support of their funds, appearing in the triple role of conductor, composer and singer. Many noted conductors have made the transition from the ranks of the orchestra to the rostrum, but at the time few musicians pursued a dual career – Casals was a notable exception – and the idea of a singer doing so, let alone fulfilling both roles at the same concert, was decidedly novel. Few people were aware that Tauber had prior experience as a conductor and doubts were expressed about the wisdom of agreeing to his proposal, but to the doubters' surprise the concert was successful, leading to further invitations to conduct, both in London and the provinces. Tauber had a limited repertoire, but within those limits proved a more than capable practitioner. Malcolm Sargent supposedly commented that 'If Tauber is going to conduct, he (Sargent) would take to singing', to be chastened by the riposte, 'By all means do so – if you can'.

The number of younger people attracted to their concerts, the warm reception given to *Philharmonic Post*, and the overwhelming response to the 'Musical Manifesto', supported the view that it should be possible to attract a much wider audience, extending well beyond the narrow boundaries of those who normally attended concerts before the war. With their financial uncertainties resolved, at least for the immediate future, the next task was to find a way to harness the enthusiasm of this new public. The solution lay just around the corner.

Shortly after the 'Musical Manifesto', Russell received a mysterious telephone call asking if he would be interested in what was described as a novel proposal for taking the orchestra on tour. The caller was unwilling to divulge the identity of the backer or give further details, but assured that it would not involve the LPO in any financial risk, Russell agreed to a meeting at which the scheme would be outlined. The intermediary was identified as Brian Michie, well-known from radio and the world of entertainment, but until the last minute Russell was in the dark as to the author of the proposal. To his surprise he found it came from one of the country's best-known dance band leaders, Jack Hylton, who had recently gone into theatrical management, with a string of theatres and variety theatres up and down the country.

Hylton had been greatly impressed by the 'Musical Manifesto', and the public response, and proposed to Russell that the LPO should undertake a national tour on very different lines from their pre-war provincial tours, playing twice nightly in music halls or variety theatres, located in some of the largest industrial cities in the country, mostly in the North and Midlands. Hylton was quick to stifle any doubts as to his intentions by giving assurances, first that he had no ambitions to conduct, and second, there was no question of the orchestra sharing the stage with anyone else. There would be no comedians, jugglers, snake charmers, song and dance acts, sword swallowers, young ladies being sawn in half by magicians, or any of the acts normally associated with music hall and variety. The LPO would be responsible for choosing the programmes and conductors, and the tour would have the support of the Hylton publicity machine. Hylton undertook to ensure that the visual presentation of the orchestra would be made as attractive as possible, especially important for a public likely to include a high proportion of people who had never been to a symphony concert. The Hylton team were to construct a special set, which would travel with the orchestra; as well as being visually attractive, this was designed to overcome the boxed-in sound resulting from playing on an enclosed stage. Hylton proposed a tour lasting ten weeks, offering the players considerably more employment than they had enjoyed for some time. Coupled with the fact that Hylton guaranteed full financial backing, this was enough to convince Gregory and Russell that while purists might look askance at the idea of the LPO playing in variety theatres, Hylton's proposal matched their objective of trying to attract a wider audience.

After mulling over various names it was agreed to invite Malcolm Sargent to undertake the bulk of the conducting, relieved once a week by Basil Cameron. Undoubtedly Sargent had faults. He was less than diplomatic in his handling of musicians, often treating them as schoolchildren rather than as skilled professionals, and his career was punctuated by disputes with orchestras and managements. But whatever those faults, he was the ideal person for a venture of this nature. His dapper appearance, with never a hair out of place, brisk platform manner and an ability to talk in simple terms about the music being played, were calculated to appeal to audiences making their first acquaintance with a symphony orchestra. He was moreover highly practical, not just in his approach to the preparation and rehearsal of a substantial quantity of music, but to ways in which the lighting and the stage layout could improve the presentation of a concert. Sargent's critics argued that his platform manner, which included a large element of showmanship, was undignified. Undeniably he had a large streak of vanity, milking applause for all it was worth, judging to perfection the number of curtain calls that could be obtained, but for audiences used to the kind of entertainment found in a music hall or variety theatre, where showmanship played an important part, everything about Sargent's personality helped to break down barriers.

The speed at which the Hylton organisation worked was remarkable. After rehearsals in London and a Sunday concert in Harrogate, the tour proper opened in Glasgow on 12 August, barely three weeks after Russell's first meeting with Hylton. Russell wrote how he and Hylton stood at the back of the theatre on the first evening in Glasgow:

> Here at last was the ideal audience. Distinctions of class, education and money had ceased to mean anything. Everybody was represented, and the rapt, almost reverend attention was a striking proof of the faith I had always had; that music was something for everyone, and that its power was in no way restricted to a small coterie of super-sensitive souls.

If this overlooked that most cosmopolitan of audiences, the Prom audience, which cast its net over all sections of society – Ferruccio Bonavia, one-time music critic of *The Daily Telegraph*, told how he was once overtaken by an errand boy whistling the last movement of the Beethoven Violin Concerto, and in response to an enquiry as to where he learned his Beethoven, received the reply, 'At the Proms, of course' – the tenor of Russell's sentiments was widely shared. Barbirolli, after his return to England, expressed pride in the fact that he and his orchestra were bringing music to 'the people'.

The Glasgow concerts were followed by weeks in Manchester, Bradford, Edinburgh, Newcastle, Birmingham, Leeds, Sheffield, Nottingham, Liverpool and Oxford, several of which received return visits, and similar weeks took place in other towns and cities including, in June 1941, a three-week season at London's Coliseum Theatre. The opening of the tour coincided with the start of the Battle of Britain, followed in the autumn by night-time raids on many of the major centres of population. During the next eighteen months most of these cities suffered heavily at one time or another, the tour ever after referred to as the Blitz Tour. In the face of heavy bombing during the previous week the visit to Liverpool was postponed, but with this exception the Hylton weeks never coincided with the worst attacks, and whether performing for Hylton, or under their own banner, it was only on rare occasions that concerts were cancelled.

As the bombing of London intensified, long absences from home, family and friends caused much anxiety and cost many a phone call to ensure all was well. Mercifully none of the players suffered injury. One Monday morning a message was received to say that the house belonging to Wynn Reeves had been destroyed, and there was alarm when he failed to turn up at Euston in time to join the other players, who were departing for the north of England. To Russell's relief he arrived in time to catch a later train, he and his wife having spent the night staying with a relative. Berta Geissmar was also bombed out. She too escaped without harm, having spent the night in an air raid shelter. Putting the short break resulting from cancellation of the planned week of concerts in Liverpool to good use, one player and his fiancée, who had been bombed out of her own home, used it to bring forward their planned wedding. With several weeks of touring starting almost immediately afterwards, husband and wife enjoyed only a brief honeymoon, but on returning home it was to find the area cordoned off because of the danger from an unexploded bomb, preventing them from entering his apartment and obtaining both the change of clothes necessary for an absence lasting several weeks, and his dress suit. Fortunately, at least on this occasion, his instrument had been temporarily stored at Queen's Hall, but it was several days before the dress suit caught up with him in the Midlands.

The opening week in Glasgow was an outstanding success, which was repeated elsewhere, providing justification for all the heartache attendant on the decision to keep the orchestra in being. By its end thirty thousand people had flocked to hear the twice-nightly programmes, and if there is a point marking the start of the boom in concert giving which was to run for the rest of the war, this was it. The Hylton publicity machine worked wonders, but almost certainly part of the audience came because they habitually went to the music hall each week, regardless of the names on the bill. One teenager, who always climbed to the gallery on a Monday, to sample whatever was on offer, was so struck he returned every night for the rest of the week. This was no isolated experience. A letter in *Philharmonic Post* from a young trainee naval officer, Sidney Dell, related how he would have expected less than half the members of his mess to be interested in attending a concert, yet when the opportunity arose, all but one wanted to go, one of his colleagues expressing astonishment 'that it was possible to find it so enjoyable'.

Twice-nightly was something of a misnomer. The exigencies of wartime soon required earlier starting times, and whereas in August concerts at the Palace Theatre Manchester began at 6.00 and 8.15, on their return visit in November the starting times had been brought forward to 3.30 and 5.45. Inevitably the repertoire was based on the most popular standard classics, bringing complaints that it was not adventurous enough. But if symphonies by Beethoven, Dvorak, Schubert and Tchaikovsky were familiar to regular concert-goers, these were uncharted waters for newcomers, though some of the shorter pieces, *Finlandia, Pomp and Circumstance* and Berlioz' *Hungarian* March, might have been familiar from arrangements for brass band. Though Sargent was far from enthusiastic, Hylton successfully pressed for the inclusion of Gershwin's *Rhapsody in Blue*; Eileen Joyce contributed piano solos, and Thomas Matthews played the solo part in items such as Kreisler's *Caprice Viennoise*. One provincial paper printed a letter bearing several signatures, complaining about the familiarity of the Beethoven and Tchaikovsky works and pleading for more varied programmes. A day or two later another correspondent wrote to say that while he agreed, 'how shall we explain the queue of more than a hundred people that renews itself all day long at the theatre box office?' As Russell repeatedly pointed out, 'one seemingly harmless piece of unfamiliar music will sway the minds of perhaps two hundred people against attending a concert'.

Admission prices were modest, an ancient playbill from the Leeds Empire showing a top price of three shillings, with some seats at under a shilling, but even with full houses the order of the day, and Sargent appearing for a fraction of his pre-war fee, receipts were never sufficient to make ends meet. It was estimated that the first ten weeks cost Hylton around a thousand pounds, modest by comparison with the sums spent by Samuel Courtauld and Robert Mayer, but crucial in the struggle to balance the books.

Gregory and Russell had misgivings about venturing into territory that could have been regarded as belonging to the orchestras resident in Glasgow, Liverpool and Manchester, but in general these were put to rest by the warmth of the reception given them by the local managements. Manchester was an exception, the LPO's activities in and around that city giving rise to concern. In April 1939 Sargent had accepted an invitation to become Conductor-in-Chief and Musical Adviser to the Hallé, and his appearances with the LPO, in Manchester and elsewhere, were viewed with concern by members of the Hallé, who regarded him as their 'chief'. After some correspondence, and a meeting between Sargent and representatives of the Hallé Executive Committee and their orchestra, the matter was resolved. Most of the Hallé Committee, though not all, took the view that because their orchestra only operated on a part-time basis they could hardly restrict Sargent's freedom to conduct elsewhere. On nights when Sargent was conducting the Hallé the LPO gave Basil Cameron an increased share of the workload, with occasional evenings entrusted to Edric Cundell and Charles Hambourg.

With the Battle of Britain changing course, London began to experience nightly raids. Concert-giving in the capital became increasingly restricted, and for most of the following winter it was only possible for concerts to take place in the afternoon. The war put paid to the Courtauld-Sargent concerts, but the Royal Philharmonic Society gave six concerts on Saturday afternoons. With the LPO engaged in a Hylton week at Sheffield, the opening concert was given by the LSO, with the remainder undertaken by the LPO, two conducted by Cameron, with Boult, Leslie Heward and Dr Reginald Jacques responsible for one apiece. The Society's concerts provided some welcome variety. Dr Jacques conducted a Bach programme, Heward's concert included the Violin Concerto of Delius and Elgar's Second Symphony, and Cameron conducted the first British performance of the Second Symphony of the American composer Randall Thompson. Despite the conditions in which orchestras and concert-giving organisations were operating, the wartime Proms, the concerts of the Royal Philharmonic Society, and those promoted by the LPO itself, were more varied than might have been expected.

5

Tours and Tribulations 1940–42

By comparison with the spring and summer, when engagements had been few and far between, the LPO was now carrying out an exhausting schedule, and in the course of the next twelve months the orchestra gave over four hundred performances. The intervening Sundays between Hylton weeks were often filled by concerts in such places as Blackpool, Grimsby, Harrogate, Leeds and Llandudno, while other weeks were occupied by a series of one-night stands. After Hylton weeks in Birmingham, Leeds and Sheffield, rather than return to London the orchestra criss-crossed the Midlands and north-east with concerts in Wolverhampton, Hanley, Malvern, Cheltenham, Oxford, Northampton, Nottingham, Coventry, Bolton, Rochdale and Wigan. After well over a month away from home, it was inevitable that once-white shirts and ties were no longer in pristine condition.

To begin with, touring often involved tedious, and apparently illogical, cross-country journeys, but with greater experience it was possible to plan on a more rational basis. Wherever possible the amount of travelling and its cost were minimised by arranging concerts in towns located reasonably close together, avoiding journeys that involved changing trains, trying to ensure that if the orchestra was playing in London on Sunday, the previous night's concert did not involve a long overnight journey. Altrincham, Buxton or Liverpool to London, with an afternoon concert in Queen's Hall next day, could be a daunting prospect, offering only a few hours at home before the players resumed their travels.

The threat of invasion, and its close proximity to enemy-occupied France, placed the South Coast out of bounds. Even so, the first two years of touring activity involved concerts in nearly a hundred different towns and cities, ranging from the very largest, like those visited during the Blitz Tour, to some of modest size, such as Trowbridge and Woking. With much of the population engaged in shift working, lunchtime concerts were sometimes arranged for factory workers. One such concert took place at midnight, a picture by the artist Kapp showing the LPO playing to an enormous audience in a factory canteen, though it was presumably for reasons of security that the caption does not identify the location. Despite travelling difficulties, long slow journeys in overcrowded trains, unheated in winter, the windows blacked out, making it difficult to read station names, and with no refreshment facilities, it was a rare occurrence for a concert to be cancelled. Once, due to severe winter weather, the orchestra was twelve hours late arriving in Preston, and on the same tour the music and instruments failed to arrive at Wakefield in time. On another occasion Sargent's car became stuck in a snowdrift, Thomas Matthews finding himself called on to conduct at five minutes' notice, no easy task when the programme included the first British performance of Copland's *Theatre Overture*. But these were isolated instances: Wally Knight, who set up and cleared the platform, and saw that everything travelled safely from one location to the next, worked a daily series of small miracles to ensure audiences were not disappointed.

If travelling caused problems, even greater difficulties could be encountered when players tried to find a bed for the night. These were less acute when the orchestra stayed in one place for a week, but it was another matter when they were engaged in one-night stands, particularly in some of the smaller towns, where at the best of times there was limited accommodation for visitors. Sometimes the audience came to the rescue. There was an overwhelming response to an appeal made by Sargent after a concert in Swindon, with more beds on offer than bodies to fill them, but it was not unknown for players to bed down on the floor of the hall where they had been playing. Occasionally, as a last resort, some resorted to the waiting room at the station. Winifred Cockerill, the orchestra's harpist, was once thankful to find a spare bed at the local maternity home. In a broadcast talk Sir Adrian Boult recalled that 'one of the most popular towns visited by the LPO was Cheltenham. The concert hall is also the spa building, and the spacious corridors are well provided with most comfortable sofas – no one bothered about digs on these nights'.

Obtaining proper meals was also a recurring problem, with many a concert given on short commons. Russell related how, during the apparently interminable journey to Preston, in an unheated train, with passengers huddled together for whatever warmth they could obtain, one of his colleagues related, in detail, the meal that, had it been available, would have put paid to his misery. Soup, a Dover sole, sirloin of beef, a pint of Guinness, course followed course before he was interrupted by an ironic voice from the corner of the carriage, 'Would you like a roll, sir?' Given the circumstances it was amazing that the players' health stood up to the life they were leading, though the difficulties they encountered, particularly in winter, were no worse than those experienced by industrial workers, for many of whom the war was a succession of interminable weeks, with long hours, much overtime and the prospect of a miserable night in an Anderson shelter. During the winter of 1940–41, with the Blitz at its peak, audiences and players alike found all their physical and mental resources put to the test.

The make-up of concert programmes also acquired new importance. For a time it was possible to accept the programmes offered by conductors, but with the increasing number of concerts given outside London, and the growth of touring by other orchestras, it became necessary to exercise stricter control, with a range of factors to be taken into account. Had any of the works under consideration been played in those towns recently? Had the orchestra played them under another conductor? Did the schedule allow sufficient rehearsal time? Later, as some towns and cities were visited on a more regular basis, there were requests for specific works to be performed. Initially the work of compiling programmes was undertaken by Russell and Aprahamian, but after a time it was handed over to a formal programme committee. With democracy a keynote of their affairs, this committee was elected from the ranks of the orchestra.

By contemporary standards the marketing appears naive. When in July 1941 the LPO visited Rhos in South Wales, giving concerts in the Miners Institute, the posters read:

> Musical Culture Limited presents
> FOR THE FIRST TIME IN HISTORY
> Special Visit of the Entire
> LONDON PHILHARMONIC ORCHESTRA
> (70 Master Players)

Full houses were essential and it was important not to overprice tickets, the most expensive seats rarely costing more than five shillings, often less, and at afternoon performances several hundred were often set aside for schoolchildren at a shilling a head. The concerts in Rhos formed part of a Welsh tour for which the conductor was Richard Tauber, notable, according to Berta Geissmar, for his 'Tauber cocktails', a concoction of his devising which, for all the fact that it was non-alcoholic, proved extremely popular with the orchestra.

Despite the bombardment suffered by London the lunchtime concerts at the National Gallery continued without interruption, and from the end of November the LPO appeared regularly on Sunday afternoons at Queen's Hall, where Harold Holt still presented their concerts under the title of 'The Beecham Sunday Concerts'. As a contribution to London's efforts to cope with the bombing Keith Douglas, the Secretary of the Royal Philharmonic Society, and the Hon. James Smith, a member of the Committee of Management, raised funds to purchase a mobile canteen, which bore the name of the LPO. The brainchild of Mrs Dora Strang, who acted as driver and manager, the canteen provided refreshment for ambulancemen, firemen and rescue workers. At weekends it was stationed outside Queen's Hall, plastered with posters advertising concerts by both the LPO and the LSO. Before and after the concert, and during the interval, it served tea and biscuits to concert-goers, with the profits donated to the Lord Mayor's Fund set up to assist those made homeless as a result of the bombing.

The Royal Choral Society resumed its activities in January 1940, performing *Messiah*. With many people bombed out or called up, there was no guarantee that the Society's membership records were still accurate. Advertisements were placed in a number of newspapers, inviting members to turn up on the day of the concert, for which there was a short rehearsal starting at noon. To general amazement two hundred and fifty arrived by the start of the rehearsal, with more turning up as it progressed. Encouraged by this response, they too began to give concerts on a regular basis, including the customary Good Friday performances of *Messiah*. On Saturday, 10 May 1941, in what was to be the last concert in Queen's Hall, the Society gave Elgar's *Dream of Gerontius*, with Muriel Brunskill, Webster Booth and Ronald Stear as soloists, accompanied by the LPO. With a concert of their own the following afternoon, many players left their instruments in the hall, some in the band room and others, mostly the brass, upstairs in the press room. That night London suffered its worst raid of the war. At around eleven o'clock two members of the staff on fire-watching duty heard an incendiary bomb hit the roof. Initially they tackled the fire which broke out with one of the hosepipes in the hall, and for a time thought they had succeeded in putting it out. However it had only been damped down, and when flames broke out again the fire-watchers found to their dismay that the water pressure had failed, a common occurrence that night. Once the fire took hold, it spread quickly. Soon the whole roof was ablaze, and by morning, Queen's Hall was practically gutted. The fire-watchers tried to summon help, but the London Fire Brigade was swamped with calls, their resources stretched to the limit, making it impossible to respond. Queen's Hall was not the only famous building hit that night. The House of Commons debating chamber was destroyed and many other famous buildings were damaged, including the British Museum, the Law Courts, the Mansion House, the Tower of London and Westminster Abbey. Fourteen hundred civilians were killed and nearly eighteen hundred injured. As well as being the worst, this was also the last major raid on London. Hitler's eyes were turning east, and henceforth most of the Luftwaffe's activities would be directed elsewhere.

When the players arrived on Sunday morning they found a scene of desolation. The instruments left in the press room survived the blaze, but of those left in the bandroom all that remained were some blackened pieces of metal. Some members of the LSO also lost instruments, their principal bass player suffering a double loss, one instrument being destroyed at Queen's Hall, his second meeting a similar fate at Denham Film Studios, which were also badly damaged that night. One item recovered undamaged was the bust of Sir Henry Wood, which to this day is placed at the back of the platform during every Prom season. In keeping with the oft-used slogan 'Business as usual', the orchestra immediately set out to resurrect their afternoon concert, Charles Gregory securing an alternative venue in the shape of the Duke's Hall of the Royal Academy of Music. To enable players who had lost instruments to obtain alternatives, the rehearsal was cancelled. Some had spares at home, which they could use themselves, or lend to colleagues, others benefitting from the generosity of members of the public who either loaned or gave them instruments. Charles Taylor, the Manager of Queen's Hall, set up shop on a table outside the hall, selling tickets and directing concert-goers to the new venue, and at three o'clock, half an hour after the advertised time, Maurice Miles walked on to the platform to conduct before a packed house, with several hundred would-be concert-goers turned away. To those present it was ironic, or significant, depending on their point of view, that the concert consisted almost entirely of music by German composers, a far cry from the xenophobia of the First World War, when some organisations placed an almost total ban on German music. In this war it was possible to take a more balanced view, distinguishing between Germany's cultural heritage and the evil of Fascism. No doubt many would have echoed the sentiments of an elderly lady who, after one concert, announced with some vehemence, 'Doesn't Beethoven make Hitler seem silly.' The programme that afternoon comprised:

> Beethoven: Overture, Coriolan; Haydn: Symphony No. 104 in D (*The London*); Franck: Symphonic Variations (**Soloist – Moura Lympany**); Brahms: Symphony No. 1 in C min

The plight of musicians who lost instruments was highlighted by the BBC and produced an overwhelming response. The London Cello School loaned a number of instruments, help came from the provincial orchestras, and the office was inundated with telephone calls and letters. Berta Geissmar recorded a touching gift from a bus driver who travelled up from Kent with a violin wrapped in brown paper. 'I cannot bear to think a player should be out of work,' he said, 'I know what that means.' Over three thousand offers of help were received and around a thousand instruments loaned or donated, many times the number needed. With the consent of the owners, it was possible to use many of these to help members of the LSO and other musicians who lost instruments as a result of the war.

Apart from nostalgia for a building in which many players had spent much of their working lives, destruction of the hall deprived the LPO of a venue in which they could promote concerts on their own account. The early months of 1941 had increasingly found the orchestra spending the weekend in London, performing on Saturdays for the Royal Choral and Royal Philharmonic Societies and at concerts under the young British conductor Maurice Miles, and though Sunday afternoon concerts were promoted by

Harold Holt, the LPO was beginning to give concerts in the hall on its own account. Like other concert-giving organisations, they had to face the problem of finding an alternative home. Various possibilities were considered, but the matter was decided by the example set by Keith Douglas, the Secretary of the Royal Philharmonic Society, who was once again responsible for staging the Proms, and who booked the Royal Albert Hall for a six-week season, engaging the LSO to perform throughout.

Prior to the war the Proms traditionally began on the Saturday immediately following the August Bank Holiday, which in those days fell on the first Monday in August. This was the case in 1940, when Wood and Douglas even adhered to the pre-war starting time of 8 p.m. Taking advantage of the fact that during summer the nation's clocks were now set two hours in advance of Greenwich Mean Time, the 1941 season began considerably earlier, on 12 July, running until 23 August, a starting time of half past six allowing the audience to reach home before it became dark. The police would not allow use of the upper gallery; even so, the hall's capacity was twice that of Queen's Hall and, after initial hesitation on the part of the public, within a short space of time the audience grew to a level far outstripping that of Queen's Hall. Other concert promoters followed Douglas' example, and for ten years the Albert Hall served as London's principal concert hall. The hall's acoustics were notorious, and Douglas asked an acoustic expert, Mr Hope Bagenal, to devise ways of overcoming the problem; he advised placing screens at the back of the orchestra, and a plywood canopy was suspended over the platform. These measures improved matters, but it was 1967 before the 'mushrooms' which now hang from the ceiling were installed, giving a marked improvement in the quality of the sound.

As a matter of prudence the LPO made no attempt to compete with the Proms. June was occupied with concerts given in conjunction with Jack Hylton, three weeks at the London Coliseum and a week at the Finsbury Park Empire. Opening on Whit Monday, the Coliseum season proved a huge attraction, drawing over twenty thousand people during the first week. Thereafter concerts were arranged in out-of-town centres, including weeks in Bristol, Cardiff and Hull, and ten days spent touring under the baton of Richard Tauber.

One serious disadvantage of the move to the Albert Hall arose from the fact that Harold Holt secured its use on Sunday afternoons. During the previous winter his concerts included a number of departures from the standard repertoire, including the first performance in this country of Britten's Violin Concerto, a work previously rejected by the Royal Philharmonic Society on extra-musical grounds. Discarding the title 'The Beecham Sunday Concerts' the programmes became increasingly stereotyped, giving rise to complaints about the repertoire, many directed at the orchestra rather than the promoter, complaints it was prudent to grin and bear. Financially the work was valuable, and it was against their interests to publicly disown the programmes. To do so ran the risk that another orchestra would be engaged in their stead. This did in fact happen two years later, but fortunately another venue became available, and when the time came it was a relief to escape from an unwelcome, if necessary, chore.

If the Sunday concerts stayed within the confines of a narrow range of music, those of the Royal Philharmonic Society continued to provide much-needed variety. During 1941–42 Leslie Heward conducted the Symphony by E.J. Moeran; Henry Holst gave the first performance in Britain of Walton's Violin Concerto, conducted by Cameron, and a concert under Boult included the Piano Concerto by Arthur Bliss. The following year Vaughan Williams conducted two of his own works, *A Sea Symphony* and *Dona Nobis Pacem*; Boult was in charge of the first performance of a revised version of Bartok's Concerto for Two Pianos, Percussion and Orchestra; Sir Henry Wood's concert included Moeran's Violin Concerto, and Cameron conducted Alan Rawsthorne's *Symphonic Studies*.

Towards the end of 1941 Thomas Russell received a phone call from the lessee of a theatre in Golders Green, the Orpheum, offering its use for concerts. The theatre, with a seating capacity rather larger than that of Queen's Hall, was often unoccupied, and the lessee was looking for business. The acoustics appeared satisfactory when the theatre was tried out in early December, and with London enjoying relief from the air raids of the previous winter, a series of Sunday evening concerts was arranged for January. Almost immediately these ran into difficulties, the lessee disappearing from sight, together with the receipts from the last two concerts. Though the LPO was left in possession of the theatre, the legal position was uncertain. Russell was keen to continue. Despite the fact that the building was unheated, the January concerts attracted sizeable and appreciative audiences, including a high proportion of young people, and despite being outside the centre of London, the Orpheum offered the prospect of providing the LPO with a home of its own. Against this had to be set the risk to be run from taking on full financial responsibility for the building, the burden of a Sunday evening concert on top of afternoon concerts for Harold Holt, and the difficulty of keeping the theatre occupied for the rest of the week. Russell was prepared to take a long view, envisaging the Orpheum as an arts centre for the local community. Others were less enthusiastic, concerned that running it would take up too much of their slender management resources, and that a venture which would have carried risks in more peaceful times was best avoided in wartime. After much debate it was decided to go ahead, and the experiment continued.

Concerts at the Orpheum continued to attract good audiences, and it was here that in 1942 the LPO celebrated its tenth birthday. In the absence of their founder, and despite the rivalry between the two men, it was Sir Henry Wood who took charge of the celebrations, given to a packed house, with many turned away, the concert opening with the first piece ever played by the orchestra, the Overture *Le Carnaval Romain*. When the LPO was engaged elsewhere, other orchestras took their place, including the LSO and the New London Orchestra, a short-lived body which played for opera seasons given by the impresario Jay Pomeroy at the Cambridge Theatre. Pomeroy was a colourful character who enlivened the London musical scene for a time, his money derived from an ingenious scheme which enabled Pomeroy and his associates to avoid Excess Profits Tax, levied at a rate of 100 per cent. The government and its tax inspectors were, however, more ingenious, and when Parliament passed retrospective legislation to disallow the scheme Pomeroy's activities came under the microscope of the Inland Revenue. Despite a long battle through the courts the inevitable result was bankruptcy, abruptly terminating his artistic activities.

Filling the theatre during the week was a never-ending problem. Visiting opera and ballet companies proved successful, the Carl Rosa Company attracting capacity audiences, and Christmas 1942 saw performances of *The Streets of London* by Dion Boucicault, a Victorian melodrama, at which the audience were invited to 'hiss the villain and cheer the heroine'. But despite pioneering work with local employers, offering ticket concessions aimed at increasing mid-week audiences, attendances for straight theatre were never large enough. With the theatre sometimes empty during the week, continued occupation placed too great a strain on management time and the always slender financial reserves. With varying degrees of reluctance, the experiment was brought to an end.

One survivor from the Orpheum was the London Philharmonic Arts Club, whose existence continued for several years, until declining membership led to it being wound up. The club became the responsibility of John Amis, who arranged recitals, talks, lectures and brains trusts, involving a distinguished list of musicians, broadcasters and actors. Orchestras may have been thriving, but many solo performers and chamber groups were only too pleased to obtain an engagement, even though it was impossible to offer more than a minimal fee. Membership cost a guinea (£1.05), with free entry to every meeting, a bargain when at one time an average of two meetings a week were being arranged, or alternatively half a crown (12½p), with an extra shilling (5p) for every meeting the member attended.

Guest conductors included a number of refugees from the Nazi domination of Europe, including Vilem Tausky and Dr Heinz Unger, but in general there was no opportunity to hear the work of overseas musicians. However 1942 saw the return home of John Barbirolli, whose perilous Atlantic crossing brought him to Liverpool in May of that year. For a month or thereabouts he divided his time between the LSO and the LPO, as well as giving a single studio concert with the BBC Symphony Orchestra. Barbirolli paid his own passage, and whatever modest fees he might have received were either donated to the orchestra he was conducting at the time, or given to a wartime charity.

Apart from some mild departures from the beaten track, a couple of his own arrangements of music by Bach, Debussy's *Petite Suite* and Delius' *Song of Summer*, the music Barbirolli brought with him was largely drawn from the repertoire performed up and down the country for the past two years, Beethoven's Seventh Symphony, Brahms' Second, the *Enigma* Variations, Tchaikovsky Four and Five, with helpings of Rossini, Tchaikovsky and Wagner to round out the programmes. If some of these had been played too often for the orchestra's good, he was nevertheless a tonic to players and audiences alike. When working in London Barbirolli used buses or trams, and on tour travelled with the players, sharing their discomforts of wartime travelling, the difficulties in finding accommodation and the poor, and sometimes infrequent, wartime meals. Back in the United States he was to chide American audiences for grumbling about the minor restrictions imposed on them by the war. The convoy in which he travelled took longer than anticipated, and he was unable to fulfil all the engagements planned for him, other conductors having to take his place at Bristol, Halifax and Leeds, but elsewhere, in Cambridge or London, Sheffield or Walsall, he and the orchestras he conducted received a rapturous reception. It was a foretaste of the success which was to attend his work with the Hallé Orchestra when he returned home for good the following year.

In 1942 the LPO performed at the Proms for the first time. Sir Henry Wood had been far from happy with Keith Douglas as his Manager. Wood was upset by Douglas' attempt to impose reduced fees on soloists and by the fact that, with the Albert Hall an untried venue, Douglas played for safety in planning the programmes. In 1941, despite the fact that the season lasted only six weeks instead of eight, many works received more than one performance, with the Eighth Symphony of Beethoven played three times. Much to Wood's relief, in 1942 management of the concerts reverted to the BBC. Lasting a full eight weeks, the season started earlier than ever, on 27 June; the BBC Symphony Orchestra was brought back to London for the second half of the season, but the first four weeks were entrusted to the LPO, providing some relief from the constant round of travelling which occupied much of the year. Wood was now well past his seventieth birthday, and though appearing every night, accepted the need for an associate conductor. In 1941 these duties were undertaken by Basil Cameron, who in 1942 continued to provide assistance for concerts given by the LPO. For the second half of the season, when the BBC Symphony Orchestra took over, Sir Adrian Boult shared the conducting.

The programmes were more adventurous this year. The LPO premiered Alan Bush's Symphony and Rawsthorne's First Piano Concerto, conducted by their composers; Wood accompanied Arthur Catterall in Moeran's Violin Concerto; Cameron conducted the first performance in this country of

Britten's *Sinfonia da Requiem*, and there were pieces by Mary Anderson-Lucas, Harry Farjeon and William Leonard Reed, composers who are now barely footnotes to history. In a change to the originally published programme, Tchaikovsky's Fourth Symphony was replaced by the *Leningrad* Symphony of Shostakovitch. The symphony should have been performed by the BBC Symphony Orchestra, but the parts were delayed and the performance was postponed until 22 June, the first anniversary of the German invasion of Russia, when it was broadcast from the BBC's Maida Vale Studios, with the LPO playing under Wood.

There is a degree of notoriety about this performance. The score and parts arrived by air in the shape of several hundred slides of microfilm, containing numerous errors, and there was a race against time to correct them. It was then discovered that the work was far longer than the hour leading up to the nine o'clock evening news which had been allotted to it. As the nine o'clock news was sacrosanct, and overrunning out of the question, Wood set out to fit the music to the time available, speeding passages up and making cuts, the performance beating the clock by a matter of seconds. Wood had a reputation for cutting works he deemed too long to hold the listener's attention, and in the early days of the Proms, with only three rehearsals a week, there was perhaps some excuse, but whatever Wood's satisfaction at beating the clock – according to his biographer, immediately the studio broadcast was over he declared with considerable satisfaction, 'We've done it! And not a second either way' – his actions, and those of the BBC who concurred in them, were a disservice to Shostakovitch. The studio performance and that given at the Proms the following week can only have been a travesty of the composer's intentions.

As time progressed there were further changes in personnel, with more players called up by the armed services, including Geoffrey Gilbert and Bernard Walton. Gilbert's position as first flute was filled by Richard Adeney, and Walton was succeeded by Terence MacDonagh, and then on a more permanent basis by Michael Dobson. A new face in the trumpet section was that of the twenty-one-year-old Malcolm Arnold, appointed principal in the following year, a post he held, apart from a brief interval, until 1948, when he resigned in order to devote himself to composition. 1942 also saw the departure of Thomas Matthews, who had been offered the post of Music Director to the Malay Broadcasting Company. Fortunately for Matthews, the fall of Singapore led to his ship being diverted and he escaped internment, spending the rest of the war in New Zealand. Reginald Morley took over on a temporary basis, but shortly afterwards the BBC disbanded its Salon Orchestra. A number of its leading members opted to join the newly formed Liverpool Philharmonic, but in addition to restoring Victor Watson to his position as principal double bass the LPO was able to persuade Jean Pougnet to accept an invitation to become leader. Pougnet was a fine violinist who made his reputation as a soloist and chamber player, but he had virtually no orchestral experience, with the result that he found himself playing works unfamiliar to him as a performer. At one rehearsal he asked Basil Cameron if they could play through parts of Tchaikovsky's Fifth Symphony, a request which brought understandable groans from his colleagues. Assured that the work should pose no problems, Pougnet replied, 'Yes, I know, but as a matter of fact I've never played it before.' Some years later in a radio broadcast, Cameron commented that there were a number of over-played works which were apt to bring groans from the orchestra when he announced them at rehearsal: 'I always try to get my groan in first,' he added.

Despite a schedule leaving little, if any, free time, during the autumn of 1942 the orchestra was involved in making a film based on their wartime experiences. The original concept was a full-length feature based on the history of the LPO, with a script by Priestley. This failed to get off the ground, but a little later the Ministry of Information agreed to production of a documentary showing how the orchestra had survived the outbreak of war. Matters seemed to be progressing smoothly, but at almost the last moment the Ministry backed down, apparently on grounds of cost. The producer, Donald Taylor, was reluctant to drop the idea, and having secured the rights to the script, found sufficient backing to enable him to embark on filming *Battle for Music*. Russell, Priestley and Hylton took part, as did many of those who had performed with the LPO on tour, including Boult, Sargent and the pianists Eileen Joyce and Benno Moisewitsch, with several members of the orchestra taking cameo parts, notably John Kuchmy and Maurice Ward. The producers had to use a degree of dramatic licence, Constant Lambert standing in for Beecham in a recreation of the first wartime concert in Cardiff – did this supposedly expert Tchaikovskian always take the opening bars of *Romeo and Juliet* quite so slowly? – and Warwick Braithwaite took Cameron's place in a scene depicting the 'Musical Manifesto', with what appears to be the London Coliseum serving as the location for scenes meant to represent concerts both in Queen's Hall and several provincial cities. The best thing that can be said about the acting of Russell and his colleagues is that it is wooden, and it is hardly surprising that Priestley, with his experience of broadcasting, was more at home in front of the camera than most other members of the cast. For all its faults, half a century later the film, now in the possession of the British Film Institute, provides an insight into the conviction that kept the LPO in being.

6

The King Returns 1942–44

In 1942, as a modest contribution to the war effort a scheme was instituted, designed to encourage servicemen and women to attend concerts: officers could obtain two seats for the price of one, with NCOs and privates admitted free. There was at best limited reciprocal assistance from the public purse, Russell constantly complaining that official circles failed to recognise that the work of the LPO had any positive value. The support given by the LCC was restricted to promotion of a concert given in 1940, in the Central Hall, Westminster, to which the Mayor of every borough in Greater London was invited, their attitude in sharp contrast to that of some other local authorities. In October 1942, in recognition of the value to the community of the regular concerts given by the LPO, Watford Council guaranteed a four-day festival against loss, their investment rewarded when, as the Mayor proudly remarked during the interval of the final concert, 'the only seats remaining empty were the chandeliers'. Elsewhere, Liverpool was showing outstanding generosity to the orchestra bearing the city's name, and the Hallé Orchestra received help from a number of sources.

Up to a point the LCC's attitude was understandable. The Hallé and the Liverpool Philharmonic had a closer identity with the cities which were their home than the LPO could claim with London. Prior to the war the LPO was the personal fiefdom of its conductor, an outspoken opponent of municipal or government support, and since the middle of 1940 the greater part of its activities had lain outside the capital, opportunities for developing its work in London severely restricted by the destruction of Queen's Hall and the difficulty in obtaining weekend bookings in their own right at the Albert Hall. Limited help came from the Carnegie Trust, mostly in the form of guarantees against loss on specific concerts, but funds provided by the Trust, and by the Council for Education, Music and the Arts (CEMA), represented no more than a tiny percentage of the budget. To keep the orchestra financially viable meant accepting an exhausting touring schedule which severely taxed the resources of the players and would at any other time have been artistically unacceptable.

There were, however, some positive developments, one of these being the formation of the National Association of Symphony Orchestras. The LPO were anxious to see a co-operative body set up but reluctant to take it upon themselves to set the wheels in motion. The Musicians Union were, however, willing to do so, and it was through their good offices that the Association was formed with the Hallé, the Liverpool Philharmonic, the LPO, the LSO and the Scottish Orchestra as founder members. The BBC were invited to join but preferred to stand aside, keeping themselves informed but taking no active part. Despite being funded by the public, through the licence fee, the BBC appeared reluctant to give other orchestral organisations the whole-hearted support that might have been expected from the national broadcasting authority, preferring to go its own way, co-operating only when this suited its own plans, a stance that has changed little over the years.

By now there had been a considerable increase in touring by other orchestras, one of the first tasks tackled by the Association being the compilation and publication of a concert calendar, enabling members to avoid unnecessary clashes of dates and programmes. The Association also stipulated that to qualify for membership an orchestra must employ a minimum of sixty players, a move aimed at promoters trying to cash in by means of pick-up bands of forty to fifty players.

For as long as the BBC Symphony Orchestra were resident in Bristol it was impossible for other orchestras to perform there, but in 1941 the BBC moved its orchestra to Bedford, and the LPO acted quickly to ensure a succession. They were greatly helped by Sir Adrian Boult, whose actions were often in marked contrast to those of the Corporation itself, and who at the last concert given in Bristol by the BBC Symphony Orchestra made a short speech, asking the audience to welcome the LPO in their stead. Working in co-operation with the local impresario, Charles Lockier, the LPO opened their activities in the city with a week of concerts. These were highly successful, and for some years the LPO made three annual visits of a week, with other concerts arranged in between. In 1945 the Colston Hall was destroyed, not by enemy action, but by a fire which apparently started accidentally, and concerts in the city were transferred to the Central Hall, a considerably less satisfactory venue. Part of the audience seemed loath to transfer their affections to the new venue, there supposedly being an east-west barrier within the city which a section of the population deemed it beneath their dignity to cross. Whatever the reason, audiences fell away, and thereafter the number of concerts in the city steadily declined. Other provincial centres which were regular ports of call included Birmingham, Coventry, Leicester, and Nottingham, while nearer home concerts were being given in Guildford, Hornsey, Walthamstow, Watford and Wembley. Regular visits strengthened the relationship between audience and orchestra, and from links with the Nottingham Music Club it was possible to broaden the scope of programmes given in that city to include the Fourth Symphony of Bax, Debussy's *Nocturnes*, Respighi's *Fountains of Rome*, Walton's Symphony and Vaughan Williams' *London Symphony*. These may not have represented the last word in modernity, but went some way to satisfy the criticism that programmes were too stereotyped.

The 1943 Proms were planned on the same lines as those of 1942, but lasted longer than usual, for nine weeks rather than eight, the LPO playing for the first four weeks, with the BBC Symphony Orchestra taking over for the remainder of the season. Cameron and Boult again acted as associate conductors, and in the event Cameron found himself, at extremely short notice, shouldering almost all the burden during the weeks when the LPO was on the platform. The season started even earlier, on 19 June, allowing Wood, whose conducting schedule would have taxed the resources of many younger men, little time to rest and recuperate before it began. Partway through the second concert he suffered what must have been a slight stroke, leaving the platform after Brahms' Second Symphony with his body bent to the right, telling his wife, 'I had to direct beneath the desk – I couldn't get my arm upright.' Wood was ordered to bed for a month, and it says much for Cameron's musicianship that the remaining twenty-two concerts given by the LPO, for which he immediately assumed full responsibility, took place without mishap.

After engagements in Torquay and Hastings, which earned him appearances at concerts of the Royal Philharmonic Society, Cameron spent several years in the USA, conducting in San Francisco and Seattle. Despite success in America he was largely unknown when he returned home shortly before the war, and it was from association with the Proms that he made his name. Cameron was an essentially modest man, too much so for his own good, who for much of his career worked in the shadow of other men, Wood and Sargent. Musicians complained that his rehearsal manner was indecisive and that he bored the orchestra, but he was a fine interpreter of Bax and Sibelius, and with Sargent unwilling to tackle more than a minuscule proportion of the contemporary repertoire, Cameron shouldered much of the burden of learning and performing works new to the Proms. He deserves better from posterity than Arthur Jacobs' verdict, that the Proms 'propelled that essentially dull musician to a questionable prominence'. Maurice Pearton's judgement that he was 'a superbly equipped musician and the leading contender for the honour of being the most underrated British conductor of his time', who had difficulty in establishing 'the right enduring personal rapport with players', is an objective tribute to a conductor held in some affection by audiences.

During the 1943 Proms the LPO gave eleven works their first performance, or first performance in this country. Britten's *Scottish Ballad* for Two Pianos and Orchestra was among the works given a first hearing, but many of the composers whose music was premiered are barely remembered, if at all, the list of new compositions including music by Inglis Gundry and Alec Rowley, the Americans Walter Piston and Lamar Stringfield, and the Russians

Alexandrov, Budashkin and Shebalin. One work which had immediate and lasting success was the Fifth Symphony of Vaughan Williams, of which the composer conducted the first performance. Modern commentators have pointed to darker aspects of this outwardly serene work, but in 1943 it was the reflective side of the symphony that made a deep impression on audiences and performers. The work was immediately taken into the orchestra's repertoire, receiving several further performances during the ensuing winter.

The association with Harold Holt was broken in 1943. Despite the absence of foreign artists, the level of soloists engaged by Holt remained at a high level, including Ida Haendel, Myra Hess, Moura Lympany, Moiseiwitsch, Pouishnoff, Solomon and Eva Turner, even if there was a degree of predictability about the works they performed. Conductors were another matter. Boult, Cameron, Heward and Wood were always welcome, but there were others, such as Sidney Beer and Charles Hambourg, whose competence was questionable. Hambourg, unkindly nicknamed King Kong on account of his size, was the subject of a story in *Philharmonic Post*, though with the conductor's identity hidden, recounting his difficulty, throughout one provincial tour, in beating the opening bars of the Overture to *The Bartered Bride*. Night after night he failed to bring the players in together, resulting in some extremely ragged playing. Thomas Matthews and others did their best to help him solve the problem and finally, at the last concert of the tour, their efforts bore fruit, Hambourg successfully bringing in the musicians as one, only to fall off the rostrum in the process.

The person of Mr Sidney Beer was encountered some time ago. During the winter of 1942–43, in addition to conducting for Holt on Sunday afternoons, Beer conducted a series of Saturday concerts, largely a rerun of over-familiar Beethoven, Rachmaninov and Tchaikovsky, but with an occasional departure from the beaten track. Just how much Beer's ambitions exceeded his ability was demonstrated during a performance of *Petrushka*, when Beer, caught out by the tricky rhythms of the score, failed to beat one bar, creating such chaos that the performance came to a standstill, the embarrassing silence which followed broken by a percussion player who, oblivious to what was happening around him, delivered a resounding clash of his cymbals. Beer continued to pursue his ambitions to conduct, at one point proposing that the LPO should enter into a full-time contract with him, under which he would become their artistic director, and when his advances were rejected, formed an orchestra of his own, the National Philharmonic, giving Sunday afternoon concerts in a London theatre. Beer subsequently came to an agreement with Harold Holt under which his orchestra replaced the LPO on Sunday afternoons. Weekend concerts, and Sunday afternoons in particular, attracted by far and away the best audiences, and the LPO faced the prospect that, apart from concerts for the Royal Philharmonic and Royal Choral Societies, their activities in the capital might have to be restricted to suburban cinemas and halls. Once again

Jack Hylton came to their rescue, offering the use of one of his London theatres, and after careful consideration of the respective merits and demerits of each, it was decided to accept the Adelphi Theatre as a temporary home.

Though the seating capacity of the Adelphi was restricted the acoustics proved satisfactory, and during 1943-44 the LPO presented a series of wide-ranging programmes. Instead of concerts in which the most popular piano concertos were played with monotonous regularity, many were given without a soloist of any kind. The Fourth Symphonies of Bruckner and Mahler, still light years away from any kind of audience popularity, were performed, and the Sixth Symphony of Shostakovitch was played twice, offering a second opportunity of evaluating a new work, a practice that could with advantage be followed more often. Vaughan Williams' new Fifth Symphony was played at the opening concert, conducted by Cameron, and other living British composers included Arthur Bliss, John Ireland, and Michael Tippett, whose Oratorio *A Child of Our Time* received its first performance under Walter Goehr, with the combined choirs of Morley College and the London Regional Civil Defence Force, and a distinguished quartet of soloists, Joan Cross, Margaret MacArthur, Peter Pears and Norman Walker. Wartime restrictions on the use of newsprint meant there was only minimal space for coverage of this and other important musical events, many correspondents being unable to do little more than announce that the performance had taken place. That it was possible to present such adventurous programmes was partly thanks to modest financial assistance from CEMA and to Boosey and Hawkes, who underwrote a concert of American music, the works performed including the First Symphony of Roger Sessions, Gershwin's *Rhapsody in Blue* and a Suite from Walter Piston's ballet *The Incredible Flutist*. One movement of Piston's score is a short march representing a circus coming to town, the score containing the instruction 'Members of the orchestra who are not playing during the Circus March will make sounds as of a crowd hailing the arrival of the circus parade'. Harold Schoenberg of the New York *Musical Courier*, in England as Lieutenant Schoenberg, US Army, drew an unfavourable contrast between the 'Redskin-like yells' of the Boston Pops Orchestra during this piece and the gentlemanly 'Whoopee' of the LPO.

The artistic success of this season was not matched by the box office returns and, despite the theatre's modest seating capacity, only one concert was sold out, a poor reward for enterprise. For all the growth in concert audiences the public was still extremely conservative in its tastes, unwilling to run any kind of risk. Fortunately in the following winter, 1944-45, it was possible to return to the Albert Hall, the LPO giving three out of every four Sunday afternoon concerts, with the BBC Symphony Orchestra on the platform for the fourth week. The concerts remained under Harold Holt's management, but the LPO were able to exercise a degree of control over the choice of artists and music, though the repertoire fell short of the degree of adventure shown at the Adelphi

Theatre. There was also continuing concern about the quality of some conductors, including the pianist Pouishnoff. No objection was raised directly, but there was no doubt of the players' view that his credentials as a conductor were far from apparent.

The Royal Philharmonic Society continued to include a major British work in almost every programme, and musically 1943–44 proved to be one of the most stimulating wartime seasons. There was, however, one unfortunate cloud on the horizon. The Society's opening concert was conducted by Barbirolli who, to the great concern of the LPO, expressed the hope, after the concert, that the day would come when the Society again had its own Royal Philharmonic Orchestra. His words were to foreshadow a change in policy. In the following year the Society increased the number of concerts from six to eight, dividing the work between five orchestras, the LPO performing at three, the BBC Symphony Orchestra at two and the Hallé, Liverpool Philharmonic and LSO at one apiece. Now that the LPO was again promoting concerts in London, the loss of engagements which had formerly been their prerogative was not as serious as it would have been when Sunday afternoons were committed to Harold Holt. It was nevertheless poor recompense for the considerable sacrifices they had made, including their generosity in giving a concert on the Society's behalf at a time when the LPO was engaged in a struggle for survival.

The resurgence of the Hallé under Barbirolli quickly gave rise to unfavourable comparisons between their playing and that of the London orchestras. Undoubtedly there was some justification for this; the strain of playing day in day out had taken its toll, and the quality of the string playing in particular had fallen away, but in making comparisons there were a number of factors to be taken into consideration. The conditions under which the Hallé worked were little better than those of the London orchestras. Manchester had also lost its concert hall, the Free Trade Hall, which was taken over as a store before it too was destroyed in an air raid, forcing the Hallé to find other venues, cinemas, the Belle Vue arena and Manchester's Albert Hall, a large Methodist mission hall. Once the orchestra was placed on a full-time basis, its touring schedule was every bit as gruelling as that undertaken by the LPO. But the Hallé had a number of advantages. In the first place it 'belonged' to Manchester, a relationship denied the London orchestras by the circumstances of concert-giving in the capital. The BBC's lack of co-operation in releasing players from the BBC Northern Orchestra may have been one of the catalysts leading the Society to employ its own orchestra all the year round, but it would be many years before the Corporation increased its provincial orchestras to full symphonic proportions. For the time being the activities of the BBC presented no threat, while the occasional concerts given in Manchester by other orchestras provided only marginal competition. Nor were there private promoters to complicate the situation. But undoubtedly the Hallé's greatest asset was Barbirolli himself. Habitually travelling with the orchestra, sharing the trials and tribulations of wartime with his players, doing everything within his powers to raise their morale, Barbirolli continually inspired them to give more than they themselves imagined they were capable of. It may have been to his advantage that when he arrived in Manchester in June 1943, he had to rebuild the orchestra, recruiting more than forty players and shaping the Hallé in his own image. Moreover, not only were his players on average younger – his second flute was in her mid-teens – they had not been constantly on the road for three years. It should have been no surprise that they sounded fresher than their London colleagues. For the next decade and more the Hallé were the touchstone against which other orchestras were judged.

It was not only the LPO who were adversely affected by the conditions under which they found themselves working. The LSO also suffered from a constant round of touring and the BBC Symphony Orchestra, which had lost many of its best players, was a pale shadow of its former self. It was not that Gregory and Russell were unaware of the problem, but they had to face the fact that not only was it necessary to give more performances than was good for an orchestra, there was also a dearth of top-class conducting talent. For several years the LPO adopted a policy of apportioning work between a number of conductors, giving many younger Englishmen, or refugees who had made their way to Britain, an opportunity to demonstrate their worth. Conductors who appeared at the Orpheum Theatre included Warwick Braithwaite, Mosco Carner, Edric Cundell, Reginald Goodall, Alec Sherman and George Weldon, several of whom also conducted at the Adelphi Theatre, where concerts were also given under Richard Austin, Walter Goehr, Vilem Tausky, Dr Heinz Unger and Hugo Weisgall, most of them also working with the orchestra on tour.

Nevertheless in 1943 the time seemed ripe to appoint a new Principal Conductor, though any such appointment was still regarded as temporary, since it was anticipated that when Beecham returned he would again take over the reins. But despite the many opportunities given to the younger generation, the field was strictly limited. Of those with greater experience, Boult was tied up at the BBC; the relationship with Sargent, who was in any event considerably occupied with the activities of the Liverpool Philharmonic, had long since come under strain, while Cameron lacked the charisma they were looking for. The man chosen was Anatole Fistoulari, of Russian birth but French nationality. Born in Kiev in 1907, he reputedly conducted Tchaikovsky's *Pathétique* Symphony at the tender age of seven, and at twelve was conducting opera in Bucharest and concerts in Holland and Germany. The family moved to Paris before the outbreak of the Russian Revolution, and Fistoulari took French nationality. Joining the French army at the outbreak of war, he escaped to Britain, where in 1942 he married Anna Mahler, daughter of the composer. But Fistoulari's abilities fell far short of those of Barbirolli, while he reputedly had the disadvantage of a relatively small repertoire. In the event the appointment was short-lived, barely outlasting the winter of 1943–44.

The reason for the parting of the ways with Fistoulari is not hard to find. Great plans were in fact afoot in the spring of 1944, pride of place going to the news that at last, after too long an absence, Beecham was planning to return home in the autumn. Arrangements were put in hand for him to conduct an extended provincial tour, and the possibility of a tour of the United States under Beecham's baton was also mooted. In the face of news of this kind Fistoulari quietly dropped out of the picture, so much so that while the announcement of his appointment merited a full-page article in *Philharmonic Post*, the magazine failed to record its termination. The spring of 1944 also brought a move to new office premises. Despite the extremely small office staff, space had always been at a premium, and the search lit upon Number 53 Welbeck Street, on which they were able to secure a long lease for the not inconsiderable sum of £9000. This proved a prudent investment, and it was here that the orchestra's official home was to be found for the next forty years.

In March 1944, as part of Henry Wood's seventy-fifth birthday celebrations, the BBC Symphony Orchestra, the LPO and the LSO joined forces for a concert at the Albert Hall. The Queen and her daughters were among the audience, and Wood shared the conducting with Boult and Cameron. Sargent should have taken part, but the concert had to be postponed for three weeks, the result of bomb damage which temporarily closed the hall, another engagement preventing him from appearing on the new date. To coincide with Wood's birthday the LPO produced a booklet of tributes entitled *Homage to Sir Henry Wood: A World Symposium*. Edited by Thomas Russell, contributions came from far and wide, from composers, conductors, and soloists. It was the first of a number of pamphlets on diverse musical subjects published by the LPO during the next few years.

As well as celebrating Wood's seventy-fifth birthday, the 1944 Proms also marked the fiftieth anniversary of his first Promenade concert, given in 1894. The LPO were booked for the first two weeks, followed by the LSO for a fortnight, with the remaining weeks allotted to the BBC Symphony Orchestra. The celebrations were however marred, first by a new form of aerial attack on London and finally by the illness and death of Wood himself. This new menace was the V1, or flying bomb, a pilotless plane packed with explosive, aimed indiscriminately at London and the south-east of England, a form of attack many Londoners found even more nerve-wracking than the Blitz. The attacks started in earnest on 15 June, five days after the opening night of the season. Large numbers crashed on take-off, or were shot down, but despite the best efforts of the RAF, London was hit by seventy-three that day, with the loss of more than fifty civilian lives. The LPO completed its allotted fortnight, but a week later the authorities concluded that, even if the audience was willing to accept the risk, the possibility of a V1 crashing on the hall would result in a disaster too awful to contemplate, and the season was abruptly terminated. Wood travelled to Bedford, where the BBC Symphony Orchestra gave studio performances of those parts of each concert which the BBC had included in the broadcast schedules – not every concert was broadcast in full – and after a performance of Beethoven's Seventh Symphony, into which Wood threw every last ounce of his physical resources, he was again taken ill, was unable to conduct the fiftieth anniversary concert, Boult taking his place, and died a few days later, widely mourned by musicians and public.

For the weeks following their fortnight at the Proms, concerts had been arranged in and around London. Even during the Blitz Tour it was the exception rather than the rule for concerts to be affected by bombing, the next few weeks providing the players with some of their most uncomfortable moments since the start of hostilities. Travel was still a recurring problem. The railways were no longer suffering as much from enemy action, but they were badly run down, leading to long delays. Once the orchestra arrived over an hour late at Boston, to find the audience still patiently waiting, yet despite all the difficulties it was only rarely that individual players failed to arrive in time: the prize for dedication to his art must surely go to the second horn, Vincent Burrows, who, missing the half past twelve train to Peterborough, and with no other train which would get him there on time, hurried home, got out his bicycle and pedalled the seventy-four miles, arriving with a quarter of an hour to spare, confessing to being 'a bit blown' by the experience. History does not relate whether he used the same method of transport for the return journey.

As 1944 progressed, not all the plans under discussion earlier in the year could be brought to fruition. Uncertainties about shipping postponed any thought of touring America. Faced with the possibility that while they might be able to travel from east to west, a shortage of places in the opposite direction could have left the orchestra stranded, a risk they could not afford to take. Difficulty in securing a passage also delayed Beecham's return, the arrangements for his tour of the provinces having to be amended, other conductors taking charge of the earlier concerts. His first concert after returning home therefore took place at Watford on 2 October, a fortnight later than originally intended. It was, however, a triumphant return, orchestra and audiences alike welcoming him back with open arms. Felix Aprahamian wrote of his homecoming: 'No absent king was ever treated with greater deference or respect than Beecham returning to his LPO. Thanks to the administrative genius of Thomas Russell, the orchestra had survived the war and its founder's absence. It had its own offices, house journal and Arts Club. And, lest it be suggested that it had lost a few eminent players, one can recall some concerts of those days that were among its greatest.'

Further concerts followed in Leeds, Huddersfield and Sheffield before Beecham brought the orchestra to London, the programme reminiscent of many he had given before the war:

> Berlioz: Overture, Le Carnaval Romain; Delius: Brigg Fair; Mozart : Symphony No. 34 in C; Sibelius: Symphony No. 6 in D; Chabrier: Rhapsody, Espana

The reception given to Beecham on his reappearance in the capital was rapturous, the audience having little difficulty in persuading him to round out the evening with encores in the shape of the Elegy from Elgar's *Serenade for Strings* and a Strauss Waltz. By now there was a new generation of both concert-goers and critics to whom Beecham was but a name. One such was Patricia Young, who wrote afterwards, 'It was with a biased mind – biased against the great man – that I went to the Albert Hall to see and hear "Tommy" Beecham conduct the LPO, since other people's enthusiasm always induces in me scepticism.' Her scepticism was soon laid to rest, for 'here was an interpretation of Mozart of a kind I had never before heard; each note was silver clear, each perfect phrase seemed to be drawn from the instruments, moulded in the conductor's hands and sent winding on its way to the audience.'

Beecham conducted the LPO in twenty or more concerts that autumn, the relationship between conductor and orchestra apparently prospering. And in contrast with the experience of pre-war provincial tours, when many concerts attracted less than full houses, the autumn of 1944 saw Beecham and the LPO playing to packed and enthusiastic audiences.

The Allied failure to seize a crossing of the Rhine at Arnhem was a severe disappointment, and bitter fighting at the end of December, as Hitler launched a last desperate counter-attack in the west, meant it was too soon to predict how long the war in Europe would last. Nevertheless the omens at the turn of the year were more favourable than for many a long day. For the LPO the long-awaited return of their chief offered hope that they were about to enter a new era, rich with promise.

7

Competition 1945

Beecham returned to North America in mid-January, where he spent the early months of 1945, and it was close to midsummer before he again conducted the LPO. In consequence guest conductors were again the order of the day, and with much of France liberated they included many distinguished French musicians. In the autumn of 1944 Russell and Aprahamian accepted an invitation from the Provisional French Government to visit Paris. Curiously there was opposition from the British Council, who argued that booking artists should be left to the concert agents, but whereas the agents had done little to promote French music, Aprahamian had been active in its cause, arranging numerous concerts of chamber music on behalf of the French Embassy, who wrote to the Foreign Office supporting their application to travel.

The first fruits came in the shape of concerts with Charles Münch and the young pianist Nicole Henriot, who performed with the LPO as early as November 1944. The early months of 1945 saw further concerts under Münch, other French artists including the conductors Roger Désormière and Paul Paray. Désormière and another guest artist, the violinist Jacques Thibaud, had both been involved in the French Resistance, and Thibaud, who throughout the occupation continued to teach his Jewish pupils, even presented some of them in public, though taking the precaution of advertising them under carefully chosen Aryan names. Another visitor from across the Channel was Francis Poulenc who, with Benjamin Britten as his fellow pianist, took part in a performance of his own Concerto for Two Pianos. Britten also appeared in the role of conductor, directing the orchestra in performances of his *Sinfonia da Requiem* in the Albert Hall and several provincial centres, including Birmingham, Leicester, Nottingham and Wembley. The liberation of France also made it possible to visit towns on the South Coast, with Eastbourne and Hastings added to the touring schedule, Brighton and Folkestone following later.

April was largely taken up with a three-week season at the Coliseum during which the LPO performed each evening, the LSO undertaking the two matinee performances given each week. The programmes included a cross-section of British music, including works by Delius, Elgar, Rawsthorne, and Walton, and the first performance of Geoffrey Bush's Overture *Resolution*, though the inclusion of *Falstaff* and Walton's Symphony gave rise to criticism from within the ranks of the orchestra that they were unsuitable, not just because opportunities for rehearsal were limited, but because they were out of place in concerts that were designedly popular in content. The Sixth Symphony of Shostakovitch was revived and the final concert given over to a re-creation of the 'Musical Manifesto' of 1940, with the conducting undertaken by Albert Coates, Basil Cameron and Edric Cundell, and an address from the platform by J.B. Priestley. British music was also to the fore when the LPO performed at the first Cheltenham Festival. This began in a modest way with three concerts, each including a British work conducted by its composer, the *Sea Interludes* from *Peter Grimes*, Walton's *Sinfonia Concertante* for Piano and Orchestra and the *Phoenix March* of Arthur Bliss, with the other works conducted by Cameron.

The summer of 1945 saw the first steps taken towards the formation of another orchestra, the Philharmonia. This was the creation of Walter Legge, one of Beecham's former assistants at Covent Garden, who in pre-war days produced some notable records for EMI. After initial recordings by a chamber ensemble, the full orchestra met for the first time at the end of August to record Tchaikovsky's First Piano Concerto. Their first public concert took place on the afternoon of Saturday, 27 October 1945, Beecham conducting a programme of music by Mozart. Beecham's flirtation with the Philharmonia was short-lived. At a lunch with Legge he offered his services as Musical Director and was firmly turned down. Legge was as independent-minded as Beecham and had no intention of compromising his freedom of action by appointing a permanent conductor, let alone a Music Director.

So far as concert work was concerned, the Philharmonia posed no immediate threat. Of more concern was the fact that through patronage of the new body EMI appeared to be shutting the doors of the recording studio to the LPO, who in consequence entered into a contract with Decca. Once the Cinderella of the record industry, this company, thanks to a series of technological advances, was about to become one of its leaders. Using a technique described as full frequency range recording, Decca produced a series of 78 rpm shellac recordings which set new standards, one of them, the LPO's recording of *Petrushka*, made under the baton of Ernest Ansermet, greatly admired both for the performance and the improvement in sound resulting from the new method of recording.

The conditions in which concerts were given in London continued to be unsatisfactory. There were hopes that Queen's Hall might be rebuilt, and a fund had been set up for that purpose, but the amount raised was pitifully small, and the priorities of post-war reconstruction meant that concert halls occupied a very low place. There was little likelihood that the newly elected

Labour Government, burdened by debts accumulated from the war and with a major programme of social reform to implement, would be in any position to offer help. Arrangements in the Albert Hall during the previous winter fell short of giving the LPO independence, and in order to regain control of their affairs a new venue was tried out during 1945–46, the long-since demolished Stoll Theatre, situated close to Kingsway, seating around two thousand people, where concerts were given on Sunday afternoons. At the same time a weekday series was launched in the Albert Hall, comprising popular repertoire, concerts in the Stoll following a more adventurous pattern.

Beecham conducted several concerts at the Stoll Theatre, and in view of disparaging comments he made later about Benjamin Britten, it is intriguing to find the *Sea Interludes* from *Peter Grimes* putting in an appearance. Fewer in number than the previous autumn, his provincial concerts received an equally enthusiastic reception; at Wembley in early October, for a concert comprising Mozart's *Paris* Symphony, his own arrangement of Handel pieces for the ballet *The Great Elopement*, and Tchaikovsky's Third Suite, he had a delighted audience clamouring for encores, an experience repeated up and down the country ever since his return to Britain

The end of October was a period of hectic activity for Beecham. The Philharmonia's initial concert took place on a Saturday afternoon. The same week saw him at Oxford with the LPO, and the day after the Philharmonia concert, he conducted a Sunday afternoon concert in the Stoll. A week later he crossed the Channel to conduct the LPO on its first post-war visit overseas, a 'Victory' tour, with concerts in Paris, Antwerp and Brussels. While the LPO performed in France and Belgium, Charles Münch and the Paris Conservatoire Orchestra paid an exchange visit to Britain, performing in both the Albert Hall and the Stoll and giving concerts in Birmingham, Southampton and Walthamstow. The Paris orchestra's concerts were given under the auspices of the LPO, and immediately after his Brussels concert, Beecham swapped rostrums with Münch, returning to London to conduct Münch's orchestra at the Stoll, the LPO giving a second concert in Paris, during which Münch conducted Walton's Symphony.

Though the war was over, opportunities for visiting the continent were still limited, many players finding a degree of unreality about going abroad for the first time in over five years. There was no doubt as to the warmth of their reception by audiences. Cellist Boris Rickelman recalled the long queue waiting for admission at nine in the morning for a Paris concert with the unusual starting time of 10 a.m., and despite the discomfort of an unheated hall, the experience of playing in the Palace des Beaux Arts in Brussels gave rise to regret that with the destruction of Queen's Hall, London had nothing comparable to offer its concert-going public.

Beecham's brief involvement with the Philharmonia was evidence that his interest in the LPO was on the wane. With the relationship increasingly uneasy, an attempt was made to persuade him to enter into a contract, a course doomed from the start. It was not Beecham's nature to enter into contracts; in any event it seems likely that he was already bent on having an orchestra of his own, where he would not have to concern himself with the views of an elected Board of Directors. Following the tour of France and Belgium his work with the LPO petered out: a concert for the Royal Philharmonic Society in November, a couple of provincial dates in December, and a Sibelius concert for the Royal Philharmonic Society in the middle of that month. He was due to conduct the LPO over the last weekend of the year, in Brighton on Saturday and at the Stoll the following afternoon, his place at both taken by Basil Cameron.

A year earlier, on his return from America, Beecham had nothing but praise for the LPO:

> 'My first meeting at rehearsal with the LPO was an unalloyed pleasure. My concern before resuming my association with it was that it should have preserved what was its prime and fundamental characteristic, the capacity to understand the nature of good music and to communicate that understanding through its executive ability to the public ear. It was this capacity that had made the orchestra famous throughout the world before the war. Five minutes only served to reassure me that this all-important essential was to be discovered as perceptible as ever in the playing of the London Philharmonic Orchestra. I find that I can today, just as before the war, make music to my entire satisfaction with the London Philharmonic Orchestra, and I can think of no greater compliment that can be paid to any group of musicians.'

Now it seemed the orchestra would no longer do. The reason for this change of heart is not hard to find. He was no longer in charge of the LPO's affairs. In an interview given jointly by the conductor and his wife some time later Beecham expressed the view that 'All over the world conductors select their players and choose their own programmes. In no other country but Britain can orchestras hire and fire conductors, as is possible under such co-operative ventures as the London Philharmonic', a statement that was demonstrably untrue, as witnessed by the example of the Berlin and Vienna Philharmonic Orchestras. To Beecham's comments his wife added her own:

> 'Music is as much a business as anything else, and what business man would be refused the right to pick his own employees? Since the LPO had formed itself into a co-op, he could no longer have the administration he wanted.'

The answer to this was that where the LPO was concerned, Beecham's right to hire and fire was lost when he absconded to the USA for four years, leaving his orchestra to its own devices. While the LPO remained loyal throughout his protracted absence, their loyalty was not reciprocated.

During the early months of 1946 Beecham was laying his plans, beavering away to secure engagements, notably those of the Royal Philharmonic Society, and recording sessions for EMI. With the connivance of Keith Douglas, Secretary of the Society, he secured the Society's title for his use, enabling him to announce his new creation as the Royal Philharmonic Orchestra, though both he and Douglas were fully aware that this would sow even further confusion between the LPO, the RPO and the Society itself.

As an interpreter Beecham was a magician, a weaver of spells, with the gift of taking second-rate music and persuading an audience that here was a masterpiece. He breathed life into the music of Delius, indeed it is within the bounds of possibility that but for Beecham, Delius would have languished, largely unplayed. His pre-war recordings of Mozart and his post-war recordings of Haydn may not please purists, but are a glorious reminder of the quality of the pre-war LPO and the post-war RPO. Neville Cardus, one of Beecham's greatest admirers, may have perhaps unconsciously touched on a flaw in Beecham's musicianship. 'It is beyond doubt,' he wrote, 'that Sir Thomas did not conduct, at his best, the profoundest sorts of music', and comparing his interpretation of *Tristan* with that of Fürtwangler, he concluded, 'Sir Thomas is interested mainly in the score as a gorgeous medium for so much sumptuous instrumental playing and fascinating conducting.' Concerned more with the moment than with the long term, it is doubtful if Beecham's horizons ever extended to the long haul which was inevitably the lot of the post-war LPO.

For some musicians Beecham could do no wrong. But their idol had feet of clay. It was not just that Beecham was possessed of a chronic inability to work with anyone else but, where the plans of others failed to coincide with his own, there was an open and freely expressed contempt for those plans and the abilities of those responsible for them. The breach with the LPO was probably inevitable, arising from irreconcilable philosophies on the conduct of musical affairs. Moreover, Beecham had to face the unpalatable fact that Gregory and Russell succeeded where he failed, rescuing his orchestra from bankruptcy and placing it on a sounder footing than he ever found possible. But Beecham was temperamentally incapable of subordinating his opinions to those of anyone else, his sense of responsibility apparently beginning and ending with himself; to be subordinate to the dictates of a Board of Directors, especially one drawn from the ranks of the orchestra, was an affront to his dignity. He was openly resentful of Russell's success in managing the LPO, his criticisms leading the Board to issue a declaration of their confidence in and support of Russell. Barbirolli's success in rebuilding the Hallé thrived on the strength of his partnerships with Philip Godlee, the Society's Chairman, and T.E. Bean, appointed General Manager when Barbirolli insisted the Society improve and strengthen its management structure. One can only feel a sense of regret that Beecham was incapable of emulating such relationships. Had he done so the post-war story of orchestral music in London would have been very different.

The philosophy behind the LPO was far removed from that of its two new rivals, the Philharmonia and the RPO, as constituted at that time. The advent of the LP record would in time lead to such a growth in recording work that many players would spend as much time, if not more, in the recording studio as on the concert platform, but in 1946 engagements for the two new bodies were few and far between; some players were to be found in the ranks of both, and to make a living they had to rely heavily on freelance work with chamber orchestras and other ensembles. So far as the Philharmonia was concerned, Legge's primary interest lay in making high-quality records, with public concerts a by-product, and the interests of EMI and the Philharmonia were interlinked, the concert-giving activities of the orchestra acting as an advertisement for EMI, the royalties paid by EMI enabling Legge to promote concerts. The Philharmonia came into being to serve Legge's interests, and through him those of EMI, not those of the public.

Nor was Beecham's RPO designed to serve the public. Rather it was the public who served Beecham, providing him with an audience, and for all its days of brilliance the RPO never enjoyed the level of success enjoyed by the pre-war LPO. Moreover, from holding undisputed sway as the leading British conductor of his generation he now faced competition from several directions. Barbirolli's Hallé was generally held to set the standard by which others should be judged, and Sargent was no longer content to be an acolyte, his position further strengthened when in 1948 he assumed Wood's mantle at the Proms. Nor was Sargent any longer able, or even willing, to deliver work for Beecham's players. There were no Courtauld-Sargent or Royal Choral Society concerts, and apart from recording sessions for EMI the only guaranteed engagements were a handful of concerts for the Royal Philharmonic Society though, faced with mounting costs, fewer subscribers and increasing competition, the Society's concerts were declining in number and importance. There was also Legge's Philharmonia to take into account, with its cast of international conductors, including Cantelli, Fürtwangler, Karajan, Kubelik and Toscanini. Following the appointment of Josef Krips as principal conductor, the LSO was also resurgent. Beecham may not have been sidelined, but no longer held centre stage by himself, while his words and actions closed many doors against him. There is an air of tragedy about this last period of Beecham's career. Possibly he felt threatened, which may explain the hint of bitterness, even venom, pervading many of his speeches and actions. Aiming his shafts at others, laughing at them rather than with them, he made enemies where he needed friends. He was openly contemptuous of the new management of Covent Garden, and engaged in an unnecessary squabble with the Hallé, leading Barbirolli to threaten that if Beecham was ever invited to conduct the Hallé he would immediately resign. He was uncomplimentary about Glyndebourne, though happy enough to let his orchestra play there, and to keep them employed hired out his players for under-rehearsed concerts under inferior conductors.

The LPO of 1945 was far removed from the orchestra of 1932. Like the Hallé and the Liverpool Philharmonic it was in every sense full-time, with clearly defined aims, even if conditions meant those aims could not be fully achieved. Gregory and Russell, concerned that the musical life of the country should not revert to a situation where for the population of many towns and cities concerts took place only once or twice a year, eked out by local choral societies performing with scratch orchestras, set out to retain and develop the long-term interest of a wider audience than had ever attended concerts before the war. That the orchestra had no proper home of its own was a major stumbling block which would remain a source of frustration. In the meantime it was necessary to continue giving concerts in halls that were less than adequate for the purpose.

A feature of the year-end concerts conducted by Cameron in Beecham's stead was that they brought together as soloists a former leader of the orchestra, Thomas Matthews, and a man about to take over this position, Andrew Cooper. With the war over Jean Pougnet decided the time had come to resume his solo and chamber music career, and his successor was chosen from the ranks of the orchestra itself. Born in Glasgow, Cooper studied in Germany under one of the most distinguished teachers of the day, Willy Hess, and after playing as a member of the Verbruggen Quartet, gained orchestral experience in the United States, where he was sub-leader of the Minneapolis Orchestra under Eugene Ormandy. Returning to this country he joined the LPO in 1941, sitting with Wynn Reeves at the second desk of the first violins. His appointment marked the start of a new era.

8

Guests 1945–49

In the immediate post-war era the LPO played under a galaxy of distinguished international musicians. Ernest Ansermet travelled from Switzerland and Eduard van Beinum from Holland; Wilhelm Fürtwangler, having gone through the process of de-Nazification, was allowed to conduct again; Erich Kleiber returned to Europe after spending the war years in exile in South America; visitors from France included Roger Désormière, Jean Martinon, Charles Münch and Paul Paray; Italy was represented by Victor de Sabata, and another exile, Bruno Walter, now living in America, crossed the Atlantic. Other lesser-known maestros yet to make their reputation included Leonard Bernstein, Sergiu Celibidache, and Erich Leinsdorf. Nor were their appearances confined to the Albert Hall, nearly all of them conducting out-of-town and suburban concerts.

A number of younger British conductors were engaged, including the Liverpool-based Louis Cohen and James Robertson from Sadler's Wells Opera, and approaches were received from numerous aspiring maestros, the Board minutes of the day recording more than once that 'It was agreed Mr X would be offered an engagement to conduct the orchestra when a suitable opportunity occurred'; somehow the occasion never arose. It would be several years before the successors to Barbirolli, Beecham, Boult, Cameron, Sargent and Wood emerged.

The early months of 1946 found the LPO playing under Ernest Ansermet, Eduard van Beinum, Basil Cameron, Albert Coates, Gregor Fitelberg and Karl Rankl, with the list of overseas soloists still primarily drawn from the ranks of French musicians, including Marcel Dupré, Pierre Fournier, Maurice Gendron, and a teenage violinist Blanchette Tarjus. Two concerts were notable for the reappearance of Marjorie Lawrence, one of the few singers to have made her exit in the last act of *Götterdämmerung* on horseback, riding off the stage of the Metropolitan Opera House in the direction of the funeral pyre seen blazing behind the backcloth. In the intervening years she had been afflicted by polio and was now confined to a wheelchair, yet she continued to sing, and there was much in her voice to remind the audience of pre-war glories. The LPO also arranged a tour by the Concertgebouw Orchestra, whose concert at the Stoll Theatre was attended by the Home Secretary, Herbert Morrison, and the Foreign Secretary, Ernest Bevin. This tour, like that of the Paris Conservatoire Orchestra the previous autumn, was planned to complement music-making in the capital. Subsequent visits by other foreign orchestras were arranged in a less satisfactory fashion, leading to unnecessary and avoidable programme clashes.

Of all the guest musicians appearing with the LPO in the early months of 1946, it was Victor de Sabata who made the most outstanding impression. He began his first rehearsal by taking the players straight through *Le Carnaval Romain*, receiving an almost unique tribute, a standing ovation from the orchestra. According to Felix Aprahamian, 'where Beecham beguiled, de Sabata, looking, according to one player, like a cross between Julius Caesar and Satan, terrified the orchestra. But they played for him like gods.' His memory was said to rival that of Toscanini, for he was never seen with a score in front of him, at rehearsals or concerts, and his rehearsals could be exhausting for he spared neither the orchestra or himself. Maurice ('Bill') Cody, newly appointed as first clarinet and still unfamiliar with much of the repertoire, was deeply appreciative that de Sabata gave him time to find his feet, before he too was subjected to the demands made on his colleagues. De Sabata's performance on the rostrum gave rise to considerable comment. According to C.B. Rees he 'exploded into an astonishing paroxysm of postures – leaping, heaving, dancing, boxing, crouching, waving and at any moment apparently about to take off into the roof. I personally had never before come across a conductor who nearly stood on his head – and produced magnificent results', a verdict confirmed by George Dannett, who wrote of his 'absurd rostrum-gyrations, which would be pathetic if it were not for the fact that his interpretation of southern European composers is electrifying', describing the LPO's playing in Beethoven's Fifth Symphony as 'a revelation'.

If Beecham's defection was a blow there were distinctly better things in store, notably the LCC's decision to award a grant of £10,000 to the orchestra, covering their work during the twelve months from 1 April 1946. This was made in the light of a memorandum submitted by the LPO, a condition of the grant being that the orchestra should present twelve concerts a year for children attending schools for which the LCC was responsible, the first such concert taking place in October before a packed Albert Hall. The fact that London's elected body had accepted the case for official support argued by the orchestra raised hopes of a long-term relationship between the orchestra and the city whose name it bore. The LCC's grant was considerably greater than the £4000 awarded to the LPO in the autumn of 1945 by the newly constituted Arts Council, but taken together they provided the orchestra with a greater degree of financial security than it had ever known.

Less happily the orchestra's playing was attracting some criticism, notably from Ralph Hill, who wrote for the *Daily Mail* and the *Evening Standard* and edited the short-lived *Penguin Music Magazine*. In the May 1947 issue he drew unfavourable comparisons between the Hallé and the LPO, commenting adversely about the fact that the BBC paid the same level of broadcast fee to every orchestra. Hill argued that the Hallé:

> 'is the finest ensemble in the country and is in a different class from the LPO, or for that matter any other orchestra in the country. The ultimate aim of the Society is to bring its orchestra into line with the great orchestras of the Continent. This object can be achieved only by reducing the number of public concerts so that more time is available for intensive rehearsal. The loss of revenue must obviously be made up by increased fees from outside organisations that wish to engage the high-quality services of the Hallé Orchestra. One might imagine that the BBC would have supported such a laudable ideal. After all, the BBC should set the highest standards in the country. On the contrary, the BBC refuses to broadcast a Hallé concert or to utilise the services of the orchestra unless the Hallé is prepared to accept the same fee that is given to all other orchestras, none of which can or will offer the quality maintained by the Hallé. The BBC ought to welcome the payment of high fees in return for high quality, and it should insist on getting high quality all the time.'

This begged a great many questions, not the least of which was that the BBC had no mandate to make such judgements, while any system of differential payments based on a subjective assessment of the standard of performance would provide constant fuel for controversy. It was not just the Hallé who were in dispute with the BBC over fees. The BBC were offering £120, less than the fee paid by the Corporation before the war, and because the Musicians Union had negotiated higher payments for the players, which had to be met from the overall amount paid for the broadcast, the net revenue going to the orchestra's funds, after the musicians had been paid, was substantially reduced. The LPO held out for £150, the pre-war figure, which took no account of inflation. The 1945 Proms were originally planned on the same lines as the cruelly shortened season of the previous year, the LPO and the LSO each playing for a fortnight, with the BBC Symphony Orchestra undertaking the remaining four weeks, but the BBC's refusal to increase fees meant the LPO took no part in the Proms in 1945 or 1946. For their part the Hallé were asking for £150 net, i.e. excluding the fees paid to the musicians, the dispute with the BBC depriving licence payers of broadcasts by that orchestra for eighteen months.

With the exception of the BBC Symphony Orchestra, every orchestra in the country was, to a greater or lesser extent, underfunded and heavily overworked and would have benefited from additional finance, whether from fees paid by the BBC or any other source. De Sabata had been forthright in his condemnation of the working conditions imposed by the LPO's financial position, which he compared unfavourably with those in continental orchestras, where it was unusual for the musicians to perform in public more than three times a week; for most orchestras, other than those employed by the BBC, such conditions were no more than a pipe-dream.

The activities of the BBC were giving rise to concern, one source of irritation arising from the fact that, even if another venue could have been found in central London, it was impossible to promote concerts in competition with the Proms. For two months of the year the BBC, funded by the licence payer, with greater financial resources than those of any other orchestral employer, monopolised the promotion of orchestral music in London, and when for some years the Corporation presented a fortnight of Winter Proms, for which the LPO and the LSO were offered a minimum of engagements, sometimes none at all, they controlled the capital's music for nearly 20 per cent of the year. The growth of provincial festivals was in its infancy, and though the orchestra's annual holiday could be taken during this period, the LPO were left in a position where, unless they were engaged by the BBC, their activities in London were severely restricted for a large part of every year.

There was also increasing suspicion at the predatory way in which the BBC was securing engagements that had formerly been the province of other orchestras. The manner in which the BBC had whisked its orchestra away from London at the outbreak of war; the reduced fees offered for broadcast relays; their reluctance to co-operate with other orchestras in the co-ordination of programmes and out-of-town visits, and the fact that the BBC Symphony Orchestra was subsidised by the licence payer, enabling them to offer terms other orchestras could not match, fuelled suspicions that the Corporation would have no scruples in launching a take-over bid for the capital's music.

It was the summer of 1946 before the dispute over fees was resolved, too late for the LPO to take part in that year's Proms, for which arrangements had been finalised. There was, however, compensation in the shape of a week of concerts at the Finsbury Park Open-Air Theatre. These formed part of the package agreed in return for the grant awarded by the LCC, and were given in the week leading up to the August Bank Holiday. Sound amplification equipment was used to try and improve the acoustics, especially for those seated furthest from the orchestra, though this aspect was only partially successful. Nevertheless, despite generally unfavourable weather – it was a miserable summer, described by one writer 'as the worst in living memory' – the week as a whole was a success, these concerts occupying a regular place in the calendar for the next few years.

This venture had something in common with the early weeks of the 'Blitz Tour', the programmes following well-worn paths, leading to another attack from the pen of Ralph Hill, who complained, in the columns of the *Daily Mail*, about the absence of any music by British composers, living or dead. An editorial in *Philharmonic Post* defended the choice of music, Russell arguing that the programmes were designed for an audience 'keen to hear works of proved worth, and to make their first agreeable contact with a symphony orchestra'. Hill responded in Penguin Music Magazine:

'Does Mr Russell really mean that Elgar's *Enigma Variations, Wand of Youth* Suite, *Chanson de Matin* and *Chanson de Nuit*; Delius' *Brigg Fair* and *Serenade* from *Hassan*; Ireland's *Epic March* and *A London Overture*; Vaughan Williams' *Tallis* and *Greensleeves* Fantasias; Walton's *Façade* Suites; German's *Welsh Rhapsody*; Balfour Gardiner's *Shepherd Fennel's Dance* and Percy Grainger's *Molly on the Shore* and *Shepherd's Hey* are not of proved worth. The L.P.O. lays claim to be a "national institution". Very well there can be no excuse for neglecting British music. No "national institution" would be allowed to neglect national products or the term "national" becomes a misnomer. Any form of subsidy given through the Arts Council must carry a certain responsibility toward the propagation of music by British composers. In no other country would public money be spent to subsidise an orchestra to play exclusively foreign music as the L.P.O. did at Finsbury Park and continues to do so in many other places as well.'

Possibly Russell should have followed the example of Sir Adrian Boult who, when the BBC were criticised by a group of British composers for the amount of broadcasting time devoted to the music of foreigners, responded by asking, 'what are the names of some of these foreigners? Here are some of them: Bach, Handel, Mozart, Beethoven, Schubert....' Apart from the unreasonableness of condemning the LPO's programming on the basis of a single week of concerts, many of the pieces listed by Hill were unsuitable for open-air performance; indeed with two or three exceptions, it was an insubstantial collection, many of which have failed to stand the test of time. Where British music was concerned the LPO had not in fact been idle. Earlier in the summer they had again been engaged to perform at the Cheltenham Festival, where this year the number of concerts was increased to four, each concert again including a work from the pen of a living British composer, Britten, Rubbra, Moeran and Tippett, with Sargent responsible for the other items in each evening's programme. The concerts given at the Stoll Theatre also offered considerably more substantial fare than *Chanson de Matin* or *Molly on the Shore*. Britten, Delius, Elgar, Tippett, Vaughan Williams and Walton were represented by major works, other unusual repertoire including Mahler's Fifth Symphony, Martinu's First, Prokofiev's Cello Concerto, Roussel's Ballet *Le Festin de l'araignée*, Stravinsky's Symphony in C and music from Szymanowski's Ballet *Harnasie*. It was not a record to be ashamed of, but as any critic worth his salt should have known, programmes such as these were all too often rewarded by rows of empty seats. Diversification of the repertoire was only possible because the financial situation had been eased thanks to grants from the Arts Council and the LCC.

Concern about performing standards was evidenced by an exchange of correspondence with the Royal Choral Society, following an enquiry as to their availability for three concerts during the following season. Russell responded that his Board had asked him to ascertain how much rehearsal time would be allowed for these performances, as during the previous winter they had taken part in performances of *A Mass of Life* and *Belshazzar's Feast*, for which the time allotted was 'inadequate for the difficulty and complexity of the works concerned'. Some months later the Society informed the LPO that 'After careful consideration of the whole matter it was decided to make other arrangements'. The relationship between Sargent and the LPO had long since cooled, his appearances with them confined to concerts promoted by the Royal Choral Society or engagements such as the Cheltenham Festival. This exchange of letters was hardly designed to improve the situation, and the concerts at Cheltenham were the last given by Sargent with the LPO for many years. The stand taken on this matter was a sign of greater financial security, and while the loss of these engagements was regretted, they were no longer crucial to the LPO's survival.

The acoustics of the Stoll were a marked improvement on those of the Albert Hall, and there were hopes that the theatre might provide the LPO with something approaching a long-term home. The Arts Council had visions of mounting seasons of opera and ballet, but a proposal to lease the theatre proved unacceptable to the owners. The autumn of 1946 therefore found the LPO returning to its pre-war home, the Royal Opera House, Covent Garden, which was to be their platform on Sunday afternoons for the next two years. For the first time since the war tickets were offered on a subscription basis, the success of the subscription scheme guaranteeing a full house when Bruno Walter conducted Mahler's Fourth Symphony. Walter's first post-war concerts in Britain proved an enormous attraction, the demand for tickets so great that the first of his Albert Hall concerts, comprising Mozart's G minor Symphony, the *Tallis Fantasia* and Brahms Two, had to be repeated the next evening, and a Beethoven programme, including the *Pastoral* Symphony and the *Eroica*, first performed at the Albert Hall in November, received a second performance at Covent Garden on the last Sunday of the old year. Other conductors appearing on the stage of the Opera House included de Sabata, van Beinum and Ansermet, and the LPO promoted return visits by the Paris Conservatoire Orchestra and the Concertgebouw Orchestra.

A review of the orchestra's work during 1946 revealed that, even if the schedule was less demanding than that of the war years, nobody could complain of being underworked. Two hundred and twenty-three public concerts had been given in nearly fifty different venues, a figure taking no account of children's concerts or recording sessions. Sixty-eight concerts had been promoted in central London, thirty-two concerts on Thursday evenings at the Albert Hall, and thirty-six on Sunday afternoons in either the Stoll Theatre or the Royal Opera House. The Albert Hall concerts continued to concentrate on the popular end of the repertoire, and despite the number given in the hall only seventy-five works were performed, the *New World* Symphony, Grieg's Piano Concerto, the *Nutcracker* Suite and *Romeo and Juliet* each receiving four performances, with *The Variations on a Theme by Goossens* composed by Ten American Composers and Rawsthorne's *Street Corner* Overture the only departures from a narrow range of music. Sunday afternoons offered a wider choice, works by British composers including Britten's *Variations and Fugue on a Theme of Purcell*, better known as *The Young Person's Guide to the Orchestra*, the first performance of Malcolm Arnold's Horn Concerto, conducted by Ansermet, with Charles Gregory as soloist, and pieces by Doreen Carwithen, John Ireland, Matyas Seiber, Bernard Stevens, Tippett and Walton. The Sunday programmes also included, in a far from exhaustive list, Bartok's Concerto for Orchestra, Bloch's Violin Concerto and Mahler's song-cycle *Lieder eines fahrenden Gesellen*. Depressingly, most of the unfamiliar music fell into the category known by the LPO's concert department as 'house-emptiers'.

Charles Gregory's solo performance in Arnold's Horn Concerto was almost his swan-song with the LPO. He had already surrendered the Chairmanship, in which role he had been succeeded by Thomas Russell, who added these responsibilities to those he exercised as Managing Director. Gregory's influence in the orchestra was, however, such that after standing down as a Director, the Board asked him to assist them in a co-opted capacity, appointing him Deputy Chairman, and with Russell absent on protracted sick leave during the last part of 1945 and the early months of 1946, Gregory found himself back at the helm. Part of Russell's former burden had been lifted in the autumn of 1945 when, coinciding with a change in the name of the company, from Musical Culture Limited to London Philharmonic Orchestra Limited, Victor Haynes was appointed Company Secretary, taking over work which had previously fallen to Russell. Though the decision to combine the posts of Chairman and Managing Director was taken democratically, placing so much power in the hands of one man was to sow the seeds of future conflict.

Much time and effort was spent trying to improve the quality of the orchestra. One of the factors affecting performance was the strain imposed on the principal players by the orchestra's workload. Proposals were tabled aimed at reducing this burden by the appointment of co-principals, an arrangement which operated in almost all of the great European and North American orchestras, an aim as much frustrated by the difficulty in finding players of sufficient quality as by the fact that increased financial assistance from the

Arts Council and the LCC was eaten up by the cost of additional rehearsal time and employment of additional players, particularly in the string sections, for concerts in Central London. Gregory was one of the principals most concerned, and it may well have been the impossibility of providing the level of relief he believed to be necessary that led him to join the substantial body of Britons making a new life for themselves in Australia, where he joined the horn section of the Sydney Symphony Orchestra.

In 1947 the LCC, pleased with the artistic return for their first year's grant, approved an increase, from £10,000 to £25,000, the LPO in recording their thanks commenting that 'the effect of the last three months has threatened orchestras no less than industry'. That threat arose from the fact that the early months of 1947 were bitterly cold. For several weeks Britain lay under a thick blanket of snow. Time and again the railways were blocked, seriously interrupting deliveries of coal, still the main source of energy, giving rise to fuel shortages and power cuts. It was not unknown for people to go to the cinema several times a week to keep warm, and newspapers published photographs of musicians rehearsing in their overcoats. Only one concert was cancelled but audiences were adversely affected, the LPO's revenues suffering by well over a thousand pounds, the losses met by an advance from the LCC of part of the following year's grant. According to the *Evening Standard*, the office staff briefly kept the cold at bay by putting to the torch a considerable quantity of unsold programmes, ticket stubs and even some old chairs which were being stored in the cellars.

Regardless of the weather travelling was always a burden; few players had cars, though some had motorbikes, and out-of-town concerts meant travel by rail. Mercifully the long wartime journeys to the Midlands and the North were a thing of the past, this area of the country being left to the Hallé, the Liverpool Philharmonic and the short-lived Yorkshire Symphony Orchestra. But whether the concert took place outside London, or in one of the outer suburbs, most evenings involved a tedious journey home. If ten o'clock in the morning sounded a luxurious time for starting the next day's rehearsal, it hardly felt like it to a musician putting his key in the door at close to midnight.

For those present February 1947 brought one abiding memory to warm the heart, if not the body, the return of Kirsten Flagstad to the London concert platform, singing the *Liebestod* and the final scene from *Götterdämmerung*. In securing her services the orchestra were greatly helped by Berta Geissmar, who wrote a long personal letter to the singer. Karl Rankl, newly installed as Music Director of the Royal Opera House, conducted, and the LSO Horn section played the Wagner Tubas. It was an emotional occasion, matching the appearance of Marjorie Lawrence the previous year. A second concert, every bit as successful as the first, took place in March, Flagstad's contribution on this occasion being arias from *The Flying Dutchman, Lohengrin* and *Tannhäuser,* and in May she sang in a complete performance of the last act of

Die Walküre, followed after the interval by the Funeral March and Immolation Scene from *Götterdämmerung*.

In the years leading up to the war a number of different choirs and choral societies performed with the LPO, including Charles Kennedy Scott's Philharmonic Choir, a name which gave rise to yet further confusion, for the choir had no connection with the LPO or the Royal Philharmonic Society. The existence of this choir ended with the outbreak of war, and in 1947 a new choir, the London Philharmonic Choir, was formed, with members of the old choir as its nucleus, and Frederick Jackson as chorus master, a position he was to hold for twenty-five years. The choir made its debut in May 1947, performing the *Choral Symphony*, under de Sabata. They approached his first rehearsal with some trepidation, but to their surprise de Sabata only made two small stops to correct their rhythm, turning to Frederick Jackson afterwards with the words, 'You have already done everything'. The second rehearsal was more demanding, de Sabata testing them with constant changes of tempo, but despite minor mishaps he finished the rehearsal satisfied that they could cope with the demands of the work. The preparatory work put in by Jackson and his choristers helped put the seal on a Beethoven cycle which, for all that memories have been erased by later cycles given by, among others, Fürtwangler, Otto Klemperer and Josef Krips, aroused great excitement at the time.

The LPO returned to the Proms in the summer of 1947, when a plan suggested by Russell was given a trial. It was not until 1927, when the BBC assumed responsibility for the Proms, that Wood was given the luxury of a daily rehearsal. Even so, with only one orchestra employed, the standard of playing deteriorated as the season wore on. Employment of a second orchestra relieved the pressure, but because the orchestras were booked consecutively rather than concurrently, playing for four weeks at a stretch, concerts of considerable length and complexity still received only one rehearsal, the quality of performance deteriorating as the weeks went by. In 1947 a radically different approach was adopted. Two orchestras were booked concurrently, one playing on Monday, Wednesday, Friday and Saturday, the other on Tuesday and Thursday, with the pattern reversed the following week, enabling each concert to be given an average of three rehearsals. The BBC Symphony Orchestra performed throughout, the LSO playing for the first four weeks, and the LPO during the last four, resulting in a higher standard of performance than was ever possible under the old system of block bookings. Boult conducted the BBC Symphony Orchestra, with Stanford Robinson as associate conductor, Sargent the LSO and Cameron the LPO. Works performed by the LPO included the Seventh Symphony of Arnold Bax; the Symphony *Harold in Italy* by Berlioz; Delius' Nocturne *Paris* and Gershwin's *An American in Paris*, though not in the same programme; and a new Piano Concerto by the American composer William Schuman. The LPO also gave what may have been the first performance at the Proms of the *Rite of Spring*, for which the

Albert Hall was all but sold out, drawing attention to the fact that the Proms could attract audiences for programmes that at any other time would have emptied the house.

The increased grant awarded by the LCC enabled the LPO to continue its policy of wide-ranging Sunday afternoon concerts mixed with popular Thursday evenings, and ensured adequate rehearsal time for difficult or unfamiliar works. The autumn of 1947 saw further concerts with Bruno Walter, who conducted more Mahler, the First Symphony and Beethoven's *Choral Symphony*, other guest conductors including Ansermet, with whom the Choir sang Stravinsky's *Symphony of Psalms*, de Sabata and Georges Enesco. It was, however, a pointer to the future that Russell's end-of-season review in *Philharmonic Post* gave pride of place to performances of two works by Ravel, *Le Tombeau de Couperin* and the Second Suite from *Daphnis and Chloé*, for which Eduard van Beinum was given the benefit of five rehearsals, an investment fully justified by the results. Van Beinum had been invited to work with the orchestra for a spell of three weeks, conducting at several out-of-town locations as well as at the Albert Hall and Covent Garden, his musicianship impressing everyone.

The engagement of Wilhelm Fürtwangler, who appeared with the orchestra during March, gave rise to some criticism, his concerts with the LPO prompting Bruno Walter to write from America expressing concern. Rightly or wrongly Fürtwangler, more than any other musician who remained in Germany during the war, had been tarnished by what was believed to be a closer association than necessary with the Nazi party. So far as the LPO was concerned, the barriers to his reappearance in this country were removed when he completed the de-Nazification process required by the occupying powers. The employment of German and Italian musicians was an area where the LPO had to tread with care, the LCC having asked for reassurance that none of the conductors engaged to perform at concerts in the Royal Opera House could be accused of political collaboration.

Fürtwangler's concerts included a cycle of the Brahms Symphonies and a performance of the *Choral Symphony*. For members of the choir, taking part in their third performance of Beethoven's masterpiece within the space of less than twelve months, it was an opportunity to reflect on their good fortune in taking part in so short a space of time in three such diverse interpretations as those of Fürtwangler, de Sabata and Walter. Other conductors who worked with the orchestra during late spring and early summer included Sergiu Celibidache, Jean Martinon, Carl Schuricht and Erich Kleiber, whose concert moved Eric Blom to write 'The playing in Schubert's little B flat Symphony and especially in Berlioz' *Fantastic* was truly wonderful.' Unfamiliar music included the *Prelude and Fugue* of Francis Chagrin, premiered at the Proms the previous year, a welcome instance of a new work by a British composer being given the benefit of a second hearing.

Apparently the BBC found the format adopted for the 1947 Proms too expensive and 1948 followed a different pattern, the BBC Symphony Orchestra and the LSO playing for a week at a time, with three or four days of rehearsal in the intervening week. The LPO was excluded, the BBC making no enquiry as to their ability or willingness to take part. Instead they performed at the Three Choirs Festival. This was usually the province of the LSO, but with that orchestra fully occupied with the Prom season the organisers had to look elsewhere, inviting the LPO to take their place.

Though the policy of working under a succession of distinguished guest conductors led to many fine performances, the appointment of a Principal Conductor, able to devote a substantial part of his time to the LPO, had been occupying the Board for some time. In the autumn of 1947 Russell travelled to the USA with a view to entering into negotiations with Dimitri Mitropoulos. When these proved unfruitful, eyes were turned to the continent. Of those with whom they had worked since the war the Dutchman, Eduard van Beinum, possessed the attributes they required, though there were two stumbling-blocks, his wish to continue working with the Concertgebouw Orchestra, and the restrictive attitude adopted by the Ministry of Labour to the appointment of overseas musicians to posts in this country. Nevertheless the Board regarded themselves as fortunate that van Beinum was prepared to commit himself to the LPO for several months at the start of each year.

Van Beinum would also be working with a new leader. Difficulties had arisen over Andrew Cooper's relations with a number of conductors, including Dr Leslie Russell, who as the LCC's Director of Music was responsible for planning and conducting the children's concerts given on behalf of the Council, and Cooper's relationship with his front-desk partner Henry Datyner was also causing friction within the First Violin section. It was an unhappy situation which led to Cooper's suspension, and though he was reinstated it was reluctantly concluded that harmony could only be restored by a new appointment. Hopes were initially centred on Henry Holst, who had a distinguished reputation as a solo performer, but Holst was not at that time a British citizen, and it was therefore decided to invite David Wise, who had spent the past five years leading the Liverpool Philharmonic Orchestra, to fill the vacancy. Like Cooper, Wise was a pupil of Willy Hess, and was an experienced chamber player, having spent six years as a member of the Brosa Quartet, with whom he had toured the United States. Consideration was given to the appointment of Henry Holst as joint leader, but delays over Holst's naturalisation papers and concerns about the financial implications put paid to what had been a highly desirable development.

The year also saw the formation of the LPO Council, set up to act as a liaison body between the orchestra and its public. J.B. Priestley accepted an invitation to become Chairman, and while the Council had no specific terms of reference, Priestley set out a number of limited aims, including advice and criticism, to be given short of direct interference; to endeavour to secure the public recognition the orchestra deserved; and to explore areas where the LPO's policies might need to be brought into greater harmony with the wishes of the public. Priestley anticipated that if ever the LPO acquired a home of its own, these tasks would be considerably increased. The Council continued to occupy an ambivalent position, with no direct responsibilities, but the expectation that its opinions would be listened to with respect.

Three years of Sunday afternoon concerts at the Stoll Theatre and Covent Garden had shown that the public remained indifferent to adventurous programmes. It was no longer possible to continue losing money on this scale, and Sunday concerts were confined to the suburbs, the Thursday evening series at the Albert Hall becoming the LPO's principal shop window in Central London. Most of the autumn's concerts were given under Martinon, Malko, and Celibidache. Martinon's programmes included a cycle of Beethoven's Piano Concertos with Solomon as soloist; Malko concentrated on Russian music, and Celibidache conducted the *Psalmus Hungaricus* of Kodály and a popular Boxing Day concert, an experiment that was not repeated. One of Malko's programmes included the Fourth Symphony of Tchaikovsky. The Berlin Philharmonic were touring Britain, one of their concerts, given two days after Malko's, advertised as including the Fourth Symphony of Brahms. At short notice the promoters, a charitable body, one of whose aims in arranging the tour was to advance the cause of reconciliation between Britain and Germany, deleted the Brahms Symphony, substituting the Fourth Symphony of Tchaikovsky. The feelings of the LPO about this were understandably less than charitable.

Though the autumn was not without interest, inevitably there was a degree to which it was the curtain-raiser to the arrival of Eduard van Beinum as Principal Conductor.

9

Eduard van Beinum 1949–50

Born in 1901, Eduard van Beinum received his first conducting appointment in 1927 with the Haarlem Symphony Orchestra, joining the Concertgebouw Orchestra four years later as assistant to Willem Mengelberg. During the Nazi occupation many Dutchmen stayed away from concerts given by the Concertgebouw, a passive protest against the occupation, the treatment of the Jewish community, the ban on music by Jewish composers, and the presence in the hall of German officers and Nazi sympathisers. Mengelberg was absent for long periods, leaving van Beinum to undertake much of the orchestra's work, but his fears that he would be penalised for carrying out his duties proved groundless. Dutch public opinion placed full responsibility for acceptance of the restrictions imposed by the occupying forces on the shoulders of Mengelberg, who made no protest at the removal of the Jewish members of the orchestra or the banning orders placed on the music of many composers. When the war ended Mengelberg was branded a collaborator, disgraced and dismissed from his post, retiring to Switzerland, where he died in exile in 1951. His successor was van Beinum.

Van Beinum's health was always a matter of concern – he was fifty-eight when he died in 1959 of heart failure – his term as Principal Conductor of the LPO lasting only eighteen months, from January 1949 until June the following year. In this short time he made a great impact on the orchestra, which by now had attracted a number of younger recruits to its ranks, including, in addition to Maurice Cody, the deputy leader Howard Leyton-Brown and Roger Lord, who succeeded Sidney Sutcliffe as principal oboe. In addition to concerts in the Albert Hall van Beinum undertook a heavy schedule in the suburbs of London and the provinces. Brighton, Chatham, Croydon, East Ham, High Wycombe, Hornsey, Ipswich, Lewisham, Nottingham, Reading, Southampton, Watford and Wimbledon were among the places receiving regular visits, and van Beinum conducted in all of them. With five or six performances a week, the schedule was too crowded for him to conduct every night, and from time to time he was relieved by another conductor, usually Basil Cameron. Russell wrote a long appreciation in which he summarised some of the reasons for the esteem in which the players held their new Chief:

> 'However willing to play the general "on the box", and he has the personality to command discipline and obedience in artistic matters, he becomes at one with the players when work is over. He does not wish for a life of solitary grandeur, and is happier when travelling third class with the other musicians, sharing a game of cards, or discussing the domestic affairs of this or that member of the orchestra. A conductor may succeed by spreading fear and even hate; van Beinum practices the slower method of gaining their confidence. A rehearsal finished he does not stalk in dignified silence from the platform, but is available for the many who approach him as he walks off, so that he misses little that passes through their minds.'

Despite his assertion that he felt more at home in London than in Paris, van Beinum was considerably more fluent in French than English, his problems with the language of his hosts providing moments of light relief during rehearsals, especially when, at a loss for the right English word, he lapsed into his native Dutch. Rehearsing *Das Lied von der Erde*, with the Australian singer Kenneth Neate as tenor soloist, he was unable to summon up the word 'vowels', his instruction to the soloist to 'be careful with your klinkers' bringing the proceedings to a temporary halt.

In 1949 van Beinum's Albert Hall programmes rarely strayed from the familiar. Concerts in January and February were devoted to a Beethoven cycle, but March offered more varied fare, including Bruckner's Third Symphony and Bartok's Concerto for Orchestra, and on Easter Saturday he adopted a tradition followed in Amsterdam every year, giving a complete performance of the *St Matthew Passion*. Bruckner's Symphony was featured in a long article about the composer in *Philharmonic Post*, but as with so many previous attempts to expand the repertoire this concert proved an expensive luxury, the takings barely covering the cost of hiring the hall.

Audiences at the Albert Hall gave cause for concern, but there was steady growth in places such as Croydon, East Ham, Hornsey, Lewisham, St Pancras and Watford, providing ample justification for the policy of trying to present music to the widest possible audience, at prices comparing favourably with those charged at cinemas. In addition to the grant from the LCC several local councils provided support for concerts in their borough, with Lewisham a case in point, the council's decision to subsidise seat prices, supporting the series with lecture recitals arranged by the LPO, leading to a gratifying increase in audience support, with most of the concerts in the Town Hall sold out.

Concerts in these suburban halls were given at intervals of between four and six weeks, and programme planning, for generally unsophisticated audiences, many of whom would be unlikely to venture as far afield as the Albert Hall, had to be undertaken with care. In the early months of 1949 the programme committee felt confident enough to include the *Symphonie Fantastique* of Berlioz at several suburban concerts, and whereas in the not-so-distant past this work might have spelt financial disaster, they were rewarded with full houses. There was from time to time another side to the coin. The continuing burden of so many concerts, with many Sundays involving both afternoon and evening performances, led to periodic lapses of discipline, players arriving late for rehearsals and concerts, or failing to take the platform in good time. Periodically the Board had to issue reminders that to its audience every concert was a special occasion, and a high level of discipline was essential to retain goodwill.

At the end of March a week was spent at the People's Palace in the Mile End Road, accompanying performances of Rutland Boughton's Opera *The Immortal Hour*, given under the direction of the composer, with Frederick Jackson as assistant conductor. Boughton's work had been performed in London before the war, running on an extended basis rather than in repertory, and the 1949 performances were successful enough for it to be revived the following year. This brief spell in the pit was followed by concerts under Erich Kleiber. Though limited to standard fare, Mozart 40 and the *Eroica* in one programme, Haydn's *Surprise* and the *Pathétique* in the other, Kleiber conjured fine playing from the orchestra. Faced with yet another performance of the *Pathétique*, which had been played endlessly up and down the country for the last ten years, and of which most players would have said that they could play the notes in their sleep, the orchestra were astonished to find Kleiber making them look afresh at the music in a way they would hardly have believed possible.

From the outset van Beinum's work attracted a string of favourable notices. At the opening concert of the Beethoven cycle the *Observer* found the LPO 'as eager as greyhounds', and later in the cycle the *New Statesman* wrote of the partnership between conductor and orchestra that 'Mr van Beinum has the great virtue of equanimity of control – control of himself as well as his players. The LPO could hardly have made a wiser choice and their development will be uncommonly interesting to watch'. Subsequent concerts found an equally enthusiastic response, the *Liverpool Post* writing of a 'beautifully balanced and eloquently articulated performance of Bruckner's Third Symphony', the orchestra's achievements during the year summed up by the *Daily Telegraph*, who commended Kleiber's 'strong and purposeful performance' of the *Eroica*, and went on, 'this orchestra is in finer form than it has been for years'. Most satisfying of all was Ralph Hill's verdict: 'In the past I have said some hard things about the LPO. But not now. Its personnel has been strengthened by many excellent young players and van Beinum has done a magnificent job of training. The London Philharmonic is a well-rehearsed, keen and alive ensemble, which is a credit to London.'

The summer was given over to guest conductors, de Sabata, Georg Szell and Martinon. The last-named was always popular with the orchestra; when they toured during the summer some players, rather than bed down in yet another set of provincial digs, took camping gear with them, and Martinon would join them under canvas. Martinon was engaged to conduct the last Albert Hall concert of the year, but though the orchestra's playing was being widely acclaimed, there was disquiet about the small audiences drawn to concerts in that venue. Ticket prices were similar to those charged for concerts at Queen's Hall before the war, ranging from 3/- (15p) to 12/6 (62½p) but despite real growth in wages and salaries, it seemed that seats cost more than the average concert-goer was prepared to spend on an evening's entertainment. As an experiment it was decided to drastically reduce ticket prices for this concert, the orchestra announcing that:

'In common with other organisations, the London Philharmonic Orchestra has been worried by the consistently small size of audiences at the Royal Albert Hall in recent months, and by this experiment hope to find out whether it is merely shortage of money which is keeping people away, or whether there is no longer a public for the Albert Hall and for a well-designed – as opposed to a catch-penny – programme.'

Ticket prices were reduced to either 2/- or 3/6d, the programme comprising:

Mozart: Symphony No. 31 in D – *The Paris*; Elgar: Serenade for Strings; Roussel: Bacchus and Ariane, Suite No. 2; Berlioz: Symphonie Fantastique

As a means of attracting an audience the experiment proved highly successful, with the Albert Hall all but sold out, the orchestra reporting that:

'Although there was no soloist, and the programme itself made no concession to box-office appeal, three times as many people as had normally attended on Thursday evenings took advantage of the lower prices. It was interesting too, to see the high proportion of young people enjoying the unaccustomed comfort of the best seats. Unfortunately at these prices it is impossible to cover even the costs of a concert if it is to have proper rehearsal. Our expenses have gone up as drastically as your own. A compromise must therefore be struck. We would far rather build (and the orchestra would far rather play to) a good-sized audience of people who come to our concerts regularly and pay a moderate price, than rely on a possibly meagre and casual attendance at the normal rates of admission.'

The outcome was a decision to reduce ticket prices for concerts in the Albert Hall during the following winter. For the more popular concerts seat prices ranged from 2/- to 7/6d, those for other concerts from 2/- to 5/-, a considerable saving on the previous price range.

Berta Geissmar died in the autumn of 1949. Ever since Beecham's departure for America in 1940 she had devoted herself tirelessly to the LPO's interests, and when the war ended it was through her good offices that it was possible to issue invitations to many of the distinguished musicians who came to conduct. Beecham's defection was a cruel blow, for she never understood how he could desert a band of players who remained consistently loyal to him throughout the years he spent in America. In a footnote to her obituary in *The Times* Russell wrote:

> 'She took all LPO troubles and difficulties deeply to heart, and turned her affection and critical acumen upon its members. She was rewarded by the friendly response of the musicians, especially those who worked closely with her during the darkest days of the war.'

During 1949–50, the orchestra's work was concentrated in the hands of a small group of conductors. October, November and December were entrusted to Nicolai Malko, van Beinum was in charge from January to the end of May, and Martinon was responsible for many of those given in June and July, with Basil Cameron regularly standing in to give one or another of these a much needed night off. Malko conducted forty-three concerts, van Beinum sixty-four, Martinon twenty-three and Cameron thirty-nine, including a week at the Proms, these four undertaking around 80 per cent of the public concerts given during the year. Others conductors included Sir Adrian Boult, who was in charge of their second week at the Proms, Ernest Bloch, Serge Koussevitzky and Georg Solti. On his first visit to this country for more than a decade, Solti's work was limited to some recording sessions for Decca, the fruits of which were a set of Haydn's *Drum Roll* Symphony and a record of the Overture to *The Force of Destiny*. It would be the autumn of the following year before he first appeared with the LPO on the concert platform, conducting some out-of-town concerts.

Ernest Bloch had last conducted the orchestra in 1934. In the summer of 1949 he appeared at the Proms, conducting the LPO in the first London performance of his *Concerto Symphonique*, and in October he directed a complete concert of his music. Somehow Bloch's work had made little headway with the public; as far back as 1935 Sibelius, a great admirer of his fellow composer, had commented, 'I cannot account for the general neglect of Ernest Bloch. He is a greatly gifted man whose music is both modern in the best sense and within the grasp of the contemporary musical mind.' Born in Switzerland, Bloch had been resident in the United States for upwards of twenty years and the major work in his programme was the first British performance of the *Sacred Service*, a setting of Hebrew texts from the Old Testament, used mainly in the Sabbath Morning Service of the Reformed Temples of America. The *Sacred Service* enjoyed a limited popularity with choral societies, but despite the interest aroused by his visit Bloch's music largely remained on the sidelines. Rehearsing for the Proms Bloch expressed amazement at the players' sight-reading facility, commenting that an American orchestra would have taken far longer to come to grips with the music. One of his rehearsals brought a query from trumpet player Eric Bravington as to whether a note in his part should be F or F sharp: Bloch peered carefully at the score before delivering his verdict that 'it must be F sharp or we will not achieve the right cacophony'.

Apart from the annual performance of *Messiah*, under Frederick Jackson, the remaining Albert Hall concerts leading up to Christmas were conducted by Malko. The First and Ninth Symphonies of Beethoven were performed at a Sunday evening concert, and it is a commentary on the orchestra's economic position that, despite the importance of this concert, the dictates of finance compelled them to give an afternoon performance in Croydon. Walter Legge was expanding the Philharmonia's concert-giving activities, and a few days later that orchestra gave a performance of the *Choral Symphony*, conducted by Karajan, but following so soon after the LPO's concert with Malko, this took place in an almost empty hall. It was another example of the chaotic conditions which continued to apply to music-making in London. Programme clashes were in nobody's interest, but there was no forum which would enable concert-giving organisations to co-ordinate their plans.

Malko's other Albert Hall concerts consisted entirely of Russian music, a miscellaneous programme, and six devoted to Tchaikovsky. It had been intended to include a contemporary Russian work in each programme, but the likelihood that this would have been detrimental to box office receipts led to the idea being shelved. In addition to a cycle of the symphonies, there was an opportunity for hearing a number of rarities, including *The Tempest*, the Introduction to *The Opritchnik*, the Overture to *Christmas Eve*, and the duet Tchaikovsky fashioned from his Fantasy Overture *Romeo and Juliet*. There were difficulties in tracing the score and parts for *Christmas Eve*, until a set was located in the Edwin M. Fleischer Music Collection of Philadelphia, who loaned them for these performances. Though several of these lesser-known works were played at out-of-town concerts, the programmes given in the weeks leading up to Christmas make depressing reading, consisting of an almost unrelieved diet of Tchaikovsky, a piece of programme planning which might have been expected to sap the players' interest in their work. Nevertheless Malko proved popular with the orchestra. Eric Wetherell, a member of the horn section, recalled how he first played under Malko at a concert in Reading, where to his surprise the conductor came across to greet him with the words, 'I do not think I know this face. I am pleased to meet you.' Without in any way undermining his authority, Malko's approach to the players was on a par with that of van Beinum and Martinon, treating them as colleagues.

The autumn also saw a further experiment with lunchtime promenade concerts, given this time in the Seymour Hall, a venue more noted for its use by boxing promoters than for any kind of association with the arts. The acoustics of the hall were found to be satisfactory, but the concerts were no more successful than previous experiments of this nature. Though a regular series had been mooted, the idea was quickly abandoned.

In place of weekly Thursday evening concerts in the Albert Hall, the early months of 1950 saw a new pattern: fortnightly concerts on Thursdays and an irregular series on Sunday evenings. Sundays were given over to extremely popular works, Tchaikovsky, evenings of ballet music and programmes built around the most popular concertos, but those on Thursdays presented a wide range of unfamiliar or rarely performed music, van Beinum conducting *Das Lied von der Erde*, Beethoven's Mass in D, the first British performances of Prokofiev's Sixth Symphony and Britten's *Spring Symphony*, Bartok's Concerto for Orchestra, Bruckner's Seventh Symphony, the Third Symphony of his fellow Dutchman Willem Pijper, and Mahler's song-cycle *Kindertotenlieder*. Though performances of their music were on the increase, Bruckner and Mahler were still a largely unknown quantity in this country, and despite the advocacy of Neville Cardus and a handful of others, many critics had neither sympathy for, or understanding of, their music. One contemporary writer dismissed Bruckner with the comment that 'although I enjoyed stretches of the music I found the ideas too protracted, the method too obvious and the design inadequate for concentrated attention'. It may well have been performances of Mahler's Ninth Symphony by Barbirolli and the Hallé Orchestra in 1954 which did much to turn the tide in that composer's favour, but the pioneering work done on Bruckner and Mahler's behalf by, among others, van Beinum and the LPO, Boult and the BBC, and Krips and the LSO, played a part in arousing the interest of the concert-going public.

Though the popular programmes on Sundays were of no especial interest, one of them involved another unnecessary clash between the LPO and a visiting foreign orchestra. The Valencia Orchestra, with whom José Iturbi appeared as conductor and soloist, were the subject of a protest by the Musicians Union and the Orchestral Employers Association, on the grounds that they were of unproven merit. So far as the LPO was concerned, fuel was added to the flames when they discovered that one of the Spanish orchestra's concerts included Ravel's *Bolero*, a piece already announced as the concluding item for a Sunday concert. In itself Ravel's piece may not have been of great consequence, but it was a further demonstration of the frustration caused by the activities of independent concert agencies, whose actions had little or no regard to the overall health of orchestral music. It was small consolation that the Valencia Orchestra's playing came in for some particularly harsh criticism, or for the fact that to perform Ravel's piece adequately they had to hire several British players as extras.

Britten's *Spring Symphony* was the subject of an introductory article in *Philharmonic Post*. The work had been given its first performance in Amsterdam the previous year, with van Beinum conducting the Concertgebouw Orchestra. After the Amsterdam performances Scott Goddard wrote, 'A rehearsal left me without a clue. Then two performances. By the end of the second there was sufficient daylight to see where one was being taken... the work had come alive. And it had become immensely attractive.' Artistically the London performance was extremely successful, yet even with a good house and a relay fee from the BBC, it was impossible to cover the cost of putting on this concert. Twelve rehearsals for the choir, five for the orchestra, rehearsals for van Beinum with the singers, a boys' choir to be trained and the necessity of recruiting additional players required by the score resulted in a loss of £600. One critic wrote that it was surprising the work only received one performance, a comment showing that he was unfamiliar with the economics of concert-giving. Britten's score included a part for an instrument new to the ranks of the orchestra, a cowhorn. As no instrument could be found to produce the sound Britten had in mind, Boosey and Hawkes were commissioned to construct a specially designed instrument, the playing of which was entrusted to horn-player Eric Wetherell. The specification stated that the instrument should be 'capable – theoretically – of the harmonic series on fundamentals C, G, and F, more than adequate for the mere two notes required by Britten', the question as to what the instrument sounded like receiving the tongue-in-cheek answer, 'Well, cowhornish, if that means anything to you.'

The *Spring Symphony* proved an exception to the general rule that concerts offering adventurous programmes were a recipe for an empty hall. The balance of the cost involved in putting on concerts such as these was of course met by the grants made by the Arts Council and the LCC. The Arts Council was now allocating £10,000 a year to the LPO and the Hallé. Excluding children's concerts and recording sessions, the Hallé and the LPO gave over two hundred concerts a year, their Arts Council grant equivalent to less than £50 a concert. Though there were no direct Arts Council grants for the Philharmonia or the RPO, each of whom gave only about thirty public concerts, both orchestras were hired by organisations which themselves received grants, the Philharmonia playing for six concerts given by the short-lived New Era Concert Society, the RPO appearing at six of the eight concerts given by the Royal Philharmonic Society. Each received £1000 from the Arts Council, equivalent to £125 a concert for the Royal Philharmonic Society and £165 for the New Era Society, a disproportionate reward for organisations which at best served a limited public. Concern about the basis of allocating funds led Ernest Bean, General

Manager of the Hallé, to ask for information about the way in which the Arts Council allocated funds to its clients, an approach that was firmly rebuffed, the Council flatly refusing to enter into any kind of discussion of the subject.

The activities of the Philharmonia and the RPO were in fact far from being universally welcome. Geoffrey Sharp, in a review of London concerts during 1949–50, wrote, 'The Philharmonia and Royal Philharmonic share a serious disability: that neither is a permanently constituted orchestra. Both assemble and disperse more or less at random, and play under various conductors for all sorts of occasions, including recording music for films. There is no style which is distinctively RPO or Philharmonia: they are in fact musical chameleons.' The existence of these orchestras was to have a serious impact on the fortunes of the LPO as plans for a new concert hall, commissioned by the LCC and now being built on the South Bank of the Thames, began to take shape.

A concert in March 1950 celebrated the tenth anniversary of the first concert given in Watford by the LPO. Basil Cameron conducted the identical programme to that which he gave with the orchestra in March 1940, and to mark the occasion J.B. Priestley spoke about the orchestra's work. The borough had then been the proud possessor of a newly opened public hall, blessed with good acoustics and the tenth anniversary concert was the seventy-first given there, the promotion of concerts on a regular basis helping to build up a loyal and stable audience, with the relationship between the borough and the LPO a matter of civic pride. These activities were underwritten by the Local Government Act of 1948, which empowered authorities to raise a rate of up to 6d in the pound for the purpose, and in addition to making a grant in support of the LPO's concerts, Watford Council purchased a block of seats for distribution to schools and youth clubs, a move designed to build the audience of the future. Many artists of distinction appeared on the platform of the hall: Boult, Heward, Sargent, Tauber and Wood were early wartime visitors. Beecham's first concert on returning from America took place there, and in the post-war years a list of eminent names included those of van Beinum, Fürtwangler, Martinon, Münch, Malko, and Walter, whose concert in Watford was his only suburban appearance.

In May 1950 the LPO undertook a week-long tour of the Low Countries, giving two concerts in Brussels, two in Amsterdam and one each in Arnhem and Utrecht. Foreign tours do not necessarily allow much opportunity for sightseeing, but most of the music included in van Beinum's programmes had been performed at concerts given in and around London, and the relatively short journeys allowed more free time than is often the case, their Dutch hosts going out of their way to show the visitors something of the country. At s'Hertogenbosch their arrival was greeted by the British and Dutch national anthems played on the carillon of the cathedral, and after lunch in the city, hosted by members of the Brabents orchestra, they were sped on their way by the strains of 'Auld Lang Syne'. The concert at Arnhem provided an opportunity for a visit to the nearby British cemetery at Oosterbeeck, the last resting place for so many men of the British First Airborne Division, where the LPO's Deputy Leader, Howard Leyton-Brown, who served as a bomber pilot during the war, laid a wreath. Overnight accommodation in Arnhem was provided by the townspeople themselves, and in Amsterdam there was enough time for a trip on the city's canals. The hospitality heaped on the players was such that once or twice there was only just time to change and get back to the hall for the day's concert.

The opening concert in Brussels, conducted by Sir Adrian Boult, included Brahms' Second Symphony and the *Enigma* Variations, with the remaining concerts, under van Beinum, based on a miscellaneous programme comprising *The Water Music*, Mozart's *Haffner* Symphony, Brahms' *Variations on a Theme by Haydn*, Debussy's *Faune* Prelude, Holst's Ballet Music *The Perfect Fool* and Elgar's Overture *Cockaigne*, described by one Dutch paper as 'containing much concussion and bells'. At the first of two concerts in Amsterdam Mahler's song-cycle *Kindertotenlieder*, sung by Kathleen Ferrier, replaced the works by Debussy and Holst, and at Utrecht the Dutch pianist Jan Smeterlin appeared as soloist in Rachmaninov's Second Piano Concerto. If the programmes entrusted to van Beinum look rather slight, at least on paper, the orchestra was received enthusiastically in both countries, the tour providing further evidence of the high standards being achieved under their Principal Conductor.

For all that van Beinum's concerts included a wide range of refreshingly unfamiliar music, the climax of the year came at its end, four concerts under the 76-year-old Serge Koussevitzky, until recently conductor of the Boston Symphony Orchestra. Koussevitzky had last conducted in Britain in the mid-1930s when, in addition to concerts with the BBC Symphony Orchestra, he made a number of records with the LPO. This was, however, his first public appearance with the orchestra. Koussevitzky acquired a great reputation as a champion of the living composer, and one contemporary work considered for performance under his baton was the First Symphony of the young British composer Peter Racine Fricker, which had been given an award bearing the conductor's name. Disappointment at the poor audiences for the enterprising series of concerts given earlier in the year meant that once again the dictates of the box office led to his four concerts with the LPO, three at the Albert Hall, one at Croydon, consisting of well-known works, Debussy's *La Mer*, Prokofiev's *Classical* Symphony, Tchaikovsky Five, Brahms Four, Sibelius Two and Beethoven's *Choral*. But there was nothing routine about the performances, the *News Chronicle* writing of his opening concert that the partnership provided 'some of the most electrifying playing heard in this hall for a decade or so'. Here was further confirmation of the LPO's enhanced status.

Artistically the past two years had given cause for satisfaction, the critical reaction to concerts under van Beinum, Malko and Koussevitzky, and the reception given to the orchestra in Belgium and Holland, reward for the decision to appoint van Beinum Principal Conductor, while the LPO's relationship with the LCC appeared to be progressing to the satisfaction of both parties. The Council had renewed its grant every year, and hopes were rising that within the foreseeable future the LPO would have a home it could call its own. Though the likelihood of Queen's Hall being rebuilt had receded, the LCC had commissioned a new hall, now being built on the South Bank of the Thames, at an estimated cost of two million pounds, and it was widely anticipated that the LPO would be appointed as resident orchestra. To outward appearances the LPO had every reason to feel justified in looking to the future with a considerable degree of confidence.

There was, however, an unhappy tailpiece to van Beinum's time with the LPO. The long round of suburban and provincial concerts, and the attendant travelling, was a considerable strain, even for a man in good health, and van Beinum was suffering from the onset of heart disease. He therefore tendered his resignation, intending to return as often as possible as a guest. His last concert as Principal Conductor took place in the Albert Hall on 2 June. Almost immediately he was taken seriously ill, and it was over a year before he was fit enough to return to conduct again. Subsequently he accepted a post in Los Angeles, which he occupied in tandem with his conductorship of the Concertgebouw, but this was less taxing than his work with the LPO, involving fewer concerts, and without the physical grind involved in continual travelling from one hall to another.

Even had ill-health not intervened, it had been appreciated from the outset that van Beinum's appointment was likely to be of limited duration, and the question of a successor had been under consideration for some time. Among the names considered by the Board were those of Alceo Galliera, Josef Krips, Rafael Kubelik, Rudolf Schwartz and Georg Solti. Events elsewhere were however to play a significant part, and though van Beinum's resignation was a matter for regret, it was the orchestra's good fortune that there was a candidate immediately available who welcomed the opportunity to step into his shoes.

10

Sir Adrian Boult 1950–57

In 1950 Sir Adrian Boult stepped down as Principal Conductor of the BBC Symphony Orchestra, giving his last public concert with that orchestra in April 1950. Boult had worked with the LPO on numerous occasions. During the 1949 Proms he conducted the LPO for a week, and that autumn, while still with the BBC, recorded Elgar's First Symphony with them. Boult was therefore well acquainted with Thomas Russell who, shortly after the news of Boult's impending departure from the BBC became public, invited him to succeed van Beinum. Boult was delighted to accept, his transition from the ranks of the BBC bringing to the LPO a man whose character was in marked contrast to that of its founder. The pre-war rivalry between the two orchestras had given rise to a degree of antipathy between the two men, largely concealed on Boult's part, less so by Beecham, and the fact that Boult now inherited the rostrum that had once been Beecham's was an indication of just how much the character of the orchestra had changed over the course of the past decade.

The nature of Boult's role as Principal Conductor of the BBC Symphony Orchestra meant that much of his time was spent in the studio rather than the concert hall. Wood's death required him to undertake a major role at the Proms, but it was not one he professed to enjoy, and he was almost certainly relieved when in 1948 Sargent became the central figure at these concerts. So far as the musical public was concerned, he lacked the charisma of his fellow musical knights, Barbirolli, Beecham and Sargent, and by comparison with the array of distinguished guest conductors who had worked with the LPO during the past few years, his appointment to succeed van Beinum did not at first sight seem particularly exciting. Yet as events unfolded over the next year, the LPO found they had recruited a man who was to be a doughty champion on their behalf at a critical point in their affairs.

Boult's departure from the BBC was an unhappy episode. The BBC Symphony Orchestra was adversely affected by the war, with improvement slow to come, impeded by the fact that many players returning from the forces were lured away by the Philharmonia and the RPO, with adequate replacements in short supply. By 1948 the orchestra was much improved, but the Corporation's newly appointed Director of Music, Sir Steuart Wilson, saw replacement of Boult as the solution to the orchestra's problems. The situation was complicated by the fact that Boult had married Wilson's first wife, a fact of which the higher management of the BBC were apparently unaware. Whether this played any part in Wilson's determination to find a new conductor is far from clear, but much of Wilson's correspondence with Boult was couched in terms which were far from courteous, and it seems unbelievable that such a senior member of the BBC's staff should have been notified of the termination of his services by what Boult himself described as 'a two-line chit from a clerk'.

Yet beneath an apparently urbane exterior Boult's character contained a core of steel. The manner of his departure from the BBC might have undermined the confidence and ability of a lesser man, but appears instead to have acted as a spur. Boult was far from happy at the prospect of freelancing, holding the view that he 'preferred saying fresh things to the same people, rather than saying the same old things to different people all the time'. The invitation to succeed van Beinum was therefore opportune, and from the outset he threw all his energies into the service of the LPO, assuming a workload that would have taxed the resources of many younger men.

Though taking no part in the 1950 Proms, at which the LPO was conducted by Cameron, Boult began work during the summer, visiting several of the towns appearing regularly on the schedule, Brighton, Croydon, Guildford, Hackney and Southampton. Boult and the orchestra also recorded Elgar's Symphonic Study *Falstaff*, and Mahler's song-cycle *Lieder eines fahrenden Gesellen*, sung by Blanche Thebom, but though Beethoven's First Symphony was also taped, the records appear never to have been released for sale. For some years most of the LPO's records had been made for Decca, who were in the process of issuing the first LP records but, as with the Elgar Symphony the previous autumn, these sessions were carried out for HMV, with the records originally issued in 78 format.

The autumn was spent building up a repertoire, with the Festivals at Malvern and Swansea providing an opportunity for Boult to introduce a wider range of music than that normally offered to suburban and out-of-town audiences, including Elgar's First Symphony, Mahler's song-cycle *Kindertotenlieder*, with Kathleen Ferrier, and Walton's Symphony. After a rehearsal at Malvern, where Boult had been working in his shirt-sleeves, a cleaner approached a member of the orchestra with the comment, 'Funny job you lot have got: your gaffer's the only one of you 'as takes 'is coat off'. In the light of the previous winter's experience when, despite lower ticket prices, audiences for concerts in the Albert Hall had been disappointing, the number given in that hall was greatly reduced, to about one every three weeks. Boult therefore spent much of the autumn 'on the road', writing in *Philharmonic Post* about his experiences in coming to terms with the various halls in which performances were given:

> 'Outside Central London there are about twenty halls which the LPO visits at intervals of four to ten weeks. Some give a pleasant mellow quality to the strings; some tend to let the woodwind get swamped; some emphasise the brassiness of the brass; in one hall we know that about twelve members of the orchestra cannot see the beat at all if they play in a normal way – well, they must manage somehow because it so happens that the quality of sound is lovely in that hall, and the audience is one of the largest and most stable that we know. The worst and unfortunately the most general trouble that we meet is inadequate space for actual playing. There are really only about half-a-dozen halls where the orchestra can be arranged in a satisfactory way so that every member is playing in comfort with ample room and clear visibility.'

Audiences in the Albert Hall remained unsatisfactory, and Bach's B minor Mass, *The Dream of Gerontius* and Vaughan Williams' *London Symphony* were performed to rows of empty seats; in marked contrast with the experience in the Albert Hall, a performance of Vaughan Williams' symphony, given two days later in Chatham, attracted a full house. Guest conductors included Solti, whose first public concerts in this country took place in Brighton, Eastbourne, East Ham and Watford. Though Solti was Principal Conductor of the Munich State Opera, as yet few people in this country knew much about his background. His recording of Haydn's *Drum Roll* Symphony had been released in June, the performance prompting the *New Statesman* to the view 'He must be one of the best conductors alive', a pointer to a future in which reputations would be made as much in the recording studio as in the concert hall.

In January 1951 the LPO toured Germany, giving concerts in Essen, Hanover, Berlin, Hamburg, Münster, Dortmund, Düsseldorf, Nuremburg, Munich, Stuttgart and Heidelberg. Travelling in Germany was a great deal more comfortable than was often the case at home, the railway authorities providing a special train, complete with dining-car and, where overnight journeys were involved, sleeping-cars. However this train could not be used for the journey to Berlin, which was of course a divided city, deep inside the Russian zone of occupation. The best method of travel to that city would have been to take the train, controlled by the British military authorities, which ran daily from the British Zone into Berlin. There were, however, insufficient sleeping berths available, and half the party took the train and the remainder flew, the first time the LPO had taken to the air. Consideration had in fact been given to using air travel from the UK to Germany, but Boult and a number of players were averse to the idea and it was dropped. The German press was uniformly enthusiastic and full houses were the order of the day, except in Düsseldorf, where the large British military community was disappointed by the failure of the local welfare officer to exchange British currency for German marks, preventing many of those who wanted to from attending. As if the German tour was not gruelling enough, after returning overnight by boat to Harwich, Boult and the orchestra broke their homeward journey at Ipswich to give an afternoon concert.

Sargent's many guest appearances led to long absences from the BBC Symphony Orchestra's rostrum, and the BBC engaged Boult to work with his old orchestra for much of February and March. Van Beinum was to have conducted during his absence, but was still convalescing, and it would be July before he again took up the baton. Boult tried to withdraw from his BBC engagements, and when this proved impossible the vacant dates in February were taken over by Cameron and Stanley Pope, with Jean Martinon undertaking most of those in March, while Boult gave up some of his free days between concerts with the BBC Symphony Orchestra to undertake an occasional LPO date. There were even fewer Albert Hall concerts than in the autumn, one in February, another in March, at which Martinon conducted the Brahms *Requiem*, and one in April.

For some time eyes had been fixed on London's new concert hall, whose foundation stone was laid in October 1949 within the site to be used for the 1951 Festival of Britain. Yet however welcome the new hall, before it opened the LCC changed their mind about the policy to be adopted for its usage in a way that was heartbreaking. There had been good reason to believe the hall would provide the LPO with a permanent home. Though the number of London orchestras had increased to five, the LPO could justifiably lay claim to be the only orchestra giving public concerts all the year round. They had apparently developed a satisfactory working relationship with the LCC, and it was not unreasonable to hope that they might be given some preferential treatment, hopes buoyed up by the fact that the LPO was consulted about facilities for the new hall, some planning meetings even taking place at the LPO's offices in Welbeck Street.

Regrettably it was not to be. Certainly there was considerable opposition from within the ranks of the musical profession, especially from those who believed their own position would be threatened if the LPO was given primacy. Nor did it help that the LCC chose to second an officer from its housing department to act as manager of the hall. The LCC sought advice from several quarters on how to make the best possible use of its facilities, those consulted including Sir Thomas Beecham and Sir Malcolm Sargent, whose opposition to the LPO could be taken for granted, and in the light of this advice the LCC announced that, rather than appoint a resident orchestra they would give equality of treatment to the LPO, the LSO, the Philharmonia and the RPO. Instead of receiving preferential treatment the LPO, whose responsibilities to players and public extended all the year round, found itself competing on unequal terms with orchestras whose responsibilities were exercised on a concert-by-concert basis. As it happened the BBC dragged its heels about transferring its concerts to the new venue, condemning their orchestra to another winter playing in a sparsely filled Albert Hall, and for the next year Sargent's appearances on the South Bank were few and far between. Beecham for his part rewarded the Council with some scathing criticisms of the building, though he was not averse to conducting there.

In fact the LPO never envisaged having sole use of the hall, which would have curtailed their continuing responsibilities to audiences in and around the capital. In addition to such organisations as the Bach Choir and the Royal Philharmonic Society, who transferred their activities to the new hall, there was ample scope for a second orchestra to play a major role, with the LSO regarded as the most likely contender. In addition to their own annual series of concerts the LSO appeared regularly at the Proms and with many of London's leading choral societies, the breadth of its activities giving it a strong claim to be awarded an important place in the hall's activities.

Even more serious was the LCC's decision to withdraw their annual grant of £25,000, offering instead the sum of £10,000 in respect of the children's concerts, the open-air concerts in Finsbury Park and a number of concerts in a subscription series to be presented by the LCC itself. With an annual budget of £130,000, on which they made a loss of £4,500 the previous year, this could have been disastrous, and it provoked an immediate outcry, the conflicting views taken on the subject spilling over into the columns of *The Times*. In response to the case argued on the LPO's behalf by a distinguished list of signatories, the Leader of the LCC replied in the following terms:

> 'During the last few years the Council's contribution to the promotion of good music has been a grant to the LPO of an increasing amount, which for the present year stands at £25,000. When the Council undertook the heavy capital commitment of building the Royal Festival Hall on the south bank it was clear the amount and nature of the Council's assistance to music must be reviewed. When the Council considered its policy for the Royal Festival Hall for its first normal year two major questions had to be determined: first whether any particular orchestra should become what is usually understood by the term a resident orchestra. After taking expert advice from the highest sources the Council decided that this should not be ruled out but that it ought to gain first-hand experience over an experimental period before committing itself, and that until the time was ripe for such a decision it was inappropriate that the Council should be specifically committed to one orchestra rather than another.

> 'Secondly, the Council considered whether it should itself promote

concerts and make itself financially responsible for them. It was decided that the Council should and during the year ending October 1952 the Council should promote some 65 concerts and offer engagements to all the leading orchestras. Besides this the Council is offering concessions in the matter of rent to concert promoting societies and other bodies operating on a non-profit making basis. The value of these commitments represents a heavy financial burden considerably in excess of the grant hitherto paid to the LPO. It was in these circumstances that the Council's decision to discontinue its grant to the LPO was taken and, in my view, fully justified. Nevertheless, anxious to afford the orchestra the best possible opportunity to make the inevitable readjustments which the discontinuance of the grant would entail, the Council besides offering the orchestra a generous share of the engagements for the concerts the Council is itself promoting, has decided to continue to engage the orchestra on a commercial basis, if the orchestra is willing, for the children's concerts and open-air concerts in Finsbury Park which the orchestra has hitherto given without specific payment in part return for the Council's grant. The value of these engagements may be said to be in the region of £10,000.'

As many voices were quick to point out, there was a world of difference between a grant of £25,000 and work valued at £10,000: the LPO's policy of giving concerts throughout the capital was endangered; the LPO were the only orchestra serving the capital in this way; the Council had failed to understand the difference between an orchestra operating on a full-time basis and orchestras paid engagement by engagement; and the LPO had been left with minimum time to reorder its affairs and counter the damage resulting from this black hole in its finances. Moreover, whatever the arguments advanced by the LCC, the Council had no business going into concert promotion, setting itself up in competition with other users of the hall. The position was summed up in an article in the Hallé Orchestra's house journal under the heading 'Bad Diagnosis, Doubtful Cure':

'If we understand the LCC's position aright the Council is in fact restoring with one hand to several orchestras what it has taken away from the other with one, and that London as a whole will benefit from the adjustment. The flaw is that this policy has been pursued by impresarios for the last twenty years with the result that musically speaking London is generally admitted to be the most chaotic city in Europe.'

The LPO appealed against the decision, a deputation led by Sir Adrian Boult visiting County Hall for the purpose, an appeal that was turned down, the General Purposes Committee recommending to the Council as a whole that the decision should stand. The affair now took a new turn, for it emerged that the hall's acting manager had proposed that the LCC should form its own orchestra, citing the Bournemouth Municipal Orchestra and the Yorkshire Symphony Orchestra as examples. This proposal was condemned from all sides, the critic of *The Times*, in an article which appeared on 8 June 1951, concluding with the words 'It is an open secret that the debate (between the LCC and the LPO) has been influenced by personal and political animosities that have little connexion with music', an assertion immediately denied by the Leader of the LCC.

Denial or no, the cat was now out of the bag. Behind the scenes there were many who believed the real reason for the LCC's change of heart over appointment of the LPO as resident orchestra, and withdrawal of their grant, had never been made public, that it lay in objections to the political sympathies of the LPO's Chairman, Thomas Russell. Like many young men of his generation, Russell's response to the rise of Fascism had been to join the Communist Party, and while the emergence of the truth about Soviet Russia persuaded many to withdraw their allegiance, Russell remained a paid-up party member. But whatever his political views, there was no question of these intruding on his management of the LPO, indeed he was punctilious in conducting the orchestra's affairs openly and democratically. The first hint of trouble had arisen in 1949, when Russell accepted an invitation to visit Moscow. In return for their grant, the LCC were invited to send an observer to meetings of the LPO's Board, and when Russell informed his Board of the invitation the Council's representative, Francis Holland, warned Russell that acceptance 'might disturb some of your friends at County Hall'. In view of later events it is significant that the Board, concerned that the visit might reflect unfavourably on the LPO, instructed Russell that on no account was the name of the LPO to be linked to his visit. His decision to go to Moscow marked a turning point in relations with the LCC.

In his statement denying the charge that the LCC was politically motivated, the Leader of the Council referred to a letter signed by the LPO the previous autumn, in which the LPO accepted that the Council had been 'acting in good faith', asserting there was nothing in the minutes of the Council or its sub-committees to substantiate the claim that the decision had been made on political grounds. His version of events was challenged by Sir Steuart Wilson, who pooh-poohed the idea that in conducting what he described as a witch-hunt against Russell, the Council would have allowed the facts to be recorded in a minute, his letter published in *The Times* on 15 June stating that:

'Mr Hayward can have for the asking a dossier of the events from the time a leading member of the South Bank Committee took panic at the visit to Moscow of Mr Thomas Russell. This councillor, or alderman, may have known Mr Russell's views, though in my years of professional association with him they have never been obtrusive. Sir Adrian Boult and I have, at the BBC and elsewhere, cheerfully accepted Mr Russell as a colleague, an expert authority and a friend. I will have produced for Mr Hayward the document the clerk of the LCC asked the LPO to sign in recognition of their receipt of extended grant – a document that is purely political.'

The charge of discrimination was further elaborated by J.B. Priestley who, at a Press Conference called by the LPO, produced a document sent to the LPO following Russell's visit to Moscow in 1949, which they were required to sign as a pre-condition of the continuance of the LCC grant. That document contained six points:

- The orchestra was not to be used for purposes of political propaganda;
- no discrimination might be made on political grounds in respect of any employee, musician, soloist or conductor;
- there must be no discrimination on political grounds in respect of the choice of music;
- payment of a grant by the LCC was not to be represented as acquiescence in any party allegiance on the part of members of the orchestra or its staff;
- those responsible for the orchestra must use reasonable discretion in exercising their private political activities;
- the placing of advertising was to be governed by commercial criteria and not influenced by the political affiliation of the advertising media.

Priestley outlined the circumstances which led the LPO to sign the letter referred to by Hayward, in which they accepted that 'the LCC had been acting in good faith'. In the autumn of 1950, following the LCC's decision not to renew their grant, the LPO submitted, in support of their case for its continuance, papers purporting to show that advice given to the Council by its representatives on the South Bank Committee was politically motivated. Faced with this evidence, and with £10,000 of the current year's grant still outstanding, the Clerk to the LCC wrote to the LPO, advising them that before receiving payment the LPO would have to provide the letter referred to by Hayward, in which as well as accepting the LCC's 'good faith' they were required to state that 'no allegation to the contrary effect will be made, authorised or instigated by the London Philharmonic Orchestra Limited or any person associated with it'. With so large a sum at stake, the LPO believed they had no alternative but to give in to what was in effect blackmail.

Priestley further claimed that, questioned directly, a member of the South Bank Committee, Councillor Walter Boys, admitted his attitude had been changed by Russell's Moscow visit and that he, Boys, would not recommend payment of a penny to the LPO while Russell remained a Director. Faced with wholly contradictory versions of events, general opinion was that one or other of the parties could not be telling the truth, cynically concluding that the balance of probability was that it was more likely to be the politicians who were failing to do so than the musicians. And there the matter rested, Hayward and his colleagues putting their heads down, ignoring the furore in the belief, rightly as it turned out, that the majority of councillors and electors were only marginally interested in such matters.

In fact so far as management of the hall was concerned, the early weeks were marked by a series of mishaps which could at best be put down to inexperience and teething troubles. The Philharmonia sat in semi-darkness for half an hour, because there was nobody available to turn on the main stage lights. The LPO were embarrassed to find that the box office, unaware that Britten's *Spring Symphony* was a choral work, had put the choir seats on sale. The Hallé, advised that a concert was not selling well, booked coaches in order to bring some of their audience down from Manchester, only to be told when they applied for tickets that the hall had been sold out for some days, and more than once members of the public were turned away by the box office, even though seats were still available. There were also complaints of discourtesy to musicians and management. Players trying to obtain refreshments were told sandwiches were only for sale to the public, not to musicians, and management staff of the BBC Symphony Orchestra and the LPO were refused complimentary tickets to enable them to hear their orchestras perform.

Teething troubles or no, matters went from bad to worse. The LCC's commitment to promoting concerts quickly petered out, but far from appointing a resident orchestra they continued to place all four orchestras on the same footing and, to the dismay of many, opened up the hall to private promoters, awarding them a significant number of dates. Few private promoters were prepared to give concerts more than one rehearsal; many were given under conductors whose qualifications were doubtful, and most were devoted to a handful of the most popular works in the repertoire. For several years it had been LPO policy only to accept engagements for which there was a proper allowance of rehearsal time. Loss of the LCC grant meant this was a stance they could no longer afford, even though, paradoxically, by accepting such engagements they put themselves in competition with their own concerts. The LCC belatedly replaced the original manager with Ernest Bean, the highly experienced Manager of the Hallé Orchestra; had Bean's appointment been made earlier he might have taken a stand against this free-for-all policy, but by the time of his arrival the die was cast and he was committed to the policy adopted by the Council.

The 'inevitable readjustments' anticipated by the LCC proved painful in the extreme. The office staff at 53 Welbeck Street, which had never been lavish, was reduced by 40 per cent and the orchestra's workload grew even heavier. The players gave up the right to be paid for their holidays, not that the schedule over the next year permitted much time off, and accepted a proposal that players called for a recording session, but not required to perform, would forfeit their right to session fees. Quite independently a petition was organised asking the Council to think again. The petition attracted eighty thousand signatures, a correspondent pointing out that if each signatory contributed five shillings a year, it would more than cover the shortfall. This avoided the question at issue whether or not the Council, by acting as a concert promoter and spreading engagements among a number of orchestras, was using public money to the best advantage.

A new Appeal Fund was launched with a concert in the Albert Hall, and numerous groups of Friends of the London Philharmonic sprang up, mainly centred on places receiving regular visits. These produced some modest sums to help bridge the gap, and several guest artists offered reduced fees, while Boult threw himself whole-heartedly into the struggle to keep the orchestra solvent, arguing the LPO's case at every opportunity, surrendering fees to which he was entitled and making over royalties due to him from recording work.

Up to a point it was the very source of their problems that proved their immediate salvation, the opening ceremony of the Royal Festival Hall marking the start of the summer-long festivities which formed the 1951 Festival of Britain. In addition to concerts in the new hall the LPO played at Festivals throughout Britain, including Bournemouth, Cambridge, Canterbury, Edinburgh, Liverpool, Llanwrst, Malvern, Rochester, Swansea and York, as well as the 1951 Proms, and throughout the summer of 1951 and the ensuing winter, audiences remained at an exceptionally high level.

Russell, who made numerous speeches from the platform, reminded his listeners that the most practical way of helping the LPO was regular attendance, trying to ensure that every last seat was filled. Many suburban and provincial halls had limited seating capacity with even a full house, and a subsidy from the local authority, unable to provide sufficient revenue to cover the full cost of a concert. In the unlikely event that every last seat was sold for every single concert, out-of-town activities during the next year would still have incurred a deficit of more than £10,000 (see Appendix B). A typical concert in Hornsey, before a well-filled Town Hall, produced receipts of £306, including a grant from the local council. After deducting incidental expenses, £92 for conductor, soloist and two extra players, £40 for hire of the hall, £7 for hire of music and £37 for advertising, the accounts department was left with net receipts of £129, against an estimated £288 to be earned from every engagement if the salary bill was to be met, a loss of £159 on the night. These losses had to be covered by grants, broadcast relay fees, royalties from the sale of records and occasional profits on concerts in the Albert and Festival

Halls. In the light of past experience that programmes containing anything adventurous usually spelt financial disaster, most programmes were planned on a conservative basis, eschewing any kind of risk.

The Royal Festival Hall was formally opened on 3 May 1951 in the presence of King George VI and Queen Elizabeth, the orchestra at the opening ceremony including representatives of all the London orchestras. The initial week of concerts provided one major disappointment. Toscanini had been invited to conduct the BBC Symphony Orchestra, and his concerts were sold out long in advance. Two months before the opening ceremony, Toscanini was taken ill. According to his biographer, Harvey Sachs, the eighty-four year old conductor acquired, at his doctor's suggestion, an exercise bicycle and, as a result of pedalling too vigorously, suffered a slight stroke. Toscanini's concerts were taken over by Sargent, the opening week including performances by the London Mozart Players, under their founder and conductor Harry Blech, the LPO conducted by Boult, and the LSO under Clarence Raybould. Efforts to try and ensure that the acoustics of the new hall were satisfactory were not wholly successful: compared with the excessive reverberation of the Albert Hall, the new hall went to the other extreme, providing a dry sound, even a hint of coarseness, and its acoustics were particularly harsh on the quality of string playing. Nevertheless it was a vast improvement on the Albert Hall, and full houses were the order of the day.

May and June were designated the London Season of the Arts, with attention concentrated on the new hall. The LPO gave eight concerts, including a further hearing for Britten's *Spring Symphony*, first heard under van Beinum the previous year. The performance was conducted by the composer, who on facing the orchestra at rehearsal observed, 'I find I've completely forgotten all this. You see, I've written so much music since.' Disappointingly only four London critics were present; perhaps the rest were bemused by the volume of music to be heard in London. Certainly some were having difficulties coming to terms with the work. Reviewing the first London performance, *The Times* found 'both singers and players appeared to know their way about the score and to appreciate its subtle cleverness... every poetic image find(ing) a musical counterpart as cunning as it is vivid', a verdict contradicted when the paper asserted that the same performance was 'so unsatisfactory as to leave doubts in the minds of many people sympathetic to modernism whether Britten had not overstepped the mark in the devising of strange new sounds and dissonant figuration'. The hall management was to poke fun at the press by quoting, in the monthly diary of events, a selection of similar contradictory notices, infuriating their authors but giving quiet amusement to audiences and performers.

One evening was devoted to music by Ravel, conducted by Victor de Sabata, including a concert performance of the opera *L'enfant et les Sortilèges*, of which Mosco Carner wrote:

'I cannot recall hearing this orchestra rise to such a pitch of dazzling brilliance as it did under the maestro's hypnotic command. One-composer programmes run the risk of monotony, and Ravel in particular cannot be said to command a wide emotional range or a great variety of style. Yet the lovely sounds de Sabata got from his players, his almost infinite scale of dynamic nuances, and the cunning way in which he allowed rhythm and colour to interplay made this programme seem almost too short.'

In conjunction with this concert the hall staged a complementary exhibition of watercolours by the artist Gerard Hoffnung, inspired by and illustrating the work. The London Season of the Arts was brought to an end by a concert including several pieces connected with the capital, Haydn's London Symphony, Elgar's *Cockaigne* Overture, and an Overture, *The Smoke*, by their erstwhile principal trumpet, Malcolm Arnold.

This concert should have been conducted by Boult, but he had been laid low by illness, which forced him to cancel all his engagements for the best part of six weeks. In the space of less than twelve months, with barely a break, he had conducted over a hundred LPO concerts, and in addition to his stint with the BBC Symphony Orchestra, undertook other engagements as guest conductor; during the summer he paid the price. Among those called in to replace him was a young British conductor, Norman Del Mar, a former horn player in the RPO and a protege of Beecham. Boult was to have conducted the first part of a programme of British music, with a repeat performance of Britten's *Spring Symphony*, conducted by the composer, scheduled in the second half. In the event Britten was also forced to cancel, the disappointment of a capacity audience alleviated by the fact that in Boult's absence the works he was due to conduct were given under the direction of their respective composers, Richard Arnell, Ralph Vaughan Williams and William Walton. Britten's place was taken by Del Mar, who earned plaudits for a first-class performance and an invitation to conduct further concerts during the autumn and winter. As if their efforts during the evening were not enough, the orchestra also played for a post-concert ball, where they shared the honours with Tommy Kinsman and his Orchestra, the LPO giving an hour of old-time dances under the baton of Eric Robinson.

Boult returned to the rostrum at the end of July, one of his first appearances after his illness taking place at an open-air concert at Cambridge. It was a hot day, and before starting the rehearsal Boult asked Patrick Hadley, the Professor of Music, if he could find some kind of hat to keep the sun off his head. A suitably academic piece was produced and, as the rehearsal was by now under way, this was placed at the conductor's feet, where a little later Boult was delighted to find the humorists in the orchestra had rewarded his efforts with the baton by placing a few coppers in it.

The opening concerts of the 1951 Edinburgh Festival were among the many engagements during the summer. The musical element of the Festival was dominated by the appearance of the New York Philharmonic, but the LPO were by no means overshadowed by their American colleagues. There was, however, a degree of controversy, not of their making, surrounding the opening concert, which included the first performance of the Second Symphony of William Wordsworth. The composer, a descendant of the poet's brother Christopher, originally submitted the symphony to the BBC for consideration by their reading panel, who rejected the work, apparently on the grounds that the manuscript was in pencil. Wordsworth then entered the work for a competition organised by the 1950 Edinburgh Festival for a new symphony, winning first prize, and inclusion in the opening concert the following year. The BBC relayed most of the New York Orchestra's concerts, but declined to broadcast Wordsworth's Symphony, even though the performance took place on a Sunday and was not competing against the Proms, for which Sunday was still a day of rest. The BBC came in for some harsh criticism, and it is hard not to conclude that their decision contained an element of pique that the reading panel had been made to look foolish.

So far from occupying a position as resident orchestra, financial problems restricted the LPO to promoting no more than a handful of concerts in the new hall on its own account. Apart from concerts included in the subscription series promoted by the LCC, their appearances in the hall during the autumn and winter of 1951–52 were few and far between. Boult conducted *Gerontius* and Solti made his first appearance in the hall, but by far the most interesting concert given before Christmas was one shared between Boult and former principal trumpet player, Malcolm Arnold, fast making his mark as a composer.

Arnold's First Symphony, completed two years previously, was premiered at the 1951 Cheltenham Festival, with the composer conducting the Hallé Orchestra. In November Arnold conducted the first London performance of the Symphony, this time with his old orchestra. Audiences were sometimes amused by the extravagant gestures used by Arnold when he was conducting, but he was a highly capable interpreter, not only of his own music but, given the opportunity, those of other composers. For those familiar with his music through the film scores, or pieces such as *Tam O'Shanter*, the First Symphony is a disturbing work, inhabiting a very different world, even the apparently extrovert finale shot through with darker undercurrents. The other side of Arnold's character was demonstrated when Boult and the LPO gave the first performance of his first set of *English Dances*, not as might have been expected in the Festival Hall, but at a concert in East Ham. These immediately attractive pieces were a welcome addition to the range of music performed at out-of-town concerts.

The subscription concerts presented by the LCC during the summer of 1951 concentrated on well known repertoire, but those given during the winter were more adventurous. A concert of British music in December included Parry's *Overture to an Unwritten Tragedy*, Lambert's *Rio Grande* and Vaughan Williams' *Sea Symphony*, and in January Boult conducted two performances of Elgar's *Falstaff*, as well as works by Francis Chagrin and Bernard Stevens. February brought the welcome return, after his protracted illness, of Eduard van Beinum, whose major Festival Hall offering, also forming part of the LCC subscription series, was a pair of concerts at which Bruckner's Fourth Symphony was performed. However the level of activity over the past eighteen months had taken its toll. Asked to report on the playing of the orchestra, van Beinum felt obliged to comment adversely on several aspects, notably the quality of the horn section.

Boult's illness during the summer of 1951 was a sign that he could not be expected to continue working at the same pace, and though continuing to conduct many concerts in and around London, other conductors took an increasing share of this work. Boult was not alone in finding it difficult to keep up with the demands placed on him by the continual round of concerts and travelling, and in the spring of 1952 David Wise was forced to tender his resignation as leader. Andrew Cooper briefly returned to his old position, before it was filled on a permanent basis by Joseph Shadwick. Brought up in Canada, Shadwick served with the Canadian Cavalry during the First World War, and spent several years with the Minneapolis Orchestra, where he was successively principal second violin, assistant leader and finally leader. Subsequently he led the Sadler's Wells and Covent Garden Orchestras.

The spring of 1952 was almost a throwback to wartime. Following hard on the heels of a tour embracing Dublin, York, Newcastle, Middlesbrough, Kircaldy, Aberdeen, Dundee and Edinburgh, a fortnight was spent in South Wales, travelling up and down the valleys, visiting Newtown, Merthyr Tydfil, Abergavenny, Llanelly, Neath, Tredegar, Ferndale, Maesteg, Gwaen-cae-Gurwen, Cardiff and Chepstow, many concerts involving participation by local choral societies. The Welsh tour was intended as a stepping stone towards the formation of a National Orchestra. Between twenty and thirty local authorities voted funds in support of the project, but despite its success, and a similar round of concerts the following year, it was not until many years later, with the enlargement of the BBC Welsh Orchestra to fully symphonic proportions, that these hopes were fully realised. Returning for concerts in and around London, any spare time was taken up by appearances in the pit at Covent Garden accompanying the ballet, while the Covent Garden Orchestra was on tour with the Opera Company.

But if the Festival Hall was a source of disappointment in terms of frustrated ambition, the advent of the LP record was steadily increasing the amount of time spent in the recording studio. In January 1952 Boult and the orchestra embarked on a cycle of the Vaughan Williams symphonies, starting with the

London Symphony, highly praised on its release. The sessions for the *Pastoral* Symphony took place in December, with the remaining symphonies, up to and including the *Antartica*, recorded in December 1953, and the Eighth in 1956, the year of its first performance. In the past Boult had recorded almost exclusively for EMI, for whom he continued to make occasional records, but the advent of Legge's Philharmonia and the fact that Beecham was recording for that company meant that for a time EMI's interest in his work was marginal. The Vaughan Williams cycle was therefore made for Decca, and several other records of British music followed, but despite the acclaim with which they were received, Decca never developed the relationship with Boult to the extent that might have been expected. For some reason Decca left the Vaughan Williams cycle incomplete, and Boult's first recording of the Ninth Symphony was made for the Everest label. There was, however, one other highly prized record. In October 1952 Boult and the LPO accompanied Kathleen Ferrier in arias by Bach and Handel, which immediately became one of the best-selling of the early LP records. It was one of the singer's last records, the inexorable onset of cancer cutting her career short a few months later. After the advent of stereo, Boult and the LPO recorded a new accompaniment, with Ferrier's voice taken from the original tapes, a record later reissued in CD form.

By the autumn of 1952 Thomas Russell had been managing the orchestra for more than a decade. Despite the problems arising from his visit to Moscow, so far as any outsider could tell his politics never interfered with his management of the orchestra, or his devotion to it, but during the summer of 1952 a fresh crisis arose when he accepted an invitation from the Britain-China Friendship Association to visit China, in a party including several left-wing Labour MPs. In considering subsequent developments it should not be forgotten that the Cold War was at its height and the Korean War was in progress, with British troops engaged against the Chinese army. Dealings with China were if anything even more suspect than those with Russia.

Russell informed the Board that he intended accepting the invitation, and that to do so he would be absent for six weeks, taking his full annual holiday entitlement of four weeks, together with two weeks due to him from the previous year, and announced his intention to the orchestra as a whole during a meeting held in Wolverhampton on August 19, prior to a concert in the Civic Hall. The orchestra supported Russell throughout the dispute with the LCC, but the events of the last two years had aroused concern about the impact of his political affiliation. Russell's announcement provoked a prolonged discussion, notes written shortly after the meeting by one of the Directors, Alfred ('Tony') Moore, indicating the difficulty he and others found in reconciling their belief in Russell's right to travel freely, with concern that his visit was foolish in the extreme, against the best interests of the orchestra, and likely to further alienate those whose support was vital to the LPO's survival. In addition to chairing the Wolverhampton meeting Russell was responsible for recording the proceedings, his minute stating that 'certain members of the orchestra expressed some apprehension', a version of events challenged by a majority of the Board who considered that around three-quarters of those present at the meeting were 'seriously disturbed' by his proposed course of action.

Russell chose to ignore the opposition, but though the Board had no powers to prevent him from visiting China, he was instructed that on no account was there to be any publicity linking his visit to the orchestra. Despite this, the day of his departure saw a news item in the communist newspaper, *The Daily Worker*, accompanied by a photo of Russell and three other members of the party, the caption describing him as 'Chairman and Managing Director of the London Philharmonic Orchestra'. A day or two later a report in *The Times*, based on a news release by the Chinese People's Institute of Foreign Affairs, announced their arrival, describing Russell as 'Manager of the London Philharmonic Orchestra', the only person whose affiliation with an organisation in Britain was mentioned.

Tony Moore's notes indicate that as well as harbouring doubts about the wisdom of Russell's decision, he and other members were disturbed that while, in addition to Russell, only two players were known to be communists, Russell's earlier foray into communist territory had led to the LPO being tagged 'the red orchestra'. These concerns, allied to the difference of opinion about the views expressed at the Wolverhampton meeting, and the news item in *The Daily Worker*, brought to the surface a number of criticisms, notably the adverse effect on working conditions arising from loss of the LCC grant, giving rise to an increased work-load, to which, because coach travel had replaced the railways as the means of travelling to and from some out-of-town concerts, was added the burden of additional travelling time, while at the same time holidays had been reduced. There was also criticism of the way Russell ran the company. The fact that he was Chairman and Managing Director placed considerable power in Russell's hands, and whereas he was always fully briefed, there had been complaints that the first other Directors often knew of plans on which he was working was when they were unveiled in finished form; at one point a Resolution was passed instructing him to give the Board an opportunity to express their views before any plan was finalised.

Four Directors, the Principal Trumpet Eric Bravington, Principal Clarinet Maurice Cody, trombonist Tony Moore and tuba player John Wilson, concluded that the only way of protecting the orchestra's interests was to remove Russell from office, deciding to force the issue by resigning, a move necessitating an emergency general meeting of shareholders. Though Russell retained the support of Vice-Chairman Frederick Riddle, and viola player Simon Streatfeild, a meeting of the Board on 9 September found the Directors unanimous in their view that 'in the light of publicity which has appeared in *The Daily Worker*, it is apparent that the Chairman's visit to China was unwise' and it was agreed that 'the Directors present should offer their resignations to the Shareholders at an extraordinary general meeting, to be held as soon as possible after the Chairman's return'. The Company Secretary, Thomas O'Dea, was instructed to write to Russell, outlining the concerns within the orchestra, advising him that the Board intended resigning, offering him the opportunity of following their example, leaving it to Shareholders to re-elect him if they thought fit. To add to their concerns Russell extended his already protracted absence for a further week, breaking his journey home in Prague, but though telephoning his private secretary from that city, no message was conveyed to the Board as to the date of his return. Concluding that Russell would not willingly resign, and advised that the only way of preventing him taking the chair at an extraordinary general meeting, even though his own conduct would be under review, was for the Board to remove him by majority vote, the Directors opposed to Russell took steps to do so, appointing Eric Bravington acting Chairman in his place.

Russell fought long and hard to reverse the Board's decision, arguing that he could only be dismissed as Chairman by a majority vote of the members. Though the LPO Council had no powers to intervene, this was felt to be a matter on which their advice should be sought and they met twice to consider the matter, the fact that Russell had overstayed his leave adding weight to the argument that 'outside interests and frequent absences' were adversely affecting his work'. His political affiliation was not mentioned, and after hearing the arguments of both sides the Council concluded that Russell's departure would be in the best interests of the orchestra.

Outside pressure was also being brought to bear. Russell twice clashed in print with Mr, later Sir, William Williams, the Secretary-General of the Arts Council, in the columns of the *New Statesman*, and over an article in *Philharmonic Post* in which Russell criticised the attitude taken towards the arts by central and local government, pointing out that grants had been frozen for several years. Williams, an authoritarian, who successfully ousted his predecessor and equally successfully neutered the Council's Chairman, Sir Kenneth Clark, gathering the reins of power unto himself, saw the article as an attack on the Council, responding in somewhat intemperate terms. Rather than turn the other cheek, Russell replied in similar vein and while he may have got the better of the argument, the wisdom of involving the orchestra in acrimonious public debate with its chief provider was questionable.

Though they had no right to intervene the Arts Council, as the major provider of financial support, had a considerable interest in a situation where a major difference of opinion was seriously de-stabilising one of their clients, even to the extent of putting its future at risk, and it was not unreasonable for the Council to seek permission for observers to attend the extraordinary general meeting. There is however evidence that Williams went further, prevailing on Boult to write to Shareholders, supporting Russell's dismissal, arguing that his re-instatement could be prejudicial to the orchestra's relations with the Council. Though as Boult acknowledged, he was not directly involved, 'he was a servant of the Company', nevertheless he concluded by saying while he 'had no wish to put pressure on shareholders, I think I have shown a number of reasons why I now suggest to you who have votes, that your future is more precarious if Mr Russell resumes control'. Frederick Riddle and several of Russell's supporters responded, inviting Boult to justify his letter, pointing out that their earnings during the past year had been higher than at any time since 1939; that increased absences from work on Russell's part, a point on which Boult specifically commented, had arisen from a troublesome medical condition, while the decision to use coach travel, a point raised by Russell's opponents, was as much due to an increase in rail fares as to the orchestra's financial position.

The extraordinary general meeting took place on 14 November. Russell conducted an effective defence, making a strong case that the action of the four dissident Directors had been illegal and irrational. The turning point in the debate was a statement by the Secretary, Thomas O'Dea. His position throughout had been invidious, leading him to write to Shareholders explaining that his actions were governed by his responsibility to ensure they were kept informed of their rights, and his statutory duty to ensure that the Directors complied with the provisions of the Companies Act. As an officer of the company O'Dea had no direct right to intervene, but speaking by invitation, he informed those present that he held statements to the effect that, during the earlier controversy with the LCC, Russell attempted to induce members of staff to resign, should he be removed as Managing Director; that evidence had been given by two members of staff that Russell's personal secretary, Miss Margot Phillips, had been instructed to listen in to the Secretary's telephone conversations, and report on their content to Russell, and Miss Phillips had confirmed that she had acted in this way.

Yet despite the dubious light cast on Russell's behaviour by O'Dea's statement, when a vote was taken it showed how divided the orchestra remained, twenty-seven votes being cast for Russell's dismissal, with twenty-two in his favour, the fact that the votes cast fell short of the playing strength of the orchestra partly explained by the fact that a number of players had yet to serve the qualifying period of a year necessary before they could be elected as Shareholders. The meeting was also presented with opposing lists of candidates as Directors, a group who supported Eric Bravington, and a group loyal to Russell, Bravington's supporters winning the day by much the same margin as had been the case in the vote over Russell's dismissal, Russell, Frederick Riddle and Simon Streatfeild losing their places to Samuel Lovett, George Maxted and Maurice Pepper.

There was considerable sympathy for Russell, and it is possible to conclude that in a Scottish court of law the case against Russell might have been held 'not proven'. Yet he was to a great extent reaping where he had sown. However much his political views were a personal matter, in the context of the times, and with the problems associated with his earlier visit to Moscow in mind, the best that can be said of his decision to visit China is that it was insensitive. It was equally insensitive to seek six weeks' leave of absence when the crisis brought about by withdrawal of the LCC grant was far from being resolved, the office staff had been drastically pruned, the players were forgoing holiday pay, and fulfilling an increased work schedule. His action in overstaying his leave of absence by a week, for which he offered no explanation, supported the argument that he was putting his political interests ahead of those of the LPO, while his assertion, on his return, that he was 'the only member of the orchestra with the brains to run it', prompted the response from his opponents that they were no longer prepared to work with a Chairman and Managing Director who 'treated the views of members with contempt, in the assurance that his indispensability places him above criticism'. Nor was his dispute with Williams an isolated instance of Russell's wish to have the last word on any subject, using the forum provided by *Philharmonic Post* to this end. Many years later Russell was invited to contribute to the Yearbook produced for the LPO's Fiftieth Anniversary, in which he wrote, 'My position as secretary and later chairman and managing director was somewhat equivocal as I was known to hold left-wing views which few of our members would support. I realised I had been chosen not because of those views but in spite of them'.

Russell was replaced as Chairman by Eric Bravington, the Company Secretary Thomas O'Dea stepping in as General Manager. O'Dea carried out a detailed review of the administrative activities, greatly improving co-ordination between departments, 'always something of a weakness in this company', by the institution of a House Committee, comprising the heads of each department, which met weekly to review work in hand, ensuring that all parts of the organisation were fully informed of developments as they occurred.

Whatever the outcome, it was inevitable that the affair, coming in the wake of the dispute with the LCC, could only harm the LPO and its reputation. There was a lengthy list of resignations with the Concerts Director Adolph Borsdorf and the Deputy Chairman Frederick Riddle among those who departed, Riddle subsequently joining the ranks of Beecham's RPO. Had the vote gone the other way, with Russell reinstated, Bravington and his supporters might well have found their position equally untenable. The vacancies were quickly filled, but it was to take much hard work on the part of the new team, and another near disaster, before the LPO was restored to financial and artistic health.

The Friends of the London Philharmonic was an early casualty. Very much Russell's brainchild, the funds raised by this organisation were minuscule, and the new management saw no justification in expending further effort for such a modest return. *Philharmonic Post* was another of Russell's projects to come under the microscope. The magazine had never paid its way, and with every penny of expenditure under close scrutiny it too had to go.

With the LCC promoting fewer concerts, the winter of 1952–53 saw an increase in the number of LPO promotions in the Festival Hall. There were, however, few departures from a narrow range of music, Tchaikovsky's First Piano Concerto receiving three performances, with numerous other popular works performed more than once. The unwillingness of the public to take risks was amply demonstrated by two concerts in December, each of which included the first London performance of a symphony by a contemporary British composer, the *Nottingham* Symphony of Alan Bush and William Wordsworth's Second Symphony, premiered in Edinburgh the previous summer. Despite the presence of Myra Hess, playing the Fourth and Fifth Piano Concertos of Beethoven, the culmination of a cycle of the concertos, Bush's Symphony only attracted a 40 per cent house, Wordsworth's Symphony doing a little better, with 56 per cent of capacity.

The record of poor rewards for anything adventurous continued the following year, van Beinum's interpretation of Bruckner's Fifth Symphony filling only 44 per cent of the seats in the hall. Disappointment was aptly summed up by the concert department's comment, 'We sincerely hope the much-maligned Tchaikovsky will preserve his unbroken record of paying for such follies.' The only other departures from this artistic straightjacket were a concert of American music under Gail Kubik, including his own Violin Concerto and the Third Symphony of Roy Harris, and one of British music, at which Malcolm Arnold's Second Symphony received its first London performance. Neither required much activity on the part of the box office.

There was, however, one new venture which was proving successful. In September 1952 a concert was arranged in Thaxted Parish Church, which was filled to overflowing. Subsequent visits to Thaxted continued to attract capacity audiences and were followed by equally successful concerts in the Parish Churches of Abingdon, Andover and Dedham, and in Selby Abbey. From these beginnings the church concerts steadily grew in number. Initially programmes were arranged along standard lines, but gradually a different pattern emerged. Rather than start with an overture, the brass players would climb the tower to perform an opening flourish, or an arrangement for brass of the '*Tower Music*' by the eighteenth-century composer Petzel. This might be followed by Vaughan Williams' *Tallis Fantasia* and a concerto played by one of the LPO's principals, the soloist sometimes playing from the pulpit, accompanied by the orchestra in the choir. As a mark of respect to the incumbent and his congregation, and for the practical reason that by this time an audience sitting on hard pews was likely to become restive, these items were usually followed by a hymn, allowing the audience an opportunity to stand and stretch its legs – was it with tongue in cheek that one programme prefaced Holst's *Planets* with 'All people that on earth do dwell'? In place of an interval the hymn would be followed by a short pause of two or three minutes, the concert ending with the evening's major work.

Audiences usually fell away during the summer, and in 1953 the takings at several concerts failed to cover the marginal expenses of conductor and soloist, hire of music and publicity. The church concerts were one way of solving the problem, and 1954 saw a much enlarged schedule of around forty such performances, with the LPO divided into two sections, one of twenty-four players, the other of forty-five. Two concerts were given each evening in churches ranging from Bexhill in the south to Thame in the north, from Chelmsford in the east to Godalming in the west, the conducting shared between Basil Cameron, Charles Groves, Maurice Miles and George Weldon. The soloists were drawn from the ranks of the orchestra, and wherever possible the concert included an item from the choir of the church they were visiting. The church concerts continued for many years, though never again on quite the same scale.

The church concerts provided an opportunity to give younger British conductors a chance to appear in public, away from the pressures of the Albert Hall or the Festival Hall. A scheme was introduced enabling applicants with some experience to conduct part of a concert, while others were given an opportunity to rehearse the orchestra, Boult, ever ready to offer a helping hand to the younger generation, willingly surrendering part of the time allocated to him for this purpose. The number of applicants far outstripped the ability of the LPO to offer more than a minority an opportunity to demonstrate their abilities. Many called, but few were chosen. Those who appeared in public included Colin Davis, Harry Newstone and Lawrence Leonard, general opinion being that of all the participants Colin Davis showed by far the greatest promise, though the conclusion that he needed more experience might have applied to any young man at the start of a career.

Another important development took place in the autumn of 1953, with the launch of a series of Industrial Concerts at the Albert Hall. Industrial Concerts, with tickets sold to groups from commercial or industrial concerns, sometimes subsidised by employers, at well below the normal box office price, had been pioneered in Liverpool, with Birmingham and Manchester following suit later. The LPO gave its first Industrial Concert on 20 November 1953, conducted by George Weldon, with tickets sold to groups drawn from major firms in and around London, Civil Service departments, local government and the nationalised industries.

With every seat in the hall sold at a uniform price of five shillings, half a crown for the under-18s, the Industrial Concerts were an immediate success, so much so that the last concert, conducted by Boult, had to be given twice. Despite a high level of attendance receipts were never sufficient to balance expenditure, but following the demise of the Finsbury Park open-air concerts, discontinued after 1953 because of dwindling audiences, the Council extended their support to these concerts as well as the continuing series of LCC children's concerts. With the passage of time the nature of the groups coming to the concerts began to change. Many still had an industrial or commercial background, but new groups were formed whose members were drawn from sports and social clubs, churches, gramophone societies or simply comprised groups of friends. By 1974 the original title of Industrial Concerts no longer seemed suitable, and it was changed to Classics for Pleasure. By the early 1980s the Albert Hall was proving a less than satisfactory venue, and in 1985 the series was transferred to the Festival Hall.

During December 1953 and the early weeks of 1954 Boult and the players were kept busy in the recording studio, completing the Vaughan Williams cycle, to which was added *Job, A Masque for Dancing*. They also recorded a much admired set of Handel's *Messiah*, and later in the year taped a miscellany of music by British composers, including Elgar's Violin Concerto, with Campoli as soloist, and shorter pieces by Arnold, Bax, Elgar, Holst, Vaughan Williams and Walton. These sessions were carried out for Decca, but Boult and the orchestra had also begun to record for Nixa, though for contractual reasons they could not appear on that label as the London Philharmonic Orchestra, using instead the pseudonym of The Philharmonic Promenade Orchestra. Their work for Nixa began in September 1953 with *Belshazzar's Feast*, *The Planets* and several works by Vaughan Williams. The following year saw the start of a long string of sessions for this company, the music committed to disc including all the symphonies of Brahms, Elgar and Schumann, Mendelssohn's *Scottish* and *Italian*, Schubert's Ninth, overtures by Berlioz and Suppe, tone poems by Sibelius, ballet music by Delibes, and pieces by Bartok, Britten and Elgar. These records were all conducted by Boult, whose recording work compensated for the fact that he was appearing at fewer out-of-town concerts.

The pattern of the orchestra's work was in fact changing. The opening of the Festival Hall, coupled with a shift in population from some of the inner London boroughs, adversely affected the economics of concert giving in many of the smaller halls. The Festival of Britain year saw audiences at record levels, but these were not maintained: in the space of two years the audience at Lewisham fell from well over 90 per cent of capacity to under two-thirds. Audiences at a number of centres, including Croydon, Eastbourne, Hastings and Watford, still justified regular visits, but many of the inner London boroughs and towns with smaller halls were dropped from the calendar. The church concerts and the Industrial Concerts were one way of filling the gap, but increasingly time spent in the recording studio became an economic necessity. As the volume of recording grew it was in the interest of orchestra and recording company for sessions to be arranged in conjunction with concerts, a practice that has attracted much ill-directed criticism, an indication of a failure to understand the economics of concert-giving. Time and again, even with a full house, a properly rehearsed public concert is only a feasible proposition thanks to allied recording sessions.

Apart from a concert of French music under Jean Martinon, including the conductor's own *Ouverture pour une tragédie greque* and Roussel's Choral Ballet *Aenéas*, the autumn of 1954 offered little of more than passing interest. However, after a Beethoven cycle under Boult, which attracted huge audiences, the new year offered more variety, including Barber's *Prayers of Kirkegaard*, the *Music for strings, percussion and celeste* by Bartok, and the first performance of a work by a member of the orchestra, Leonard Salzedo's Symphonic Poem *Gabble Rechtit*. Overshadowing all these in importance was the first European performance of the Tenth Symphony of Shostakovitch, given in the presence of the Soviet Ambassador, only the second hearing given to the symphony outside the Soviet Union.

The music of Shostakovitch had not made the headway in this country that might have been expected, even arousing antipathy in some quarters. The first British performance of the Ninth Symphony led one writer to comment 'it proved as puerile a milk-and-water affair as the pestiferating other eight', while Fritz Reiner's pioneering recording of the Sixth Symphony prompted a reviewer to deliver the verdict that 'on present showing I don't see Shostakovitch moving up into the company of the truly great'. With the Tenth Symphony it seemed that the tide began to turn in the composer's favour. Though the performance showed that the two rehearsals allocated to this concert were insufficient for conductor and players to come to grips with this long and complex score, nevertheless the symphony was an outstanding success, quickly staking a place for itself in the repertoire. If Boult was not fully at ease with this piece, Holst's *Choral Symphony*, given in June, saw him on ground where he was in his element, though whereas Shostakovitch was accorded an excellent house, the almost predictable response of the public to the revival of Holst's work was to stay away in their multitudes.

Much of the autumn was occupied with a project reminiscent of some of the worst excesses of the war years, five concerts at which Artur Rubinstein performed a total of seventeen piano concertos, but whereas Rubinstein attracted capacity houses, departures from the beaten track continued to have a dismal effect on the box office. In November three works by Holst, the *Scherzo from an Unfinished Symphony*, the *Somerset Rhapsody* and the *Hymn of Jesus*, with the first performance of Stanley Bate's Fourth Symphony forming the second half of the concert, met with an all too predictable result at the box office, while later in the season Beethoven's *Emperor* Concerto failed to draw an audience for the Sixth Symphony of Bax, and a concert including the First Symphony of Robert Simpson and the Fourth Symphony of Vaughan Williams met with an equally dismal response.

The winter of 1955–56 saw the launch of a series of Historic Concerts, under the title 'From Bach to Bartok'. Devised by Herbert Menges, who shared the conducting with Boult, this provided a survey of the orchestral repertoire, ranging from the First Suite of Bach to the Concerto for Orchestra by Bartok, with a spoken introduction to each concert by the critic Scott Goddard. Both time and venue, Saturday mornings in the Central Hall, Westminster, adversely affected attendances; even the *Choral* Symphony, which would have drawn a capacity house on any evening across the river, was performed to a meagre audience. Nevertheless this attempt to break out of the narrow confines of standard classics signposted the way forward to more adventurous offerings.

As the 1950s progressed the BBC broadened the scope of the Proms, engaging the RPO, the Hallé, the Bournemouth and the Liverpool Philharmonic orchestras, with a consequential reduction in the number of concerts offered to the LPO and the LSO. The problem of filling the summer months was partially resolved by their engagement in 1955 to play for London Festival Ballet's summer season at the Festival Hall, an engagement later extended to cover the annual performances of *Nutcracker* given during the Christmas holiday period. The orchestra pit created for the ballet season could not accommodate a full-sized orchestra and initially a string section of only nineteen was employed, increased in later years to twenty-nine. Though it was singularly unprestigious work, under less than inspiring conductors, the ballet performances fulfilled a double function. In addition to providing work during some of the most difficult weeks of the year it allowed flexibility in holiday arrangements, enabling these to be taken on a staggered basis, with the added advantage that the summer season of church concerts could be undertaken by players not required for the ballet. Working for the ballet also opened up the possibility of arranging recording sessions during the day, and Sundays were sometimes given over to open-air concerts in Holland Gardens.

It was five years since the LPO had visited the continent, and the autumn of 1956 was occupied with a heavy schedule of overseas touring. In quick succession, they became the first British orchestra to perform in Soviet Russia, toured Germany and visited Paris. Because Boult disliked flying – as late as 1966 he still travelled to the USA by sea – he did not feature in the original plans for the tour of the Soviet Union. The Russians asked for three conductors to accompany the orchestra, intimating that they would like Fistoulari and George Hurst to take part. Hurst, who had been acting as Assistant Conductor, understudying Boult and taking a number of Industrial and out-of-town concerts on his own account, was an obvious choice as a representative of the younger generation, and Fistoulari was acceptable to the LPO, despite the fact that his connection with them in recent years had been somewhat tenuous.

In the absence of Boult the LPO were anxious to find a conductor of international repute to take his place. Sir John Barbirolli was the first to be invited, and when he intimated that prior engagements with the Hallé would prevent his acceptance, Eduard van Beinum, Paul Kletzki, Josef Krips, Sir Malcolm Sargent and Hans Schmidt-Isserstedt were all canvassed. Subsequently, when it proved impossible to secure the services of any of these,

Munich 17 November 1936, conductor Sir Thomas Beecham. Note first and second violins on opposite sides of the platform. Later in his career Beecham sat firsts and seconds to the left of the rostrum.

The Blitz Tour 1940–41. Dr Malcolm Sargent conducting the LPO in the Nottingham Empire. The orchestra is led by Thomas Matthews.

The poster for the film telling the story of the LPO's survival during the Second World War.

Thomas Russell, Chairman and General Manager, with J.B. Priestley and Mrs Priestley at a dinner hosted by the LPO, 8 October 1948.

```
CABLEGRAM VIA NORTHERN
       THE  GREAT  NORTHERN  TELEGRAPH  CO.
              (LIMITED) OF DENMARK

1949 AUG 9  23  17                              L 154

              GN
MOSCOW YM148 87 10 0044 NORTHERN
- ELT - THOMAS RUSSELL C/O SCR 14 KENSINGTON SQUARE
              LONDON/W=8 =

AT INITIATIVE OF SOVIET PUBLIC TRADEUNION AND CULTURAL
ORGANISATIONS ALLUNION PEACE CONFERENCE BEING CONVENED
MOSCOW AUGUST TWENTY FIFTH STOP BEHALF ORGANISATIONAL
COMMITTEE INVITE YOU AS ACTIVE PARTICIPANT PEACE
MOVEMENT BE GUEST AT CONFERENCE STOP YOUR PRESENCE AT
  CONFERENCE WILL BE NEW PROOF COMMON EFFORTS PEOPLES
USSR AND BRITAIN ENSURE DURABLE AND LASTING PEACE
THROUGHOUT WORLD STOP PLEASE INFORM US EARLIEST
CONVENIENCE DATE YOUR POSSIBLE ARRIVAL FOLLOWING
ADDRESS TEN KROPOTKIN STREET MOSCOW STOP ACADEMICIAN
BORIS GREKOV CHAIRMAN ORGANISATIONAL COMMITTEE
```

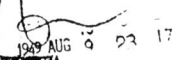

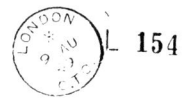

The telegram inviting Thomas Russell to Moscow, setting in train a chain of events leading to loss of the LCC's grant and failure to secure appointment as resident orchestra when the Royal Festival Hall opened in May 1951.

Eduard van Beinum Principal Conductor 1945–50 at rehearsal. The orchestra is led by David Wise; the sub-leader is Howard Leyton-Brown and the timpanist Peter Allen.

Sir Adrian Boult conducting in Thaxted Parish Church on 11 May 1953. The orchestra is led by Andrew Cooper. A. Garth Jones and John Kuchmy are prominent at the second and third desks of the first violins. (Photo: Erich Auerbach).

Eric Bravington. Principal Trumpet from 1948. Chairman from 1952, subsequently Managing Director, a post held until his retirement in 1980.

May 1972. Bernard Haitink and Alfred Brendal recording a Liszt Piano Concerto with the LPO. (Photo: Donald Cooper).

China 1973. John Pritchard addressing an impromptu remark to the audience during a morning rehearsal. Leader Rodney Friend. Marie Wilson is at the second desk of the first violins.

Klaus Tennstedt, Sir Georg Solti and Managing Director Stephen Crabtree at a press conference to launch a new LPO season.

Kirstenbosch Botanical Gardens, Cape Town, February 1995. The audience gathering for an open-air concert. (Photo: Laurence Watt).

Music Director Franz Welser-Möst (runner 14009) completing the London Marathon, April 1992.

Hannover, September 1996. Sir Georg Solti acknowledging the applause for a concert performance of *Don Giovanni*. Leader Joakhim Svendheden; Co-Leader Duncan Riddell, with Sub-Leader Tina Gruenberg and Chairman Robert St. J. Wright immediately behind. Principal Second Violin Gina Beukes is partly hidden by Solti; the Cellos are led by Co-principal Cellist Susanne Beer. (Photo: Eberhard Franke).

The London Philharmonic, conducted by Avi Ostrowsky, playing in the open-air at Leeuwin Wine Estate, West Australia. 23 February 1985. (Photograph Laurence Watt).

Participation is an essential element of education work! (Photo: Mike Hoban).

Rudolf Schwartz, then working with the City of Birmingham Orchestra, was considered as an alternative. At a late stage, however, an official from the Soviet Embassy asked to see the programmes and, noting the absence of Boult's name, delivered an ultimatum that if he did not take part the tour would be cancelled.

It was impossible to discover if the official concerned had the authority to make such a statement, or whether it was a self-important piece of bluff, but it was enough to set alarm bells ringing in the offices of the LPO, the Arts Council and the British Council, leading to an appeal from the Foreign Office to Boult to reconsider his decision. With the LPO's finances on a knife edge, cancellation of the tour would have carried incalculable consequences, possibly leading to the bankruptcy of the orchestra. At the last minute Boult therefore agreed to take part, insisting however that he travelled overland. Of nine concerts given in Moscow he undertook four, repeating one programme in Leningrad. British music was strongly represented, Boult's programmes including the *Meditations on a Theme of John Blow* by Sir Arthur Bliss, Holst's *Planets*, the Fourth and Fifth Symphonies of Vaughan Williams and Walton's Violin Concerto, with Alfredo Campoli as soloist. Fistoulari conducted the *Overture to a Picaresque Comedy* by Bax, the *Symphonic Studies* of Alan Rawsthorne, and Britten's *Sea Interludes*, and George Hurst the Second Symphony of Malcolm Arnold, Elgar's Violin Concerto and Walton's Symphony. Every concert was sold out, and it is a sad reflection on the state of musical life in London that most of the programmes offered to Russian audiences would have been unlikely to attract anything like a good house at the Festival Hall.

The tour took place at a tense period of international affairs, with the Suez crisis working up to a climax, but there was nothing unfriendly about the reception given to the LPO; indeed on the outward journey the players were embarrassed to discover their presence on the train meant the dining-car was closed to ordinary passengers, though it is possible that this arose from Russian suspicion of any unsupervised contact between their own people and foreigners. Few Westerners had the opportunity of visiting Russia, and the timetable was flexible enough to allow the players a sight of the Kremlin, as well as the reconstruction work taking place in Leningrad to repair the damage done by the retreating Germans to some of the great architectural treasures of the city. Audiences and the Russian press were enthusiastic, the players surviving the tour without diplomatic incident and without totally succumbing to the rigours of Russian hospitality.

One upshot of the Russian tour was that it led Boult, who was not only averse to flying but found that long journeys gave him trouble with his back, to tender his resignation, unwilling to risk a repetition of the circumstances that forced him, against his will, to reorder his schedule, cancelling a planned, and very necessary, holiday period. In practice he continued to work with them frequently, usually allocating time to the church concerts, of which from the outset he had been an enthusiastic supporter, and though he now had greater freedom to record with other orchestras, most of his work in the recording studio continued to be with the LPO. The early summer of 1957 found them working for the American company Vanguard, taping performances of several Beethoven symphonies and a number of overtures, and at the end of July a section of the orchestra travelled to Warwickshire to spend a week accompanying the American organist E. Power Biggs, who recorded Handel's complete Organ Concertos on the organ of Great Packington Church, some players risking the vagaries of the English weather by camping in the grounds of Great Packington Hall, the home of Lord Alresford, within whose boundaries the church was situated. The following year saw sessions for the Everest label, with recordings of symphonies by Hindemith, Mahler, Shostakovitch, and the first recording of the Vaughan Williams Ninth Symphony. The latter was a melancholy occasion, Ursula Vaughan Williams phoning Boult the morning the sessions began with the news that her husband had died during the night. The sessions included a remake of Vaughan Williams' *Job*, recorded in the Albert Hall, but this was generally felt to fall short of the performance recorded by Decca.

The standing of the LPO improved throughout the 1940s, peaking during Eduard van Beinum's term as principal conductor, a peak which carried them through the Festival of Britain year of 1951. Their ability to build on these achievements was undermined by the withdrawal of the LCC grant and the damage inflicted by the Russell affair. Under Boult, van Beinum, Martinon or de Sabata performances were generally respectable, and often a great deal more, but with van Beinum and de Sabata dropping out of the picture the LPO lost out in terms of the quality of guest conductors. Where once they worked with the leading European conductors, they had been overtaken by the Philharmonia, whose line-up included Guido Cantelli, Wilhelm Fürtwangler, Herbert von Karajan, Otto Klemperer, and Wolfgang Sawallisch. The need to reduce the burden undertaken by Boult, and to economise in terms of fees, led to many out-of-town dates being allocated to Basil Cameron, Norman Del Mar, George Hurst, and George Weldon, who lacked the inspiration needed to lift an orchestra into the front rank. Nor were Festival Hall concerts under Fistoulari, Massimo Freccia and Hans Swarowsky likely to set the Thames on fire. An attempt to solve the problem was made by appointing Alceo Galliera and Jean Martinon as Associate Conductors, but this was short-lived. During the mid-1950s the LPO was at best marking time.

11

Interregnum and William Steinberg 1957–60

The 1950s were a troubled time for Britain's orchestras. When the local council threatened to withdraw its backing, assistance from the Arts Council and the Winter Gardens Society led to the rebirth of the Bournemouth Municipal Orchestra as the Bournemouth Symphony Orchestra, but there was no such help for the Yorkshire Symphony Orchestra, also funded municipally, which was disbanded. Elsewhere the City of Birmingham Symphony Orchestra, the Hallé and the Liverpool Philharmonic all encountered serious financial difficulties. Withdrawal of the LCC grant could have dealt the LPO a mortal blow, but for six years the orchestra survived, just. Nevertheless, despite drastic economies, a modest increase in the Arts Council grant, support from the LCC for their children's concerts and the Industrial Concerts, and an artistically damaging work schedule, it was impossible to make ends meet. Despite sacrifices, artistic and personal, by the end of 1956 the accumulated deficit had grown to over £40,000. The LPO's continued existence was again in the balance.

To raise short-term cash the members agreed to wind up the pension and sick funds and transfer the proceeds to the LPO; the administrative staff was again slimmed down, with the orchestra's General Administrator Thomas O'Dea among those whose services were dispensed with, and because the costs involved in choral concerts meant less employment for the London Philharmonic Choir, permission was given for them to accept, or promote, other engagements, provided that when appearing with another orchestra reference was made to the LPO. Savings were made by using coaches for the longer journeys, this method of transport reducing the cost of a concert given in Bristol by £70, and overheads reduced by letting part of the premises at 53 Welbeck Street to a subsidiary of the Dowty engineering company. But these economies did no more than nibble at the edge of the problem.

It was calculated that to maintain the LPO on a salaried basis required external finance of £45,000 a year, with no likelihood of obtaining support at anything like this level. After much heart-searching the Board was forced to the conclusion that it was no longer possible to operate on a salaried basis and that in future the players would only be paid engagement by engagement. In addition to work for concert promoters, performances for Festival Ballet, recording sessions and children's concerts, the LPO's plans for the next twelve months involved eighty concerts promoted on its own account, fifty in venues in and around London, ten Church Concerts, eight Historic Concerts and twelve Industrial Concerts, for which the Arts Council was prepared to make an annual grant of £21,000, of which £10,000 was to be allocated to the provincial concerts, £2000 to the Church Concerts, £3200 to the Historic Concerts, £1800 to the Industrial Concerts, £2800 awarded to meet the cost of twenty additional rehearsals, with £1200 provided for the Young Conductors scheme. A scheme of arrangement offered members the maximum possible employment, the players asked in turn to give assurances that they would perform at all Albert Hall and Festival Hall concerts, BBC engagements and recording sessions, with 85 per cent attendance at other times. It was estimated that these would provide an average of three and a half days' work each week.

Paying the players engagement by engagement reduced the overhead cost of running the orchestra. PAYE records could be discontinued for all but the office staff and, acting on advice given by John Cruft, General Secretary of the LSO, discussions with the Ministry of Health and Social Security confirmed that, as the musicians now ranked as self-employed, the LPO was no longer liable to pay National Insurance contributions on their behalf. A small increase in fees compensated the players for the increase in National Insurance contributions, which they had to pay personally.

There remained the daunting task of finding an injection of finance to meet the claims of creditors. There was considerable sympathy for the LPO's plight, and various offers of assistance were received. Royalton Kisch was prepared to meet 50 per cent of the outstanding claims from creditors in return for the title of Principal Conductor, an offer that would only have merited consideration *in extremis*, for despite his foothold in the Festival Hall, Kisch was a conductor cast much in the mould of Sidney Beer. Harnessing themselves to his uncertain talents was unlikely to restore the LPO to its former prestige. An offer meriting more serious consideration was a proposal put forward by Wilfred van Wyck, acting on behalf of Massimo Freccia. In return for a loan of £28,000, secured against the premises at 53 Welbeck Street, the music library and instruments owned by the LPO itself, the LPO would enter into a five-year agreement with Freccia, offering him a minimum of forty concerts a year. In the event, the parties were unable to agree on terms. The LPO were only prepared to offer him fifty guineas a concert, well short of the £4000 a year sought by his agent, who also requested changes in the structure of the company, allowing the appointment of Directors from outside the ranks of the membership, with responsibility for the orchestra's artistic direction placed in Freccia's hands. These demands, which would have undermined the orchestra's independence, proved insurmountable stumbling blocks.

The solution to their problems came through the good offices of Ibbs and Tillett, an anonymous donor, widely believed to be Sir Adrian Boult, offering an interest-free loan sufficient to meet the demands of the creditors. Together with the generous stance taken by Boult in respect of outstanding conducting fees, and assurances from the Arts Council about further losses that might arise before the new scheme came into force on 1 April 1957, this timely injection of cash ensured the LPO's survival. The relationship with Ibbs and Tillett, who were working in close alliance with Harold Holt Limited, was to bear considerable fruit, and a Board of Trustees was set up to co-ordinate future activities. Chaired by Sir Adrian Boult, this comprised Eric Bravington and Samuel Lovett from the LPO, with Mrs Emmie Tillett and Major Denzil Walker representing Ibbs and Tillett.

The brunt of the complex negotiations involved in putting together the rescue package fell on the shoulders of Eric Bravington who, in addition to his duties as Chairman, had still been taking his seat in the orchestra. This was an impossible burden, and it was agreed that Bravington should be released from his playing duties until a new General Manager was appointed. Relief came with the recruitment of Stephen Gray, who took up his new post in July, but the pressure on Bravington continued to be such that in the following year he felt obliged to ask the Board to temporarily relieve him of his duties as Chairman. Ultimately an ear infection put paid to his playing career, and on Stephen Gray's departure to work for the Philharmonia, Bravington temporarily added the post of Managing Director to that of Chairman. Past experience having shown the undesirability of concentrating these responsibilities in the hands of one man, the Chairmanship passed to John Coulling, with Bravington's post retitled General Manager.

Yet despite these new financial difficulties, the artistic tide was beginning to turn. The first task was to find a new leader. Joseph Shadwick had been taken seriously ill in the spring of 1956, dying in hospital shortly afterwards, and though numerous candidates were considered, the post of leader remained unfilled for over a year, programmes for the orchestra's concerts usually bearing the legend 'Led by Harold Parfitt'. This was an unsatisfactory situation, brought to an end when Henry Datyner accepted an invitation to fill the vacancy. Datyner had been a member of the LPO from 1945 to 1948, serving as sub-leader, before joining the Liverpool Philharmonic, which he led until 1955, thereafter playing in the ranks of the Philharmonia. Datyner took up his position in the autumn of 1957, but before doing so on a full-time basis had to fulfil outstanding obligations to the Philharmonia, and for concerts at which he was unable to be present the orchestra was led by David McCallum. Sharing the front desk with Datyner was the burly figure of Arthur Davison, who was to make a modest reputation as a conductor, occasionally taking the LPO's rostrum. Sir Adrian Boult's place was filled by an announcement that William Steinberg, chief conductor of the Pittsburgh

Symphony Orchestra, was to become Principal Conductor and Musical Director, as from the autumn of the following year, 1958.

Steinberg belonged to the generation of European conductors, including Erich Leinsdorf, Georg Szell and Bruno Walter who, after Hitler came to power, emigrated to America. Born in Cologne in 1899, he had held a succession of operatic posts, in Cologne, Prague and Frankfurt, and was involved in the formation of the Palestine Symphony Orchestra, forerunner of the Israel Philharmonic. His first post in the USA was with the Buffalo Philharmonic, but it was in Pittsburgh, where he remained from 1952 to 1976, that he built his reputation. With the advent of the jet aeroplane it was feasible for conductors to hold more than one post simultaneously, and in appointing Steinberg the LPO had to accept that his services would only be available for a limited number of weeks in any year.

Undaunted by the failure of 'Bach to Bartok' to attract audiences, January 1957 saw the launch of a far more ambitious series of historic concerts. Entitled 'Music of a Century', each was designed to draw attention to a different aspect of music during the previous hundred years, the series concentrating on the twentieth century rather than the romantic masterpieces of the nineteenth. In a bid to attract audiences to programmes containing much unusual repertoire, each concert was given its own individual title, 'Retreat from Wagner', 'Adventures in Tonality', 'Strange Orchestras', 'Nostalgia', 'Once Upon a Time', 'Voice and Verse', 'Primitive Strength', 'Diversions', and 'Signs and Portents'. (Programmes of the Historic Series will be found in Appendix D.)

Audiences were variable, but though given on Mondays, generally considered a poor night for theatres and concert halls, ticket sales were encouraging, with average takings of £650, justifying the financial help specially allocated to the series by the Arts Council and the LCC. Especially good houses were attracted to 'Strange Orchestras' and 'Voice and Verse'; no doubt pre-concert publicity had much to do with this, especially where some of the sensational aspects were concerned, such as the fact that George Antheil's *Ballet Mechanique* included the sound of aeroplane propellers, though in the event this was disappointingly reproduced by a percussion player lifting the arm of a record deck and placing it on a record. A small section of the musical press adopted a slightly superior attitude to marketing music in this way, but with average takings well in excess of anything earned in the past from more adventurous programmes, the public response was an indication that good presentation had a major role to play in attracting an audience for well-thought-out programmes offering very different fare from the run-of-the-mill concerts which were all too often given in the Festival Hall.

Conductors employed during the series included Sir Adrian Boult, Paul Kletzki and Hermann Scherchen, the opening concert introducing a conductor new to this country, Constantin Silvestri, who attracted a string of favourable notices. Neville Cardus wrote of Debussy's *Nocturnes*, 'seldom has the LPO achieved so much imaginatively nuanced tone and shading', and Desmond Shawe-Taylor, prevented from attending this concert by the necessity of reviewing a new production of *The Mastersingers* at Covent Garden, commented after an Industrial Concert at the Albert Hall, 'I have no doubt his (Silvestri's) conducting is the genuine thing'.

A concert in October 1957 marked the LPO's twenty-fifth birthday, the celebrations muted by the fact that Boult was laid low with bronchitis, forcing him to cancel appearances at both the Silver Jubilee concert and a concert given to mark the eighty-fifth birthday of Ralph Vaughan Williams. It was a tribute to Basil Cameron's musicianship that he was able to step in and undertake both concerts with little or no warning. Given the opportunity to take the limelight, he delivered satisfactory accounts of programmes tailor-made for the man into whose shoes he was temporarily stepping, with Holst's *Planets* the major work in the Silver Jubilee concert and Vaughan Williams' birthday celebrated by performances of the *Pastoral Symphony* and *Job, A Masque for Dancing*.

In the wake of 'Music of a Century', the Historic concerts presented during 1957–58 were given under the title '*Grand Tour de la Musique*', featuring concerts of Hungarian, Spanish, Russian, German, French, British, Scandinavian and American music, all the works performed having been written in the twentieth century. These titles did not have the same immediacy as those of the previous year, the programmes devoted to Hungary and Scandinavia respectively suffering from the fact that a substantial proportion of each was given over to composers almost unknown in this country, the Hungarians Weiner and Lajtha and the Scandinavians Alfven, Sæverud and Valen. Paul Hindemith was prevented by illness from conducting the concert of German music, his place taken by Boult, and from an audience point of view the most successful was the Spanish programme, with the great Spanish guitar player Segovia as soloist in the Guitar Concerto by Ponce.

In complete contrast, Sunday evenings were given over to popular concerts under the title 'Masterworks'. Advertised as being 'in association with Ibbs and Tillett Limited and Harold Holt Limited', the LPO agreed that in return for financial backing from the agents they would share any profit from these concerts with them. Opening with the Silver Jubilee concert, the series thereafter comprised some of the most familiar works from the standard repertoire, Dvorak's *New World*, Tchaikovsky's Fifth and Sixth Symphonies, Brahms' Fourth, *Scheherazade*, and the annual performance of *Messiah*.

Steinberg made his official debut as Principal Conductor in the autumn of 1958; his work with the orchestra concentrated in three spells of three to four weeks, the first at the start of the season with return visits in mid-January, and late May. Steinberg's appointment was well received by the press and coincided with a new pattern of concert-giving, reflecting the fruits of the burgeoning relationship with Ibbs and Tillett and Harold Holt. 'Masterworks' on Sunday evenings again concentrated on standard classics; Thursdays were given over to 'International Celebrity Concerts', promoted by Harold Holt, the cover of each programme bearing the logo of that company rather than that of the LPO, with each concert built around the appearance of a distinguished soloist, those appearing including Daniel Barenboim, Shura Cherkassky, Annie Fischer, Zino Francescatti, Leonid Kogan, Hephzibah Menuhin, Yehudi Menuhin and Isaac Stern. The Historic Concerts bore the overall title 'Music of the Twentieth Century', each concentrating on works from one decade, except that the 1940s were divided in two, with a concert of music written between 1940 and 1945 and another of works composed between 1946 and 1949. Elsewhere the Industrial Concerts continued to attract sizeable audiences, but apart from Boult and Silvestri, the list of guest conductors was less imposing than the names of the solo artists.

The partnership with the agents heralded the formation in 1959 of the London Philharmonic Society, under whose auspices the LPO's concerts were now given. Modelled on the Royal Philharmonic Society, this was the brainchild of Eric Bravington, its formation, in association with its new allies, a bid to restore the LPO to the front rank of London's orchestras. Sir Gilmour Jenkins was invited to become the Society's Chairman, with Eric Bravington and Ian Hunter, Managing Director of Harold Holt Limited, as joint Managing Directors, and in addition to players elected to the Board of the LPO, the Directors included Sir Adrian Boult, the Hon. James Smith and Mrs Emmie Tillett. The Society set out its stall in the programme for the opening concert of the 1959–60 season:

'It has been said that the pattern of London Music is a couple of dozen standard works played innumerable times, with a few less familiar works thrown in from time to time. This Society has been formed to make some contribution, through imaginative programme building and planning, to giving London something better than that. We are offering concerts in well thought out series which, while still giving a proper place to well-known masterpieces, will greatly extend the range of works available to London music-lovers, and will enable them to hear less familiar works of all periods. We hope also to be able to give more time to rehearsal, particularly of new and difficult works. Our ambition is, in short, to provide London with a choice of programmes and with a standard of orchestral playing second to none in the world. This is to aim high, but no higher than proper for the greatest city in the world. The programmes advertised, and the world famous names of the artists, give an earnest of our intentions. To carry them out we need support from patrons of the Arts; already we are receiving support from the Arts Council and the LCC and we hope for other help. We require even more the consistent support of a permanent music loving audience seriously interested in taking part in an enterprising musical venture. On them we shall depend for our financial stability and it is for them and for the enrichment of their musical experience that the Society exists.'

The link with Harold Holt Limited ensured a list of guest artists as distinguished as that of the previous year, including Robert Casadesus, Annie Fischer, Yehudi Menuhin, Ruggiero Ricci, Artur Rubinstein, Rudolf Serkin, and Rosalyn Tureck, and in addition to Steinberg, guest conductors included Franz Konwitschny, Jaroslav Krombholc and Sir Malcolm Sargent. After a long absence from the LPO's rostrum Sargent began to appear regularly with the LPO. He conducted an International Celebrity Concert in October, and a lengthy spell of work in February and March involving two further concerts in the Thursday series, a popular Sunday evening programme, a Twentieth-Century concert entitled 'A Tale of Two Cities', several out-of-town concerts and a pair of Industrial Concerts at the Albert Hall, these concerts bringing to an end a rift between orchestra and conductor whose origins were long forgotten. It was a feature of the year's work that several other conductors, including John Pritchard, Jaroslav Krombholc and János Ferencsik were engaged for spells of work lasting two or three weeks, an arrangement designed to improve playing standards.

In late March the LPO left for an extended tour of Germany and Switzerland, and in their absence the LSO gave a concert in the Thursday series, with Wilhelm Backhaus as soloist. The concert was marred when Basil Cameron collapsed, shortly after launching the LSO into the opening tutti of Beethoven's *Emperor* Concerto. Fortunately Cameron was suffering from no more than a severe gastric upset, but it necessitated the leader Hugh Maguire taking over the baton to restart the concerto, and by the time the interval arrived the London-based conductor Harry Newstone had been summoned to attempt the thankless task of conducting the Fourth Symphony of Sibelius and Ravel's *Alborada del Gracioso*. Despite a newspaper report that he had leapt from his seat at the piano to catch Cameron as he fell, Backhaus appeared unperturbed, and despite some shortcomings of ensemble delivered a finer account of the concerto than might have been expected.

As a result of abortive negotiations for an earlier tour, which would have involved what was described as a 'Mozart-sized orchestra', the itinerary for the tour of Germany and Switzerland included more smaller towns, Coesfeld, Hamm and Herford, than would normally have been the case, adversely affecting its finances. It was originally intended that Hugo Rignold, sometime Principal Conductor of the Liverpool Philharmonic, now working with the Royal Ballet, and shortly to become Principal Conductor of the City of Birmingham Symphony Orchestra, would conduct throughout. Because he was largely unknown outside Britain the agents requested that five concerts should be given under Henrich Hollreiser, subsequently conceding that had they fully appreciated Rignold's abilities they would never have sought Hollreiser's participation. Even as late as 1960 travel was still being undertaken by train and ferry, and the prestige of the agents suffered a further blow when, after the last concert, there was a misunderstanding over arrangements for transportation of the instruments, which were only transferred to the care of the German railways in the nick of time. Sadly the programmes were almost wholly lacking in adventure, with the musicians committed to the chore of performing Beethoven's *Emperor* Concerto at twenty-two of the twenty-four concerts.

Relationships with the LPO's new Music Director were not, however, going according to plan. It was understandable that Steinberg found it necessary to draw attention to weaknesses in the orchestra, but of greater concern was his insistence that press comment during his first year in office was damaging his standing in the USA. This heralded a series of problems, including his insistence on limiting the amount of rehearsal he would undertake on any one day to no more than four hours, and his refusal to take a morning rehearsal if there had been a concert the previous evening. After protracted negotiations the stipulation of no more than four hours of rehearsal a day was conceded, but rather than accept a proposal that the remaining time should be taken by a young conductor, Colin Davis or John Avison, it was decided that it would be entrusted to the leader, Henry Datyner.

A further problem arose when Steinberg asked to be released from concerts arranged with him in January and February 1960. Steinberg was booked to appear with the Boston Symphony Orchestra during the first part of January, concerts he insisted were of considerable importance to his future career in the USA, and as he had been suffering from a recurring arm problem, his doctor advised him that rather than visiting Europe he should take a break from conducting. The orchestra could not countenance a situation where their Music Director regarded guest appearances in the USA as of more importance than his obligations to them, and there is more than a suspicion that Steinberg was either unable, or unwilling, to steel himself for the long haul still needed to raise the LPO to international status. The problem was resolved by a mutually agreed announcement that for health reasons Steinberg would relinquish his title of Music Director in the summer of 1960.

Steinberg's final report to the Board acknowledged that standards had improved over the past eighteen months, but highlighted areas where there were still serious weaknesses. Concern about playing standards led John Coulling to write a lengthy letter, which he requested should be placed on record, detailing criticisms of the orchestra, a matter of some embarrassment to all concerned when one of those whose playing was felt to be wanting was serving as a Director. It was, however, a nettle that had to be grasped, and much time and energy was spent trying to recruit players who would improve the standard of performance. One major problem in attracting players was the fact that the LPO were not obtaining sufficient recording work. EMI's doors were largely closed to them, and Decca were turning to a revitalised LSO. The problem was only partially resolved by a contract with the American company Miller International. This proved fraught with difficulties, and as time passed many planned sessions were either postponed or even cancelled, considerable difficulty being experienced in obtaining outstanding sums due under the contract.

Changes in public taste were demonstrated by the fact that Steinberg could open the Thursday series with Bruckner's Fourth Symphony, and include Mahler's Sixth as the main work in his last concert. He also opened and closed another series of 'Music of the Twentieth Century', with each concert again given an individual title: 'The Elements', 'The Philosopher', devoted to a concert performance of Busoni's *Doktor Faust*, 'Personal Protest', 'Humour', 'Primavera' and 'Present Thoughts', for which the LPO was joined on the stage by the Johnny Dankworth Orchestra, for the *Improvisations* for Jazz Band and Symphony Orchestra, a product of the combined talents of Johnny Dankworth and Matyas Seiber.

From the earliest days of the Festival Hall's existence there had been dissatisfaction with the haphazard nature of programme planning, which could lead to several performances of the same work within a short period of time, a situation benefiting neither the audience, the hall or the orchestras concerned. In a bid to improve the position Ernest Bean invited representatives of London's orchestras to a meeting, to determine what, if anything, could be done to improve matters. Partly arising from the fact that the Philharmonia was rebalancing its activities, increasing the number of public concerts, the independent orchestras were bidding for more dates than were available. The root of the problem lay in the decision to allow private promoters a sizeable share of the available dates: of 170 evenings available in any year for orchestral concerts, around 40 per cent were in their hands. Bean was prepared to offer the orchestras more dates in their own right, but only on condition that there was a greater degree of co-ordination in programme planning, and orchestras whose concerts had kept to a fairly narrow repertoire should begin to provide opportunities for the presentation of new music. His modest proposals were generally welcomed.

The LPO could lay claim to have been in the forefront so far as innovative programming was concerned, but the cost of rehearsing and performing so much unfamiliar music was a considerable burden. One further series of Historic Concerts took place in 1960–61, by which time the appointment of William Glock as the BBC's Controller of Music was making itself felt. Given the financial problems which had so recently beset the LPO, the Historic Concerts represented a remarkable venture, but while the LPO would continue to offer wide-ranging programmes, henceforth it would be the BBC, with their considerably greater resources, who would set the pace in the presentation of contemporary music.

In January 1961, a concert was offered as a tribute to Sir Adrian Boult, marking ten years of association with the LPO. Yehudi Menuhin was to have been the soloist in Elgar's Violin Concerto, but to the disappointment of audience, conductor and soloist, illness prevented him from doing so, his place taken by Alfredo Campoli. The programme opened with the first performance of the Dance Concerto *Phalaphala* by the South African composer Priaulx Rainer, and was completed by the *Colour Symphony* of Sir Arthur Bliss. Menuhin was able to attend the concert, before which he presented the conductor with a score of the symphony, signed by those taking part. The programme book included a sketch of the conductor written by Frank Howes, as well as the LPO's own tribute:

'The London Philharmonic Orchestra and the London Philharmonic Society take this opportunity of honouring a great man; for those of us who have had the privilege of working with Sir Adrian Boult know that he is one of the outstanding musicians of his day, selflessly devoted to the realisation of the scores he undertakes to conduct. With him duty and inclination are one. No task is too difficult, none too menial for him. In Sir Adrian we salute an ambassador, a public servant and a great artist, as well as a human being of warm sympathy and deep understanding.'

It was an indication of the affection and respect in which he was held throughout the ranks of the orchestra, that in 1965 the Directors invited him to become the LPO's President. It was a post which this most self-effacing of conductors occupied with distinction, ready with advice when asked, and always willing to undertake tasks which prouder men might not think worthy of their attention.

The Historic Concerts might have run their course, but the LPO was far from standing still, and 1960–61 was notable for the greatly increased stature of the guest conductors. It had been intended that Steinberg would open the season, but when he cancelled Jascha Horenstein was engaged in his stead, other guest conductors including Kirill Kondrashin, Josef Krips, Pierre Monteux and Charles Münch. The following year saw further concerts under Krips, the roster of visiting names including those of Ferenc Fricsay, Paul Kletzki and Hans Schmidt-Isserstedt. Though the process still had some way to run, here was evidence of the LPO's improved standing and the benefits derived from the link with Ibbs and Tillett and Harold Holt.

12

John Pritchard – a Changing Scene 1960–66

The choice of Steinberg's successor fell on a member of the younger generation of British conductors, John Pritchard. Born in 1918, Pritchard cut his musical teeth as an accompanist while working for the Prudential Insurance Company, appearing with among others, Arthur Catterall and Leon Goossens. He also conducted the largely amateur Derby Philharmonic, a body of somewhat variable quality, and the fully professional Derby String Orchestra, these appointments giving him opportunities to work with local choral societies. A performance of *Elijah* so impressed the singer Roy Henderson that he wrote to John and Audrey Christie at Glyndebourne, recommending them to give him an opportunity to gain experience. Starting at the bottom of the ladder in 1947, it was not long before Pritchard was asked to conduct, his work with the company opening other doors, including those of Covent Garden and the Vienna State Opera. In 1952, following the Ministry of Labour's refusal to provide a work permit allowing them to appoint a musician from abroad, the Liverpool Philharmonic were looking for conductors to fill gaps in their calendar. Pritchard was one of those invited to do so, and after sharing a season with Efrem Kurtz, was appointed Principal Conductor in his own right.

Pritchard's orchestral experience was still limited, and the Liverpool appointment was a golden opportunity to broaden his repertoire, away from the critical glare of the London press. He continued working at Glyndebourne, and in 1961 brought Glyndebourne Opera to the Albert Hall for the first time, conducting *Don Giovanni*. When the LPO began looking for a successor to Steinberg, Pritchard commended himself as a musician with a broad range of musical sympathies.

Pritchard took up the reins with effect from 1962-63, though it was not until the end of that season that he surrendered his post in Liverpool. Before then he took part in the most ambitious tour undertaken by the LPO. Lasting from late February 1961 until the first week of April, this involved thirty thousand miles of travel, taking the orchestra to India, Hong Kong, the Phillipines, Australia and Ceylon: not only were the LPO breaking fresh ground, they were the first British orchestra to visit these countries. The tour opened in Bombay with two concerts in the Raj Bhavan open-air theatre, where a special shell was built to house the orchestra; the audience at the first concert included Mr Jawaharlal Nehru and Mrs Indira Gandhi. The concerts in India, Hong Kong, and the Phillippines were conducted by Sargent, and in Hong Kong the orchestra were given the privilege of inaugurating the newly completed City Hall. For audiences largely unaccustomed to symphonic music Sargent's programmes were primarily based on standard classics, with a sprinkling of British works. It was left to Pritchard, who shared the conducting during the Australian leg of the tour, to introduce an element of more demanding twentieth-century fare in the shape of symphonies by Nielsen and Walton.

The start of Pritchard's term coincided with a temporary diminution in the quality of the LPO's guest conductors. In 1962–63, when Pritchard was still working in Liverpool, the opening concerts were undertaken by Josef Krips, who closed the year with a Beethoven cycle, and there were concerts under Boult and Sargent, but the supporting cast, Dietfried Bernet, Arthur Fiedler, Massimo Freccia and the chorus master Frederick Jackson, was not one to excite the public. An exception must be made in the case of the thirty-three-year-old Bernard Haitink, who made his debut with the LPO conducting two unlikely bedfellows, Rachmaninov's Third Piano Concerto and Bruckner's Third Symphony. Apart from Haitink and Horenstein, most of the following year's visitors were equally unexciting, the former child prodigy Roberto Benzi, now aged twenty-six, Dietfried Bernet, George Malcolm, Hermann Michael and Norman Del Mar, though when Pablo Casals conducted his Oratorio *El Pessebre* (*The Manger*), a setting of a poem by the Catalonian poet Juan Alavedra, the evening provided an opportunity for a display of affection for a great artist, whose love of country compelled him to go into exile while Franco remained in power in Spain.

Events elsewhere were making a major impact. Sir Thomas Beecham died in 1961, shortly before his eighty-second birthday. He had been ailing for some time, and it was nearly a year since his last concerts with the RPO. His death could well have brought about the demise of that orchestra. After two difficult years it came close to collapse, before the musicians took the path followed by those of the LPO, turning themselves into a self-governing co-operative.

The difficulties faced by the RPO on the death of their founder were hardly unexpected. Not so Walter Legge's announcement in March 1964 that he was suspending the Philharmonia Orchestra. Whatever the public reasons announced by Legge, there seems little doubt the reality lay in Legge's resentment of the way in which his work was being regulated in the recording studio, where EMI were imposing greater control, and in the concert hall following implementation of Ernest Bean's proposals for introducing a degree of planning, and sanity, into the Festival Hall's calendar of events. Legge's arbitrary action aroused considerable indignation, Boult giving the Philharmonia a public declaration of support at its first concert after the announcement of its suspension, an action prompting Legge to get up and walk out. Immediate backing from the Philharmonia Chorus, support from within the musical profession and an indication of financial backing stiffened the players' resolve, and within days they too declared their independence, making the Philharmonia London's fourth self-governing orchestra.

The change in status of the Philharmonia and the RPO placed new demands on the resources of the Arts Council. In the face of the financial problems faced by all London's orchestras the Council set up a committee, chaired by Lord Goodman, whose terms of reference required it to consider whether the London orchestras should be maintained or reduced, and how concerts in the capital could be better organised and co-ordinated, consistent with a high level of artistic achievement and satisfactory standards of employment. The Goodman report concluded that there was insufficient work for four orchestras but fought shy of proposing disbandment of any of them, which would most probably have meant blackballing the RPO. Though the LPO had made great strides during the past few years, the RPO was arguably the better orchestra. Bearing in mind its founder's opposition to public funding, and that much of the RPO's work was carried out for concert promoters, rather than on its own account, it is within the bounds of possibility that had the position been reversed the committee might have reached a different conclusion. In practice they recommended a basic grant of £40,000 for each orchestra, with additional amounts allocated on a per concert basis. It also recommended channelling grants via a new body to be set up for that purpose, the London Orchestral Concerts Board, which came into existence in April 1966, the Board also assuming responsibility for co-ordinating the allocation of dates in the Festival Hall.

With four orchestras bidding for dates there was increasing pressure on the facilities provided by the Royal Festival Hall, a problem exacerbated by its closure for eight months to allow a major programme of refurbishment and improvement. The hall's main entrance should have been built on the north side of the building, facing the River Thames, but it proved impossible to complete this in time for the opening, and in the interim an entrance on the east side had sufficed. In addition to relocating the main entrance, which involved resiting the box office and the cafeteria facilities, the closure was used to improve the quality of the sound, using modern acoustic techniques designed to introduce a greater degree of reverberation.

While the hall was closed London's orchestras had to cope as best they could, using the Albert Hall and the newly opened Fairfield Hall in Croydon. The LPO's autumn schedule was filled in a variety of ways, although it proved impossible to balance Pritchard's view that the workload was too heavy, with the need to provide work from engagements that would not leave the orchestra heavily out-of-pocket. October opened with a short tour of Denmark under

Colin Davis, one Danish reviewer writing that 'the LPO's fame is only overshadowed by that of the Beatles'. Church concerts were arranged at Spalding, Lincoln Cathedral, Southwell and Thaxted; two concerts were given in Swansea as part of the annual Festival, and there was a short Welsh tour. As a result of the rapprochement with Sargent they were again accompanying the Royal Choral Society, dates which this autumn were of especial value, and the London Philharmonic Society promoted concerts in the Albert Hall, the Fairfield Hall, Croydon, and the Regal Cinema, Edmonton.

These expedients, including Festival Ballet's Christmas performances of *Nutcracker*, performed this year at the New Victoria Theatre, served to tide things over until the Festival Hall reopened in February 1965. It did so with three special concerts, the LSO playing under Colin Davis and the Philharmonia under Klemperer, the LPO contributing a concert at which Boult accompanied Menuhin in Elgar's Violin Concerto, and Michael Tippett conducted *A Child of our Time*.

By comparison with the unremarkable fare which bridged the gap while the hall was closed, the concerts now encompassed a wider repertoire. It was a sign of changing public taste that whereas van Beinum's 1949 performance of Bruckner's Third Symphony attracted minimal public interest, it was possible for Horenstein to conduct not one but two performances of the work. Silvestri's programme included Walton's *Partita* and the Tenth Symphony of Shostakovitch, repeated two days later for Sir Robert Mayer's Youth and Music. Rafael Frühbeck de Burgos accompanied Victoria de los Angeles in the *Four Last Songs* of Richard Strauss and arias from Falla's Opera *La Vida Breve*, and Yevgeni Svetlanov and Christoph von Dohnányi made their debuts with the LPO. Pritchard conducted Bach's Mass in B minor, a concert at which the LPO was joined by the Johnny Dankworth Orchestra, and a Musica Viva concert comprising Bartok's First Violin Concerto and the *Second Fantasia on John Tavener's In Nomine* by Peter Maxwell Davies.

Pritchard was a man of great energy and enthusiasm, and from the day he joined the LPO supported the orchestra in every way possible, both on and off the platform. He made time to attend members' evenings arranged by the London Philharmonic Society, and while there were musicians, some within the ranks of the LPO, who looked down on the Industrial Concerts, Pritchard never saw them as a chore, playing a full part in both their planning and performance. Yet despite successful tours with the LPO and the acclaim given to his work at Glyndebourne, he never enjoyed the same success as the leading overseas conductors appearing in London. This was a poor reflection on the judgement of London audiences, for if he had a special affinity with Russian and French music, and a particular sympathy for contemporary composers, he was a conductor with a wide-ranging repertoire, whose performances were never routine. Moreover, regardless as to whether he was conducting the *Carmen Suite* and the 1812 Overture at an Industrial Concert, or a contemporary work in the Festival Hall, he had the gift of communicating his enjoyment of the piece to which his energies were directed at the time. Nevertheless, for all the virtues of his work it was impossible to avoid the uncomfortable feeling that for all the improvement in the quality and standing of the orchestra, the LPO were still playing second fiddle to the LSO and the Philharmonia. In the event it was by mutual agreement between conductor and orchestra, and without acrimony, that he stepped down from his position at the end of 1965–66.

Viewed superficially, Pritchard's term of office looks disappointing. He was, however, involved in two developments which had a significant impact. The first lay in the recruitment of a new leader and personnel changes designed to improve the orchestra's playing. Henry Datyner's leadership had given rise to problems arising from his less than sympathetic approach to a number of conductors and soloists. He therefore tendered his resignation, though when this was withdrawn he led the LPO throughout their tour of India and the Far East. In the following year serious health problems necessitated his absence from a tour of Germany, during which the orchestra was led by Arthur Davison, and he resigned shortly afterwards. Dissatisfaction with Datyner's leadership focused attention on the quality of the violins, which had been the subject of much criticism, leading to a major reorganisation of both sections.

The schedule worked by the LPO placed a great strain on any leader, with David Wise, Joseph Shadwick and Henry Datyner all succumbing to health problems. It was therefore a happy solution that from among the various candidates the choice fell on the twenty-four-year-old Rodney Friend, whose experience included eighteen months as co-leader of the LSO, and who joined the LPO in September 1964, Pritchard playing a major part in persuading him to accept the post. In addition to the influence exerted from the leader's chair, he was involved in the recruitment of a number of younger players, leading to an improvement in the quality of the string sound.

Other comings and goings were also taking place. Uncertainty over the future of the Philharmonia and the RPO led several members of those orchestras to make enquiries about the possibility of joining the LPO, presenting a unique opportunity for making judicious changes designed to eliminate weaknesses. Of longer-serving members Peter Allen, timpanist for fifteen years and sometime member of the Board, died in harness in 1963, his place taken by Christopher Seaman, a graduate of the National Youth Orchestra, and another significant change of personnel saw Bernard Walton replace John McCaw as Principal Clarinet. Walton had played in that position as long ago as 1937, but following war service he joined the Philharmonia and was elected Chairman of that orchestra when the players determined that it should not, as Sir Adrian Boult put it, 'be snuffed out like a candle'. Disagreement over policy led to Walton's resignation, and subsequently he left the Philharmonia, Walton and John McCaw swapping their respective positions, Walton joining the LPO and McCaw the Philharmonia.

Undoubtedly, however, the greatest change in the composition of the orchestra lay in the fact that whereas in the past, with the exception of its harpist, the LPO had been a male preserve, the opposition to women as members of the orchestra began to crumble. One of the players recruited to strengthen the violins was Marie Wilson who, before Paul Beard arrived to take up his new post, led the BBC Symphony Orchestra for the 1936 Proms. Joining the LPO in February 1963, she occupied the third chair in the first violin section. That discrimination was far from dead is revealed by a paragraph in the London Philharmonic Society's newsletter which stated 'her appointment does not signify the sudden incursion of the fair sex into the ranks of the orchestra, but (is) an indication that if there is available a woman of outstanding ability for any post vacant she will receive equal consideration'. It was to be another two years before the Annual General Meeting approved a proposal allowing women instrumentalists to join the orchestra on a permanent basis.

But arguably the most far-reaching development of all, in which Pritchard played a major part, was the engagement of the LPO to perform for the opera season at Glyndebourne. Pritchard had steadily worked his way to the top of the Glyndebourne hierarchy, where he now held the title of Music Counsellor and Principal Conductor. He was thus in a position to exert considerable influence when fears that the RPO might be about to collapse faced Glyndebourne with the prospect that, unless they looked elsewhere, they would be without an orchestra in 1964. On Pritchard's recommendation an approach was made to the LPO, and Bravington was quick to seize the opportunity of securing work that was considerably more prestigious than performing for the ballet.

The transition was far from straightforward. The Musicians Union intervened on the RPO's behalf, at one point issuing an ultimatum to the effect that members of the Union, other than those employed by the RPO, would not be allowed to perform at Glyndebourne. For their part Glyndebourne refused to back down, threatening that unless their engagement of the LPO was confirmed they would cancel the entire season, making public their reason for doing so. The situation was only resolved after some difficult negotiations, for which Gerald McDonald of the Liverpool Philharmonic acted as an impartial adviser. Glyndebourne were fully entitled to engage the orchestra of their choice, yet astonishingly a settlement was only reached by the extraction of Danegeld, £10000 from Glyndebourne and £5000 from the LPO, for which it was necessary to raise a bank loan, the money paid to Rophora, the parent company under which the RPO was operating. For their first year in the pit the orchestra was described in the programme book as the Glyndebourne Festival Orchestra, though it was made clear that all the players were members of the LPO, and it was not until the following year that they performed in the opera house under their proper title of the London Philharmonic Orchestra.

The LPO's calendar now reverted to that of the pre-war orchestra, the autumn and winter months spent in the concert hall, late spring and summer in the opera house. There was, however, one significant difference, for whereas the pre-war International Seasons at Covent Garden staged as many operas as possible within a limited period of time, each opera being given only a handful of performances, Glyndebourne's concern for artistic standards limits the number staged each year, with most operas performed a dozen or more times. The relationship with Festival Ballet was not terminated overnight. For some years the LPO continued to provide the accompaniment for the Christmas performances of *Nutcracker*, and in 1966, when the opera season was shorter than usual, even provided an orchestra for Festival Ballet's summer season, though the players engaged for those performances did not appear as the LPO.

There were a number of teething troubles to be solved, including the fact that the repertoire and style of playing were one with which the players were largely unfamiliar. The operas performed in 1964 comprised *Macbeth* (Verdi), *L'incorazione di Poppea* (Monteverdi), *La pietra del paragone* (Rossini), *Capriccio* (Strauss), and two operas by Mozart, *The Magic Flute*, conducted by Vittorio Gui, a great favourite at Glyndebourne, who had last worked with the LPO at Covent Garden in 1939, and *Idomeneo*, works few of them had encountered before.

It took time to adjust to working in the Opera House. Performing in an orchestra pit is never as comfortable as doing so on the concert platform, and Glyndebourne's pit was extremely cramped, making it difficult for players to hear each other, with those at the back, under the stage, seriously affected by extraneous noise. One player described it as performing in a cardboard box, and the pit was sometimes referred to as 'the green grave'. Surprisingly, a suggestion that the players should be allowed to wear less formal attire was rejected, a majority voting to remain in dinner jackets. Another problem lay in the fact that for good reason Glyndebourne occasionally hands over a number of performances to younger conductors, enabling them to cut their conducting teeth on a production that has already settled down in performance, part of the process that has encouraged numerous budding maestros at the start of their career, but one that is not necessarily welcome to the musicians playing under them.

The size of the orchestra which could be accommodated was smaller than that which usually appears on-stage in the Festival Hall, giving rise to concern about possible loss of earnings. The task of ensuring everyone receives an equitable share of the season's work is complex. Most players perform in three or four operas, and while Concert Management and the Personnel Manager try to meet players' preferences, a degree of compromise is necessary to ensure every opera has a full complement, and that principals or co-principals are available to cover every performance.

The LPO's relationship with Glyndebourne has proved of immense value, giving management the stability of guaranteed work during the summer months, with bonuses in the shape of broadcast and television relays, as well as engagements to perform at the Proms, the orchestra benefitting from the element of variety introduced into their work. Some operas are performed with a degree of regularity, notably those of Mozart, but whereas full-time opera orchestras may find it hard to enthuse about the umpteenth revival of *Butterfly* or *Traviata*, the repertoire has evolved in a way that reduces the risk of staleness. Productions of *Carmen, Bohème*, and *Traviata* are exceptions to the rule that in general, Mozart excepted, the company steers clear of the more popular repertoire. The pre-war Festivals concentrated on Mozart, but the post-war years saw Glyndebourne branching out in new directions, performances at the Edinburgh Festival including a memorable production of *La Forza del Destino*, then relatively unknown in this country. The 1950s saw an exploration of Rossini's comic operas, *Cenerentola, Compte Ory* and *Turco in Italia*, and the 1960s the first twentieth-century opera, Henze's *Elegy for Young Lovers*. Since taking their place in the pit the LPO have performed a repertoire ranging from *L'incorazione di Poppea* to contemporary British works, including the premiere of Nicholas Maw's *The Rising of the Moon*, and Harrison Birtwistle's *The Second Mrs Kong*. There has been much Strauss, including rarities such as *Intermezzo* and *Die schweisgame Frau*, and several operas by Britten, among them a magical *Midsummer Night's Dream*, while performances of *Albert Herring* demonstrated that the company's comic talents were not limited to Mozart and Rossini. Year in, year out, the LPO's contribution has added lustre to the company's work, attracting considerable critical acclaim.

Despite Glyndebourne's heavy rehearsal schedule, the fact that each opera requires less than the full orchestra makes the season something of an oasis in an otherwise hectic year of activity. Afternoons are nearly always free, and the final weeks, when the last opera has been brought into production, bring the luxury of days with only an evening performance, or days with no performance at all. Travelling to and from Lewes is still a burden, though some players emulate the singers by renting property in the area. 'What do they of music know, who only music know?' The orchestra's summer residency in Sussex has the merit of allowing its members time to recharge their batteries by engaging, at least briefly, in pursuits unconnected with their music-making.

Changes were also taking place away from the platform. Towards the end of 1962 members of the public were invited to join the London Philharmonic Society, which offered a range of benefits, including priority booking, attendance at rehearsals, a newsletter and a number of social functions and meetings. Within a short space of time the Society attracted a membership in excess of eight hundred. Recruitment owed much to John Pritchard, who in impromptu speeches at an Industrial Concert, on a Sunday evening in the Festival Hall and at out-of-town concerts in Eastbourne and Folkestone, offered the inducement of a free record for every twenty-fifth member recruited that evening. The LPO had a longstanding relationship with Eastbourne, where in 1963 they performed at the opening concert in the newly completed Congress Theatre and the Eastbourne branch of the Society organised its own programme of activities. In 1968 members, concerned at the sub-standard rostrum used for concerts in the Congress Theatre, subscribed to a replacement, which was also employed for other out-of-town concerts given by the LPO.

The nature of the Society was in fact changing, and from 1965 the orchestra reverted to promoting concerts under its own name. At the same time the status of the LPO Council was enhanced, with members of the reorganised Council mostly drawn from the ranks of those who had served as Directors of the London Philharmonic Society. The Council's first Chairman was Sir Nicholas Sekers, with the Earl of Shaftesbury as Vice-Chairman, the two men swapping roles shortly afterwards, the Earl of Shaftesbury proving himself one of the LPO's most active and influential supporters. From being a consultative body the Council was given new responsibilities, with primary importance given to the task of raising the outside funding essential to the artistic health of the orchestra, and in a move foreshadowing the increasingly important part that commercial sponsorship was to play, the tobacco firm of W.D. & H.O. Wills began to give direct financial support.

One of the first actions taken by the Council was to launch a new National Appeal to enable them to set up a Trust Fund which would:

- Maintain the LPO's ability to present a wide series of public concerts at the highest possible level with the greatest artists and given with adequate rehearsal facilities.
- Provide the LPO musicians with a stable annual income including a paid holiday period, payment in the event of illness and a pension scheme.
- Assist in the financing of the many invitations the LPO receives to tour abroad.
- Enable instruments of outstanding quality to be purchased as they become available.
- Give to the London Philharmonic the overall security which is enjoyed by its sister orchestras, the Vienna Philharmonic, the Berlin Philharmonic and the New York Philharmonic.

Though it has been impossible to fulfil these aims in full, the activities of the Council, and more recently those of the orchestra's Trustees, have done much to underwrite many of the artistic achievements of the past thirty years.

John Pritchard's last season as Principal Conductor, 1965–66, saw a distinguished line-up of guest conductors, including Rafael Frühbeck de Burgos, Colin Davis, Antal Dorati, Bernard Haitink, Paul Kletzki, Eugene

Svetlanov and Sir Adrian Boult. Pritchard conducted ten concerts, and though Elgar was not a composer one immediately associated with him, gave a fine account of *The Dream of Gerontius*. He accompanied John Ogden in Busoni's rambling Piano Concerto, and was joined by Johnny Dankworth and his Orchestra for a programme in which Dankworth played Stravinsky's *Ebony Concerto*. For several years the Labour Party and the Musicians Union jointly sponsored a Festival Hall concert. Attended by the Prime Minister, Mr Harold Wilson, the Minister for the Arts, Miss Jennie Lee, and several members of the Cabinet, this year's, at which the LPO performed, marked Pritchard's last appearance as Principal Conductor, with John Ogden as soloist in Bartok's Third Concerto, sandwiched between Walton's Overture, *Portsmouth Point*, and a work in which the conductor was always heard to advantage, Holst's *Planets*.

Though Pritchard severed his official links with the orchestra in 1966 he continued working with them at Glyndebourne, in the concert hall and, with more frequency than before, in the recording studio. During his time as Principal Conductor he engaged in little or no recording work, but when EMI introduced a budget label, Music for Pleasure, later retitled Classics for Pleasure, a number of recordings were conducted by Pritchard, mostly of popular repertoire, but including Bartok's Concerto for Orchestra, and Britten's Violin Concerto, with Rodney Friend as soloist. The commercial support provided by W.D. & H.O. Wills was extended to records made by the LPO for this label, the records known as the Embassy Master Series. In addition to concerts in this country, Pritchard continued to accompany the LPO overseas. In the autumn of 1966 he conducted a tour which opened in Vienna, the itinerary embracing Innsbruck, Freiburg, Stuttgart, Munich, Ludwigshafen, Mulheim, Hannover, Berlin and Kiel, concluding with a concert in Paris, the programme in the French capital including the first performance in that country of Walton's Second Symphony. Pritchard also took part in tours of the Far East and North America, and had the distinction of conducting the LPO in 1973 when they were the first Western symphony orchestra to visit mainland China. Pritchard undoubtedly played a major part in improving the quality of the LPO, but his greatest legacy was to introduce the orchestra to Glyndebourne.

Meanwhile the Directors identified the man they wanted to take over from Pritchard. In March 1966 they were able to announce that Bernard Haitink had agreed to take up the position of Principal Conductor and Artistic Adviser as from 1967-68. Eighteen months would elapse between the announcement of Haitink's appointment and his joining the orchestra, and during 1966–67, in addition to Boult, Haitink and Pritchard, an impressive line-up of conducting talent included the names of Karel Ančerl, Antal Dorati, Jascha Horenstein, Constantin Silvestri, Georg Solti and Eugene Svetlanov. It was a season rich with Mahler, Silvestri conducting the First and Third Symphonies,

Haitink the Fourth and Horenstein the Fifth, while Svetlanov's four concerts, spread throughout March, were largely devoted to Russian music. Without breaking new boundaries it was an adventurous enough set of programmes to avoid the label of routine, a further indication that management and players had put the problems of the 1950s behind them.

13

Bernard Haitink – Years of Achievement 1967–72

Bernard Haitink's appointment coincided with that of Colin Davis as Principal Conductor of the BBC Symphony Orchestra, and with André Previn assuming a similar position with the LSO the following year, these three appointments represented a vote of confidence in the younger generation of conductors. Colin Davis, not long turned forty, was the oldest, with Haitink a few months short of his thirty-ninth birthday, and Previn, who like Haitink was born in 1929, a month or two younger. Colin Davis' tenure at the BBC was relatively short-lived, but for the next decade and beyond Haitink and Previn made a significant impact on the orchestral life of London, the concert-going public benefiting from the fact that the repertoire in which each was particularly gifted only overlapped to a marginal extent.

Haitink had been at the helm of the Concertgebouw for six years, and for the LPO his arrival was the start of an era in which their achievements were to match, even surpass, those of Beecham's pre-war orchestra. Each concert became a special occasion, a fact acknowledged by audiences to such an extent that within a short space of time the management could report that, on average, they were selling over 90 per cent of the capacity of the Royal Festival Hall's two thousand nine hundred seats, well in excess of anything achieved by the other London orchestras.

The days when an orchestra could look to its principal conductor to take on a high proportion of each season's work were long past. Haitink remained Principal Conductor of the Concertgebouw, and in order to fulfil his commitment to the LPO greatly reduced his guest conducting with other orchestras; even so, the amount of time he could devote to London was limited to around ten weeks a year. The pattern of this season, two to three weeks in the autumn, a similar period shortly in the new year, and short spells in March and April, was largely followed in later seasons, with additional weeks occasionally squeezed in, allowing him to tour overseas or make festival appearances. In 1967–68 Haitink's schedule included eleven Festival Hall concerts, one of them the Royal Concert in aid of the Musicians Benevolent Fund, at which he shared the conducting with Boult, an Industrial Concert at the Albert Hall, and concerts at various halls in and around London.

An additional engagement shouldered by Haitink was a concert at Eastbourne which should have been conducted by Sir Malcolm Sargent. In December 1966 Sargent underwent major surgery, but by the following spring was able to undertake concerts in Australia and the USA. On his return home in July he was again a sick man, and though taking the preliminary rehearsals for the 1967 Proms, was forced to cancel his appearance at the concerts themselves, entering hospital for another operation. One by one his concerts were handed over to other conductors, but on the Last Night, by a supreme effort of will, he made a final platform appearance, not to conduct, but to make a valedictory speech, receiving an emotional farewell from the audience. He died a fortnight later. His final concert with the LPO, almost one of his last in England, had been in October 1966, at Hastings. During the 1967 Proms he should have conducted the LPO in a concert of British music, his place on the night taken by Charles Groves.

The autumn began with concerts under Horenstein, Boult and Silvestri, Haitink's debut as Principal Conductor taking place on 9 November, with the following programme:

Berlioz: Overture, Benvenuto Cellini; Stravinsky: Symphonies of wind instruments; Beethoven: Piano Concerto No. 3 in C minor (**Hans Richter-Haaser**); Bartok: Concerto for Orchestra

An attack of flu forced Haitink to cancel his first concert in the New Year, Brian Priestman taking over a programme including Beethoven's Seventh Symphony and excerpts from Mussorgsky's *Boris Godunov*, in which Boris was sung by the Chinese bass Yi-Kwei Sze, supported by the New Opera Chorus. Disappointingly, Priestman felt unable at such short notice to learn Janacek's *Taras Bulba*, substituting Tchaikovsky's *Romeo and Juliet*. In general it was a year for building the relationship between conductor and orchestra, and to this end Haitink's programmes trod well-known paths, including symphonies by Beethoven, Brahms, Bruckner and Dvorak, with Britten's *Spring Symphony* and Stravinsky's *Capriccio* for Piano and Orchestra the major departures from the normal run of the repertoire. Concerts were also given under Antal Dorati, Christoph von Dohnányi and Yevgeni Svetlanov. Richard Bonynge was engaged for a performance of *Messiah*, with his wife Joan Sutherland as the soprano soloist, and Maxim Shostakovitch, son of the composer, conducted two works by his father, the Concerto for Piano and Trumpet and the Fifth Symphony.

The number of out-of-town concerts had been steadily declining, and by 1967–68 had fallen to twenty-seven, six in Croydon, Eastbourne and Hastings, four at Watford and single engagements in Bournemouth, Brighton, Greenwich, Hornsey and Oxford. The halls at Chatham, Folkestone and Margate were considered to have unsatisfactory staging, and these places, once regular ports of call, were dropped from the calendar. A decision had also been taken that, so far as possible, out-of-town concerts would not be arranged the day before a Festival Hall concert, especially where anything in the way of a long journey and a late arrival home was involved. That this was possible stemmed from growing demand for the LPO's services in the recording studio, evidenced by the fact that in 1966, despite the fact that Glyndebourne's season was shorter than usual, with performances of only four operas, the calendar was so well filled that apart from days set aside for the players' annual holiday, there were only thirty wholly free days.

Record companies for whom they worked included a new label, the Lyrita Recorded Edition, which concentrated on music by British composers, much of it neglected. The LPO played a major part in the company's recording programme, with several symphonies by Bax among the works recorded. Sir John Barbirolli and Basil Cameron did much to champion his work during the post-war era, but the appearance of a Bax symphony on the programme usually spelt poor box office returns. With the advent of the Glock regime at the BBC, and emergence of a younger generation of music critics more interested in the newer school of British composers, Harrison Birtwistle, Alexander Goehr and Peter Maxwell Davies, the music of Bax fell further out of favour, yet the commercial success of the records indicated a sizeable public for these unashamedly romantic works whose immediate appeal was to the heart rather than the head.

In the autumn of 1967, in preparation for some of the Lyrita sessions, Boult, who had already recorded several works by John Ireland for this company, treated the audience at Eastbourne to *November Woods* by Bax, performing Moeran's *Sinfonietta* in Hastings, and at Watford the London Philharmonic Choir sang John Ireland's *These Things Shall Be*, a work once popular with choral societies, which had also fallen out of fashion. Boult also conducted new recordings of the Elgar symphonies for Lyrita, but instead of following his usual practice of seating the first and second violins opposite each other, with the basses spread across the back of the platform, he was persuaded to adopt the layout followed by most conductors, seating both first and seconds to the left of the conductor's rostrum. Boult believed that placing the violins together gave an unbalanced sound, concentrating the treble to one side of the platform and, if the strings fanned round the platform in order, the bass sound on the other. He supported his argument by quoting the many examples, particularly in music by classical composers of the eighteenth and nineteenth centuries, where passages played by the first violins are answered by the seconds, an effect which is lost if the violins are seated together. Nineteenth-century orchestras almost always placed the first and second violins opposite each other, and Boult cited Klemperer, Monteux and Walter as conductors who remained faithful to this practice. Whether or not it was the layout with which he was persuaded to work, these did not rank among the best of his recorded performances of the symphonies.

One performance which did give great satisfaction was Elgar's *Dream of Gerontius*, recorded by BBC Television in March 1968 at Canterbury Cathedral, and transmitted on Easter Sunday, with Janet Baker, Peter Pears, singing the role of Gerontius for the first time in twenty years, and John Shirley-Quirk as soloists. Vernon Handley acted as assistant conductor, a role he undertook for several of Boult's recordings of large-scale choral works. Boult professed to being disappointed with the transmission, which he felt compared unfavourably with the sound achieved in the Cathedral itself, but for many of those who watched the recorded performance, it was a moving experience.

Boult's wonderfully productive Indian summer in the recording studios was proceeding apace. The LPO was not always available, and in December 1965 it was with the New Philharmonia Orchestra that he accompanied Yehudi Menuhin in the Elgar Violin Concerto, recording *The Planets* with the same orchestra in July of the following year. Boult also commenced work on a new cycle of the Vaughan Williams symphonies, with the New Philharmonia engaged for the *Pastoral* and Fourth symphonies, and the remaining works undertaken by the LPO. There were also sessions for the World Record Club, for whom, in addition to more traditional fare, a day was spent recording a dozen well-known marches, including several by Sousa, Kenneth Alford's *Colonel Bogey*, Eric Coates' *Dambusters March* and Walford Davies' *Royal Air Force March*. It was a break with routine, allowing conductor and players a chance to let their hair down, especially the brass, woodwind and percussion sections, some of whom had played these pieces while serving in military bands. The autumn of 1968 was occupied with more serious matters. Vaughan Williams' *Sea Symphony* was recorded in September, prefaced by a performance in the Fairfield Hall, Croydon. A Festival Hall programme including Rubbra's Seventh Symphony was followed by a recording of that work, and in December Boult took the LPO and its Choir to Eastbourne, for Elgar's Oratorio *The Kingdom*, also preparatory to recording sessions.

The year saw the introduction of a scheme of Corporate Membership of the London Philharmonic Society, to which eighteen companies subscribed, a number which steadily increased over the next few years. Companies were offered two alternative packages, a payment of £105 securing two stall seats for every Festival Hall concert in the next calendar year, or for £250 the company had the right to four box seats; Corporate Members also enjoyed the benefits offered to ordinary members of the Society. The scheme proved a valuable way of interesting companies in the work of the LPO, with the added benefit of obtaining advance ticket sales. For the first time the LPO also published a yearbook. At the outset this consisted largely of a listing of the orchestra's concerts, but its scope was gradually enlarged, with reports on activities ranging from the orchestra's overseas tours to those of the LPO's football team. Unhappily the LPO's success on the football pitch was not always of the same order as that achieved on the concert platform.

At this point in his career Haitink was known in this country for his interpretation of the mainstream German repertoire, with an affinity for French music and for Stravinsky. 1968–69 saw his repertoire expand in two directions. He continued his exploration of British music, one concert featuring Britten's Violin Concerto and *Belshazzar's Feast*, his most intriguing programme comprising Mozart's Symphony No. 33 in B flat, Bruckner's Mass in E minor, and the Fourth Symphony of Vaughan Williams, the harshest and in many ways the most demanding of the composer's symphonies. A second point of departure took place in the last concert of the season, before the orchestra forsook the Festival Hall to spend the summer at Glyndebourne, the evening concluding with the Fourth Symphony of Shostakovitch. As with the Vaughan Williams, this hugely disturbing work is not one that comes naturally to mind as the first of the composer's symphonies a conductor might wish to tackle. The Tenth Symphony entered Haitink's repertoire shortly afterwards, but for a time that was as far as his exploration of this composer went; several years were to elapse before, prompted by Decca's interest, he performed and recorded a complete cycle of the Shostakovitch symphonies.

The year included two performances of music drawn from the opera *Arden Must Die* by the young English composer Alexander Goehr, the practice of repeating a new work at a subsequent concert one which was to be followed on several occasions, and in the following year, 1969–70, Richard Rodney Bennett's *Aubade*, Elgar's *Enigma* Variations, and Holst's *Planets* entered Haitink's repertoire, illness preventing him from conducting Robert Simpson's First Symphony, for which the composer took his place. This was not just lip service to the music of his hosts. A growing school of overseas musicians has long disproved the theory that the music of Elgar, Holst, Vaughan Williams and Walton contains qualities that cannot be fathomed by anyone born outside these shores; Haitink was in the vanguard of those who both performed their music in public and were anxious to record it. His other concerts included the *Choral Symphony*, Bruckner's Ninth, Mahler's *Resurrection* Symphony, Sibelius' Second, performed in the Festival Hall and at an Industrial Concert, *Ein Heldenleben*, and Tchaikovsky's Fourth, another work to receive two performances, at a Sunday concert in the Albert Hall in January, and in the Festival Hall in May. Conductors new to the orchestra included Eugen Jochum and Jerzy Semkow, and there were concerts under Dorati, Krips and Solti, the LPO's sixth tour of Germany, which took place in April 1969, also being given under Solti's baton.

Boult's eightieth birthday was marked by a special concert, given on Tuesday, 8 April 1969 in the Albert Hall, for which he and the LPO were joined by Yehudi Menuhin, as soloist in Elgar's Violin Concerto, the choir including members of the London Philharmonic Choir and representatives of other choral societies with which he had enjoyed a close association, the Bach Choir, the BBC Choral Society, the Croydon Philharmonic Choir, the Goldsmiths' Choral Union and the Ripley Choir, Bromley. The programme comprised:

> Parry: Unison Song, England, Blest Pair of Sirens; Elgar: Violin Concerto in B minor (**Yehudi Menuhin**); Vaughan Williams : A London Symphony

Boult's professional career started in earnest in the early months of 1918, when he conducted four concerts with the LSO, at which the *London Symphony*, a piece for which he had become a famed interpreter, was performed twice. But however appropriate its inclusion, the reflective ending was hardly the way to end an evening of celebration. Boult and the orchestra therefore brought the concert to a rousing conclusion with Eric Coates' *Dambusters March*. In a personal note included in the programme for the evening Boult wrote:

> 'This concert is a gesture of thanks to the very many people who have supported a career lasting fifty-one years. Friends in audiences, colleagues on platforms, backroom boys and girls have all, under Providence, made heavy contributions to a life of almost unclouded happiness, domestic, social and professional.'

To which a major contributory factor was the unswerving loyalty and support given to the players with whom he worked, and his unfailing generosity in matters great and small. It had been his hope that the concert would produce a useful contribution to the funds of Oxfam, but due to circumstances outside his control, the final accounts showed a deficit. Nevertheless it was wholly in character that in addition to a cheque from the orchestra, representing fees returned by many of the players taking part, Oxfam received a generous donation from Boult himself.

Overseas touring was playing an increasingly important part in the calendar, raising the international profile of the LPO as well as its marketability in the recording studio. The autumn of 1969 took the orchestra to the Far East, and in the spring of 1970 they broke new ground, performing for the first time in the USA. Because Haitink was prevented from doing so by other commitments, John Pritchard and Jerzy Semkow conducted the opening stages of the Far East tour, which embraced Singapore, Hong Kong, Manila, and Seoul. Their concerts in Singapore contributed to celebrations marking the one hundred and fiftieth anniversary of the founding of the British colony, and those in Manila were the first to be given in the newly opened Arts Centre.

Haitink joined the orchestra in Japan, where, with the Empress in the audience, their performances in Tokyo took place during British Trade Week, the LPO also performing in Hiroshima, Matsuyama, Nagoya and Sendai. Almost every programme included a British work, Haitink conducting the *Enigma Variations* and Richard Rodney Bennett's *Aubade*, Pritchard's concerts including either the *Dance Scene* by Peter Racine Fricker or the Suite from *Checkmate* by Sir Arthur Bliss. The reports sent back to London spoke highly of the orchestra, confirming the view of management and players that the LPO's playing was now fit to be judged alongside any of the great orchestras of the world.

Overseas travel is rarely as glamorous as it sounds. Like the business traveller, musicians rarely see more than the airport at which they touch down, the hotel in which they are staying that night and, in the musicians' case, the hall in which the day's concert takes place. Few tours are however without mishaps, moments of light relief, or even dramas. The audience in Singapore were far from being the first to be misled by the opening drum-roll of the Overture to *La Gazza Ladra* into believing that this was the start of the National Anthem; concerts in Manila took place against the background of an election campaign, the volatile politics of that country periodically erupting into gun battles between rival factions, while after a concert in Seoul, Barrie Iliffe, a senior member of the British Council's staff, who was invited to accompany the orchestra as a measure of thanks for the support given by the Council, was taken aback when he was buttonholed by a Korean lady, unfamiliar with the workings of a symphony orchestra, anxious to know how all the players managed to obtain their employer's permission to take time off work simultaneously in order to go on tour.

The Far East tour involved eighteen concerts, lasting the best part of a month, a schedule which on the surface may appear relaxed, but in practice allowed only one day without either a concert or travel from one centre to another, several days in Japan involving both. The American tour the following April was no less hectic. Fourteen concerts were given, all conducted by Haitink, with an itinerary which embraced several of the principal eastern cities, New York, Philadelphia and Washington, and took the orchestra to Charleston and Columbia in South Carolina, Ashville, Charlotte and Durham in North Carolina, Athens in Georgia, as well as Hershey and the steel centre of Bethlehem, in Pennsylvania. After a performance of Bruckner's Second Symphony in New York Haitink was presented with the Medal of Honour of the Bruckner Society of America, and New York also heard *The Planets*, which featured in his Festival Hall programmes during the winter, and the Fourth Symphony of Shostakovitch, which had not. Other cities were deemed to require less daunting fare, the remaining programmes comprising standard classics.

Financial assistance was again provided by the British Council and the LPO set up an American company, the London Philharmonic Society (USA) Inc, with Lord Shaftesbury as President, and a number of influential Americans as members of the Board, thanks to whose efforts it proved possible to obtain the benefit of two days' rehearsal in Carnegie Hall before the opening concert took place. Lord Shaftesbury, who had accompanied the LPO on their Far Eastern tour, was with them in America, and as a gesture of thanks to their American supporters, hosted a supper-ball at the St Regis Roof, which took place after the opening gala concert in Carnegie Hall. The success of this tour led to an immediate invitation to return, plans being put in train for a more extended visit embracing Canada and Mexico as well as the USA.

During 1969–70 Haitink conducted *Taras Bulba*, postponed from January 1968, three works by Mahler, *Das Lied von der Erde*, the *Resurrection* Symphony and the Ninth Symphony, concluding one of his concerts in a somewhat unusual fashion with Bartok's *Music for strings, percussion and celeste*. In a further contrast with past experience of performing Bruckner to half-empty halls, the decision to schedule two performances of Bruckner's Fifth Symphony, conducted by Jochum, was fully vindicated. Much of the choral contribution was out of the ordinary, Prokofiev's *Alexander Nevsky*, under Svetlanov, Franz Reizenstein's *Voices of the Night*, conducted by Edward Downes, and a Boult speciality, Holst's *Choral Symphony*. A distinguished list of soloists included Vladimir Ashkenazy, Shura Cherkassky, Clifford Curzon, Christoph Eschenbach, Ingrid Haebler, Wilhelm Kempff and Artur Rubinstein. Rodney Friend's talents were displayed when he joined forces with Henryk Szeryng in a Concerto for Two Violins by Vivaldi, and in company with the co-leader Gerald Jarvis, performed Bach's Concerto for Two Violins at a pair of Industrial Concerts.

Despite some improvements in working conditions, including higher payments for holiday periods and sickness, the inadequacy of the Social Security arrangements was brought home by the death in harness of John Cload, the last founder member still playing in the ranks of the LPO. Because it had not been possible to re-establish the pension scheme his dependants, and those of another member who died during the year, Richard Bradley, could only be given limited financial assistance. The shortcomings of the Social Security provision for the players was a recurrent theme for many years to come.

Concerns about the financial stability of Britain's orchestras led the Arts Council to commission a further report, from a committee chaired by Sir Alan Peacock, which was given a wide-ranging brief to study orchestral resources throughout Britain. Their report recommended the appointment of players to the Boards of those orchestras which were not self-governing, and composers-in-residence to work with each orchestra. More controversial was a proposal that the Arts Council should select two of the London orchestras to receive increased grants, the implication being that the other two would suffer a reduction in funding. It was not the first time such a proposal had been aired, nor would it be the last. The likelihood of it being implemented disappeared when, in his preface to the report, Lord Goodman distanced the Arts Council from this recommendation. Nevertheless the idea of a super-orchestra for London continued to resurface in different guises.

In 1970 the LPO returned to the Edinburgh Festival, where for the next decade they were one of the most regular visiting orchestras. Georg Szell should have conducted, but died in July, his place taken by Carlo Maria Guilini, conducting the LPO for the first time. For many years Guilini's concerts in this country had been with the New Philharmonia, but Guilini was unhappy about developments within that orchestra, allowing the LPO to temporarily lure him into their camp.

Successive seasons brought fresh triumphs, as well as occasional disappointments. Haitink opened 1970–71 with *The Rite of Spring*, and in November Boult conducted a concert performance of Vaughan Williams' *The Pilgrim's Progress*, deferred from the previous February. Boult and the cast, led by John Noble as The Pilgrim, went on to record the opera, issued initially on five sides with the sixth taken up by recorded extracts from the rehearsals. These sessions overlapped with two performances of Mahler's Third Symphony, conducted by Haitink, a work which was to feature in the orchestra's programmes with a fair degree of regularity. Disappointment came in January, particularly for members of the London Philharmonic Choir, illness forcing Haitink to cancel two concerts, the first taken over at such short notice by Brian Priestman that the only item remaining from the original programme was the First Piano Concerto of Liszt, with Dvorak's *Symphonic Variations* substituted for Janáček's *Sinfonietta*, and the *Four Sacred Pieces* of Verdi replaced by *Scheherazade*, and at the second concert, which should have included Mahler's First Symphony, Georg Solti substituted the composer's Ninth Symphony, which had constituted the entire programme on the previous Sunday. Other guest conductors included Daniel Barenboim, Jascha Horenstein, Josef Krips, Lorin Maazal and Hans Schmidt-Isserstedt, with several of the most enterprising programmes of the year given under John Pritchard, who led performances of the American composer Gunter Schuller's *Seven Studies on themes of Paul Klee*, Iain Hamilton's *Circus* for Two Trumpets and Orchestra, and Malcolm Williamson's Second Symphony.

Pritchard was again to the fore in the autumn of 1971, when the LPO crossed the Atlantic for an extended tour that opened in Canada, moved down the West Coast of America, and included concerts in Mexico, before terminating in Carnegie Hall. In Mexico the demand for tickets was so great that to accommodate at least some of those clamouring for admittance, additional chairs filled virtually every inch of space in what should have been the aisles, the enthusiasm of the audience reaching such a pitch that the first encore of the evening had to be given before the interval. Because other commitments prevented Haitink from appearing until the tail-end of the tour, the earlier concerts were shared between Pritchard and Erich Leinsdorf.

Once again appearances were deceptive. A schedule of nineteen concerts in twenty-seven days might appear leisurely, but the distances involved meant that almost every day without a concert was spent travelling: with the outside temperature well over a hundred degrees Farenheit, the six-hour journey across the Californian desert, travelling from Fresno to Santa Barbara, underlined the advantages of air conditioning for the modern traveller. The orchestra had to travel without the Orchestral Manager Ted Parker, who was taken ill shortly before the tour opened and died soon afterwards. Recruited by Beecham in 1936 as a member of the cello section, Parker was appointed Orchestral Manager in 1957, for a time carrying out his new duties while still playing in the orchestra. Another long-serving member, he had been with the orchestra for thirty-five years.

That the total cost of £100,000 was met without recourse to the orchestra's own finances was partly thanks to the British Council, who guaranteed the expenses incurred in Canada, San Francisco, and Mexico. The concert in San Francisco formed part of British Week in that city, and was attended by Princess Alexandra, underlining the ambassadorial aspect of touring work. The remaining concerts in the USA were underwritten by the continuing efforts of the London Philharmonic Society (USA) Inc, and the generosity of the LPO's American supporters.

The year brought a closer association with Georg Solti, who took up an appointment as Principal Guest Conductor, in which capacity it was intended that he would give six to eight Festival Hall concerts a year. Solti was now Principal Conductor of the Chicago Symphony Orchestra and the Orchestre de Paris, and, having made his home in this country, chose the LPO as the British orchestra with which he wished to be specially associated. The first fruits of his appointment were seven concerts, which included Elgar's First Symphony, Haydn's *Creation*, and two performances of Mahler's Seventh Symphony. Already honoured by the Queen, Solti had recently applied for British citizenship, an announcement from the platform during the concert at which the Elgar was performed giving the audience the news that his application had been granted, and that he could in future be known as Sir Georg.

For his part Haitink conducted thirteen Festival Hall concerts, more than in any previous year. He was steadily building a repertoire with the LPO, repeating past successes, including the Tenth Symphony of Shostakovitch and Mahler's Third, with Tippett's *Praeludium* for brass, bells and percussion, and the Song Cycle *Notturni et Alba* by John McCabe, among pieces new to him. The year's most unusual work, the first of a series commissioned from British composers, David Bedford's wonderfully titled *Star Clusters, Nebulae and Places in Devon*, scored for two eight-part choirs and brass, was however conducted by John Alldis. The programme note, written by the composer, explained that the text for Choir One was taken from various astronomical catalogues, and that for Choir Two from signposts in Devon and maps of the county, leaving the reader little the wiser as to his intentions, since the note said nothing about the music itself. For his annual pair of Industrial Concerts, a duty he never shirked, Haitink chose the *Pastoral* Symphony and, in discussion with Edward Greenfield he rated this as the most difficult of Beethoven's symphonies to conduct, explaining that 'though the slow movement is marvellously poetic, it is hard not to get the feeling that the audience is going to sleep. That inhibits a performance.'

Yet for all that concerts in the Festival Hall were attracting capacity or near-capacity audiences, success in this area carried a penalty. Under the scheme operated by the London Orchestral Concerts Board, the orchestras undertook to perform a proportion of music by contemporary British composers. This commitment was backed by a British Music Guarantee Fund, but under the rules governing their financing, the orchestras could only call on this fund if all other guarantees had been paid in full. The LPO found itself in a position where, because a number of concerts were so successful that the guarantee was not fully drawn, they were unable to obtain so much as a penny towards their performance of contemporary British music, this despite the fact that they were losing money, £3,000 in 1971–72, on the concerts at which it was performed.

With much of the work undertaken by Haitink and Solti, there was less scope for guest conductors. William Alwyn conducted his Third Symphony, the prelude to a recorded cycle of his symphonies for the Lyrita label: Josef Krips was given two concerts, and Eugen Jochum commenced a cycle, spread over three seasons, in which he conducted, in sequence, the twelve *London Symphonies* of Haydn. These were also recorded, by DGG. Regrettably international politics prevented the appearance of David Oistrakh as both conductor and soloist, his visit cancelled by the Russian government on the grounds of the 'extremely abnormal measures taken by the British government towards official Soviet representatives in England', a reference to the recent expulsion of various members of the KGB.

Concerts at the 1972 Edinburgh Festival, under Guilini and Daniel Barenboim, formed an auspicious start to the Fortieth Anniversary Season, but there was a melancholy aspect to their Prom appearances. Bernard Walton, who should have performed Mozart's Clarinet Concerto, had died from a heart attack earlier in the summer, his experience, as a player and as a member of the Board, being greatly missed. Other orchestral changes saw a new face behind the timpani, Christopher Seaman, who had always intended pursuing a conducting career, having taken up the post of Assistant Conductor of the BBC Scottish Orchestra, his place filled by Alan Cumberland; Nicholas Busch, formerly principal horn in the New Philharmonia, took over this position in succession to Ronald Harris; Robert Hill was appointed principal clarinet, David Watkins replaced Elisabeth Fletcher as harpist, and Santiago Sabino Carvalho took up a position in the cello section.

Before launching the season in the Festival Hall, the LPO gave two concerts in Berlin, where Haitink conducted Bruckner's Eighth Symphony and a piece fast becoming one of the his calling-cards, the Tenth Symphony of Shostakovitch. Both symphonies had been performed at the Proms, helping to ensure that these works were deep in the players' consciousness. The many tributes to the orchestra included *Der Tagenspiegel's* appreciation of 'the noble tone of the London orchestra', their reception showing the LPO had nothing to fear from comparisons with the home team of Karajan and the Berlin Philharmonic. The fee quoted to the LPO for these two concerts was 100,000 Deutschmarks, then the equivalent of £12,000, a far cry from today's rate of exchange.

The Anniversary Season opened with a gala concert, given in association with the Variety Club of Great Britain, at which Barenboim conducted Elgar's Second Symphony, with Pinchas Zuckerman as soloist in Mozart's First Violin Concerto. Haitink's contribution to the celebrations included a second gala concert, given in support of the LPO's National Appeal Fund, with Artur Rubinstein as soloist; Mahler's Sixth Symphony; the first London performance of Ligeti's *Lontano*; the premiere of Iain Hamilton's Concerto for Orchestra, commissioned by the LPO, and two performances of Bruckner's Fourth Symphony. He conducted two additional concerts in January. The first, part of a poorly attended season of Winter Proms, was largely taken up by Mahler's Sixth, and in the second, which formed part of the musical element of the celebrations marking Britain's entry to the EEC, Haitink and the LPO performed Elgar's Overture *In The South* and the Fourth Symphony of Vaughan Williams, and were joined by members of his Glyndebourne cast in excerpts from *Il Seraglio*. Later in the month Haitink and the orchestra made another short continental visit, performing the Mahler Sixth in Rotterdam and Amsterdam, the enthusiasm of the Dutch matching that of the audience in Berlin the previous autumn.

Guest conductors included Jochum, who gave two further concerts in his unfolding cycle of Haydn's *London* Symphonies, Krips, and Kurt Sanderling. Solti conducted Bruckner's Seventh, which was performed twice, a Bartok programme, and *The Damnation of Faust*; Yevgeni Svetlanov brought the State Choir of the USSR to Britain for the *Oratorio Pathétique* by the hitherto unknown Russian composer Sviridov, which made no great impression; and Boult's contribution included two Vaughan Williams Centenary Concerts.

Above all, the year included an overseas tour unlike any other undertaken by the LPO. The calendar included, during March, ten concerts forming part of the Hong Kong Festival, three conducted by Edo de Waart, three by Erich Leinsdorf and four by John Pritchard, with Ida Haendel, John Lill and Michael Roll as soloists. In October 1972, during the course of a visit to Peking by the Foreign Secretary, Sir Alec Douglas-Home, one of the subjects discussed was the improvement of cultural relations. In return for an exhibition of their treasures in London the Chinese asked for a visit by the LPO, an invitation immediately relayed to the LPO by the Foreign Office. Fortuitously John Pritchard was scheduled to be working with the LPO in London, and Ida Haendel was free to travel as soloist. By cancelling an Industrial Concert and a Festival Hall concert and postponing a concert in Hastings for a month, it was possible to extend their stay in the Far East to embrace concerts in Peking, Shanghai and Canton.

China was a closed book to all but a minority of Westerners. The regime frowned on contacts with foreigners, and apart from diplomats and a few businessmen, almost the only visitors allowed were members of the Communist Party or known Communist sympathisers. Bearing in mind the circumstances surrounding Thomas Russell's dismissal, it was more than a little ironic that Eric Bravington now found himself leading the orchestra to China in his role as Managing Director.

The Cultural Revolution had rendered performances of Western music all but non-existent, but if players or management harboured doubts about their reception, these were put to rest at the frontier, where customs formalities were dispensed with and the first of a succession of lunches and banquets preceded the train journey to Canton and a flight to Peking.

Hosts and visitors were equally curious about each other. The first encounter with the Chinese public came the morning after their arrival, with a packed hall for the rehearsal, a feature of their visit being that rehearsals were as well and enthusiastically attended as the evening concerts. Two programmes were given, the first comprising *Cockaigne*, Brahms' Violin Concerto, in which Ida Haendel played the solo part, and Beethoven's Seventh, and the second the *Academic Festival* Overture, Vaughan Williams' *Tallis Fantasia*, Haydn's Trumpet Concerto, played by Gordon Webb, and the Eighth Symphony of Dvorak. Each programme was given in Peking and Shanghai, and the first was also played in Canton. In addition to the planned programmes the orchestra added a number of unscheduled items, including an excerpt from a Chinese revolutionary ballet *The Red Detachment of Women*, which their hosts invited them to perform and which was thereafter played each night as an encore. These additional items were introduced by John Pritchard, whose enthusiasm and enjoyment readily communicated themselves to the audience, one of his throwaway comments providing one of the few sources of embarrassment. Introducing Johann Strauss' *Radetzky March*, he described Count Radetzky as a freedom fighter from an earlier age, only for his interpreter to explain that so far as China was concerned Radetzky was not regarded as a friend of the people.

As well as visits to the Great Wall and the Forbidden City, a packed itinerary included a cruise down the Whangpoo River, a tributary of the Yangtze, a visit to Canton Zoo, entertainment by the Canton Acrobatic Troupe and a performance of a Chinese ballet, *The White Haired Girl*. In addition to their own music-making there were opportunities for meeting with, and hearing performances by, Chinese musicians, several players trying their hand at traditional Chinese instruments, with varying degrees of success. Discussion with their Chinese colleagues revealed that as a result of political constraints, which required strict 'correctness' in artistic matters, they were only allowed to perform a very limited amount of music. It was difficult to understand how the Chinese musicians could have retained their enthusiasm when they were restricted to performing four operas, two or three full-length ballets and a handful of other pieces, and because everything was composed collectively, the music contained little or no variety, much of it sounding like a third-hand distillation of a score written for a romantic Hollywood film script.

Touring had increased to the point where it was a regular feature of the players' lives. This was the twentieth undertaken since the end of the war, sixteen of which had taken place in the last ten years, but this was a unique experience, the visit to China putting the seal on the Fortieth Anniversary Season, even if it did not mark its end.

Returning home, it was back to work with a vengeance, with six major concerts and their rehearsals in the space of ten days. Haitink contributed a pair of concerts, the first including a performance of *Also Sprach Zarathustra*, and the second given over to Brahms, with Barenboim as soloist in the First Piano Concerto. It was Josef Krips, however, who had charge of the closing concert, a programme comprising the *Unfinished* Symphony and, a fitting conclusion to the year, Mahler's *Resurrection* Symphony. Eric Bravington, whose report on the LPO's activities was a feature of each yearbook, writing with justifiable pride of their achievements, might have reflected, as Mahler's Symphony came to a triumphant close, how the LPO itself had risen from the near-disasters of 1957 to become one of Britain's most valuable artistic assets, the decision to invite Bernard Haitink to become Principal Conductor succeeding up to and beyond expectations.

14

Haitink – The Later Years 1972–79

Despite the achievements of the past six years, Eric Bravington was nursing doubts about some aspects of the relationship with Haitink. His responsibilities with the Concertgebouw meant that there were times when Haitink was unable to accompany his London orchestra overseas, while as time passed he came under increasing pressure to accept other engagements. From his association with the LPO Haitink's career began to move in the opposite direction to that of many continental conductors, who learn their trade in the opera house, progressing to the concert hall at a later stage. In 1972 he conducted at Glyndebourne for the first time, making his debut with *Il Seraglio*, returning the next year to conduct *The Magic Flute*, and in 1975 *The Rake's Progress*. These outside pressures, and continuing responsibilities with the Concertgebouw Orchestra, meant he was not always free to accompany his London orchestra overseas. The visit to Hong Kong had been one such case, for Haitink's name had been included in the original schedule, from which he asked to be released because of the pressure of other work, though when the opportunity to perform in China presented itself, it was fortuitous that John Pritchard was able to extend his stay in the Far East. This was a disadvantage that could have been foreseen; indeed it was unlikely that any other conductor of international stature would have been able to offer more time than Haitink was able to spare.

Another factor which may have affected relations was Haitink's reluctance to become too closely involved in the orchestra's business affairs. He could advise on musical policy, the choice of guest conductors and repertoire, and the recruitment of players, but despite his title of Music Director, he was in no position to dictate, even on matters of artistic policy, still less if there was a clash between artistic and business interests. Ideally an orchestra which rehearses on the morning of a concert should have the afternoon left free, but artistic ideals are sometimes subservient to business requirements. From time to time work in the recording studio, or taping the score for a film, can be sandwiched between the morning rehearsal and the concert in the evening, work which helps pay for other activities, the dictates of finance being such that it is essential to accept every possible engagement, even when some work may be thought to be of secondary artistic quality. Turn work down and there is the possibility of future sessions going elsewhere. Whatever Haitink's thoughts, and however much his stance might be open to misinterpretation, administrative and financial questions were matters on which, understandably, he deemed it best not to interfere.

What was apparently of more concern was the fact that, for all the state of excellence to which the orchestra had risen, there had been few fringe benefits, in the shape of recording sessions. Haitink was recording exclusively for Philips, and it was understandable that, based in Holland, that company preferred to work with the Concertgebouw, with whom they had a long-standing relationship. Haitink and the LPO did in fact make a number of records for Philips, notably a cycle of Liszt's symphonic poems, and the three great Stravinsky ballets, *The Firebird*, *Petrushka* and *The Rite of Spring*, and over the next two or three years there was an increase in the number of sessions undertaken for them. On balance, however, this could be viewed as an area where London was losing out to Amsterdam.

In addition to the concerns being voiced about the level of recording work undertaken with Haitink, unfavourable comparisons were being made with the high profile obtained by Andre Previn and the LSO. Following the appointment of Solti as Principal Guest Conductor, Bravington began trying to persuade his colleagues that the LPO would benefit from the higher international profile enjoyed by the older man. Initially he suggested a joint conductorship, ultimately proposing that it would be better for the orchestra if Solti were to be in sole charge. Unhappily, the internal debate on the relative merits of the two men was brought to Haitink's notice, unsettling his relations with Bravington. It would be several years before this process was finally worked out; in the meantime orchestra and conductor were still to share many days of artistic triumph.

Yet, viewed externally, it is hard to see why these concerns should have arisen. The LPO was in great demand in the recording studio. As well as recording with Haitink for Philips, and Boult for EMI and Lyrita, sessions were undertaken for half a dozen other companies, the works committed to disc including recordings of the Elgar symphonies for CBS and Decca, under Barenboim and Solti respectively, and Jochum's on-going cycle of Haydn's last symphonies for DGG. There was also a steady increase in their contribution to the Classics for Pleasure catalogue, for whom, by 1973, sales of their records had passed the half-million mark. Year in year out, the volume of work in the recording studio ensured a full diary.

One indication of the satisfactory way in which the calendar was filled was the fact that however much Boult preferred recording with the LPO, they were not always available, sometimes because they were performing at Glyndebourne, their work there apparently causing him some irritation, to the extent that he was even known to remark that the best thing that could happen to the place was that it should be burned down. Thus in August 1970 it was with the LSO rather than the LPO that Boult made new recordings of the *Enigma Variations* and Vaughan Williams' *Job*. When these were completed within the allotted span, he opted to use the remaining time to record the Third Symphony of Brahms. EMI had largely been using Boult's services to record works by British composers, but the success of the Brahms led EMI to invite him to record the rest of that composer's symphonies, followed over the next few years with music by Bach, Mozart, Schubert, Tchaikovsky and Wagner, as well as his final thoughts on the Elgar symphonies. All but a handful of these were recorded with the LPO, one major exception being *The Dream of Gerontius*, recorded in the summer of 1975, for which the New Philharmonia was employed.

Other major recording commitments in the 1970s involved Charles Groves, who recorded Delius' *Mass of Life*, Aldo Ceccato, who conducted *Maria Stuarda* by Donizetti, and Raymond Leppard and his Glyndebourne cast were in Argo's studios to repeat their performance of Cavalli's *La Calisto*. The score of this last named had been given an extremely rich arrangement by Leppard, one which might not have met with the approval of the purists but delighted the Glyndebourne audience. The volume of recording work had reached a level such that, even if Philips had wished to arrange additional sessions for Haitink in London, it would have been difficult to fit these into the diary.

It was concern to secure recording work, and the fees that went with it, that led to involvement in proposals for the creation of a 'super-orchestra', a proposal envisaging a merger between the LPO and the New Philharmonia. Impetus for the idea came from several sources. The New Philharmonia was experiencing problems. Klemperer had retired from the concert platform, Lorin Maazel had resigned as Assistant Principal Conductor, Guilini had temporarily switched his affections to the LPO, and despite generous outside support, the New Philharmonia's activities were running at a loss, their reserves depleted to a point where its continued existence was under threat. Merger with another orchestra could be their salvation. The Arts Council were supportive – a merger would reduce the number of mouths they had to feed – and EMI favoured the idea, which would have served their recording interests.

With encouragement from these sources the New Philharmonia began to develop proposals for a merged orchestra, based on the assumption that Daniel Barenboim would be the Musical Director, envisaging that by taking the best of the conducting talent working with the LPO and the New Philharmonia, it would be possible to bring together an outstanding list of conductors, both for concerts and recordings. In addition to Barenboim, the names of Guilini, Haitink, Mehta and Solti were among those canvassed. Gerald McDonald, General Manager of the New Philharmonia, and Peter Andry of EMI put their ideas to Bravington, and after preliminary discussions involving the Arts

Council, Bravington undertook to produce costings. The knowledge that discussions were taking place was supposedly restricted to a closed circle, however such matters have a habit of leaking out, as became apparent when one of the New Philharmonia's backers, who had got wind of what was afoot, expressed an interest that went well beyond providing financial support, proposing to buy the orchestra outright, on condition that while the orchestra might still have its own elected governing body, overall control would rest with him.

Bravington's attitude is interesting. Artistically the LPO were riding high, with the New Philharmonia's position considerably weaker than theirs. Viewed objectively, a merger must have involved one of the two orchestras losing its identity to the other, and with much of the financial support for the proposals coming from the other side of the table, there was no certainty it would be the LPO whose name would survive. Nevertheless, by the autumn of 1973 Bravington had completed his assessment of the scheme's viability, based on financial support from the Arts Council and other sources equivalent to half the estimated running cost of the orchestra. Even though none of the conductors had signified agreement – several had not been approached – the scheme's sponsors were all but ready to submit their proposals to various interested parties, including the Arts Council and the GLC, with a view to guaranteeing the financial support required.

It was at this point that the scheme broke on the rock that has been the undoing of initiatives to try and change the pattern of London's orchestral music – the overriding importance placed by directors and players alike on their independence. Even an orchestra much increased in size, including a doubling of principal positions and a greatly enlarged string section, would have involved widespread redundancy among the rank and file, and the stipulation by one of the scheme's backers that overall control would pass into his hands was a factor that would have further prejudiced many members of both orchestras against it. In the event, the proposals were never submitted to the players for approval. Had they been, it seems likely that even if the necessary financial support had been forthcoming, a majority could well have voted against them.

These abortive merger negotiations took place during the Fortieth Anniversary season, and it would have been surprising if rumours had not reached Haitink's ears. Nevertheless, the partnership between conductor and orchestra was achieving all that could have been asked of it. In the summer of 1973 Haitink brought the Glyndebourne production of *The Magic Flute* to the Albert Hall, and repeated one of his great successes of the previous year, Bruckner's Eighth Symphony. A few weeks later he conducted the opening concerts of a European tour embracing Austria, Belgium, Germany and Switzerland, challenging the Austrian musical community on its home ground by giving two performances of Bruckner's Fourth Symphony in Vienna.

The lion's share of work on this tour was in the hands of Josef Krips, who conducted performances of Humphrey Searle's Second Symphony and a programme combining Elgar's *Enigma Variations* with yet another Bruckner Symphony, the Seventh. His tour programmes formed the basis of the opening concerts of 1973-74, a season which could have been an anticlimax after the celebrations and excitements of the previous year. In practice this was far from being the case, the LPO continuing to offer London some fine music-making, though the year was not without its problems. The mineworkers' strike and the three-day week led to cancellation of a number of recording sessions as well as a proposed television recording of Britten's *War Requiem*, some judicious switching by the Concerts Director Rosalie Cody saving a number of sessions. One Festival Hall concert was cancelled, and because the players were paid by the session, the necessity of cancelling some work meant that the dispute adversely affected their earnings.

On the concert platform Barenboim led two performances of Elgar's First Symphony, Eugen Jochum completed his cycle of Haydn's *London* Symphonies, and Solti conducted five concerts, including two performances of Mahler's Sixth Symphony, and the British premiere of a work by Henze, *Heliogabalus Imperator*. The performance of Henze's work was not without 'mishap'. The score called for an unusual addition to the normal range of percussion instruments, a 'lion's roar', the responsibility for which was placed in the hands of Alan Cumberland, one of the few occasions when he performed on an instrument other than his timpani. All went well in rehearsal, but the performance was jinxed, the instrument coming noisily to pieces in Cumberland's hands, distracting and embarrassing the player so much that he missed his next timpani entry. The barely suppressed mirth among the back rows of the orchestra conveyed itself to the audience, which had become restless, Henze's music being some way removed from what they expected at one of Solti's concerts, Cumberland's mishap providing many of them with more enjoyment than the piece itself. The brass section also encountered difficulties during the performance and were delighted at the commendation by one reviewer of their 'impeccable entries'.

Haitink's major contribution was a Beethoven cycle, with Vladimir Ashkenazy as soloist in the Piano Concertos, the *Financial Times* reporting of the opening concert that 'the LPO's performance of the *Eroica* Symphony was so finely prepared, so clearly reasoned and ready, that it must be safe to welcome the Beethoven cycle as the high noon of the present concert season', writing a fortnight later of the concluding concert, 'The LPO's Beethoven cycle has come to a joyful and splendid end...not only were all these masterpieces done, but they were wonderfully well done too. In Haitink we have a superlative Beethoven conductor, able to command the whole range of emotional response required by such a widespread task.'

London had long suffered from lack of adequate rehearsal facilities. As a general rule the Festival Hall was only available on the day of the concert, preliminary rehearsals having to be held elsewhere, in halls whose acoustics might bear little or no relation to those of the Festival Hall, often with poor ancillary facilities. A solution was found following the deconsecration of Holy Trinity, Southwark, a building which, as a result of population movement and the decline in church-going, had been declared redundant. Permission was granted for conversion of the church into a rehearsal hall, primarily for the use of the LPO and the LSO, who formed the Southwark Rehearsal Trust, jointly headed by the Earl of Shaftesbury on behalf of the LPO and Sir Jack Lyons for the LSO. The cost of conversion was estimated at five to six hundred thousand pounds and, despite a serious fire shortly before the work was due to start, which destroyed the roof and seriously damaged the interior, the conversion went ahead. In addition to private gifts, funds were donated by the Arts Council, the Department of the Environment, the GLC, the Musicians Union, the Pilgrim Trust and the Henry Wood National Memorial Trust; after consultation with both orchestras, the Trustees decided to rename the building the Henry Wood Hall, a decision that was universally welcomed.

The work of conversion took nearly two years, the opening ceremony taking place on 16 June 1975 when, before an invited audience, members of the LPO, conducted by Haitink, performed the *Siegfried Idyll*, the LSO's Wind Ensemble contributed Mozart's Serenade K388, and their Brass Ensemble, Johann Christoph Pezel's *Sonata* and a *Canzona* by Giovanni Gabrieli. The LPO and the LSO enjoyed priority booking rights, but many other orchestras and ensembles used the hall, and as it was equipped with two recording control rooms it was soon playing host to numerous record companies. Provision had also been made to house both orchestras' music libraries, which were located in the crypt, with the players' welfare looked after by means of kitchen facilities and a cafeteria.

The Board had been looking to strengthen the roster of conductors with whom the orchestra was working, of which Solti's appointment as Principal Guest Conductor had been the first step. In March 1974, coinciding with the opening concert of Haitink's Beethoven cycle, Bravington announced that Barenboim and Guilini had agreed to work closely with the LPO. This was a major coup, the line-up of international conductors including many of the names canvassed during the negotiations with the New Philharmonia. Bravington, who came in for some criticism concerning the high fees sought by some artists, defended himself in the London Philharmonic Society's Newsletter, pointing out that it was the quality of the roster of conductors that enabled the LPO to out-sell the other London orchestras, the revenue earned from full, or near full, houses a justification for this policy. Though it would be another year before the new arrangements came fully into effect, Barenboim, Guilini and Haitink all took part in the 1974 Edinburgh Festival, Guilini conducting two performances of Verdi's *Requiem*, Haitink's programmes including *Erwartung* and Bruckner's Fourth Symphony, and Barenboim framing *Lieder eines fahrenden Gesellen*, sung by Dietrich Fischer-Dieskau, with *Falstaff* and the *Enigma* Variations.

The early months of 1975 were especially trying for the concert department, illness leading to a spate of changes. Dietrich Fischer-Dieskau, due to make his conducting debut in London, was unable to do so, and was replaced by John Pritchard, while Haitink was laid low by a debilitating virus; forced to rest on medical advice, he cancelled all his concerts in March, his place variously taken by Andrew Davis, Karl Richter, Erich Leinsdorf and Colin Davis, with a pair of Industrial Concerts taken over by the orchestra's former sub-leader Arthur Davison. Replacements had also to be found for the recently deceased Josef Krips, and to round off this series of problems the political situation in Portugal led to cancellation of a tour of that country. Nevertheless the year ended on a high note, Guilini making his Festival Hall debut with the LPO in four concerts, the *Missa Solemnis*, two performances of Mahler's Ninth Symphony, and a programme in which Janet Baker sang Berlioz' Song Cycle *Nuits d'été*, the concert concluding with the Ninth Symphony of Schubert.

The last of Guilini's concerts was given in association with the Royal Philharmonic Society, an arrangement relieving the LPO of some of the costs, and in a new departure the Yearbook for 1974-75 identified three concerts given with the aid of commercial sponsorship. This new form of support came from Philips, who were celebrating their Golden Jubilee Year. There was also commercial funding from EMI for the Industrial Concerts which, with the company's permission, were retitled Classics for Pleasure. During the interval of the opening concert a presentation was made to Wills and the orchestra by EMI, in recognition of the fact that sales of records made for Classics for Pleasure, and with the financial backing of Wills, had passed the million mark.

Financial support from companies in the form of sponsorship of specific concerts was to assume increasing importance in balancing the deficit that always existed, even with a full hall, between the box office receipts and the mounting cost of concert-giving. The number of sponsored concerts steadily grew, to five in 1975-76, and the following year, in addition to eight sponsored concerts in the Festival Hall, there was support from Courage, who took over the sponsorship of Classics for Pleasure, with Marks and Spencer providing assistance for concerts at the Fairfield Hall, Croydon. Though sponsors neither asked for, or expected, any kind of artistic input, their involvement gave rise to certain obligations, usually in the shape of a number of seats for the use of the company and its guests, together with pre-concert hospitality. There was also an increase in the number of companies joining the London Philharmonic Society as Corporate Members. With inflation at unprecedented levels, such support was invaluable.

The 1975 Edinburgh Festival involved performances of the Beethoven Ninth, under Guilini, and Rostropovitch made his conducting debut with the LPO, accompanying his wife, Galina Vishnevskaya, in the first British performance of the arrangement by Shostakovitch of Mussorgsky's *Songs and Dances of Death*. Guilini's concerts brought several principal players to the fore: Roger Winfield, Robert Hill, Neil Levesley and Nicholas Busch as soloists in Mozart's Sinfonia Concertante for oboe, clarinet, bassoon and horn, and Rodney Friend, Alexander Cameron, Roger Winfield and Neil Levesley in Haydn's Concertante for violin, cello, oboe and bassoon. The LPO also gave three Proms, conducted by Haitink: a concert performance of *The Rake's Progress*, a straightforward programme including Dvorak's Violin Concerto and Tchaikovsky's Fifth Symphony, the third concert opening with *Metamorphosen/Dance* by Alexander Goehr, premiered the previous winter, and concluding with Mahler's First Symphony.

Two contrasting tours took place during the autumn, a visit to Russia in October, and in the following month a tour of Scotland and the North of England. It was twenty years since the LPO's last visit to the Soviet Union, and concerts were again given in Moscow and Leningrad, each programme including a work by a British composer. In addition to Goehr's *Metamorphosen/ Dance*, the works chosen were Tippett's *Fantasia concertante on a Theme by Corelli*, Vaughan Williams' *Wasps* Overture and Walton's *Partita*, the tour repertoire including Beethoven's *Pastoral*, Dvorak's Eighth, Mahler's First and the Shostakovitch Tenth, the performance of which was attended by the composer's widow. As many visitors to Russia have discovered, baths and basins often lack one vital item, a plug. In Leningrad viola players Judith Swan and Irmeli Rawson found that in addition the hotel room allocated to them also lacked soap and towels. Having expressed a fair degree of indignation to one another on the absence of these commodities, they were taken aback when almost immediately afterwards both soap and towels arrived, uncertain whether to attribute this swift response to efficiency on the part of the hotel or the presence of a listening device. The absence of a bath plug remained an unresolved problem. It was most emphatically not the LPO who were the source of the story concerning the visitor to Moscow who, determined to uncover the 'bug' he was convinced had been planted in every hotel room, thought his efforts had been crowned with success when he discovered and unscrewed a metal object under the carpet, to the bewilderment of the hotel management unable to understand why a guest should have sent the chandelier in the room below crashing to the floor, a story attributed to the RPO, numerous visiting bankers and almost every visiting foreign trade delegation.

The British leg of this touring activity took them to Edinburgh, Glasgow, Manchester, Huddersfield and Liverpool. The concert in Huddersfield was presented by the local authority, and those in the other cities visited were given in conjunction with the Scottish National Orchestra, the Hallé and the Royal

Liverpool Philharmonic. The cost of touring had risen substantially since the days when the LPO had been 'on the road' on a regular basis, and these concerts were made possible thanks to Commercial Union, who undertook to meet any deficit, British Rail, who covered the cost of rail fares, and British Transport Hotels. For Haitink it added up to one of his busiest years with the LPO. Eight concerts in Russia; five in the North of England; thirteen in the Festival Hall; a pair of Industrial Concerts; three Proms; two concerts in Croydon; one each in Eastbourne and Oxford; performances at Glyndebourne, and a considerable amount of recording work for Philips, for whom Haitink and the orchestra embarked on a cycle of the Beethoven symphonies, with the *Eroica* and the Seventh committed to disc in November 1974, the sessions for the remaining symphonies commencing in August 1975 and completed the following May. Four of the Piano Concertos were also recorded, with Alfred Brendel as soloist, with the final concerto held over until the next year.

In line with the announcement made two years earlier Solti, Barenboim and Guilini played a prominent part during 1975-76. Solti's concerts were given under the title 'The Solti Series', each concentrating on the music of a single composer: Bartok, Beethoven, Bruckner, Stravinsky, and Mahler. Barenboim spent three widely spaced out weeks with the orchestra, conducting all the Schumann symphonies, Beethoven's Fifth, Tchaikovsky's Fourth, an Elgar programme with Pinchas Zukerman as soloist in the Violin Concerto, and two excursions off the beaten track, the Concerto Opus 24 by Webern, and the Concerto for Orchestra by Lutoslawski. Guilini's Festival Hall concerts were marred by illness, Edward Downes taking his place at two of them, Guilini recovering in time to lead the players in Bruckner's Ninth Symphony.

Far from being a holiday period, August was one of the busiest months of the year. In 1976, hard on the heels of the last Glyndebourne performance of the summer, the LPO took part in three Proms, spent a week in the television studios recording productions from the Glyndebourne season, and in the last week of the month were back in Edinburgh for concerts in which Guilini conducted *Das Lied von der Erde* and two performances of the *Missa Solemnis*. The LPO's Proms were the last in which they were led by Rodney Friend, who was departing to join the New York Philharmonic. His influence was recognised by an appreciation in the Yearbook for 1976-77 which recorded that 'His dynamic work in this vital position during the past 12 years was an important factor in bringing the orchestra to its present excellence'. He was succeeded by David Nolan, a former member of the first violin section, who had spent the past two years as principal second violin of the LSO.

The opening Festival Hall concerts of 1976-77 offered staple fare, two Brahms concerts under Jochum, and a Tchaikovsky cycle under Rostropovitch embracing all the numbered symphonies, *Manfred*, arias sung by his wife Galina Visnevskaya, and the First Piano Concerto, with Ilana Vered as soloist, bringing an added bonus in the shape of recordings of the symphonies.

Haitink's opening concerts included *La Mer*, the Tenth Symphony of Shostakovitch and the first performance of Malcolm Arnold's specially composed *Philharmonic Concerto*; these, and a pair of Classics for Pleasure concerts, at which the major offering was the *Eroica*, used to prepare for a tour of the USA forming part of the bicentennial celebrations.

The bicentennial tour, conducted throughout by Haitink, was made possible by financial backing from Commercial Union Assurance. Opening in Chicago, concerts were given in towns and cities in the Midwest before conductor and players arrived on the eastern seaboard, where they played in Washington, New York, Philadelphia and Boston. The tour was not one of the happiest undertaken by the orchestra: inauguration of 'The Solti Series' had sparked increased internal debate between those who placed great emphasis in Haitink's achievement in returning the LPO to the front rank of international orchestras, and those who, like Bravington, believed, for one reason or another, that the time was ripe for change. Haitink was aware that he no longer commanded the complete support of the Board, and relations between Bravington and Haitink were becoming increasingly strained. In fact Haitink still had a strong core of support among the players, but few of those outside the Boardroom had any inkling as to the way in which events were shaping.

On a lighter note, Chicago was the scene of a match between the LPO darts team and the Chicago Area Associated Darters. The darts team was one of the by-products of the Long Interval at Glyndebourne, and the match in Chicago the result of a chance meeting in the Festival Hall between trumpet player Michael Clothier and an American visitor. The Americans took the contest rather more seriously than the visitors, choosing their team by means of an eliminating contest involving 3000 players, and it was no surprise that a jet-lagged LPO team was beaten 5-2. The darts team's claim to be 'the only teetotal darts team in the world' was viewed with a fair degree of cynicism.

The arrangements for the year's work in the Festival Hall could have been interpreted as a sign that the status of the Principal Conductor was being placed below that of some of the leading guest conductors. The Business Plan drawn up by Bravington envisaged that for marketing purposes star billing would be given to the roster of guest conductors working with the orchestra, and to 'The Solti Series' was now added 'The Barenboim Series'. In contrast, there was a marked reduction in the amount of work Haitink was scheduled to undertake. Compared with the thirteen Festival Hall concerts allotted to him the previous year, he was down for eight, seven of the LPO's own concerts and one for the Royal Philharmonic Society, a reduction which was partly explained by the commitment of three weeks to touring the USA.

During the 1970s the LPO acquired the reputation of an orchestra whose programmes were firmly based on the established repertoire, yet for all that audiences were to a great extent shy of contemporary music in anything other than small doses, every year brought a clutch of unusual items, with 1976-77 no exception. Kiri Te Kanawa was the soloist in the first performance of *For Ophelia* for soprano and orchestra, a work commissioned by the World Centre for Shakespeare Studies from the Newcastle-born Italian composer, Raffaello de Banfield; Haitink conducted the London premiere of Berio's arrangement of music by Boccherini, *La Ritirata Notturna di Madrid*; there were further hearings for Nicholas Maw's *Concert Music for Orchestra*, derived from his Opera *The Rising of the Moon*, and David Bedford's *Star Clusters, Nebulae and Places in Devon*, but when Haitink was indisposed it was necessary to cancel a revival of the *Concerto for the Instruments of an Orchestra*, by John Mayer, a former member of the LPO, which had been premiered the previous year. With Barenboim appearing in Haitink's place, John Mayer's work and the *Italian* Symphony of Mendelssohn were replaced by the Ninth Symphony of Bruckner. The 'Solti Series' occupied most of February, including concerts devoted to Mozart, Elgar, Brahms and Strauss, though the latter, comprising *Ein Heldenleben*, *Don Juan* and *Till Eulenspigel*, seemed a less than ideal programme, offering insufficient variety to make a satisfactory concert, while illness prevented him from conducting the Brahms programme, for which his place was taken by Charles Mackerras. Artistically the season was a great success, and though audiences had fallen slightly, to 83 per cent of the hall's capacity, this was well in advance of the level achieved by any other London orchestra.

One result of the engagement to perform at Glyndebourne was that demand for the orchestra's services had reached a point where an invitation to take part in the 1977 Edinburgh Festival was actually turned down, the LPO having been engaged to accompany six performances of Glyndebourne's production of *Don Giovanni*, given in the Lyttelton auditorium of the National Theatre, three under Haitink and three under Andrew Davis. Haitink also took charge of the LPO's annual appearances at the Proms, a concert performance of *Don Giovanni*, a programme including the Brahms Violin Concerto and Dvorak's Eighth Symphony and Beethoven's *Choral* Symphony. This last concert was hardly over before, two days later, Haitink was conducting Mahler's *Resurrection* Symphony at the opening concert of a new season in the Festival Hall.

Though it was not immediately apparent, Bravington was by now suffering from the onset of major illness. During 1975-76 he had been advised by his doctor to rest, but it was not until some time later that a brain tumour was diagnosed, leading to major surgery and a convalescence lasting several months. It seems likely that Bravington's illness affected his judgement and had much to do with his increasing determination to replace Haitink with Solti. One straw in the wind was a recommendation to turn down an invitation from the Concertgebouw Orchestra to give two concerts under Haitink in Amsterdam, at a time when that orchestra would be occupied in accompanying opera performances, the reason given that the concerts would clash with a projected tour of Spain. In the event, negotiations for the Spanish tour proved abortive. It was a situation which could not continue, a press release in July 1977 announcing that Haitink would be relinquishing his appointment at the end of the 1978-79 season. As planned by Bravington, his successor was to be Sir Georg Solti.

Despite problems behind the scenes the year brought official recognition of Haitink's partnership with the LPO, both at home and abroad, with his appointment, in November 1977, as an honorary Knight Commander of the Order of the British Empire. Unlike Solti, who as well as making his home in London had taken British citizenship, Haitink remained a Dutch citizen, and for this reason cannot be known as Sir Bernard. On the concert platform he continued to expand his repertoire of British music. During 1977-78 he conducted Britten's *Sinfonia da Requiem*, the First and Second Symphonies of Elgar and, in line with his customary practice regarding works by contemporary British composers, two performances of Alexander Goehr's *Psalm IV*. He was also scheduled to conduct the early unnumbered Bruckner Symphony, Number 0 in D minor (*Die Nullte*), but two days beforehand he was laid low by a virus infection. At 11 p.m. that evening, less than forty-eight hours before the concert was due to take place, Walter Susskind agreed to step into the breach. Receiving the score at 9.50 the next morning, forty minutes before the first rehearsal was due to start, he secured a performance which did great credit to both conductor and orchestra.

The autumn of 1977 saw the debut of a conductor who was to become closely associated with the LPO, Klaus Tennstedt. Born in 1926, the post-war division of Germany found him living in the Communist East, where he held appointments in Dresden and Schwerin and appeared with the Dresden State Opera Orchestra and the Leipzig Gewandhaus. In 1971 he escaped to the West, disguising himself in order to do so, where, after conducting in Sweden, he obtained a minor post as General Music Director of the Kiel Opera. By now he was in his mid-forties, and it was by chance that he found himself launched on an international career. The Toronto Symphony Orchestra were in urgent need of a replacement for an indisposed conductor, and Tennstedt was invited to fill the gap. The Toronto concerts were outstandingly successful, leading to an equally successful debut with the Boston Symphony Orchestra, followed by a spate of invitations from throughout Europe and North America. His first concert with the LPO included the First Symphony of Mahler, a composer with whom he and the LPO were to become closely associated. There was an immediate rapport between conductor and players, and though Tennstedt's diary for the following year was full he entered into an agreement committing him to conduct the LPO every year for a five-year period, commencing in 1979. It was to become one of the happiest of partnerships between conductor and orchestra.

For the first time for some years the schedule for 1977-78 contained no overseas tour. It was not, however, a year without incident. London's orchestras were again under the microscope, this time from Sir Frank Figgures. Concerns about financing and programme content were never far away, and this enquiry was initiated by the London Orchestral Concert Board. The report covered much the same ground as the Goodman Report of 1965 and the Peacock Report of 1970, and in the absence of new funding initiatives it was difficult to do more than recommend the Board to continue funding London's orchestras along the lines already in operation.

It was not a report which contributed greatly to the solution of the day-to-day problems faced by management, though it led to yet another proposal aimed at creating a 'super orchestra' for London. The four independent orchestras were asked to respond to a proposal that one of them should become fully contracted, i.e. the players would be paid on a salary basis rather than for each session they worked. It was an idea which in this instance failed for lack of any kind of support from within the musical profession and, even more important, because in the event there was no likelihood of finding the additional finance which would be required by such a scheme.

Age was taking its toll and Sir Adrian Boult's concert appearances had become steadily fewer in number, and it was no surprise when in 1978 he announced his retirement from the concert platform. His last Festival Hall concert with the LPO had taken place the previous year when, in a meeting of youth and age, the twenty-two-year-old Simon Rattle conducted the first half, with Boult responsible for Vaughan Williams' Ninth Symphony after the interval. Typically the last public appearance of this most modest of conductors was a muted affair, a performance of Elgar's Ballet *The Sanguine Fan* for London Festival Ballet. There were a few recording sessions to come: he completed a fifth recording of *The Planets* in July, and started work on his final disc, devoted to the music of Sir Hubert Parry, putting the finishing touches to this shortly before Christmas 1978. EMI originally intended using *The Planets* as their first digital recording, but were prevented from doing so by technical problems. Andre Previn and the LSO earning this distinction for their recording of Debussy's *Images*. The announcement of his final retirement was delayed until 1981, but there was a sense that a great career was at an end. Fittingly, Bravington chose a photo of Boult as the cover to the Yearbook for 1978-79, a passage in his tribute to the conductor aptly summarising Boult's approach to his work:

> Working with the orchestra he gets the results he wants without recourse to the spectacular showmanship of certain more extrovert colleagues. The most sober and self-effacing of great conductors – though not necessarily the most placid when displeased at a rehearsal – he has always considered furious arm movements an unnecessary extravagance. He would hate to risk distracting the audience's attention from the music itself.'

Another name to disappear from the LPO's list of conductors was that of Guilini, whose last concerts with the LPO took place at the 1977 Edinburgh Festival, two performances of Brahms' *German Requiem*. The Philharmonia, which from the autumn of 1977 dropped the prefix New, reverting to its original name, had made great strides since appointing Riccardo Muti as Principal Conductor. The management had been determined to persuade Guilini to return to an orchestra with whom he had long been associated, and now at last succeeded in doing so.

Financial matters were still wont to raise their heads, even at moments of artistic success. In April 1978 Eugen Jochum took charge of a tour of Austria and Germany, conducting all fourteen concerts, a considerable undertaking for a man of seventy-six. Overseas touring would be impossible without considerable financial support, which on this occasion was provided by the British Council and John Player. Reporting on the tour's success – every concert was sold out – Bravington compared the enormous difference in the level of subsidy between the Berlin Philharmonic and his own orchestra, the Berliners enjoying a grant fifteen times greater than the amount the Arts Council could make available to the LPO.

Financial problems of a different kind could have arisen from a case brought by the oboe player, Roger Winfield, who appealed to an Industrial Tribunal against dismissal. The Tribunal upheld the LPO's case that as the players were self-employed it had no jurisdiction, and also dismissed Winfield's appeal, rulings that were as much a relief to the other London orchestras as to the LPO. Almost immediately a second and even more serious problem arose, the Department of Health and Social Security (DHSS) claiming that associate members of the four independent London orchestras, i.e. players who were not shareholding members, but enjoyed first claim when additional players were required, and other players recruited by the orchestras as extras, ranked as employees, giving rise to a liability on the part of the orchestras to pay National Insurance contributions on their behalf. The matter was all the more serious because a precedent case had arisen in connection with a part-time orchestra, the English Sinfonia, the court ruling in favour of the DHSS, and though the English Sinfonia had lodged an appeal, to be heard in the High Court, there was every likelihood that this would be turned down.

A ruling in favour of the DHSS would have had profound implications, bringing in its train the additional cost of employers' National Insurance contributions, and the added burden of re-introducing PAYE records. In the light of the Industrial Tribunal's ruling against Roger Winfield, and in favour of the LPO, it was decided that the best means of countering this threat was by means of a test case, to be taken through the Industrial Tribunal machinery. The LPO's solicitors, Charles Russell & Co, were asked to act on behalf of all four London orchestras, inviting some of the players who regularly appeared with the LPO as extras to act as guinea pigs. Four players, Richard

Addison, who played bass clarinet and E flat clarinet, double bass player Geoff Downes, the flautist Averil Williams and horn player Frank Rycroft, agreed to assist by writing to the LPO, asking for contracts of employment, and when their request was refused, the players appealed to the Industrial Tribunal who, in the light of the precedent set in the Winfield case, again ruled that the players ranked as self-employed, and that they had no jurisdiction. There was however a further hurdle to be cleared before the threat was finally removed. The English Sinfonia's appeal had yet to be heard in the High Court: were they to lose, the DHSS would be in a position to use the precedent set by the High Court to appeal against the ruling given by the Industrial Tribunal. A ruling given within the framework of the Industrial Tribunals appeals machinery carried equal status with a ruling of the High Court itself, and it was therefore imperative that an appeal by the four players should be heard within that framework, before the appeal by the English Sinfonia was heard in the High Court. Despite a worryingly tight timetable the LPO's legal advisers were successful, the Employers Appeal Tribunal handing down a decision in favour of the LPO, on the day the English Sinfonia case came up at the High Court. Rather than setting a precedent themselves, the High Court, in considering the English Sinfonia's appeal, took into account the precedent set by the Employment Appeal Tribunal, reversing the decision of the lower court, and ruling in favour of that orchestra. With their finances poised, as ever, on a knife-edge, the additional burden of costs arising from an adverse decision might well have led one or more of London's orchestras to disband.

During his last year as Music Director Haitink was scheduled to conduct more concerts in the Festival Hall than for some seasons past. He should have bowed out with two concerts given as a ninetieth birthday tribute to Sir Adrian Boult, but the strain of so much work had led to a shoulder problem. In January he handed over Messiaen's *Et exspecto resurrectionem mortuorem* to Gilbert Amy, retaining the other works in the programme, but despite extensive treatment his shoulder failed to respond, leading to cancellation of all his concerts in March and April, his predecessor, John Pritchard, standing in to conduct the birthday tribute to Boult.

There are members of the orchestra who even today believe the decision to replace Haitink was mistaken. But with his appointment as Music Director at Glyndebourne, Haitink's career was moving in a different direction, and bearing in mind Bruno Walter's dictum that it is of benefit to conductor and orchestra to make a change every ten years or so, after more than a decade of almost uninterrupted artistic success perhaps the time had come for a parting of the ways, even if the means were a matter for regret. During 1979-80 he fulfilled guest engagements, but for a time thereafter his London concerts were with the Philharmonia rather than the LPO. The relationship between conductor and orchestra was maintained at Glyndebourne, and the passage of time, and changes in the management team, acted as a healing process.

Haitink returned to the LPO during the Fiftieth Anniversary Year, 1982-83, since when he has been a regular and welcome guest, and in 1990 he was invited to become the orchestra's President, an office vacant since the death of Sir Adrian Boult. It is our good fortune that Haitink, third in line of a great triumvirate of Dutch conductors, Willem Mengelberg, Eduard van Beinum and Haitink himself, has, through his association with the London Philharmonic, Glyndebourne and the Royal Opera House, devoted so much of his time to the musical life of this country.

15

Sir Georg Solti and the Fiftieth Anniversary 1979–83

Several factors combined to prevent Sir Georg Solti's term as Music Director being the success hoped for by Eric Bravington. When Haitink joined the LPO he was on the threshold of an international career; choosing to concentrate his time away from Amsterdam in one city, rather than accepting a wider range of guest conducting opportunities, was a viable option. This course was not open to Solti, whose services were in demand from around the world, with a wide range of commitments from which withdrawal was not possible. Though his home was in London, the main base of Solti's orchestral activity lay in Chicago with the Chicago Symphony Orchestra, whose Principal Conductor and Music Director he had been since 1971, with that orchestra the vehicle for much of his recording work.

A further factor inhibiting the development of the relationship between conductor and orchestra was the deterioration in Bravington's health, Solti's first year of office coinciding with Bravington's departure from the post of Managing Director, the Yearbook for 1980-81 containing Bravington's last annual report on the orchestra's activities. After drawing attention to the disparity between the level of grant enjoyed by major continental orchestras and those in this country, he commented on the fact that British musicians faced a double burden. In the first place, however generous the most recent increase in their grants might appear, at around 15 per cent, this was less than the rate of inflation, running at nearly 20 per cent, while arts organisations were further disadvantaged by the increase in VAT from 8 per cent to 15 per cent, an imposition that could not be immediately recovered by increasing ticket prices. With the prospect of a widening gap between income and expenditure, Bravington announced that a Finance Committee had been set up, under the chairmanship of Mr Phillip Shelbourne, shortly to become Chairman of the British National Oil Corporation. The formation of this committee was one of a number of matters that became a bone of contention.

To outward appearances Bravington had recovered from the operation he had undergone some time previously, but his last months in office were an unhappy episode for all concerned. There is no question of the pressure under which Bravington worked, and there was general sympathy when, early in 1980, he suggested changes in the administrative arrangements designed to relieve him of part of this burden. It had already been decided that on Bravington's retirement, due in the autumn of 1983, his place would be taken by the Chairman, Stephen Crabtree, and Bravington initially proposed that he and Crabtree should act as Joint Managing Directors, giving Crabtree an opportunity to familiarise himself with the day-to-day activity before taking over in his own right. It was the prelude to a protracted and unproductive debate, during which Bravington, constantly changing his mind, produced a succession of proposals about the administration of the company, the wheel eventually coming full circle when he informed his colleagues that, after giving further thought to the matter, he had concluded that there should after all be no change in the existing arrangements, and he should continue as sole Managing Director until his retirement.

Initially there was much sympathy for Bravington, but the long-drawn-out debate brought to the surface a series of criticisms of his handling of the company's affairs, including the failure to engage Solti for the number of concerts called for by his contract, the fact that new sponsors were not being found, the LPO's publicity and public relations were falling short of the requirements of the 1980s, the Managing Director was resentful and dismissive of criticism, and was failing to keep his colleagues informed of plans and developments to such an extent that the Board were losing control of the affairs of the company. However much these problems stemmed from the fact that Bravington's powers had been impaired by his illness and operation, the loss of confidence reached a level where the only way of resolving matters was by appointing a new Managing Director or electing a new Board prepared to work with him. With general agreement that it was in nobody's interest to create a situation where the Board had either to seek Bravington's resignation or dismiss him, terms for his early retirement were approved. It was an outcome which gave satisfaction to nobody. It was appreciated that Bravington's increasingly unpredictable and irrational behaviour resulted from his illness, in no way detracting from the fact that from the time of his appointment as Chairman in 1952, he had worked tirelessly on the LPO's behalf, the respect in which he was held throughout the musical world demonstrated by the good wishes heaped upon him when he was first taken ill.

After taking up the reins as Managing Director Bravington served the LPO in this capacity for some twenty years, a record which may not be unique among orchestral managers, but is almost unparalleled in London. Unswervingly loyal to the orchestra he served, it was his energy and vision that brought the LPO through the financial crisis of 1957, thereafter lifting it back into the front rank of orchestras. Despite the level of inflation experienced during the 1970s Bravington succeeded, taking one year with another, in balancing the LPO's books, the efficiency of his housekeeping ensuring that income and expenditure were kept in such close alignment that the surplus or deficit for any year was generally of the order of no more than a thousand or two, and his work received official recognition in 1973, when he was awarded the OBE. His departure was marked by a presentation made at a Festival Hall concert on 7 December 1980, but illness had taken its toll and he was not to live long to enjoy his retirement, dying less than two years later, his passing marked by a memorial service held in November 1982 at St Sepulchre's Church, Holborn.

As intended, Bravington's successor as Managing Director was Stephen Crabtree, who was succeeded as Chairman by Nicholas Busch. One of their earliest and most urgent tasks was the need to reassure members of the orchestra and its supporters, notably members of the LPO Council, who were disturbed by rumours of Boardroom turbulence. Fears had even been expressed that some sponsors might withdraw support, while however good the intentions may have been which led to the formation of the Finance Committee, its existence in parallel with the LPO Council was a source of concern to members of the latter body, Lord Shaftesbury expressing the view that creation of the Committee robbed the Council of any valid purpose, and after many years of service as Chairman, he felt this was an opportune moment to stand down. Meetings with members of the Council and the Finance Committee led to an agreement to merge the two bodies.

Despite a small drop in the number of concerts attracting sponsors, so far from the worst fears expressed about their possible withdrawal being realised, several gave undertakings of continuing support for at least the next three years. The continuing level of corporate support was a reflection of the efforts made on the LPO's behalf by members of the Council, though the spring of 1981 saw the untimely death of one of their most valued supporters, Mr Ben Rosenfeld, whose good offices had been instrumental in cementing relations with a number of companies. His support was sorely missed, though his widow, Mrs Jackie Rosenfeld, herself a member of the LPO Council, has continued to offer generous support, sponsoring many concerts in her own right. In 1994 in recognition of her devoted service to the orchestra, Mrs Rosenfeld received the unique distinction of being invited to become an Honorary Member of the LPO.

For Solti there was a world of difference between working in Chicago and working in London. The Chicago Symphony Orchestra has the advantage that rehearsals, and recording sessions, all take place in Orchestra Hall, but even with the advent of the Henry Wood Hall it was impossible to disguise the fact that being unable to rehearse in the Festival Hall, usually until the day of the concert itself, created problems for conductor and players. Moreover, while it remains an exception rather than the rule for London's orchestras to give the same programme more than once, the Chicago orchestra, like other leading

North American orchestras, gives each at least twice, many being performed three or even four times, spreading rehearsal costs over several performances, while the idea of an afternoon session, slipped in between a morning rehearsal and an evening concert, is inconceivable.

Solti opened 1979-80 with *The Rite of Spring*, his other concerts including the *Choral Symphony*, Tippett's Fourth Symphony, commissioned by the Chicago Symphony Orchestra, and given its first performance by that orchestra under Solti, an Elgar programme and two concert performances of *Das Rheingold*, a reminder that Solti was the first to record a complete cycle of *The Ring*. Haitink's guest appearances included some distinguished programmes, including the Seventh Symphonies of Bruckner and Shostakovitch, a complete performance of *Daphnis and Chloé,* and more Tippett, the Third Symphony. Though the Shostakovitch Seventh was recorded, one result of the temporary breach between Haitink and the LPO was that the outstanding symphonies of the cycle were recorded in Amsterdam, where the Concertgebouw Orchestra were no longer recording exclusively for Philips. There was, however, growing competition for the cycle of Mahler symphonies recorded by Solti with his Chicago orchestra, from Klaus Tennstedt, whose rapport with the players appeared to grow almost every time they worked together. This year it was the turn of the Third Symphony, given two performances, a week apart, with the *Eroica* performed during the intervening period, the recording sessions for the Mahler starting part-way through the week. Other guest conductors included Sir Charles Groves, who conducted the first performance of an LPO commission, the Sixth Symphony of Robert Simpson, Kiril Kondrashin, Erich Leinsdorf, André Previn and Mtsislav Rostropovitch. Though the year brought no overseas tour as such, New Year's Eve involved an excursion to Munich for an early evening concert of light classics conducted by Solti, televised live by Eurovision. The players flew home immediately afterwards, with in-flight champagne by courtesy of their Music Director, arriving back in London in time to see the New Year in at home.

The summer of 1980 found the BBC in dispute with its orchestras and the Musicians Union, over plans for reducing the playing strength of its Scottish Symphony Orchestra. By midsummer the BBC orchestras were on strike, and with other orchestras refusing to perform the Proms were seriously affected, only getting under way towards the end of the third week. The dispute was resolved in time to allow the LPO's scheduled concerts to take place, *The Magic Flute*, conducted by Haitink, and a concert with Riccardo Chailly. The outcome was salvation for the BBC Scottish Symphony Orchestra, but it is questionable whether the independent orchestras gained any benefit, indeed they may well have been adversely affected by the outcome. Historically, orchestral music in this country has divided itself into two camps, the BBC orchestras, financed by the licence fee, and the independent sector, supported by the Arts Council. It is understandable that the BBC's frustration with the machinations of Beecham led them to form their own orchestra in London, but it is a matter for regret that in Birmingham and Manchester existing partnerships, of great value to the orchestras of those cities, fell by the wayside. The BBC National Orchestra of Wales, funded jointly by the Corporation and the Arts Council, is an example of what might have been achieved had the BBC built on the existing relationships. Instead the BBC enlarged their Northern and Scottish orchestras, the least economic solution to the broadcasting of orchestral music, with the inevitable result that the BBC placed increasing reliance on its own orchestras, with broadcast and television fees, which at best made a modest contribution to the budgets of the independent orchestras, declining further.

Of those who worked with the LPO in the 1960s and 1970s, Horenstein died in 1973 and Krips in 1974; Barenboim was involved with the Orchestre de Paris; Guilini had returned to the Philharmonia, and Haitink had withdrawn from the concert life of the LPO. Bravington had only booked Solti for five of the thirty-four Festival Hall concerts arranged for 1980-81, and guest conductors therefore assumed increasing importance: no less than four Principal Guest Conductors were appointed, Riccardo Chailly, Christopher Eschenbach, Jesús López-Cobos and Klaus Tennstedt, other conductors including James Conlon, Andrew Davis, Eugen Jochum, Kirill Kondrashin, Mstislav Rostropovitch and Kurt Sanderling. The LPO was also graced by the patronage of the Duke of Kent who attended the opening concert, conducted by Solti in what the *Daily Telegraph* described as a 'grandly energetic, darkly impressive account of Brahms' Fourth Symphony'.

During 1980-81 out-of-the-way repertoire included the *Glagolitic Mass* of Janacek, conducted by Andrew Davis, with the London Philharmonic Choir praised for their mastery of the Slavonic text. Rostropovitch introduced music by Dutilleux, the first British performance of *Timbres, espace, mouvement*, inspired by Van Gogh's painting *Starry Night*, and turned to his cello to play the solo part in Prokofiev's *Sinfonia concertante*. Bruckner and Mahler featured strongly. Kurt Sanderling conducted two performances of Bruckner's Third Symphony, Klaus Tennstedt the Fourth, and when illness compelled Solti to miss a concert, López-Cobos substituted the Seventh Symphony for the Fifth. Tennstedt continued his Mahler cycle with the Seventh Symphony, and brought the year to a triumphant close with the *Resurrection* Symphony. The programmes contained enough in the way of the unusual to give them a touch of spice, but there was a marked decline in the amount of British music.

After the hectic touring activity of the 1970s, there was a temporary slow-down in this area. With several possibilities failing to come to fruition, only one tour was undertaken during Solti's first three years in office, a visit to Japan and South Korea in November 1980. It had been intended that Solti would conduct all fourteen concerts, twelve in Japan and two in Korea, but doubts as to the wisdom of travelling with only one conductor, should he by mischance be taken ill, led to an invitation to Jesús López-Cobos to conduct four of those arranged in Japan. Subsequently Solti asked to be released from the Korean leg of the tour, López-Cobos taking over the concerts in Seoul.

For touring purposes Bruckner and Mahler, mainstays of London concert programmes, were put into storage, the music chosen comprising standard classics, with a leavening of British works, Britten's *Young Person's Guide*, the *Enigma Variations*, John McCabe's *The Chagall Windows*, and Walton's *Variations on a Theme by Hindemith*. Sue Jameson, a journalist from the commercial radio station LBC, travelled with the orchestra. She was impressed by the discipline of the Japanese audience, for whom it was out of the question to disturb the music with any kind of extraneous noise, and the fact that Tokyo could boast no less than eleven orchestras, among whom there was nothing in the way of co-operation about programme planning, the Japanese expressing astonishment that London's orchestras met together regularly to try and avoid undue repetition of the same works.

Programme planning was the subject of an article in the next Yearbook, profiling the work of the Concerts Manager, Rosalie Cody, the wife of Maurice Cody, formerly the LPO's Principal Clarinet. She described her work as being 'like fitting together a giant jigsaw puzzle', a puzzle in which the pieces can from time to time change shape. Booking conductors and planning programmes, which may require a degree of compromise between the Concert Department's wishes and ideas offered by conductors, is the first stage of a complicated procedure. As a broad rule of thumb, planning takes place on a three-year cycle. As one season opens Concert Management aim to put the final details for the following year in place, with advance planning for the third year under way. Much juggling takes place before the final details slot into place, and the best endeavours can run into unexpected difficulties. The problems of extending the repertoire are manifold, not least the adverse effect of much contemporary music on the box office. A new symphony can sometimes be slotted in 'if you combine it with one of the top international artists playing Beethoven'. Even when programmes and dates are agreed and sent to the printer, there is the risk of cancellation, sometimes for unexpected reasons; Guilini, a devout Roman Catholic, once pulled out at the last minute, having failed to realise that he was booked to work on Good Friday.

The LPO's sole contribution to the 1981 Proms was a concert performance of *Ariadne auf Naxos*, conducted by Gustav Kuhn, but later that month they were again in Edinburgh, under Raymond Leppard, Riccardo Chailly and Klaus Tennstedt. Edinburgh was the prelude to a year in which Solti's concerts, two in October, two in December and three in late winter, contained only one major departure from mainstream repertoire, Elliott Carter's *Variations for Orchestra*, performed at a Royal Philharmonic Society concert. James Conlon gave a concert of music by Mussorgsky, with an orchestration of *Pictures from an Exhibition* by the Russian composer Tuschmirov, rather than the usual version by Ravel, and Boris Christoff as soloist in the *Songs and Dances of Death*, and the Death Scene from *Boris Godunov*; Rostropovitch performed *Tout un monde lontain* for cello and orchestra by Dutilleux; López-Cobos, with Julian Lloyd Webber as soloist, gave the first performance of Rodrigo's Cello Concerto, and Tennstedt conducted Mahler's Fourth Symphony, Bruckner's Eighth and two performances of the First Act of *Die Walküre*, with Jessye Norman as Brunnhilde.

That these two seasons gave the impression of being put together on a piecemeal basis, rather than as an integrated whole, was largely a result of the after effects of Bravington's illness, which adversely affected the work of concert planning. Even more serious was the fact that arrangements for the Golden Jubilee Year fell behind schedule, one of the most obvious results being that though Solti remained as Music Director for a further year, his contribution was limited to four concerts in the Festival Hall and the lion's share of the conducting during a tour of Europe.

The Jubilee Year opened with a brief tour of Spain and concerts in Edinburgh, where Solti conducted the Third Symphony of Mahler and the *Missa Solemnis*, repeating the latter work on the penultimate night of the 1982 Prom season. Solti launched the celebrations proper in the Festival Hall on 28 September, with Mahler's Third Symphony, and on 5 October the LPO hosted a celebratory party in the Banqueting Room of the Fishmongers Hall, using the occasion to announce that, from the autumn of 1983, Klaus Tennstedt would be stepping into Sir Georg Solti's shoes as Music Director and, with both conductors present, Solti congratulated the orchestra on their choice, warmly commending their colleague to them.

The anniversary concert took place two days later, and since the London Philharmonic's first public appearance had been at a concert of the Royal Philharmonic Society, it was appropriate that it should be given in collaboration with the Society, though some tact was necessary to obtain their support, for whereas the anniversary fell on a Thursday, the Society, who had provisionally booked the hall for the previous evening, were initially reluctant to make any change from their tradition of giving concerts on Wednesdays. With the addition of an opening fanfare, Solti conducted the identical programme to that with which the LPO first announced itself to the public. Delius' *Brigg Fair* was almost certainly an addition to Solti's repertoire, but in every other respect it was a programme as much suited to his talents as it had been to Beecham's. Among the extra players hired to fulfil the orchestration of *Ein Heldenleben* was Richard Walton, who had been on the platform in October 1932, though for the Fiftieth Anniversary concert he played among the off-stage trumpets, rather than on the platform itself.

It was a season in which guest conductors again played a major role, among them André Previn, with his own work *Reflections* and two performances of the *Alpine Symphony*; Bernard Haitink, whose absence would have been unthinkable, and who took up the challenge of *The Dream of Gerontius*, with the Fifth Symphony of Mahler the cornerstone of another concert; Klaus Tennstedt conducted a Strauss programme, Mahler's Sixth Symphony and, standing in for an indisposed Eugen Jochum, a performance of the Eighth Symphony of Bruckner. Jesús López-Cobos' programmes included Sibelius' First Symphony and Verdi's *Requiem* and concerts were given under Riccardo Chailly, James Conlon, former Principal Conductor John Pritchard, Raymond Leppard, Hugh Wolff, Mtsislav Rostropovitch, and Christoph Eschenbach. Soloists engaged to perform included Vladimir Ashkenazy, Daniel Barenboim, Clifford Curzon, James Galway, Arthur Grumiaux, Radu Lupu, Anne-Sophie Mutter, Maurizio Pollini and Isaac Stern. It was a tribute to the efforts of Stephen Crabtree and Rosalie Cody, that despite working to an extremely tight timetable, they not only succeeded in putting together a roster of conductors and soloists worthy of the occasion, but one that would have been regarded as outstanding by any of the world's major orchestras.

The LPO produced several commemorative items, a pictorial album, compiled by Jerrold Northrop Moore, and a double album 'Fifty Years of the London Philharmonic', for sale to the record-buying public. The House of Hallgarten, celebrating their own and the orchestra's fiftieth anniversary, produced two specially bottled white wines, a Mainzer Domherr Kabinett and a Bernkastler Kurfurstlay Kabinett as well as Quartet, a specially blended LPO liqueur, and the Minister for the Arts unveiled a commemorative plaque in the foyer of the St George's Hotel, on the site formerly occupied by Queen's Hall. The Yearbook included a pen portrait of 1932, the year of the LPO's birth, a potted history of the orchestra and a reflection on the early years written by Thomas Russell, now in his eighties. Eric Bravington had often written ominously about the increasing gap between income and expenditure, which for an individual concert in the Festival Hall could be as much as £10,000, and the Yearbook outlined the approach devised by the LPO to financing its activities during this Jubilee year, much thought having been given to ways of underwriting the costs. Sponsorship was playing a major role in maintaining the highest artistic standards, and the previous year had seen sixteen Festival Hall concerts variously sponsored by Commercial Union, Lambert and Butler, Lloyds Bank and Pioneer High Fidelity, with Courage supporting Classics for Pleasure and Marks and Spencer continuing to give financial assistance for concerts in Croydon, Eastbourne and Hastings.

For the Anniversary Year the publicity department, in conjunction with Owen Wade Delmonte, part of the Charles Barker Group, devised a scheme designed to give companies supporting the orchestra a return for their expenditure. This was to be achieved by an advertising programme which, linking the sponsor's name with the orchestra, would raise the public profile of both. Major companies were invited to participate by purchasing 'shares', each costing £30,000, of which a third was to be set aside to cover concert expenditure, the remaining two-thirds pooled to finance a publicity campaign, not just focusing on the Jubilee, but highlighting the part the sponsors were playing in maintaining the LPO as a vital part of London's musical life. The campaign was launched at Christie's, who lent their saleroom, and the presentation was preceded by a short concert given by members of the orchestra. In the event most help came from two long-standing supporters, John Player, who sponsored nine concerts, and Commercial Union, who in addition to sponsoring six concerts provided substantial assistance for a European tour. There were, however, two new and welcome departures, Mars Limited supporting two children's concerts in Slough, and McDonald's a children's concert in the Festival Hall. For the latter, given on Halloween, children were invited to 'dress the part', the hall staff entertained by the wide variety of imaginative costumes. The children were presented with black helium-filled balloons, embossed with a skull and crossbones, and when they were invited to release them, these floated to the top of the hall. Unfortunately it proved impossible to recover all the balloons before the evening performance, given by the Philharmonia, during the course of which some of the balloons drifted down among the ranks of the orchestra, giving rise to some understandable if erroneous suspicions that this was an attempt at sabotage.

Children's concerts, long part of the orchestra's life, were breaking fresh ground, with participation increasingly important. A seed was sown in 1980, when several principals coached and then played with a wind band made up from children attending schools around the Elephant and Castle area. The final rehearsal was taken by Jesús López-Cobos and the next year, in advance of two Festival Hall performances of excerpts from *The Nutcracker*, Peter Maag rehearsed parts of the score with the combined orchestras of the William Ellis and Camden Schools. It was an approach that found favour with the ILEA, teachers and pupils. Richard McNichol, a member of the flute section, showed a special talent for this work, eventually resigning in order to devote himself full-time to it. Building on this pioneer work he developed an integrated approach to children's concerts, with preparatory workshops followed by a concert offering opportunities for participation. At one concert around two hundred and fifty children joined with the LPO to perform 'The British Grenadiers', and there was an opportunity for children to try their hand at playing the timpani or other percussion instruments.

One event only marred the celebrations, the death in February 1983 of the LPO's President Sir Adrian Boult, just short of his ninety-fourth birthday. With typical generosity he offered, after his retirement, to stand down as the President, since he felt no longer able to contribute directly, an offer that was gently declined. Sorrow at his passing was matched by gratitude for his part in supporting the orchestra during some of the most difficult years in its history. There was a time when his interpretative powers were overshadowed by the perceived brilliance of Beecham, but his stature as a musician of the front rank was confirmed and enhanced by performances and recordings during the wonderfully productive latter years of his working life. Boult's death occurred shortly after the LPO had embarked on their tour of Europe, Stephen Crabtree going on-stage in Berlin to ask the audience to join with the LPO in dedicating the concert to the memory of a great musician. The obituary note in the programme for their next Festival Hall concert recorded that the orchestra were 'very proud to have been associated with this most sober and self-effacing of great conductors and is profoundly saddened by the passing of a musician for whom it held not only the deepest professional respect but great personal affection'. It was entirely in keeping that before his death he should have requested that any memorial service should be delayed for at least a year, and that if and when one was held it should be 'jolly'.

In March 1982 David Nolan tendered his resignation, to take effect from the end of August, in order to take up a post as leader of the Covent Garden Orchestra. A number of candidates were considered as his successor, but in the event Nolan applied to rejoin the LPO from the start of 1983, in time to lead the orchestra on the Jubilee year tour. It was originally proposed that this would take the LPO into new territory, South America, but costings of the project showed that even after taking into account the generosity of Commercial Union, the expenses would have been prohibitive. In its place the LPO undertook a tour of Europe, involving seventeen concerts and embracing seven capital cities, Brussels, Paris, Stockholm, Oslo, Vienna, Budapest and Madrid, with other concerts in Hamburg, Berlin, Mannheim, Stuttgart, Munich, Frankfurt and Barcelona. Ten concerts were given under Solti, and seven under Tennstedt, for whom Ann-Sophie Mutter appeared as soloist in Munich and Frankfurt. The repertoire was largely familiar, with Solti's programmes built around the *Eroica* Symphony and Ravel's arrangement of *Pictures from an Exhibition*, and those conducted by Tennstedt, based on the First Symphony of Brahms and the Fourth of Bruckner, other works including Bartok's *Dance Suite*, Britten's *Sinfonia da Requiem* and John McCabe's Concerto for Orchestra.

The European tour was Solti's swansong as Principal Conductor. Solti himself professed that before taking up his appointment with the LPO he harboured doubts about the wisdom of accepting their invitation, hesitating before deciding that, having made his home in London, 'it was my duty to accept'. If nothing else, it was desirable that for the Fiftieth Anniversary season the LPO's Music Director should remain in post, rather than the season take place under a new appointment, or with the conductorship vacant. Despite the fact that pressure of Solti's other commitments must have made continuing in post seem 'an appointment too far', when asked by the LPO to extend his original three-year term by a further year, he put aside any misgivings he might have felt and agreed.

The unpalatable truth was that while the quality of London's orchestras made many musicians anxious to work with them on an occasional basis, the negative factors in London's musical life, financial uncertainty, rehearsal facilities that even with the advent of the Henry Wood Hall fell short of those in Europe and the United States, and the fact that except in a minority of instances programmes could only be performed once in the Festival Hall, were leading conductors to fight shy of accepting a London post. Despite these disadvantages, the LPO was about to hitch its star to a musician who was to identify himself whole-heartedly with their activities.

16

Klaus Tennstedt 1983–87

In every generation only a small handful of conductors inspire universal respect, with fewer still held in any kind of affection, usually musicians of great age and experience. Bruno Walter and Pierre Monteux were among those who had done so in the past, and it was to such a man that the LPO now turned, Klaus Tennstedt. Since his rapid rise to prominence in the West, Tennstedt had been in great demand, the LPO counting themselves fortunate in securing his services on a regular basis. The respect in which he was held by the orchestra was matched by Tennstedt's own description of the LPO as 'the great romantic orchestra, an orchestra capable of infinite flexibility'.

Tennstedt's appointment represented a break with tradition. Almost without exception, the musicians invited to preside over the affairs of the LPO were noted for their ability to train an orchestra, using rehearsal time to fashion and mould the music, without expecting every rehearsal to be a performance in itself. Van Beinum, Boult, Steinberg, Pritchard, Haitink and Solti all had this in common, but Tennstedt belonged to a different school, the class of conductor who demands their all, not only in performance, but also in rehearsal. Some members of this school obtain results by fear: however much American orchestras respected Toscanini, his rehearsal methods were unlikely to endear him to his players. Tennstedt made considerable demands on the orchestra, but he was no less demanding of himself, while so far from engendering fear in the players, his rapport with the orchestra was such that their respect for him bordered on affection.

From the outset Tennstedt identified himself totally with the LPO, exemplified during his appearance as a guest on the television programme 'Face The Music', Joseph Cooper finding great difficulty in making Tennstedt talk about anything other than the orchestra of which he was Music Director. The relationship between conductor and players seems, from the outset, to have been heightened by a sense that the thread linking them was slender in the extreme. Tennstedt, like Leslie Heward before him, was an extreme example of a chain smoker, the effects of which were to ravage his health, leading to the trauma of throat surgery and a course of chemotherapy. He was also diagnosed as diabetic and if these were not afflictions enough, underwent two hip replacement operations at a younger age than many consultants would wish their patients to submit themselves to such treatment. But over and above these physical ailments, Tennstedt suffered from self-doubt, an affliction that grew worse with the passage of time. In consequence his tenure of office was tragically brief, lasting less than four years, for part of which he was laid low by illness.

Tennstedt's reputation is based on his interpretation of the great German classics, and the limitation of his repertoire was to become a major problem, particularly in drawing up touring programmes. There was some early promise that his horizons might expand in unexpected directions. During 1983-84 he conducted works by Messiaen, Carl Orff, Stravinsky and Prokofiev, and his programmes for the following year embraced Britten and Janacek. In an interview with Nicholas Kenyon, he even talked of introducing Elgar's music into his programmes. It is only possible to speculate on what might have happened had he not been dogged by ill-health, and circumstances had allowed the relationship to develop more fully, and over a longer period. But if excursions from a limited range of music were the exception rather than the rule, there was nothing routine about the music made under his baton. Many of his performances are stamped on the memory of those privileged to take part.

In August 1983 Tennstedt conducted his first Prom, the programme consisting of one work, Mahler's Sixth Symphony, and shortly afterwards he opened the LPO's autumn season in the Festival Hall with the Eighth and Ninth Symphonies of Beethoven, the *Guardian* reflecting the general approval with which his appointment and these performances were received:

> 'Having watched this most fruitful of relationships blossom and apparently deepen over the last year or so, it was perhaps not surprising that the overriding impression here should have been one of an orchestra embarking confidently upon an important new phase in their history'.

Of thirty-eight Festival Hall concerts Tennstedt conducted ten, and in this year at least maintained a balance between the German repertoire in which he excelled and other schools. One programme brought together *Petrushka* and *Carmina Burana*, and in another the *Pathétique* Symphony was used as bait for Messiaen's *Oiseaux Exotiques*. Mahler was represented by the Fifth Symphony, and some of Tennstedt's thoughts on the composer were set down in the programme:

> 'I consider the interpretation of Mahler the most complicated activity a conductor can engage in. You have to know exactly Mahler's life, because he composed his life. One needs to know about him absolutely.

And in order to do that a conductor has to have a lot of similar experiences in his life also. A young man can conduct a Mahler symphony easily but he can't interpret it – not without experience.'

The spring of 1984 brought another highly successful tour of Japan, Tennstedt's first as Music Director, with never a whisper of complaint that the tour repertoire, Haydn's *Surprise* Symphony, Mozart's *Haffner*, Schubert's *Unfinished*, Bruckner's Fourth, the First and Fourth Symphonies of Brahms and the Fifth of Mahler, with Britten's *Sea Interludes from Peter Grimes* the solitary British composition, in any way failed to come up to their expectations. With the cost covered by the Japanese broadcasting company CBC the tour was free from financial worries, and its artistic success was of major commercial importance, for Tennstedt's reputation in Japan was reaching a point where among the record-buying public of that country he was only outsold by Karajan, with the gap between them closing fast.

Touring Japan always raised problems of language, particularly where food was concerned. This was less acute in a city such as Tokyo, where international hotels are the order of the day. Elsewhere, obtaining meals required a degree of ingenuity, with much use of what the visiting musicians hoped was sign language. One hotel assisted its guests by translating the menu into English, the dishes on offer including the exciting possibility of 'Sauteed Nackered Clam'. It must be questionable whether any British hotel would make such a good fist of translating its menu into Japanese.

Coinciding with Tennstedt's appointment as Music Director, Vernon Handley took up the post of Associate Conductor, one created specially for him. EMI's Classics for Pleasure label had come a long way from the days when the first issues concentrated on the most popular elements of the repertoire, Handley and the LPO contributing works by Delius, Elgar and Vaughan Williams, including a distinguished version of Elgar's Violin Concerto with Nigel Kennedy as soloist. A pupil of Sir Adrian Boult, Handley earned prominence from his work in Guildford, raising the part-time orchestra based in that town to fully professional status. He had a considerable reputation as an interpreter of British music, and a strong affinity with Russian composers. His contribution to the year included an Elgar concert which, given in association with the Elgar Society, took place on the fiftieth anniversary of the composer's death, with Janet Baker as soloist in the *Sea Pictures* and the First Symphony as the major orchestral work. He also conducted a performance of Vaughan Williams' *Job*, subsequently recorded for the Classics for Pleasure label. Handley also gave a concert in an ill-devised series devoted to twentieth-century British music. Entitled 'The Great British Music Festival', this was largely made up of lesser-known works, resulting in pitifully small audiences. The LPO's contribution included one piece of substance, the Second Symphony of Robert Simpson, but the venture was a disservice to the composers represented, and it was no surprise that plans for a second series were abandoned. In addition to Vernon Handley and Principal Guest Conductors Chailly, Eschenbach and López-Cobos, concerts were given under James Conlon and the Russians Rostropovitch, who led a performance of Britten's *War Requiem*, Rozdestvensky, with the Eighth Symphony of Shostakovitch, and Svetlanov, who, given a break from the Russian fare normally allotted to him, included the First Symphonies of Brahms and Sibelius in his programmes. In recognition of his services over many years Solti had been invited to accept the title of Conductor Emeritus, but other commitments restricted him to two concerts.

The summer of 1984 marked the fiftieth anniversary of the first performances given by John Christie's fledgling company at Glyndebourne, and by a happy coincidence was the LPO's twenty-first year as resident orchestra. The season opened on 28 May, fifty years to the day from the first performance given in what was then Britain's newest opera house, the company's Golden Jubilee year launched with a new production of *Figaro*, the opera with which Glyndebourne had announced itself to the public. The season comprised sixty-six performances of five operas. In addition to *Figaro*, given with two casts, the first led by Claudio Desderi as Figaro and conducted by Haitink, who handed over the baton to Gustav Kuhn for the second series of performances, the repertoire for this Jubilee season comprised *L'incoronazione de Poppea*, conducted by Raymond Leppard, *Cosi Fan Tutti*, under Gustav Kuhn, a new production of *Arabella*, conducted by Haitink, with the last four performances given to Stephen Barlow, and *A Midsummer Night's Dream*, also under Haitink, who again handed over the last four performances, this time to Jane Glover. Glyndebourne's Golden Jubilee year gave much pleasure, vocally, visually and orchestrally.

Figaro was also chosen for the company's annual appearance at the Proms, and the orchestra's second contribution was a performance of Brahms' *German Requiem*, for which the London Philharmonic Choir was joined by the BBC Symphony Chorus. It was the last concert in which Marie Wilson played before her retirement, Tennstedt cutting short the applause for himself to make way for a public presentation to a long-serving and much valued member.

The problems attendant on maintaining four orchestras in London resurfaced in 1984 with the publication by the Arts Council of their report, *The Glory of the Garden*. Faced with the prospect that the funds made available by government were unlikely to keep up with even a reduced rate of inflation, the Council had two options, to continue allocating grants in much the same way as in the past, letting each organisation bear its share of the resulting financial pain, or to engage in drastic surgery. One of the proposals mooted was that a London orchestra should relocate itself outside the capital, with Nottingham the most favoured choice to play host. The LSO were taking up residence in their new home in the Barbican, and the likelihood of any other orchestra opting to relocate was minimal, a fact which should have been apparent to the authors of the proposal. It was an idea born of a failure to comprehend that since each orchestra is a self-governing institution it is not within the gift of the management to take such a decision. Even if they could have done so, there was every likelihood that a majority of the players would have promptly resigned, choosing to join the pool of freelance players working in London rather than translate themselves, and their families, to what would in all probability have been a less financially advantageous environment.

But though the LPO had no intention of moving out of London, its offices had moved to new premises. Number 53 Welbeck Street had provided them with a home for nearly forty years. Advised that the outstanding value of the lease was declining in value, they cast around for a suitable freehold building, settling on 35 Doughty Street, a terraced house not far from Russell Square which, including the basement, contained five floors of office space and whose stairs provide a built-in fitness regime for the administrative staff. The original outlay of £9000 for the lease of 53 Welbeck Street may have seemed expensive at the time, but proved to have been a shrewd investment, the residual lease being sold for £375,000. After purchasing and refurbishing the new building the LPO was left with a useful surplus, which was transferred to the account of the National Appeal Fund.

For the LPO and the Philharmonia, publication of *The Glory of the Garden* provided an opportunity to resubmit a plan, put forward the previous year, for a joint residency at the Festival Hall. Following the re-election of a Conservative government the days of the GLC were numbered, and with the demise of that body management of the hall would pass into new hands. Whatever the political consequences of abolishing the GLC, it presented an opportunity to address the unsatisfactory situation which, even with the departure of the LSO to the Barbican, still arose when planning each year's work. While there was a degree of overlap, there were sufficient areas in which the activities of the two orchestras were complementary for the proposal to make good sense. The plan in effect resurrected the original blueprint for the hall, with the Philharmonia in place of the LSO, but rather than one orchestra having primacy it was envisaged that both would have equal standing. Yet whatever the logic of the plan, its fate was to be pigeon-holed. Instead, the Arts Council set up a working party to examine the options for running the South Bank complex after the GLC was no more.

In the meantime, pending a decision on the future of the South Bank, an announcement at the end of 1984 soured the festive season with the news that a cut in grant amounting to £280,000 would be spread across all four orchestras. It is hardly surprising that when David Marcou, who succeeded to the role of Chairman in 1984, sat down to write his contribution to the 1985-86 Yearbook, it should have contained an element of bitterness:

'Advice has been plentiful: raise more in sponsorship, as though we hadn't been engaged in this field for many years; double the price of tickets for concerts, bringing them in line with the USA – this at a time when enormous efforts are being made to reach out to and win new audiences; take more London concerts to the provinces, although local authority resources are currently being stretched to the limit. In tandem with such advice is criticism of programme content, complaints that we do not play enough contemporary music, that the orchestras lose too much money, that players are too irresponsible and the playing standards cannot compare with our European and American counterparts. Has all this been free or have we the four London orchestras had to pay £280,000 for the privilege.'

The new season opened with a twenty-four hour visit to Lyon for a Shakespeare-inspired programme conducted by James Conlon, comprising extracts from Prokofiev's *Romeo and Juliet* and the incidental music written by Mendelssohn for *A Midsummer Night's Dream*. A visit to Perugia had also been planned for later in the month, but the best endeavours of the planners were thwarted by a combination of unusual circumstances. Initially the Concert Department encountered unexpected problems over the travel arrangements, a Board minute recording that 'the orchestra was experiencing difficulties in arranging transport to Italy for itself and the choir because of a NATO exercise which was taking place at the time', and the tour was finally postponed for a year because of the devastation caused by an earthquake, the damage including destruction of the usual venue.

At home the year was launched with four concerts under Tennstedt, including two performances of the *Eroica*, and a concert at which he proudly accompanied a teenage discovery of his, the Israeli pianist Mayer Weltman, in Mendelssohn's First Piano Concerto. These performances were preparatory to a sixteen-concert tour of the United States, which opened in Texas, embraced San Francisco on the West Coast, and ended triumphantly on the East Coast with concerts in Washington, New York and Boston. There was a predictability about Tennstedt's touring repertoire and, with the exception of a performance of the *New World* Symphony, the music was similar to that given in Japan earlier in the year: the *Eroica*, Brahms First, Schubert's *Unfinished* and Mahler's Fifth, with a complete absence of British music. The opening concert in New Orleans was somewhat nerve-wracking. Given in a partially constructed auditorium which, while providing cover for orchestra and audience, still lacked a proper back and sides, the orchestra had to compete with a variety of extraneous sounds, including those of tugboat sirens from the Mississippi. New Orleans offered those inclined the chance to visit the old quarter, the cradle of jazz, and a day in Phoenix Arizona allowed time for viola player Judith Swan to organise an excursion to the Grand Canyon.

One fear of any tour organiser is that a vital member of the orchestra can be struck down by illness or injury. This could have been the case in Minneapolis, when timpanist Alan Cumberland hurt his leg in a fall. With his leg encased in plaster, he hobbled onto the platform, wearing as an alternative to his dress trousers, which would not go on over the plaster, a long black slip, and surrounded by friendly colleagues to hide this unusual form of platform attire from the audience. Despite what must have been acute discomfort, he somehow managed the pedals of his timpani without mishap. The constant travelling involved in major tours stretches physical resources almost to the limit, but however tired the players, they had something in reserve for the final concert, in Boston, the city which ten years earlier had been the launch-pad for Tennstedt's career in the West, and where Mahler's Fifth Symphony earned conductor and orchestra an ovation, putting the seal on the success of this venture.

Earlier in the year the LPO learned that Thomas Russell was terminally ill. Whatever the circumstances surrounding his dismissal, any animosity was long dead and buried. In recognition of the debt owed to him by the LPO for his years of service to the orchestra, Stephen Crabtree travelled to see him at his home in Taunton. Russell died during the autumn at the age of eighty-four his death taking place while the LPO were in America, and the programme for the first Festival Hall concert given after their return contained an appreciation by Charles Gregory: 'Blessed with a wide vision of life and an ability more catholic than is usual in a practising musician, Tom had acquired a reputation amongst his colleagues as an intellectual, a rare compliment from those who possess fanatical concentration for their art.'

The second half of the winter saw a second major tour, to Australia, where the conducting was to have been shared between Tennstedt and Yevgany Svetlanov. Unhappily Svetlanov suffered a heart attack not long before their departure. His preparatory Festival Hall concert was taken over at short notice by Yuri Terminkanov, appearing by permission of the RPO, the orchestra with whom he usually worked when in this country, while for the tour itself Svetlanov was replaced by the Israeli conductor Avi Ostrowsky. The American tour had been sponsored by Bacardi Rum, with transport provided by Greyhound Buses, and in Australia backing came from a number of sources, notably from one of the country's wine producers, Leeuwin Estate of West Australia. In recognition of their support the tour began with an open-air concert given before an invited audience of four to five thousand in the grounds of the estate, some two hundred miles south of Perth. The daytime temperature was so great that the planned rehearsal was cancelled for fear of damage to the instruments, and when the concert took place, on a beautifully warm evening, the performers found themselves competing with the far from melodious song of the numerous kookaburra birds nesting nearby. Laurence Watt, a member of the LPO Council, who had laid the initial plans for this tour during an earlier visit to Australia, subsequently wrote of this concert: 'No wonder the kookaburra has been called the "Laughing Jackass"; this is precisely what they sounded like against the mellifluous notes of Nick Busch's horn solo in the slow movement. My boys, aged seven and five, models of behaviour until the birds started, were rolling on the ground in mirth.' The birds were not the only local wildlife aroused by the music-making; Bob Wright recalled the sight of two kangaroos peering enquiringly through the perimeter fence.

It is by no means uncommon for overseas tours to include concerts marking special events of one kind or another. Those in Melbourne formed part of the one hundred and fiftieth anniversary celebrations of the founding of the State of Victoria, and in Brisbane the LPO gave the first concert in the newly completed Brisbane concert hall, though the official opening, by the Duke and Duchess of Kent, was not due to take place until the following month. Touring Australia had the advantage that several days were spent in each city, the schedule allowing time in which to enjoy the beaches of Perth and Sydney, with a little gentle exercise essential to recovery from the hospitality heaped upon them by their Australian hosts. One souvenir was a didgeridoo, presented to the Chairman, David Marcou, in Perth, which defeated the best efforts of the brass section to produce any kind of sound from it and has yet to make its debut in the Festival Hall.

Svetlanov was not the only artist whose health gave rise to disappointment in a year which, due to the American and Australian tours, involved fewer Festival Hall concerts, twenty-six compared with thirty-eight the year before. Boris Christoff, engaged to sing arias from operas by Mussorgsky, Rachmaninov and Rimsky-Korsakov, was another performer forced to withdraw, his place taken by the Russian pianist Andrei Gavrilov. There were, however, three autumn concerts under Bernard Haitink, sponsored by the Prudential Insurance Company, and promoted under the banner 'The Prudential-Haitink Series'. Two concentrated on British music, the first comprising the *Tallis Fantasia*, Britten's *Sinfonia da Requiem* and Elgar's Violin Concerto, and in the second Prokofiev's Suite from *The Love of Three Oranges* was framed by Elgar's *Introduction and Allegro* and Vaughan Williams' *Sinfonia Antartica*. Haitink's other concert was an all-Russian affair, including Rachmaninov's infrequently played Fourth Piano Concerto and the Sixth Symphony of Shostakovitch. Otherwise the roster of conductors showed little change from the previous year: Conlon, Eschenbach, López-Cobos and Solti.

Thirty years after their inception it was decided that, as from the winter of 1985-86, Classics for Pleasure would move to the Festival Hall. There were always problems attendant on giving concerts in the Albert Hall, many people failing to understand the system of privately owned seats, and there were complaints arising from the way in which the box office allocated tickets: it was not uncommon for groups to receive tickets situated in several different parts of the hall. Nevertheless, there were those for whom the move represented something of a wrench. The Classics for Pleasure organiser, Rowena Unsworth, believed many of the audience had never been to the Festival Hall, raising the possibility of audience resistance to the move, and as an encouragement to subscribers to transfer their affections to the new venue, and give them an opportunity to familiarise themselves with new surroundings, it was decided that in addition to the main series, given for the last time in the Albert Hall, there should be two pilot concerts in the Festival Hall. Doubts about audience resistance were quickly put to rest, the demand for seats at the pilot concerts outstripping the Festival Hall's capacity to such an extent that, to cater subscribers who could not be accommodated at the pilot concerts, seats were set aside for them at four other Festival Hall concerts.

The legacy of Bravington's illness had left Stephen Crabtree with a daunting task, made no easier by the cut in grant imposed by the Arts Council at the end of 1984. After five testing years in the post, Crabtree asked the Board to accept his resignation. His successor was John Willan, the first person from outside the orchestra to be appointed to the post. After qualifying as a chartered accountant, Willan changed the direction of his career, reading music at Edinburgh University before spending a postgraduate year at the Royal Academy of Music, this in turn leading him to the International Classical Division of EMI. In a world where work in the recording studio played a vital part in securing the economic health of the orchestra, his experience in this field was particularly valuable. A change in the company's Articles was necessary in order that he could be appointed a Director, the first time an employee had taken a seat on the Board.

From the day of his arrival Willan was determined to make the LPO the leading London orchestra. As a step towards raising the orchestra's profile, the principal series of concerts in the Festival Hall became known as the International Series, and to justify describing it in this way Willan set out to secure a roster of artists second to none. It was also necessary to tackle a declining financial situation. Even a well-filled Festival Hall could produce, for a properly rehearsed concert, a substantial loss, and in 1984-85 the LPO had budgeted for a loss of £5000 a concert, the reduction in the grant from the Arts Council proving all the more serious because it coincided with a fall in the level of audience, to 72 per cent of the hall's capacity, the LPO having, for the first time in many years, to temporarily surrender its position as the London orchestra attracting the fullest houses in that venue. The temporary withdrawal of one of the orchestra's most valued sponsors, Commercial Union, from this area of activity was a further blow. The combined effect of a cut in grant, a fall in the level of audience attracted to their concerts and loss of some sponsorship led to a growing deficit, necessitating urgent remedial action.

As part of a plan to improve the LPO's financial health Willan proposed seeking expert help from outside, recommending the appointment of Saatchi and Saatchi as advisers on their marketing strategy and their public image, one of their recommendations being that the initials LPO, by which the orchestra was known to several generations of concert-goers, should no longer be used in marketing and publicity material, proposing instead use of the title London Philharmonic.* Willan also took action to increase the level of corporate membership, which had temporarily declined. Setting a target of a hundred members, which was to be the ceiling for the scheme, he envisaged corporate membership as so prestigious to members, companies or individuals, that it would be to the London Philharmonic's advantage to demonstrate that there was a waiting list. His efforts to increase membership met with such success that in 1985-86 the scheme generated nearly £125,000, an increase of around 80 per cent on the previous year, with over two hundred of the most expensive seats in the hall pre-sold for every concert. There was also an increase in the number of subscribers to the Classics for Pleasure series, overall attendances during 1985-86 showing a welcome increase, from 72 per cent in 1984-85 to 79 per cent in 1985-86. The situation was further improved by an increase in the volume of recording work, with more sessions undertaken than for several years.

Though the need for sponsorship remained as great as ever, the number of sponsored concerts had fallen away, to nine in 1983-84, recovering to seventeen the following year, before falling back to thirteen in 1985-86. For many years the London Philharmonic Council had done sterling work in this area, but it was questionable whether a body of twenty or more members was best equipped to deal with the increasingly hostile financial environment in which arts organisations were operating. Willan believed the time was right to emulate the Philharmonia, whose Trustees had raised the sponsorship profile of that orchestra. Steps were therefore taken to replace the Council with a smaller Board of Trustees, the new body coming into being in 1986, its formation providing an opportunity to introduce new blood into the ranks of the orchestra's fund-raising supporters, Mr Elliott Bernerd, the Chairman of Morgan Grenfell Laurie and a Director of Stockley plc, accepting an invitation to act as Chairman. In addition to fund-raising it was envisaged that the Trustees would focus attention on the orchestra's business objectives, without however becoming involved in artistic matters, which remained the prerogative of the Board.

In 1985 Glyndebourne made one of its rare excursions into the more popular area of the repertoire, mounting a production of *Carmen*. This opera was also performed in the Albert Hall, the first of two engagements at the Proms, and a second Glyndebourne production received a concert performance in

---

*From here on the book follows the practice adopted by the orchestra, using the title London Philharmonic rather than the initials LPO.

London, at the Barbican, where Simon Rattle conducted *Idomeneo*. At the other extreme the opera season included *Albert Herring*, with an orchestra largely comprised of section principals. Had Ernest Newman been alive he might have been surprised to find *Arabella*, about which he had been so dismissive, retaining its place in the repertoire for a second year.

Tennstedt's health was already giving rise to concern. At this stage his problems were put down to overwork, and discussions took place with his agent, Ronald Welford, with a view to trying to rationalise his schedule. He withdrew from two concerts at the 1985 Edinburgh Festival, where Christoph Eschenbach and Walter Weller appeared in his place, returning to the rostrum for the orchestra's second Prom of the year, at which he conducted Mozart's *Jupiter* Symphony and Beethoven's *Choral Symphony*, and in the following week opened a new Festival Hall season with Verdi's *Requiem*. It was a year in which, with the transfer of Classics for Pleasure to the Festival Hall, the LPO promoted more concerts in that venue than in any other year since the hall first opened. In a bid to increase audiences the International Series was given a new simplified price structure, with seats for most concerts priced at £3.50, £7.00 and £11.00, subscribers to the Classics for Pleasure series, for which there was a new sponsor, the National Westminster Bank, paying a modest £14 for five concerts, with any unsold seats available from the Festival Hall Box Office at £4.50.

The visit to Perugia, delayed from the previous year, took place in September, Tennstedt conducting performances of the *Choral Symphony* and *The Creation*, but satisfaction at the success of the year's opening concerts was overshadowed by the fact that it was all too apparent that, at least for the time being, Tennstedt could no longer cope with such concentrated spells of work. Towards the end of the September, when he was due to conduct four concerts in five days, two Festival Hall concerts framing two appearances at the Swansea Festival, he was obliged to withdraw from the first pair, for which Andrew Litton took his place, retaining the less demanding programme, made up of music for the dance, given in Swansea, and repeated in London at a Charity Gala in aid of the Save the Children Fund, attended by Princess Anne and sponsored by Leeuwin Estate, sponsors of the previous winter's tour of Australia.

The worst fears about Tennstedt's health were not immediately realised, and though Vladimir Ashkenazy replaced him at one concert he was able to fulfil his other engagements in the Festival Hall, several of which were devoted to the music of a single composer: Beethoven, Brahms, Mahler and Strauss. Another of his concerts paired Stravinsky's *Firebird* Suite with Orff's *Catulli carmina*, but what was intended as an evening of Hungarian music was subjected to a late change, Mahler's Fourth Symphony replacing Bartok's Concerto for Orchestra. It was an indication of a problem causing increasing concern: far from expanding, Tennstedt's repertoire appeared to be shrinking, his reluctance to step outside extremely narrow boundaries continuing to give rise to programme changes. Within those boundaries his work continued to win almost universal approval; under another conductor the Beethoven concert with which the season came to an end might have been regarded as routine, but as the *Daily Telegraph* reported: 'Klaus Tennstedt makes things happen at his concerts. This is why he is such a tonic to London's musical life. With his alert probing presence on the podium he immediately banishes the routine that too often casts a blight on our musical scene.'

Substitute conductors had to be found at short notice when Jesús López-Cobos withdrew from three Festival Hall concerts, one of them a young Austrian, Franz Welser-Möst, with a Mozart programme including the *Haffner* Symphony and the *Requiem* attracting favourable notices, one critic going so far as to compare him to the late Karl Böhm. Solti led performances of Liszt's *Faust Symphony* and the Seventh Symphony of Bruckner, and Simon Rattle conducted two widely contrasting concerts, the first devoted to Stravinsky, with Rachmaninov's Second Symphony the major work in the second.

Vernon Handley's term as Associate Conductor came to an end this year. EMI were exploring the lesser-known choral works of Elgar, and among Handley's concerts was a performance of *King Olaf*, which was subsequently recorded. On the heels of Handley's departure the composer Carl Davis began a short association with the orchestra, a by-product of which was a four-day engagement at the London Palladium, playing the new score Davis had written to accompany the silent version of *Ben-Hur*. Davis became involved in planning the Classics for Pleasure series, composing a fanfare intended to open and close each season, the concerts including some of the music he had composed for films and television.

Problems arose in connection with a contract with a new concert agency, John Higham International Artists, who engaged the orchestra for a series of concerts in the Festival Hall and the Barbican. Given under a string of unknown conductors, these failed to attract audiences, resulting in the financial failure of the agency. The London Philharmonic were owed a substantial amount in respect of unpaid fees, and in a move widely misinterpreted by the press, who were unaware of the full background, the Board decided to protect their position by taking the company over, but despite spending considerable time in trying to recover the sums due to them, it eventually became necessary to wind the company up, writing off the debt.

The London Philharmonic's contribution to the 1986 Proms included *Simone Boccanegra*, under Haitink, who conducted two orchestral concerts, the first comprising the *Enigma Variations* and the Tenth Symphony of Shostakovitch, and the second the Third Piano Concerto of Beethoven and *Ein Heldenleben*. They were also engaged to give the end-of-season performance of the *Choral Symphony*. Conducted by Solti, this followed hard on the heels of a four-day visit to Frankfurt, where Solti and the orchestra, with the London Voices and the Welsh National Opera Chorale, gave two performances of the *Choral* Symphony and two of *The Damnation of Faust*. These four concerts were estimated to have cost the promoters around £250,000, a staggering figure to the manager of any cash-starved British orchestra, one not far short of the London Philharmonic's annual grant from the Arts Council. Work of rather different artistic quality, but no less remunerative, took the orchestra into the film studios to record the background score for *The Mission*, the premiere of the film, at the Empire, Leicester Square in October, providing one of their more unusual engagements, a section of the orchestra playing Haydn's *Drum Roll* Symphony and extracts from the film score before the curtain went up on the film itself.

Tennstedt's health broke down in the autumn of 1986. He conducted the year's opening concerts, which included much Beethoven, but in November cancelled a Festival Hall performance of Bruckner's Eighth Symphony and an Italian tour which took place shortly afterwards, and as the season unfolded, other conductors took over his remaining concerts; it would be eighteen months before he returned to the concert platform. In his absence the services of Neeme Järvi were obtained for the Italian tour, Tennstedt's withdrawal giving rise to considerable embarrassment when, despite the circumstances, the President of the Santa Cecilia Academy in Rome threatened that, in the absence of the London Philharmonic's Principal Conductor, he proposed to cancel their concert in that city. John Willan's frustration was understandable, but it was unwise to vent this so publicly, his reference to the behaviour of the 'Italian musical mafia' good for newspaper headlines but unlikely to calm troubled waters. The dispute was resolved by the intervention of Guiseppi Sinopoli, Principal Conductor of the Philharmonia Orchestra, who informed the Academy that unless they withdrew their threat, they would find that when the time came for him to conduct in Rome, later in the year, he would also be 'ill' and unable to appear. It was not the happiest of tours, the orchestra plagued by press reports of trouble in the hotel in Ravenna where the orchestra were staying, the kind of unfounded rumour which habitually plagues touring English cricketers, but which may have been unique in the annals of orchestral touring.

Despite disappointments arising from Tennstedt's absence there were compensations, including Haitink's performance of Vaughan Williams' *London Symphony*, which was recorded, the start of a still unfolding cycle, and a concert performance of *Figaro*, also conducted by Haitink and given in tandem with recording sessions, the concert itself made possible thanks to generous support from Lloyds Bank. Mahler's Fifth Symphony was played twice under Solti, the two performances taking place some three weeks apart; Okko Kamu gave London its first hearing of Aulis Sallinen's Fifth Symphony, and Kurt Sanderling conducted a majestic account of Bruckner's Seventh Symphony.

Tennstedt was scheduled to take part in a tour of Germany, sharing the conducting with Leonard Slatkin, but in the event replacements had to be found for both conductors. Franz Welser-Möst, who was among those who deputised for Tennstedt in the Festival Hall, had agreed to make himself available to stand in for Tennstedt, should this prove necessary, and Yoel Levi took the place of Slatkin. It is not unknown for orchestras to test the mettle of young conductors in one way or another, and Welser-Möst quickly showed he had their measure when, in reply to a mumbled question put to him by a player during rehearsal, he responded, 'I can't hear you, but if you are suggesting I speak too softly, I do it deliberately so that you listen to what I am saying.'

At the end of 1986 Rosalie Cody retired from the post of Concerts Director, the alarms and excursions of the year's cancellations providing a baptism of fire for her successor, Rowena Unsworth. Another long-serving member of the orchestra's staff, Jean Stephenson, whose responsibilities included the arrangements for overseas tours, had resigned the previous year, to take up charitable work. Something has been mentioned of the work of the concert management department. Touring presents a different but allied set of problems. The logistics of transporting a hundred plus players and their instruments, ensuring they take the stage in the right city at the right time, entails meticulous planning which begins many months in advance, the planning cycle for a tour generally even longer than for concerts in the Festival Hall. The tour must be costed, finance sought from the British Council and/or sponsors, flights and hotels booked, arrangements made for transport to and from each day's concert, insurance put in place for the instruments, and records kept to ensure passports are up to date, not necessarily the simplest of tasks when, apart from members carrying British passports, the ranks of the orchestra include citizens of such diverse countries as Australia, Brazil, Germany, South Africa and Sweden. The end product is a set of detailed itineraries for drivers, stage managers, players, conductors, soloists and members of the management staff travelling with the orchestra. As well as managing the orchestra's touring arrangements since 1964, Miss Stephenson had been responsible for preparing the work rotas for successive Glyndebourne seasons, ensuring that each opera had a full complement of players. In paying tribute to a quarter of a century of backroom service, the Managing Director remarked that in all probability she knew more about the workings of the London Philharmonic than any other member of the organisation.

It was a considerable coup that the concerts scheduled for the autumn of 1987 were launched through the columns of the *Sunday Times Weekend Magazine*, the newspaper's sponsorship bringing in its train a bonus in the shape of an award made under the government's Business Sponsorship Incentive Scheme. The interest generated was such that the newspaper itself recorded increased sales for the issue in question, and the public response so great the Post Office refused to deliver more than five hundred ticket applications a day. At one point there was a backlog of two to three thousand awaiting delivery. Many concerts were sold out in advance, with a minimal number of tickets returned to the Festival Hall for sale on a single ticket basis.

The roster of conductors included Haitink, Andrew Litton, Solti, Tennstedt and Welser-Möst, two conductors making their debut with the LPO, Kurt Masur and Leonard Slatkin, and an evening in lighter vein was given with Victor Borge. Solti conducted the Fifth Symphony of Tchaikovsky and, *Messiah*, and Haitink returned to a score he had performed many times with the orchestra, the Tenth Symphony of Shostakovitch. The American contingent offered a strong input of British music, Andrew Litton conducting *Dona Nobis Pacem* by Vaughan Williams, while Leonard Slatkin chose Walton's First Symphony for his opening concert, and was joined by the London Philharmonic Choir for his second, a performance of *The Kingdom*. Kurt Masur's debut with the orchestra comprised Kodaly's Suite *Háry János* and the Incidental Music written by Grieg for *Peer Gynt*, with the added attraction of speeches from the play read by Michael Jayston and Pamela Hunter.

Hopes that Tennstedt might be able to resume his place as Music Director were, however, dashed shortly before the season began. Engaged to conduct at the Proms he began the first rehearsal, but halfway through felt unable to continue, almost immediately tendering his resignation. Despite the fact that his by now frequent withdrawals from engagements were a source of much frustration, it was a decision received with regret. James Loughran took Tennstedt's place at the Proms, with his scheduled Festival Hall concerts given under Sir Charles Groves, Hans Vonk and Symon Bychkov.

Tennstedt's illness cast a shadow over a projected tour of the USA scheduled for November. With uncertainty as to his fitness the Board were in doubt as to the wisdom of going ahead, only confirming the tour at a very late date, the decision whether to proceed or not a finely balanced one. Cancellation would have left the players without much prospect of work for the best part of three weeks, but the delay in making a decision made it impossible to obtain sponsorship, resulting in an unwanted loss on the expedition. It had been intended that, to relieve the strain on Tennstedt, five of the thirteen concerts would be conducted by Bychkov, and though attempts were made to replace Tennstedt, Bychkov conducted throughout. Two further ventures abroad took place during the winter, a two-day visit to East Berlin under the French conductor Serge Baudo, with any concerns about finance allayed when the promoter undertook to pay the costs in sterling, and there was an even quicker turnaround for the second, involving a single concert in Seville under Jerzy Maksymiuk.

For the second half of the winter, concerts in the International Series had to stand on their own, without the benefit of newspaper support, one highly satisfactory feature of the year the fact that after the slump experienced in the mid-1980s, attendance figures had climbed back to over 90 per cent of the capacity of the Festival Hall. Little in the way of publicity was needed to secure packed houses for two concert performances of *Porgy and Bess*, the sensation of the previous summer at Glyndebourne, which Simon Rattle brought to London, preparatory to recording the work for EMI, and concerts were given under Andrew Davis, Riccardo Muti, making his debut with the London Philharmonic, and Kurt Sanderling. Haitink conducted Mahler's First Symphony, and the same composer's Ninth Symphony formed part of one of the South Bank's earliest thematic schemes. Entitled 'End Games' and based on the last works written by the composers represented, it was a piece of programme-building that appeared to have no particular logic or virtue, and largely failed to attract the public.

The orchestra was also kept busy working for Chandos, who were recording the complete works of Bax, conducted by Bryden Thompson. The Fourth Symphony and some of the tone poems were recorded with the Ulster Orchestra, but the remaining works were performed by the London Philharmonic, with the Seventh Symphony featuring in a Festival Hall concert. In addition to the symphonies the discs embraced two major works for piano and orchestra, the *Symphonic Variations* and *Winter Legends*, the Cello Concerto, the Violin Concerto and a number of shorter, mostly unknown pieces. Other music recorded under Thompson included new recordings of the Elgar Symphonies and works by Walton, part of a growing catalogue of British music recorded by this company.

Tennstedt returned to the rostrum for the final Festival Hall concert of the year. The programme was of a kind much despised in some quarters, orchestral excerpts from the operas of Wagner, the Overture and Venusberg music from *Tannhäuser*, the Overture to *Rienzi*, Dawn, Siegfried's Journey to the Rhine and the Funeral March from *Götterdämmerung*, the Overture to *The Mastersingers* and, as an encore, *The Ride of the Valkyries*. If the programme looked short measure, a packed Festival Hall was in no mood to concern itself with such matters, according Tennstedt a rapturous reception. Briefly, nature allowed him to resume his career. For three or four years hereafter he was able to take charge of a small number of concerts, each an occasion to be cherished.

Though without the services of a Music Director, and despite the disappointments arising from Tennstedt's health problems, the past three years had seen the London Philharmonic recover from a series of problems. Other events were, however, unfolding which were to have a profound impact on the affairs of London's orchestras.

17

From Rumour to Residency 1988–90

With the abolition of the GLC, ownership of the South Bank complex passed to the Arts Council, who received increased funding to compensate for a substantial addition to their outgoings. Rather than manage the halls directly, responsibility for their operation was placed at arm's length, with a new body, the South Bank Board, set up for that purpose, the Board taking its place as one of the Council's many clients. In addition to its management role, the South Bank Board also took over the responsibilities formerly discharged by the London Orchestral Concerts Board, becoming the channel through which grants were disbursed. The first Chairman of the Board was Ronald Grierson, formerly Chairman of the Philharmonia Trust. Grierson's appointment was a matter of some concern, giving rise to fears as to whether it would be possible for a Chairman whose past links had been with another orchestra to be wholly impartial.

At the outset there appeared to be an internal dispute as to the role to be adopted by the South Bank Board. Was it to limit its responsibilities to management of the complex, restricting its involvement in artistic matters to encouraging diversity of repertoire and assisting in the avoidance of unnecessary programme clashes, or should the Board take a more active role, seeking to influence organisations using the halls in their choice of programme, as well as promoting thematic series of its own devising? It was the latter view which prevailed, giving rise to a reappearance of the clash of interest between the hall itself and the orchestras performing in it, that bedevilled matters when the hall first opened. Because the Board have been either unable to provide sufficient finance to give certain of these ventures their full financial backing, intrusion into the area of programme planning has led to a situation where orchestras, forced into less than enthusiastic co-operation in promotions they regard as being unlikely to attract public support, can be left to foot the bill. The emergence of this policy presented the London Philharmonic with an unwelcome choice between taking part in the Board's promotions, running the risk of losing their own individuality, or standing to one side, which in turn could prejudice hopes of appointment as resident orchestra.

Whatever the faults of the GLC's management, over the years the London Philharmonic learned to live with the organisation set up by that body to operate the halls. The relationship between orchestra and hall management was generally satisfactory, but this now came under considerable strain, resulting from several factors, the South Bank's decision to influence programme planning, especially through the medium of thematic series of concerts, the unsettled question of the residency, what appeared to be hostility on the part of Grierson to Willan's attempts to break the deadlock, and the fact that Willan rightly saw it as his duty to do everything within his power to secure primacy of place for the orchestra he served, one of his main objectives being to secure the residency. Misunderstandings arose from Willan's management style, derived from experience in the recording industry, a style described in one Arts Council appraisal as 'robust'.

The snail's pace approach by the Arts Council to the proposals submitted jointly by the London Philharmonic and the Philharmonia was a continuing irritant. Despite the received wisdom that the repertoire offered to the London concert-going public fell short of the diversity offered to provincial audiences, particularly those in Birmingham, the range of music played by both orchestras covered a wide spectrum, arguably only falling short in the case of more advanced contemporary music, a gap which was to a considerable extent filled by the BBC Symphony Orchestra and the London Sinfonietta. There was nevertheless room for improvement in the way each season was planned, and on the face of it there seemed no real obstacle to prevent a closer partnership, one which would provide London with a sensibly planned and executed season of concerts, even if no cure seemed in sight for the London public's unwillingness to support programmes given more than one performance.

For all that they were in competition, relations between the two orchestras were generally harmonious, but this state of affairs was to be broken in no uncertain fashion. In December 1986 Willan submitted proposals to the Philharmonia aimed at bringing the two orchestras under joint management control. As well as strengthening their hand in dealing with the South Bank Board over such matters as allocation of dates, programme planning, choice of repertoire and booking arrangements, the proposal to bring them under the umbrella of a unified management was expected to produce modest administrative savings. But whatever the merits of the proposals, the manner of Willan's approach appeared seriously flawed, and it was with a poor sense of timing that he chose to deliver the letter detailing his proposal late on a Friday afternoon, so that it was unlikely to be read, let alone absorbed, before the weekend, an error compounded by briefing a journalist connected with the *Sunday Times* as to its contents. Any hope of constructive discussion disappeared when the paper gave the proposals front-page coverage.

Premature publication could not have been better designed to stoke the fires of opposition, the fears of the Philharmonia players fuelled by the fact that the proposals were almost universally interpreted by the media as a take-over bid for that orchestra. The proposals were immediately condemned without trial, leaving little or no scope for fruitful discussion, but ample room for conflict.

One of the major stumbling blocks to acceptance of the plan was the suggestion that management of the two orchestras should be in the hands of a holding company, to be administered by the London Philharmonic. Given the zeal with which London's orchestras guard their independence, this was in itself sufficient to set alarm bells ringing, raising fears that with day-to-day management control in other hands, the Philharmonia would rapidly lose control over its own affairs, perhaps even its own identity. Faced with outright rejection by management and players, a second attempt was made to persuade members of the Philharmonia to think again. A personal letter from David Marcou, the London Philharmonic's Chairman, was sent to the members of both orchestras, with a reply paid card which each recipient was invited to return to the Electoral Reform Society, indicating whether or not the ideas merited further discussion. In the climate created by the press, who continued to interpret the proposals as a take-over bid, there was little hope of success, most of the Philharmonia players not deigning to reply. There for a time the matter rested. But whatever the merits and demerits of the merger plan, and the manner of its publication, it had the virtue of making the Arts Council and the South Bank look afresh at the pattern of orchestral provision in London, putting the whole question of residency back on the agenda.

Meanwhile artistically and financially, and despite Tennstedt's long absence from the platform, the London Philharmonic continued to advance. The success of the *Sunday Times* subscription offer boosted audiences dramatically, and though the newspaper's support only applied to concerts given in the autumn of 1987, ticket sales remained at highly satisfactory levels. As a result of the *Sunday Times* campaign, and subsequent publicity obtained through the columns of the *Sunday Express, You Magazine,* distributed with the *Mail on Sunday* and the *Telegraph Magazine*, it was possible to build up a substantial database of subscribers, making the mailing list one of the largest available to any London orchestra, a major factor in the continuing success of subscription sales. Artistically there was growing cause for satisfaction from the steady development of the young Austrian conductor Franz Welser-Möst and, a by-product of their friendship with Klaus Tennstedt, the conducting debuts with the London Philharmonic of Kurt Masur, in December 1987, and Zubin Mehta, in January 1988.

By comparison with the previous year, the autumn of 1988 presented the marketing department with a stiff challenge. The year's opening concerts included concert performances of *Leonore*, Beethoven's first version of his opera, conducted by Roger Norrington, and *Fidelio* itself, the latter conducted by Kurt Masur, who had taken up a three-year appointment as Principal Guest Conductor. After a tour of Hong Kong and Japan, November was largely taken up with four concerts devoted to Bartok, conducted by Solti, while December involved the orchestra in one of the most costly promotions on which it had ever embarked, the British premiere of Olivier Messiaen's *St Francois d'Assise*, for which the conductor was the young American, Kent Nagano. A scheme had been introduced giving subscribers to the Classics for Pleasure series an additional bonus in the shape of priority booking for selected concerts in the International Series, offering them a substantial discount on the normal price of tickets. It was in part thanks to Classics for Pleasure subscribers taking up a proportion of seats made available in this way for two of the Bartok concerts that these attracted an attendance figure of over 93 per cent, better than the level of seat occupancy for the year as a whole. If the downside of the scheme lay in the fact that these tickets were discounted to such a level that greatly improved ticket sales were obtained at the expense of revenue, it was a valuable way of persuading part of the Classics for Pleasure audience to cross over to the International Series.

The Bartok concerts were possible thanks to the generosity of Mrs Jackie Rosenfeld and one of the London Philharmonic's American supporters, Walter J. Johnson, who jointly sponsored all four concerts. But if the Bartok series was expensive, the performance of Messiaen's oratorio was even more so. This was a mammoth undertaking, requiring an outsized orchestra, a large cast of soloists and a heavy rehearsal schedule for a work whose performance lasted the best part of four hours. Despite a house which exceeded expectations, over 80 per cent of capacity, and a fee from the BBC for televising the last three scenes, which in themselves lasted around an hour and a half, the concert was only saved from financial disaster by the last-minute provision of £50,000 of sponsorship money, including £35,000 from Yves Saint Laurent, originally earmarked for a French Festival to be promoted by the South Bank the following year. Even with financial help of this order, the orchestra were left to rue the fact that promotion of one of the most prestigious concerts of the year left them out-of-pocket to the tune of many thousands of pounds. Other major events included four outstanding evenings with Haitink. Felicity Lott sang the *Four Last Songs* of Richard Strauss, rejoining the orchestra for the Fourth Symphony of Mahler. Stravinsky's *Symphonies for wind instruments* was framed by two major French ballet scores, Debussy's *Jeux* and a complete performance of *Daphnis and Chloé*, the programmes also featuring three major pieces by British composers, Tippett's *Fantasia concertante on a Theme of Corelli*, Holst's *Planets* and Vaughan Williams' *Sea Symphony*. Tennstedt contributed two performances of Mahler's *Resurrection* Symphony, but continuing health problems prevented him appearing at the year's closing concerts, for which he was replaced by the Russian conductor Yuri Simonov.

There was another unhappy codicil to the year, the month of April bringing the untimely death at the age of fifty-four of the Principal Double Bass, William Webster, who had occupied that position for twenty-seven years. Webster was only the third player to have led the section on a permanent basis. Victor Watson, apart from his brief sojourn with the BBC Salon Orchestra, led the section from 1932 until 1952, when he was succeeded by James Carpenter, Webster taking over in 1962. Possibly there is something special about bass players, for while from one year to another there are always changes taking place in the ranks of an orchestra, it was a feature of Webster's leadership, and the loyalty of his colleagues, that the turnover of players in his section was minimal.

The London Philharmonic's success in selling tickets on a subscription basis gave rise to a further source of irritation. The sale of subscriptions was effected through the London Philharmonic's offices at Doughty Street, not the Festival Hall. However, the South Bank's terms of hire included the requirement that they should be paid 13.5 per cent of the post-VAT revenue on every ticket sold, regardless as to whether the sale was made through Doughty Street or their own box office. With no ceiling on the level of commission, the greater the London Philharmonic's success in selling tickets, the greater the benefit received by the South Bank, regardless as to whether or not their own marketing department and box office could claim any share of the responsibility. What made this all the more galling was the fact that, even with an innovative programme policy, the LPO were again outselling the other London orchestras, ticket sales averaging over 90 per cent of capacity, compared with 75 per cent achieved by the RPO and under 60 per cent by the Philharmonia, while the LSO's 87 per cent had to be set against the very much smaller capacity of the Barbican Hall. The combined effect of the nightly hire charge and the commission paid on tickets was that 37 per cent of the income from concerts promoted in the Festival Hall went to the South Bank Centre, equivalent to 40 per cent of the annual grant received from the Arts Council. It was a situation which appeared absurd and unjust, the more so when both were clients of the same body.

Two major developments taking shape had their roots in the orchestra's Five Year Business Plan, drawn up in 1986 and regularly updated. The self-governing orchestras were now required by the Arts Council to appoint directors from outside the playing ranks, providing Boards with the benefit of their business and management skills, and Bernard Rix QC was the first person from outside the playing membership to accept an invitation to serve in this capacity. A new management structure was therefore set up, aimed at improving the operation of the company, and requiring a further change in the Articles. In addition to the Orchestral Board, elected from the ranks of the playing members and responsible for artistic policy and development of the orchestra, the day-to-day responsibility for running the company was placed in the hands of an Executive Board, comprising the Chairman and Deputy Chairman and one other playing Director, the outside Directors and the departmental heads, Concert Director, Finance Director and Marketing Director. This new structure left the ultimate control of the London Philharmonic in the hands of the musicians themselves.

The second development was an improved system of payment for the players. It had been decided not to accept engagements, or promote concerts on its own account, unless these were given a minimum of two rehearsals, and for the International Series conductors were generally given as much rehearsal time as they required, with additional rehearsals allocated for works of exceptional complexity: Messiaen's *St Francois d'Assisse* received no less than fifteen. In keeping with this decision, it was decided that for their own promotions in the Festival Hall the existing 'concert fee' system of reimbursing players would be replaced by a new system of 'call fees'. Under the old system rehearsals were paid at half the fee applicable to a concert, with a complicated system of additional payments for players who doubled on other instruments, were involved in solos or called on to play special instruments. Under the 'call fee' system every three-hour session was paid at 75 per cent of the old fee, regardless as to whether it was for a concert or a rehearsal, and at the same time the arrangements for making additional payments to players came to an end. The effect of the new arrangements improved the players' earning potential while increasing the orchestra's operating costs. In the following year, therefore, the London Philharmonic launched its Development Plan, aimed at raising an additional one and a half million pounds, with success in this area likely to attract additional incentive funding from the Arts Council.

Continuing artistic and commercial success was an essential ingredient to ambitious plans of this kind, and it was a relief that in the autumn of 1988 Klaus Tennstedt was able to undertake a tour of Hong Kong and Japan, in which Leonard Slatkin also took part. Once again the programmes were far from adventurous, Tennstedt conducting the *Eroica*, a Wagner programme, and the Beethoven and Schubert symphonies with which he opened the season in the Festival Hall. Slatkin conducted the only British work, Walton's Overture *Portsmouth Point*, his programme completed by the Cello Concerto of Dvorak and Tchaikovsky's Fifth Symphony. Tennstedt's programmes were further evidence that, much as the orchestra wished to continue working with him, it was necessary to face up to the increasing limitations of his repertoire. This however was of no great concern to the Japanese who, regardless of the fact that the programmes contained little in the way of adventure, again accorded the orchestra an enthusiastic reception.

The orchestra's participation in the 1989 Proms was limited to a single orchestral concert, under Leonard Slatkin. Simon Rattle, who was conducting *Figaro* at Glyndebourne, the opera brought by the company to the Proms, had expressed a preference for a period instrument orchestra, and Glyndebourne engaged the Orchestra of the Age of Enlightenment for these performances, the London Philharmonic performing for the other four operas in the repertoire, *Kátya Kábanova, Capriccio, Falstaff* and the first staging of Michael Tippett's latest opera, *New Year*. Fears that Glyndebourne might be about to change tack and engage a period instrument orchestra for the entire season were quickly allayed, and the slightly diminished workload at Glyndebourne was offset by the fact that twenty-six recording sessions took place in August, more than in any other month of the year.

The improvement in Tennstedt's health had proved fragile, Andrew Litton and Myung-Whun Chung taking his place at the opening concerts of the new season, 1989-90, and a replacement had also to be found for concerts that he was scheduled to conduct during a tour of Japan. The sponsors had requested the participation of a British conductor, the choice falling upon James Loughran who, since resigning from the Hallé Orchestra, had been active in Japan, and Tennstedt's withdrawal led to Loughran shouldering the full burden of the tour. With the expenses met in full by the promoter, Harold Holt Limited, the only unsatisfactory feature was that the repertoire chosen by Loughran was little more adventurous than that given under Tennstedt the previous year, though it did include two major works by Elgar, the First Symphony and the *Enigma Variations*.

Happily Tennstedt was fit enough to fulfil his remaining Festival Hall engagements, including a gala concert in aid of the Royal Free Hospital, which ended with Beethoven's Seventh Symphony, his other programmes including Brahms' First Symphony, Bruckner's Fourth and Mahler's First. Mahler's symphony was taken on tour under a scheme jointly financed by the Arts Council and the Prudential, which enabled London's orchestras to give audiences outside London the opportunity of hearing well-rehearsed and out-of-the-ordinary programmes. Without such assistance it would not have been possible to include in the same programme two short works by the young British composer George Benjamin, one of which, *Cascade*, received its first performance in Hull, with further performances in York, Middlesborough, Warwick, London, Cambridge and Bristol. Despite a request that he should work to the instrumentation used by Mahler for his First Symphony, Benjamin, who conducted his own music, did in fact score this for some additional instruments, and the cost involved in preparing and performing new music was underlined by the fact that the complexity of these pieces necessitated three additional rehearsals, over and above the five already scheduled for this concert.

The year's programmes again belied the oft-spoken criticism that the repertoire programmed by London's orchestras was less adventurous than that of their provincial brethren. Kurt Masur conducted much Schumann, the First, Third and Fourth Symphonies, and the Piano Concerto, as well as the darkly brooding Thirteenth Symphony of Shostakovitch, for bass soloist, men's voices and orchestra, with more Shostakovitch from Kurt Sanderling, the Fifteenth Symphony; Rozhdestvensky's programmes included unusual repertoire in the shape of Schoenberg's orchestration of Brahms' G minor Piano Quartet and Respighi's orchestration of Rachmaninov's *Five Études-Tableaux*; Andrew Davis conducted a concert performance of *Jenufa*, and Simon Rattle the Third Symphony of Szymanowski, and a concert comprising Messiaen's *Et exspectuo resurrectionem mortuorem* and a long extract from the last act of *Die Walküre*. None of this was everyday fare. One notable absentee was Bernard Haitink, newly installed as Music Director of the Royal Opera House.

Financially the season was well supported, twenty-five out of thirty concerts in the International Series attracting sponsors, an advance on the previous year's figure of twenty-one, and the Classics for Pleasure audience had reason to be grateful for continuing support from the National Westminster Bank. Though the Bank customarily limited sponsorship of any organisation to three years, to which their investment in cricket's knock-out cup is a major exception, they had already sponsored the series for six years, and now undertook to extend their support for a further period. In building programmes for these concerts it is necessary to pay regard to the special needs of this audience, avoiding more advanced contemporary music, striking a balance between well-tried repertoire pieces and the need, for the sake of audience and orchestra, to carefully extend the range of music performed. This year's programmes contained modest adventures in the shape of Ernest Bloch's *Schelomo* for Cello and Orchestra and the Violin Concerto of Korngold, though the inclusion of the *Enigma Variations*, *Pictures from an Exhibition*, *Scheherazade* and *Also Sprach Zarathustra* left room for only one symphony, Dvorak's Seventh.

The long-drawn-out debate concerning the residency was coming to an end. In the aftermath of the bid to place the London Philharmonic and the Philharmonia under joint management, the Arts Council set up a working party, chaired by Robert Ponsonby, 'to recommend to the Arts Council's Music Advisory Panel objectives in respect of the Council's current subsidy to the four London orchestras'. Their proposals included provision of more rehearsal time in the Festival Hall, and suggested, with some reservations, that association between the South Bank and one or more orchestras should be beneficial to the parties concerned.

In June 1989 in the light of the Ponsonby report, and with the approval of the Arts Council, the South Bank Board invited bids for the residency, setting up an advisory panel under the Chairmanship of Sir John Tooley, whose members included Sir William Glock and the conductor Jeffrey Tate, to consider the applications and to report on 'the appointment of one or more resident orchestras at the South Bank Centre'. The tender document was given wide circulation and at least in theory, it was open to any orchestra in the country to submit proposals. After overcoming teething troubles the LSO had settled into new quarters at the Barbican, and the RPO were going through a troubled patch, ruling them out of contention, while so far as orchestras located outside London were concerned, none of them would have been able to take on the role without to a considerable extent turning their back on the audience they already served, making them from the outset non-starters. Not unexpectedly, the only two orchestras to respond were the London Philharmonic and the Philharmonia.

The London Philharmonic's preferred option had always been to secure a sole residency, but during earlier discussion of the subject the South Bank insisted that, while they had great admiration for the excellence of the orchestra's work, granting them sole residency was something that was not within their gift. As an alternative serious consideration had again been given to the idea of a joint residency with the Philharmonia, and though discussions proved inconclusive, the South Bank believed there was broad degree of agreement among the parties concerned that a joint residency would prove acceptable. However, in the light of the terms of the tender document, and the fact that the London Philharmonic and the Philharmonia had been unable to finalise the basis on which a joint residency might be entered into, it was decided that it was in the best interests of the orchestra to bid for a sole rather than a shared residency, a decision received with something less than enthusiasm on the part of the Chairman of the South Bank Board, Ronald Grierson, who had previously been upset by an incident arising from the circumstances of the opening concert of the 1988-89 season.

The South Bank's policy of staging as many events in the hall as possible, avoiding 'dark nights', meant it was only on rare occasions that anything other than the final rehearsal could be staged in the hall itself. The opening of the Henry Wood Hall improved rehearsal arrangements, but for all the virtues of that venue it was impossible to replicate the acoustics of the Festival Hall itself. Sir Georg Solti repeatedly expressed the opinion that, given the same conditions that applied to his work with the Chicago Symphony Orchestra, he could make the London Philharmonic the equal of any orchestra in the world, but in the existing conditions this was unattainable. The year was to have opened with the *Missa Solemnis*, conducted by Tennstedt, but it proved impossible to schedule more than the final rehearsal in the hall itself, a situation Tennstedt found unacceptable, and he declined to go ahead with the original programme, substituting the Eighth Symphony of Beethoven and the Ninth of Schubert. The programme book for the concert included a note, which John Willan had every reason to believe had been agreed by the South Bank, explaining the reason for the change from the originally advertised programme, but this had not been brought to the attention of the Board's Chairman. Despite the fact that his marketing department were consulted about the wording, Grierson interpreted the note as an implied criticism of the South Bank organisation.

From this point relations with the South Bank deteriorated, the situation complicated by the fact that Grierson was on friendly terms with Elliott Bernard, Chairman of the London Philharmonic's Trustees. Though the Trustees had no role to play in the management of the London Philharmonic, Grierson tried to arrange meetings from which Willan was excluded, but to which representatives of the Trust were invited, apparently hoping that some or all of the Trustees might be given executive authority, enabling him to deal with them rather than with the London Philharmonic's Managing Director. It was a situation as embarrassing to the management of the South Bank as to the London Philharmonic, resolved by the expedient of creating a 'standing committee', chaired by David Marcou, whose task was to resolve any further source of conflict between hall and orchestra, Grierson himself deciding to stand aside from the process of evaluating the responses made by the London Philharmonic and the Philharmonia to the invitation to tender for the residency.

The process of analysing the two bids occupied Sir John Tooley and his colleagues throughout the autumn of 1989, with their assessment of the applications expected to be completed in time for an announcement in February 1990. The review was the subject of considerable press speculation, fears about the outcome fuelled when, during the Christmas season, information was leaked to the London Philharmonic Trust to the effect that a decision had been made to award the residency to the Philharmonia. Earlier discussions with the South Bank had indicated that this was the least likely outcome but, in view of the source from which the information was received, it was considered prudent to guard against the possibility that it was accurate, and consider alternative courses of action, among the ideas discussed being the possibility of moving to the Barbican or, the most extreme solution, even trying to raise the capital to finance an entirely new hall. In the event these fears were dispelled when the advisory panel unanimously recommended appointment of the London Philharmonic as resident orchestra. It seemed as if long-cherished hopes were about to be fulfilled.

18

Homecoming? 1990–93

The conclusion reached by the South Bank's working party seemed to provide justification for the policies recommended by John Willan. After paying regard to the quality of conductors and soloists, and the high standard of performance, the panel commended the London Philharmonic's success in attracting consistently larger audiences than any other orchestra, their marketing and sponsorship plans, improvements in the terms of employment, and the level of skill demonstrated by the Business Plan. Their recommendations included appointment of a Music Director, to be in post before the residency commenced, and that the orchestra should 'commit itself to encouraging audiences for more varied and interesting programmes', an area where the marketing department had demonstrated some success, 'ensuring the repertoire was fully representative, from the classical era to the present day'. They also recommended that the residency should run for an initial period of five years, and in a paragraph touching on the financial implications commented:

> 'We have referred earlier to the significant additional costs involved in the residency and the importance of clarifying the responsibility on the part of the South Bank Board and the orchestra for meeting these. Adoption of a single resident orchestra is such an important step forward in the musical life of London that we believe it is crucial that the Arts Council of Great Britain should back this bold venture by assisting with an appropriate portion of the additional costs which are peculiar to the residency.'

The contract setting out the terms of the residency offered primacy in terms of selection of dates for rehearsal and performance, and made provision for the orchestra to perform at Glyndebourne between May and August, a quid pro quo for weeks when the South Bank played host to English National Ballet. Some advantages were offered backstage, a retiring room for the Music Director, permanent accommodation for the orchestral staff and improved locker facilities for the players. However, unlike the LSO, whose residency at the Barbican enabled that orchestra to relocate its offices in the hall, the South Bank was unable to offer administrative space, and it was necessary to retain the Doughty Street office, with its attendant overhead costs. The contract also contained a number of restrictive clauses, limiting overseas touring to thirty-one days between the beginning of September and May, precluded the orchestra from undertaking engagements, other than the Proms, within a thirty-mile radius of the Festival Hall, and specified that the first performance of every programme given by the orchestra was to take place in the Festival Hall. The most onerous clauses related to repertoire, requiring part of each year's work to be committed to thematic projects and performance of an agreed element of twentieth-century music, including a specified proportion composed since 1945. These restrictions suggested a certain lack of mutual confidence, and there was one crucial omission: despite the comments in Sir John Tooley's report, there was no mention of the financing of the residency.

The appointment of a new Music Director became a matter of primary importance, for if this was delayed it could mean postponing commencement of the residency for a year. Among the names canvassed was that of Zubin Mehta, whose term with the New York Philharmonic was ending, but who decided against taking up a new permanent post, while hopes that Kurt Masur might accept an invitation were dashed when he was appointed to succeed Mehta in New York. After much debate, the decision was taken to invite Franz Welser-Möst to act as Music Director as from September 1990. Welser-Möst had established himself as an outstanding member of the younger generation of conductors, with a growing repertoire, extending beyond the standard German classics, an important factor when the South Bank were looking for the orchestra to present a widely diversified repertoire. Overseas, his links with the Linz Bruckner Festival brought an invitation to perform in that city, while from a commercial angle there was the attraction of his recording contract with EMI. Overall, there was good reason to hope for much from this new partnership. Nevertheless it was recognised that there were risks attached to the appointment of so young a man, as much for the musician himself as for the orchestra.

John Willan's press statement announcing that Welser-Möst had accepted the London Philharmonic's invitation indicated that he would have a more prominent role than his predecessors:

'We have chosen a Music Director with whom the orchestra has an unquestionably strong relationship. This is the first time a self-governing orchestra in London has afforded its Music Director the powers that are theirs, as of right, in all other top orchestras around the world.'

These powers included membership of the Executive and Orchestral Boards with, in theory at least, the right to 'hire and fire' players. In practice the days of the great dictator conductors, Beecham, Rodzinski, Stokowski and Toscanini, who could and did dismiss players without any right of appeal, were a thing of the past; in most orchestras auditions had long involved not just the Music Director, but at least the principal of the section concerned, and the process adopted by the London Philharmonic was very similar: after hearing players in audition, and consultation with the section principal, the final responsibility for confirming an appointment resting with the Orchestral Board. Nor, except in extreme cases, can a player be summarily dismissed. There is an agreed procedure, designed to help and encourage improvement on the part of any player whose performance is thought to have fallen below the accepted standard, with dismissal regarded as a last resort. Bringing their Music Director into the process provided an additional layer of expertise to be consulted before a final decision was reached.

Though plans for the residency were being set in train, it would be two years before these came to fruition. In the meantime the orchestra had a heavy round of commitments for the next two seasons, 1990–91 and 1991–92. By now there was always an element of doubt about Tennstedt's appearances, but in August 1990 he conducted a performance of Beethoven's Fifth Symphony which left a crowded Albert Hall in raptures. Their response was echoed by the *Independent*, whose critic was moved to write, 'I thought I knew this symphony. I did not.', a comment which might have applied again and again when Tennstedt conducted. A month later, however, it was necessary to find a replacement for the year's opening concerts in the Festival Hall, Yuri Simonov appearing in his stead, and in October the young Italian conductor Carlo Rizzi stepped in to conduct Schubert's *Unfinished* Symphony and Mahler's Fourth. This was another programme taken on tour under the scheme sponsored by the Arts Council and the Prudential, the centres visited outside London including Durham, Glasgow, Liverpool, Hanley and Sheffield. The demands of the diary were such that the players went straight from the overnight train from Sheffield to London into rehearsal for a cycle of the Brahms symphonies under Simon Rattle.

Tennstedt's absences gave rise to fears about three performances of Mahler's Eighth Symphony in January 1991, the more so as these were to take place within the space of four days, the kind of schedule that had recently seemed beyond his capabilities. Whether the Festival Hall was the right venue for a work demanding such large forces is open to argument, but to the great relief of all concerned Tennstedt was able to conduct all three. These triumphant performances rounded out a public cycle of Mahler's symphonic output, the recorded cycle, which had been unfolding for more than a decade, having been completed some time before. The performances were recorded in High Definition TV and released on video disc.

If Mahler's Eighth Symphony was the centrepiece of the year's music, there was much else of note. Welser-Möst was demonstrating his ability to build intriguing programmes, one concert comprising the Second Symphony of one of his former teachers, the Austrian composer Balduin Sulzer, of which he gave the first performance with the Norrköping Orchestra, Mendelssohn's *Scottish* Symphony and a complete performance of Stravinsky's Ballet *Pulcinella*. This programme was repeated at the Linz Bruckner Festival, but so far as the Festival Hall was concerned, there was a downside to such imaginative programming: it did not attract the public, the audience amounting to 40 per cent of capacity. It was a demonstration of the Catch-22 situation regarding programme building, the Arts Council demanding that orchestras perform contemporary music, at the same time insisting they balance their books, the poor public response to such programmes making it impossible to square the circle. Nor was there a much fuller hall for a concert performance of Tippett's opera *New Year*, though in this case there was a bonus in the shape of a television recording, which took place around Christmas, a period which usually comprised part of the players' annual holiday, but which this year saw them kept exceptionally busy, those involved giving up Boxing Day to rehearse for a performance of *Messiah* promoted by the *Sunday Times* the following evening.

Further evidence of public resistance to thematic schemes was provided by the South Bank's 'Russian Spring Festival', which encompassed a broad cross section of Russian culture, including architecture, painting, sculpture, and photography. The musical content included works by post-revolutionary composers, notably Nicolai Roslavets, a contemporary of Stravinsky, whose innovative ideas – he developed his own twelve-note style of composition without having seen or heard a note of Schoenberg – brought him into conflict with the new regime. Notwithstanding conductors of the stature of Kurt Masur and Kent Nagano, and the attraction of major pieces by Stravinsky and Tchaikovsky, programmes including works by Schnittke and Roslavets attracted only modest houses, and for all the South Bank's advocacy of Roslavets his music subsequently slipped back into the obscurity from which it had been briefly plucked. Simon Rattle's Brahms cycle had greater audience appeal; Solti conducted the Second Symphony of Bruckner, and Leonard Slatkin continued to demonstrate his penchant for British music with a concert comprising Britten's Sea Interludes from *Peter Grimes*, the *Sinfonia da Requiem* and Elgar's Violin Concerto, the concert dedicated to the memory of two members of the orchestra, the oboist Harriet Bell and the violinist Maire Dillon; only in their forties, both had succumbed to cancer during the summer. The year's overseas tours, to Germany in March and Switzerland in April, were given under Charles Dutoit and Christoph von Dohnányi, and the year ended with Mahler's Seventh Symphony under Bernard Haitink, a performance repeated a few days later on a flying visit to Amsterdam.

After the many disappointments arising from Tennstedt's ill-health, the ten concerts he was engaged to conduct during 1991–92 were carried through without a hitch. The pressure on Tennstedt was relieved by arranging most of his concerts in pairs, repeating at least one major work, sometimes the whole concert, with several days allowed between each performance. Beethoven's *Eroica*, given at the opening concerts, was taped by EMI for future release; a Wagner programme, including the first Act of *Die Walküre*, was given twice, as was Mahler's Sixth Symphony, and performances of Beethoven's Fifth Symphony were supplemented by the *Pastoral* Symphony and by Berg's Violin Concerto. In general Welser-Möst eschewed the standard repertoire. For a performance of Bach's *St Matthew Passion*, the choral numbers were undertaken by the Choristers of the Abbey Church of St Albans and the Mozart Choir of Linz, a youth choir whose members' ages ranged from fourteen to twenty-two, with whom Welser-Möst had worked in the past and in which he himself once sang. The programme book contained a long and thoughtful interview in which the conductor discussed his approach to interpretation and performance of the work.

In late February the orchestra embarked on another concentrated tour, taking them to Japan, across the Pacific to Mexico, finishing on the eastern seaboard of the USA. The conducting was to have been shared between Welser-Möst and Tennstedt, but though fulfilling all his scheduled appearances in the Festival Hall, Tennstedt felt impelled to withdraw from an exacting schedule, the entire burden falling on Welser-Möst's shoulders. One unusual feature was the number of different halls in which the orchestra performed: in Tokyo concerts were given in the Shinjuko Bunka Centre, Ikebikuro Geijustso Gediko and Suntory Hall; in Osaka they played in Symphony Hall and Orchard Hall; in Mexico City performances took place in the Palacio de Bellas Artes and the Auditorio National, and in New York there were performances in both Carnegie Hall and Avery Fischer Hall, home of the New York Philharmonic.

The year's activities concluded with nine concerts under the collective title 'Diaghilev and his Circle'. As the brochure announcing the series explained, before the formation of the ballet company for which he is chiefly remembered, Diaghilev 'organised a series of concerts of Russian music in Paris, familiarising audiences with the music of composers such as Glinka, Tchaikovsky, Mussorgsky and Borodin'. Music from no less than eleven productions mounted by Diaghilev was performed, and to give the programmes balance they were rounded out with a number of mostly contemporaneous works, Walton's Viola Concerto, Gershwin's *Rhapsody in Blue* and Hindemith's *Concert music for brass and strings*. There was a large element of Stravinsky's music, the *Firebird* Suite, *Petrushka*, the Suite from *Pulcinella* and *Oedipus Rex*; Shura Cherkassky performed Schumann's *Carnival*; Poulenc was represented by *Les Biches*, Ravel by the First Suite from *Daphnis and Chloé*, and *La Valse*, commissioned by the impresario, who angered the composer by declaring it unsuitable for dancing. Other composers included Debussy, Glinka, Prokofiev and Tchaikovsky. To match the quality of the music a distinguished roster of performers was engaged, the conductors including Kurt Masur, Zubin Mehta, Klaus Tennstedt and Franz Welser-Möst, and in addition to Cherkassky the list of soloists included Dmitri Alexeev, Kathleen Battle, Cécile Ousset and Maxim Vengerov. Based on a more clearly defined logic than that of many thematic schemes, this was an imaginative curtain-raiser to the residency.

Financially the year was well supported, with sponsors for almost every concert in the International Series and continuing support from the National Westminster Bank for Classics for Pleasure. Tennstedt's opening concert was sponsored by Elliott Bernerd, a gesture showing the personal commitment of their Trust's Chairman to the orchestra, and with expectations of growing support from the London Philharmonic Trust, the omens for the residency, artistic and financial, appeared good.

Glyndebourne's contribution to the 1992 Proms was *The Queen of Spades*, conducted by Andrew Davis, and the London Philharmonic's second concert was an all-Wagner affair under Tennstedt. With a new opera house due to open in less than two years' time, Glyndebourne closed its doors earlier than usual, facilitating the acceptance of invitations to perform at Edinburgh, Naples, where two open-air concerts were given, and the Lucerne Festival. Tennstedt repeated the Wagner programme in both places, but it had been reluctantly decided, after his withdrawal from the trans-Pacific tour, that these would be his last overseas concerts with the orchestra, the risks arising from his health problems having reached a point where it would no longer be prudent to invite him to tour.

The residency was to begin under a new leader. After sixteen years at the front desk, David Nolan departed to join the ranks of the Philharmonia. The post was filled by the Swedish violinist Joakim Svenheden, who as leader of the Norrköping Symphony Orchestra had worked with Welser-Möst in the past. Svenheden's experience had also encompassed the first chair of both the Swedish Radio Symphony Orchestra and the Stockholm Chamber Orchestra, and he was in some demand as a soloist, performing many of the major concertos in the violin repertoire.

There was one other notable departure, the viola player Wrayburn Glasspool, who had joined the orchestra as long ago as 1935, deciding that after fifty-seven years, and with the London Philharmonic apparently secure in the residency, the time had come to retire. One of the great raconteurs in the orchestra, a tongue-in-cheek Board minute noted that he 'would not be sending a letter (of resignation), due to the fact that he had never had a contract in the first place'. Asked for his opinion of the many conductors under whom he had worked he singled out two, Beecham and de Sabata, delivering the verdict that 'If Beecham was red-hot, de Sabata was white-hot.'

Including the Classics for Pleasure series, the first year of the residency involved fifty concerts. Audience figures suggested, at least where mainstream repertoire was concerned, that it should be possible to sell the house twice over, and in addition to the Classics for Pleasure concerts, twelve of the twenty-eight programmes in the International Series were given a second performance. The opening concerts took place on 17 and 18 September 1992. Conducted by Franz Welser-Möst, this abnormally long programme, given on both evenings, and necessitating two intervals, started at the early hour of 6.30:

Kuisma : Three Galaxies; Beethoven : Piano Concerto No 4 in G (**Maurizio Pollini**); Schumann : Symphony No 2; Stravinsky : Symphonies of Wind Instruments; Britten : Prelude and Fugue for Strings; Prokofiev : Suite The Love of Three Oranges

The opening item, for six percussion players, was a late addition to the programme, and if its inclusion demonstrated a commitment to contemporary music, the piece proved a less than inspired choice, generally disliked by audience and press. Nevertheless these concerts were an auspicious start to the residency. They were followed by three outstandingly successful programmes, the attendance at which fully justified the decision to give each a second performance. Zubin Mehta sandwiched Bruch's First Violin Concerto between Webern's *Six Pieces for Orchestra* and *Carmina Burana*, the first performance of this programme designated a gala evening, attended by the Duke of Kent, with the concert followed by a fund-raising auction, in which Mehta participated, an event which raised a valuable sum for the Development Fund. Tennstedt conducted two performances of the *Choral Symphony*, and accompanied Nigel Kennedy in Beethoven's Violin Concerto, the evening rounded out by a performance of the First Symphony of Brahms. Other concerts were given under Haitink, a Bartok programme attracting an all but sold-out house, Mariss Jansons, and Welser-Möst, who conducted the Choir in two performances of *Messiah*. A distinguished list of soloists included Kyung-Wha Chung, Stephen Kovacevich, Radu Lupu and Victoria Mullova.

Ticket sales were boosted by the fact that the residency was launched through the columns of the *Sunday Times*, audiences prior to Christmas averaging an almost unbelievable 97 per cent. The turn of the year brought the first indication that this was something not to be taken for granted. A mixed bag under Welser-Möst, Schubert's Third Symphony, the *Burlesque* for Piano and Orchestra by Strauss, and pieces by Julius Fucik, Nicolai, Suppe and Johann Strauss showed the orchestra's Music Director in relaxed mood, but the response to what appeared an audience-friendly programme was disappointing. Thereafter only Mahler Seven, conducted by Tennstedt, and popular repertoire, under Mehta and Jansons, attracted anything like full houses; even an evening of Tchaikovsky, at one time almost guaranteed to keep the box office busy, was given to a three-quarter full hall. Returns for two thematic series given in conjunction with the South Bank were especially disappointing. A Schubert series included rarities such as Joachim's orchestration of the *Grand Duo*, for which even Ann-Sophie Mutter playing the Sibelius Violin Concerto could not fill the house, with particularly dismal results for two performances of Schubert's Ninth Symphony. This may have had something to do with the fact that the first half of each evening was given over to *Death and the Maiden*, performed by the Emerson Quartet, the recipe of chamber and symphonic music one which has often encountered audience resistance, with Tennstedt's withdrawal from these concerts a further contributory factor, uncertainty as to whether or not he would conduct adversely affecting advance bookings.

Three concerts forming part of a thematic venture entitled 'Alternative Vienna', featuring the music of two contemporary Austrians, H.K. Gruber and Kurt Schwertsik, met with an even less enthusiastic response. Gruber's *Frankenstein* had achieved a degree of near-notoriety, but proved a poor bedfellow for *Das Lied von der Erde*, with Schwertsik's Violin Concerto an equal dampener for Mahler's Ninth Symphony. The best house was achieved by the London Philharmonic's third contribution to this scheme, in which Schwertsik's *Weiner Chronik Suite* and Gruber's *Rough Music* framed Stravinsky's *Capriccio*, the evening rather oddly rounded out by *Tales from the Vienna Woods*. Even so, the hall was only just over half full.

But though additional Arts Council support was forthcoming, the grant for the year amounting to £1,100,000, an increase of £700,000, the residency was already proving a greater financial burden than had been anticipated. However imaginative the programming, concerts such as those given under the title 'Alternative Vienna' were enormously expensive to stage, and with rows of empty seats proved a considerable drain on resources, while, resident orchestra or no, it was still necessary to pay substantial hire fees for use of the hall, a significant element of the additional funding going to meet the cost of the 'dark nights', essential to a rehearsal schedule arranged without recourse to other locations, protracted negotiations securing only a modest reduction in the figure of £480,000 sought by the South Bank. Sponsorship continued to go some way to filling the gap between receipts and expenditure, but with one major sponsorship falling by the wayside, there was a marked drop in the number of sponsored concerts in the International Series, from twenty-four to eighteen.

A new venture, launched to coincide with the start of the residency, saw the formation of the London Philharmonic Youth Orchestra. Drawing its membership from the principal music colleges and young freelance musicians at the start of their careers, the Youth Orchestra provides a stepping-stone between student and youth orchestras and fully-fledged professional ensembles. Giving three concerts a year in the Queen Elizabeth Hall, with tours to other parts of the British Isles, the orchestra offers its members a carefully chosen repertoire, sectional rehearsals taken by principal players from the London Philharmonic itself, and the opportunity of rehearsing under some of the parent orchestra's guest conductors. The orchestra was established in conjunction with the Arts Council Young Conductors' Scheme, and its first Music Director was Leon Gee, a graduate of the Birmingham Conservatoire, who held the post for two years before handing over to the highly talented Andrea Quinn.

The creation of the Executive Board, with limited player representation, gave rise to concern that control might be slipping out of the shareholders' hands, and a divergence of opinion on the way the company should be run led to John Willan's departure. From a low point in the mid-1980s Willan greatly improved the orchestra's fortunes, achieving his twin aims of making their concerts the most successful in the capital and securing the residency. The chairmanship also changed hands. After playing a major role in the negotiations of the past few years, David Marcou stepped down, to be succeeded briefly by the Vice-Chairman Keith Millar, before this role was assumed by Simon Channing, one of the youngest players to have taken on the task.

With Glyndebourne closed for rebuilding, the Concerts Department successfully filled the summer of 1993 in a variety of ways, a major constituent of which was a series of concert performances in the Festival Hall under the banner of Glyndebourne Opera, with each opera chosen for this short season performed three times. Glyndebourne's Music Director, Andrew Davis, conducted *Beatrice and Benedict*, Roger Norrington took the place of Klaus Tennstedt to conduct *Fidelio*, with Jane Glover conducting an additional performance in Birmingham, and Franz Welser-Möst, who had yet to appear at Glyndebourne itself, made his company debut on the South Bank with *The Merry Widow*, this last, which was also recorded, being by general consent the most satisfactory of the three, with the discs highly acclaimed on their release by EMI some months later.

A projected tour of India, scheduled in March, had to be cancelled for lack of finance, the blank weeks filled in with some hastily arranged recording sessions, but the summer months made up for the earlier lack of touring activity, including visits to Vienna and Madrid under Welser-Möst, and to Athens, where Ivan Fischer conducted two open-air concerts in the Herrod Atticus Theatre,

By far and away the most demanding tour, taking the orchestra to hitherto unexplored territory, took place at the end of July. With the release from prison of Nelson Mandela, and slow but steady progress towards multi-racial elections, it was possible to arrange an extended tour of South Africa. The groundwork had been laid when, during the course of a visit to South Africa, Laurence Watt secured the agreement of the Pretoria Arts Centre Trust (PACT) that as and when the political climate, both at home and South Africa, would allow a tour to take place, the London Philharmonic would be the chosen visitors, though in the event when the tour took place PACT were not involved in its management. Thus when the orchestra flew to Johannesburg, they were the first British orchestra to visit the country for nearly forty years.

Concerts were given in Pretoria, Johannesburg, Durban, Cape Town, Port Elizabeth, Bloemfontein and the leisure complex of Sun City, with a day's break in Cape Town. Welser-Möst's repertoire may not have appeared over–adventurous, but was more widely based than had been the case under Tennstedt. Symphonies by Brahms, Schumann and Tchaikovsky were balanced by the inclusion of Bartok's *Dance Suite*, Kodaly's *Peacock Variations* and the First Symphony of Shostakovitch, and for a public whose exposure to orchestral music was of necessity limited, the choice of music was adventurous enough. Of equal importance was a programme of education work involving all parts of the local community, the tour itinerary including a range of education projects, devised by the Education Department in conjunction with Eugene Skeef, a South African percussion player who had made his home in London. This included coaching for string players, a percussion workshop, children's concerts and visits to schools, notably Cowan School in Port Elizabeth. Josephine St Leon, the London Philharmonic's Education Director, wrote later how their visit to this school

> 'was for many of us the highlight of the tour. Row upon row of immaculately dressed well-disciplined children became musicians; the ramshackle classroom with half its floor missing was transformed into a place of beauty as they sang. Later they performed a traditional African song, complete with movement, which was one of the most moving and inspiring performances I have ever witnessed: the children had rhythm in every bone of their bodies and sang with unselfconscious joy. The London Philharmonic has now "adopted" Cowan School, and as well as providing material support we hope to return there to work further with the children, assist with teacher training and help the music teacher realise a long-held dream – the setting up of a string group.'

Glyndebourne's closure also made it possible to accept an invitation to perform at Salzburg, though a demanding schedule meant that after the long flight home from South Africa there was only time for one day at home before leaving for that city. In the absence of adequate sponsorship, acceptance of this invitation could not be justified on financial grounds, but the public interest generated in South Africa made it possible to negotiate highly satisfactory terms for the tour of that country and, given the prestige attached to an appearance at Salzburg, justified the expense involved. The concerts given in Salzburg were based on the repertoire performed in South Africa, with the addition of concertos by Bartok and Dvorak, and a hectic month ended with appearances at the Proms and the Edinburgh Festival. Conductor and orchestra had added to their laurels, but after three gruelling weeks, fifteen concerts in twenty-one days, and several thousand miles of air travel, the late summer break was more than usually welcome.

Coinciding with the start of the residency Mariss Jansons took up the role of Principal Guest Conductor, and in the autumn of 1993 Roger Norrington joined the roster of conductors as Associate Principal Guest Conductor. Another new appointment was that of Harrison Birtwistle as Composer in Residence. While his music was to feature in concert programmes, of almost equal importance was his involvement in education work and in a new development, Family Concerts, the programmes for which included a significant proportion of music the composer himself first heard when, as a child, he attended concerts by the Hallé Orchestra. Falling into a slot part-way between the children's concerts and Classics for Pleasure, the Family Concerts were an important step in building an audience for the future, evidence that they were reaching out to a new audience shown by the fact that many of the audience were obviously uncertain of their way around the hall. Birtwistle was also involved in devising a number of contemporary concerts. Given in the Queen Elizabeth Hall, these attracted audiences which in the larger hall would have been sparse, but represented a sizeable proportion of the smaller hall's capacity.

If the second half of the year was disappointing in terms of audience numbers, nevertheless the first year of the residency attracted an average attendance in excess of 85 per cent. Given the wide-ranging nature of the programmes this was not unsatisfactory, even if the jury was still out on the experiment of giving a high proportion of the year's programmes a second performance. Unhappily, this success was not carried forward into the following year. Of their Music Director's fitness there was no doubt, for in 1992 he successfully completed the London Marathon, running on behalf of the orchestra's Benevolent Fund, a feat probably unparalleled by any other member of his profession, but in the autumn of 1993 he was laid low by appendicitis. His place at the year's opening concerts was taken by Stanislav Skrowaczewski and Michael Gielen who, in addition to conducting Bruckner's Eighth Symphony in the Festival Hall, took Welser-Möst's place for a performance of this work at the Linz Bruckner Festival. This inauspicious start was compounded by the cancellation, one by one, of all Tennstedt's concerts. The effect on audiences was disastrous: even Haitink attracted less than half-full houses for two performances of the Eighth Symphony of Shostakovitch.

Matters improved after Christmas, though Welser-Möst was again laid low, this time with back trouble, necessitating his withdrawal from two concerts forming part of a South Bank Festival featuring the music of Luciano Berio. For programme planners anxious to broaden public taste, it must have been frustrating that by far and away the best audiences of the year were those attracted by concerts featuring the more popular repertoire, the *German Requiem* of Brahms, conducted by Welser-Möst in place of Tennstedt, a programme comprising Haydn's *Clock* Symphony, the Schumann Piano Concerto and Elgar's *Enigma Variations*, and Mahler's *Resurrection* Symphony.

But if the second year of the residency was disappointing in audience terms, an even greater headache now arose in the shape of new proposals for funding London's orchestras put forward by the Arts Council's Music Panel.

19

Hoffmann and After 1993–96

In July 1992 the Arts Council and the BBC set up a joint enquiry into the provision of orchestral resources in England and Wales. The terms of reference given to the review team asked them to examine the location and distribution of orchestras, the artistic balance of their programming, the arrangements for broadcasting and the most effective management structure for the BBC orchestras. The composition of the team contained one omission. The BBC's representatives could speak on behalf of the Corporation, and be mindful of its interests; there was, however, no representative of the independent orchestras, leaving room for the possibility that the review team could reach conclusions which were not in their best interests.

This enquiry was barely under way when, in the summer of 1993, it was halted in its tracks by an announcement that, acting on the advice of its Music Panel, the Arts Council proposed withdrawing funding from two of London's orchestras. The LSO who, in addition to a grant from Arts Council, receive financial support from the Corporation of London, were given an assurance that they were not under threat, the intention being to fund one of the other three orchestras at an increased level, placing it on the same financial footing as the LSO. In announcing the enquiry, the Secretary General of the Arts Council stated that their object was to secure 'two great orchestras at the very height of international prowess, expertise and reputation, instead of four which we can no longer afford to support at an adequate level', though it was not clear whether or not other options, if any, had been considered as an alternative. Rather than take the decision itself, the task of selecting the orchestra to be singled out for increased funding was handed to an independent committee, a strategy which appeared designed to obtain external support for the Council's policy, while diverting criticism elsewhere. It was a policy that was to backfire disastrously.

The composition of the Music Panel, none of whose members had experience of orchestral music, or was directly connected with it, hardly carried much weight, and the Council's actions came in for considerable criticism. In addition to pre-empting the study put in hand jointly with the

BBC, the decision seemed to fly in the face of the conclusions reached by Sir John Tooley, and approved by the Council when they agreed to the appointment of the London Philharmonic as resident orchestra at the Festival Hall. Moreover, by whatever standard of judgement the committee appointed by the Arts Council reached its decision, it would inevitably be arbitrary. The Berlin Philharmonic were among those who protested, as did many notable British musicians, Sir Peter Maxwell Davies threatening that if the RPO lost its grant he would surrender his knighthood.

The committee was chaired by Sir Leonard Hoffmann, one-time secretary of the London Orchestral Concerts Board, now a Lord Justice of Appeal, and though it was October before the remaining members were appointed, the committee was asked to report in time for their recommendation to be considered by the Music Panel in December. Since losing its grant could well prove to be the death-knell for an orchestra, the brevity of the timetable suggested an unseemly haste on the Panel's part, likely to leave the two losers with a minimum of time in which to attempt to reorder their affairs, a matter of some concern to the two hundred or so musicians and back-office staff whose livelihood was likely to be affected. In the event, for all the wealth of detail in the report, which provided a comprehensive insight into the workings of the orchestras under review, the outcome remained undecided. The committee's conclusion that the RPO did not meet the necessary criteria underlined the arbitrary nature of the process, for while the report expressed the view that 'none of us would today choose it in preference to either of the other two', it went on to state, 'The Royal Philharmonic is an orchestra of which many a great city would be proud'.

So far as the London Philharmonic and the Philharmonia were concerned, the report summed up the respective merits of each orchestra as follows:

> 'The London Philharmonic impressed us all with its efficiency and confidence. The Philharmonia impressed with its originality, adventure and independence. These qualities are not easily weighed against each other, and the majority feel that doing so would be a great injustice to one or other orchestra.'

But while the chairman and a majority on the Committee declined to express a preference for either orchestra, the report contained a minority view put forward by two members stating, 'they are of course very aware of the fallibility of their judgement in these matters, but having formed a view in accordance with the terms of reference, they feel bound to express it', concluding that while recognising 'the excellence of the London Philharmonic, they think that in those respects in which the Philharmonia is superior are those which carry the greatest weight'. The minority view argued that the Philharmonia had consistently given more adventurous programmes, that overseas touring was more important for this orchestra, and while they were the only orchestra to have 'maintained its position as a great recording orchestra', they were also 'the only orchestra which planned to reduce its recording activity if it was awarded funding at an increased level'. Which was somewhat confusing, and without in any way wishing to denigrate the work of the Philharmonia, it was difficult to understand thinking which valued overseas activities, which were hardly within the remit of the Arts Council, higher than the London Philharmonic's success in attracting audiences, or the value of the work undertaken by the RPO in carrying orchestral music to the regions, matters which most assuredly should have been of concern not just to the Council but to its ultimate paymaster, those taxpayers who constitute the audience for orchestral music.

Publication of the report was followed by a period of intense lobbying. In the face of almost universal criticism the Council had been forced to abandon similar proposals, which would have withdrawn funding from several regional theatres, including the Bristol Old Vic, the Belgrade Theatre, Coventry and the Theatre Royal, Plymouth, proposals which so far from fulfilling the Council's task of increasing 'the accessibility of the arts to the public', would have denied a significant element of the population access to live theatre. Now, as a consequence of Hoffmann's refusal to act as executioner, the Council was forced to make a further retreat, extricating itself as best it could from an untenable position, deciding to leave well alone. The three orchestras under threat were advised that there would be no change in their funding, except that the amount awarded to the London Philharmonic to meet the cost of the residency was in future to be channelled via the South Bank Board rather than paid direct.

The Chairman of the Music Panel, Bryan Magee, set out to defend the Panel's proposals in the columns of *The Times*, claiming that assurances given to the LSO that their funding was not under threat were justified by recent performances of Sibelius under Sir Colin Davis, which he asserted surpassed anything heard in London since the war. It was a statement for which coals of fire were heaped on his head, several correspondents, without denigrating the LSO, or the conducting of Sir Colin Davis, questioning Magee's competence to form such a view, challenging the subjective basis on which it was formed, and enquiring if the author had taken into account the playing of the LPO under the likes of Haitink, Solti or Tennstedt, the Philharmonia under Karajan, Guilini or Klemperer, or the RPO under Beecham, Kempe or Ashkenazy. In the event, with its policy in tatters the Music Panel disintegrated, the Chairman and several other members submitting their resignations, the remaining members doing their best to distance themselves from proposals that had come close to making the Council a laughing-stock.

At first sight, inasmuch as the immediate financial threat had been removed, the outcome appeared satisfactory. There was, however, a price to be paid, and there is no question that the London Philharmonic was damaged by the Hoffmann enquiry. One lesson to be learned from the success of the LSO's residency in the Barbican was that this did not come overnight. Adoption of a progressive programme policy cost the LSO dear, requiring several years of dedicated commitment on the part of management and orchestra to turn the situation round. The fact that the Hoffmann enquiry was set up a year into the London Philharmonic's residency served to throw doubts on the decision-making process leading to their appointment, and while the report failed to make a clear-cut recommendation, the minority view was interpreted in some quarters as a decision in favour of the Philharmonia. Moreover, circumstances dictate that orchestras exist on minuscule management resource, and the time scale to which the Hoffmann Committee was expected to work meant that the submission of evidence required an almost full-time commitment from the management team, to the detriment of forward planning.

The enquiry also diverted attention from the marketing activity aimed at securing the additional finance essential for the presentation of well-rehearsed concerts and a diversified repertoire, while for sponsors the enquiry presented an unattractive scenario. Already the number of sponsored concerts in the International Series had fallen, only thirteen of those given during 1993–94 attracting support, and for the first time for many years there was no sponsor for Classics for Pleasure, National Westminster deciding that the time had come to terminate their involvement. Two years into the residency, it was proving impossible to sustain it in anything like the manner which had been intended. To less than full houses was added the fact that, hand in hand with the difficulty in attracting sponsors, so too the Trust, which had been a considerable source of financial strength, was finding problems in raising new money.

After guiding the orchestra through the opening months of the residency and the traumas of the Hoffmann enquiry, Simon Channing felt it was right to surrender this burden. The Chairmanship was temporarily taken over by the Deputy Chairman, Ronald Calder, before passing to Bob St. John Wright. A past member of the Board, Bob Wright returned to face a deteriorating financial situation. With the Trust unable to match its earlier fund-raising successes, temporary relief was obtained in the shape of an interest-free loan from the Musicians Union. Restoring the position was to prove a long and difficult haul.

The opening of Glyndebourne's new opera house in May 1994 was a triumph for all concerned. Sir George Christie and his colleagues were rightly proud of the fact that the new house not only opened on time, but was completed within budget, the building meeting with the approval of both audiences and performers. So far as the musicians were concerned the new orchestra pit, though still not as large as the players might have liked, was a great improvement on the cramped conditions in which they worked in the old theatre. Designed to cater for an orchestra of eighty, the pit was built with descending steps from front to back. While adding somewhat to the difficulties always experienced by players located at the back of the orchestra, and sitting under the stage, this form of construction, coupled with use throughout the auditorium of that most beautiful of building materials, wood, combined to provide a wonderfully natural acoustic. The new house also had one great advantage over its predecessor, air-conditioning. Though Andrew Davis had by now taken Bernard Haitink's place as Music Director, it was Haitink who opened this fresh chapter in Glyndebourne's history, conducting a new production of *Figaro*. Welser-Möst made his house debut with the company, and was much praised for his conducting of *Peter Grimes*, and Glyndebourne continued the policy of engaging the Orchestra of the Age of the Enlightenment for one opera, this orchestra playing for a new production of *Don Giovanni*, one of two operas performed at the Proms, with *Eugene Onegin*, conducted by Andrew Davis, the other. *Onegin* was the last of the orchestra's three appearances during the Prom season; it was hardly a surprise when Tennstedt, who was to have conducted the *Sinfonia da Requiem* and the *Eroica*, was replaced by Libor Pešek, but on a happier note Franz Welser-Möst won many friends with a light-hearted evening of Viennese music, during which Felicity Lott sang items by Heuberger, Lehar and Robert Stolz, the television cameras picking up, for those watching at home, the glint of real enjoyment in the conductor's eyes.

The orchestra's opening concerts in the autumn of 1994 formed part of a major South Bank theme, '*Deutsche Romantik*'. Bruckner's Sixth Symphony is arguably one of the least audience-friendly of his nine, and it was no great surprise that the hall was less than half-full for the opening concert; nor was there a much better house for a programme including Beethoven's Fifth Symphony and *Heliogabalus Imperator* by Henze. There was, however, an encouraging response to the experiment of a Sunday evening concert starting at 6.00, rather than the usual 7.30, the more so since Mozart's *Requiem* was preceded by the Fourth Symphony of a composer largely unknown in this country, the Austrian Franz Schmidt. Nevertheless the most successful concerts were those featuring the established repertoire, with two full houses for a programme featuring the Schumann Piano Concerto and Brahms' First Symphony, albeit conducted by Myung Wha Chung rather than the advertised Tennstedt, and for the First and Ninth Symphonies of Beethoven, conducted by Haitink.

It was eighteen months since Tennstedt had last conducted, and the announcement that he was retiring from the concert platform was greeted with a mixture of sorrow and resignation. Successive generations are apt to bemoan that the great conductors are no more, the generation that regretted the passing of Nikisch, Richter and Steinbach succeeded by those who regarded the likes of Beecham, Fürtwangler, Mengelberg, Toscanini and Weingartner as preeminent, with the names of Böhm, Karajan, Klemperer and Monteux among those thrown into the equation by concert-goers of the present generation. Few would dispute Tennstedt's claim to be included in the pantheon of great interpretative talents, or with Richard Morrison's verdict in the 1995 Yearbook:

> 'Tennstedt has brought a depth of response that has shocked, riveted and finally elated audiences the world over. To journey with Tennstedt through a symphony is to penetrate the heart of darkness, and ultimately to experience a glorious feeling of release. I just wish that his genius had been recognised when he was thirty instead of fifty; for the truth is that Tennstedt has enjoyed fewer than twenty years at the top. That makes the memory of his performances burn all the more intensely.'

As well as being financially profitable, the 1993 tour of South Africa generated much goodwill and an invitation to return at the earliest opportunity. There was every reason to anticipate that a return visit in February 1995 would be equally successful, but for a variety of reasons this tour failed to break even. One major factor was that, acting on the advice of the South African managers, ticket prices were set too high, adversely affecting audiences in several centres, a problem compounded when a major sponsorship deal provided less financial backing than originally anticipated. Yet there were many positive aspects, especially the linked educational project, involving children of all races, and a return visit to Cowan School, 'adopted' by the orchestra in 1993, where a concert took place in the open air. Welser-Möst rehearsed the Wits University String Orchestra, with a leavening of players from the London Philharmonic sitting in among the ranks of the students, and performances of the *Choral Symphony* involved members of several choirs, with both choristers and soloists drawn from a wide spectrum of the many races, described by Bishop Desmond Tutu as 'The Rainbow people of God', that make up South Africa's population. Several concerts took place in unusual locations: a Marquee was set up on Durban Village Green, where the audience responded equally enthusiastically to Warwick Tyrell's trombone playing and a demonstration of African drumming. Welser-Möst also spoke movingly of the open-air concert in Kirstenbosch Botanical Gardens, under the slopes of Table Mountain, one of the most beautiful of the many venues in which the orchestra has performed, where against a setting sun, the orchestra played Mozart's *Prague* Symphony.

A brief return home, involving five major concerts in under a fortnight, and it was off again, to Korea and Japan, with an unusual touring repertoire, built round the *Prague* and *Pathétique* symphonies, leavened by Strauss Waltzes, pieces by Bernstein, and a mixture of operatic arias and traditional Korean songs, with the Korean-born soprano Sumi Jo as soloist.

At home there was a mixed audience response to the post-Christmas concerts, Welser-Möst obtaining the best house for a programme in which Bartok's *Miraculous Mandarin* Suite was framed by the *Prague* and the *Pathétique*, but despite a high proportion of tickets taken up by members of the Classics for Pleasure audience, a concert performance of Gilbert and Sullivan's *Iolanthe* failed to attract a full house. It had become the South Bank's regular custom to hold a spring festival featuring a living composer, in which they appeared to be following a practice initiated by the BBC at the Barbican, though rather than concentrating performances over one weekend, these were spread over a longer period, mingled with music by other composers. In 1995 the spotlight fell on the Estonian composer Arvo Pärt, Roger Norrington conducting a complete concert of his music in the Queen Elizabeth Hall, and Welser-Möst opening a Festival Hall programme with the Third Symphony, which he and the orchestra went on to record.

A concert in May 1995, promoted jointly by the London Philharmonic and the RPO in aid of their respective Benevolent Funds, gave rise to further speculation that a merger between two of London's orchestras might be in the offing. Conducted by Sir Georg Solti, the RPO contributed Beethoven's Seventh, the London Philharmonic occupying the platform for Bartok's *Concerto for Orchestra*, the concert concluding with the Overture to *The Mastersingers*, performed by a composite orchestra. This speculation was heightened when Lord Young of Graffham, the newly appointed Chairman of the London Philharmonic's Trustees, announced that the two orchestras were looking into the possibility of a merged management, but hopes that bringing the administrative functions under one roof would generate substantial savings – at one point a figure in excess of £500,000 was quoted – proved unfounded.

Just how wide of the mark speculation concerning a merger with the RPO had been was shown a few weeks later. In the face of the difficulties encountered in trying to sustain the residency on its own account, the London Philharmonic put forward new proposals to the Philharmonia inviting them to take part in a joint residency. It was a move welcomed by the South Bank, who were able to announce, in June 1995, that arrangements were being worked out that would give, as from the start of September 1997, joint residency status to the two orchestras. According to the South Bank's statement, 'Since the Hoffman Report in 1993, the climate for music in London has undergone significant changes, which have brought orchestras closer together in their drive to boost audiences and maximise existing resources', which diplomatically ignored the fact that, despite the recommendation made by Sir John Tooley's Committee, the single residency foundered because it was impossible to make available sufficient financial resources to ensure its success. Whereas the LSO's residency in the Barbican has the dual support of the Arts Council and the Corporation of London, the straightjacket imposed on spending by local authorities meant that even if Lambeth Council had the will, it was not within their means to emulate the generosity shown by the Corporation to the LSO. In the current financial climate, the only way the Arts Council could have found sufficient funds to match those available to the LSO would have been by drastic pruning in other areas, an exercise which the Hoffmann enquiry had demonstrated was unacceptable to such a wide range of opinion within the music profession as to make implementation of any such proposal almost impossible.

The inconclusive outcome of the Hoffman enquiry enabled the joint Arts Council/BBC Study to be taken out of cold storage. Interviews with a wide range of those involved in the field of orchestral music, including orchestras, local authorities and independent concert agencies, led to the issue of a Consultation Document, inviting responses to a series of questions embracing the strategic purpose of the orchestras, their regional distribution, funding, education and training, and the opportunities for creative co-ordination of their activities. The responses, from organisations and individuals, were summarised by the Principal of the Royal College of Music, Dr Janet Ritterman, but announcement of the joint residency to some extent pre-empted the resulting document issued by the Arts Council, setting out a 'Strategy for the support and development of orchestras and their audiences'. This proposed the creation of yet another body, whose terms of reference would include obtaining agreed areas of responsibility for orchestras in respect of concerts, education work and community activity; the co-ordination of programming; and co-ordination of promoters' plans for visiting orchestras in Central London. No supporting evidence was offered to show why a new layer of bureaucracy would be an improvement on the network of informal communication that already existed.

Throughout the summer of 1995 the orchestra earned plaudits for its continuing work at Glyndebourne, but the autumn and winter brought a string of unwelcome problems, many arising from the hiatus in forward planning caused by the disruption of the Hoffmann enquiry. It was, however, the combined effects of a standstill in the level of Arts Council grant, and recession, which led to cancellation of several concerts, including Messiaen's *Turangalîla* Symphony and a concert performance of Birtwistle's opera *The Second Mrs Kong*. First performed by Glyndebourne Touring Opera during the autumn of 1994, Birtwistle's opera was given at Glyndebourne itself during the 1995 season, and this concert performance, scheduled to take place in the Queen Elizabeth Hall, was to have formed part of a South Bank Festival highlighting the composer's music. Despite an offer of additional financial support from the South Bank, the impossibility of securing a major sponsorship package meant that, faced with the prospect that even with a full house the concert would still have involved a loss of many thousands of pounds, the risks involved outweighed the artistic credit to be gained from proceeding.

The high cost involved in promoting choral concerts also led to cancellation of a projected performance of *Elijah*. Rather than abandon a Festival Hall date, the players agreed to forego their fees for this concert, donating these to the orchestra's funds, the revised programme, conducted by Wolfgang Sawallisch, comprising the First and Third Symphonies of Brahms.

The year opened with concert performances of *Aida*, conducted by Zubin Mehta, and Roger Norrington devised an imaginative series concentrating on the music of Berlioz, incorporating many lesser-known works; the *Tempest* scene from *Lèlio*, the *Death of Ophelia* and *Hamlet's Funeral March* from *Tristia*, and the Overtures *King Lear* and *Les Francs Juges*. Norrington introduced each programme, explaining that the unusual platform layout, with first and second violins on opposite sides of the stage and cellos and basses ranged across the back, was the layout used by Berlioz when conducting his own works. Haitink conducted twice, a Dvorak programme celebrating the hundredth anniversary of the first performance of the Cello Concerto, with his second concert given over to one work, Mahler's Sixth Symphony, and Sawallisch conducted music by Brahms and Beethoven, a partnership giving much obvious pleasure to audience, conductor and orchestra. An engagement of a different nature came in the shape of an invitation to perform at Buckingham Palace, part of the celebrations for the Duke of Kent's sixtieth birthday. The London Philharmonic's contribution to the evening, in which the Hanover Band also took part, were performances of the *Siegfried Idyll* and the Fourth Symphony of Beethoven, conducted by Welser-Möst.

The year's work in the concert hall concluded with a visit to Vienna, the concerts given in that city bringing to an end Franz Welser-Möst's term of office as Music Director. There is no denying that the relationship between conductor and orchestra had at times been difficult. Tennstedt would always have been a hard act to follow, and it was placing a considerable burden on a young conductor's shoulders to ask him, during the first year of the residency, to occupy a position of primacy in a roster of conductors that included the names of Haitink, Jansons, Mehta, Rozdestvensky and Tennstedt, a situation exacerbated by invidious comparisons from a press which for a time appeared almost uniformly hostile. The weight of criticism overshadowed the positive features of Welser-Möst's work, notably the enthusiastic reception given to his work overseas. In addition to a regular invitation to appear at the Linz Bruckner Festival, Welser-Möst's growing reputation played a part in securing invitations to appear at such prestigious festivals as those of Lucerne, Salzburg and Vienna, and he made a significant contribution to the artistic success of the tours of South Africa. His recorded repertoire ventured well beyond the mainstream of orchestral music: in addition to works by Bartok, Bruckner, Schumann and Stravinsky, this embraced symphonies by Giya Kancheli, Arvo Pärt and Franz Schmidt, their recording of Schmidt's Fourth Symphony securing fresh laurels for conductor and orchestra when it was selected by *The*

Gramophone as winner of their prize for orchestral record of the year. The announcement that Welser-Möst was to stand down, preparatory to assuming the Music Directorship of the Zurich Opera, appeared to produce a more relaxed climate and, in marked contrast to much of the criticism aimed at his conducting, Bruckner's Second Symphony and Verdi's *Requiem*, performed during his last spell of work in London, were widely praised.

The drastic curb imposed on public spending meant that after two years in which it was necessary for the Arts Council to hold grants at a standstill level, the Council found itself in the unhappy position of having to actually reduce the amount allocated to some of its clients, the London Philharmonic facing a cut of £80,000 in its grant for 1996-97. The position of the London Philharmonic matched that of many other arts organisations, all of whom were increasingly living from hand to mouth. The fact that the National Lottery was generating substantial sums of money for the arts was small consolation; with these funds earmarked for capital projects, they provided no comfort for the financially hard-pressed performing companies. However desirable such projects might be, the fact that in many instances they require associated funding from industry places them in competition with arts companies looking for sponsorship to help balance current account spending, a problem likely to be compounded by expectations that the Millennium Project would act as a further drain on the corporate sector.

The acute financial problems faced by orchestras in London were making the capital less attractive as a base for musicians of international stature. Hopes that Mariss Jansons might succeed Welser-Möst broke down on this point, the Russian conductor preferring the greater security of the Pittsburgh Orchestra. His decision reinforced the Board's concern that management was focusing on the marketing of the orchestra, to the detriment of its artistic direction, and it was essential to provide the orchestra with experienced artistic direction. Christopher Lawrence, who succeeded John Willan as Managing Director, almost immediately finding himself embroiled in guiding the orchestra through the trauma of the Hoffmann enquiry, left in the summer of 1995, and a meeting between Bob St. J. Wright and Ernest Fleischmann, sometime of the LSO, and for many years the Managing Director of the Los Angeles Philharmonic Orchestra, led to an invitation to Fleischmann to undertake a review of every facet of the orchestra's artistic activity. One outcome was a decision that the vacuum created by the absence of a Music Director, should be filled by appointing an Artistic Director, who would also act as Chief Executive. In January 1996 it was announced that the man chosen to lead the London Philharmonic into the new era of a joint residency was Serge Dorny, Artistic Director of the Flanders Festival for the past nine years.

20

Towards the Millennium 1996–98

In the autumn of 1952, shortly before his dismissal as Chairman and General Manager, Thomas Russell published a further book, *Philharmonic Project*, in which he wrote critically of Britain's half-hearted approach to public funding:

'It can be shown that we are spending too much or too little on music; too much for those who think concert-goers should pay for their own pleasures; too little for those who believe in cultural values and who want to see our standards of performance and listening raised to the highest international level. Our national mind has never been made up on whether the symphony orchestra is a necessity or a luxury. We keep our orchestras barely in existence, with no reserves to call upon and at the mercy of adverse happenings. Artistic policy is always hampered and continuity threatened. If symphony orchestras are to be finally regarded as a luxury, then it is evident that, in our straitened circumstances, it is one we cannot afford. If, on the other hand they are a cultural necessity to a civilised nation, then we must ensure the survival of their finest qualities, in spite of heavy national expenditure in other directions.'

Little has changed. The government's funding of the Arts Council remains at a level at which the grants it can afford for our orchestras, opera, ballet companies and theatres keep them at the very edge of survival. The post-war history of the arts is one of recurring financial crisis, with from time to time an organisation of real worth going to the wall. Indeed as Lord Gowrie, Chairman of the Arts Council, pointed out in his introduction to the Council's report for 1996–97, the 1990s have seen a worsening of the financial situation, the grant from public funds falling by £20,000,000 in real terms over a four-year period. The cities of Berlin and Vienna place great pride in the orchestras bearing their name. Not only does the annual grant made to the Berlin Philharmonic by the city authorities exceed the sum of the Arts Council grant for all London's orchestras, it is greater than the total grant the Council can make available to all Britain's orchestras, including chamber and period ensembles. On the other side of the Atlantic, orchestras in the

United States are not without their problems, but it is difficult not to feel envious of the endowment funds built up over the years by those in the major league.

In the prevailing circumstances it is well-nigh impossible for a performing arts company to build up working capital, with the inevitable result that any interruption in cash flow, be it from a temporary downturn in business, a standstill in the level of public funding, or some other cause, can quickly lead to a crisis. To meet the problems arising from the absence of reserves of any kind, the existence of Lottery money would seem to open up the possibility of creating endowment funds, providing arts organisations with at least a degree of protection against cyclical problems, but a suggestion along these lines produced a somewhat dusty response from the former Secretary of State for National Heritage, Mrs Virginia Bottomley:

> 'Endowments can be attractive because they represent a once and for all commitment. There are however a number of issues to consider. An endowment is an expensive way of allocating money. To endow just one of our many national flagship arts organisations would use up around 20 per cent of the available Lottery funding in one year. We must also remember that Lottery money is public money. Once a recipient is endowed, little control may be exercised over the use of the (public) funds. There is a danger that this may create bodies that operate in a way which does not necessarily serve the public interest. There are also real practical difficulties: setting and agreeing a satisfactory level of endowment to meet specific revenue requirements; the uncertainty of the stock market, or return on investments, which might for example lead the principal to be lost or diminished such that the revenue is inadequate for the original purpose.'

These arguments are spurious; an example of a nanny state mentality unable to trust the good sense of the citizens it serves. Built up over a period of years, endowments would provide that very degree of stability arts organisations so perilously lack and, in addition to providing a degree of security against the ups and downs of the economic cycle, an element of endowment funding would facilitate forward planning on a more sensible basis than is often possible in present circumstances. The concerns of government as to the security of the capital apply to any Trust or Pension Fund and, as any actuary worth his salt will testify, the crucial factor is not the periodic variations in capital value arising from the ups-and-downs of the stock market, but rather that the investments should produce a growth in income to meet the specific liabilities for which the fund was set up.*

---

*As this chapter was being finalised, the House of Lords was debating a new Lottery Bill, one purpose of which was to remove the ring-fencing surrounding lottery money allocated to the arts, restricting its use to capital projects.

Sponsorship has of course played a valuable part in keeping the wolf from the door, with orchestras and audiences alike indebted to the fund-raising efforts of Trustees, who play a major part in ensuring that artistic standards are maintained at the highest level. Even so, London's orchestras have only survived by taking desperate measures. From time to time the musicians surrender fees to help make ends meet; holidays are taken without pay; pension and Social Security arrangements remain inadequate, and orchestras commit themselves to schedules that are artistically inadvisable. It should be a matter for shame that, as revealed by the enquiry instituted by the Arts Council and the BBC, at the end of 1994 the pay of rank and file players in the best-paid provincial orchestra in the country, the Royal Liverpool Philharmonic, started at £16,700, rising to £18,500 after eight years of service. Things are somewhat better in London, where the players, other than those employed in the BBC orchestras, are paid by the session rather than the week or month, but this is only achieved by means of a gruelling work schedule and acceptance of a knife-edge existence placing additional strain on the players.

The Arts Council represents an easy target for politicians, public and the Council's clients alike. An annual grant in excess of £180,000,000 may at first sight seem handsome, especially when the arts are so often portrayed as a minority activity. In practice this sum represents less than £4 per head of population, while so far from being a minority activity, the annual paid attendance for music, in the concert hall and the opera house, exceeds that for every professional spectator sport, other than Association Football. Examination of the Council's annual report reveals how the range of artistic activity supported by the Council reaches out to almost every sector of the community, but however great the temptation to question whether this or that item is justified, and whether money could not be better spent elsewhere, robbing one area of activity, dance, drama, film, literature, music or the visual arts, to pay for another is no solution. It is perhaps understandable that, faced with a standstill in the level of grant awarded by the Treasury, which represents a cut in real terms, the Council should from time to time seek to find a partial solution to ever-increasing demands on its resources by encouraging orchestral mergers, or taking measures to 'rationalise' some areas of artistic activity.

The multiplicity of London's orchestras, and the fact that they are self-governing, is also the subject of much criticism, with declining and ageing audiences cited as justification for a policy of merger, with the self-governing status of the orchestras viewed as a barrier to what some would have us believe is progress. But if the city of Vienna can support the activities of three orchestras, the Vienna Philharmonic, the Vienna Symphony and the Orchestra of Austrian Radio, it should be within the means of London, with the far greater population both of London itself and the catchment area of the Home Counties, to finance its orchestras. The on-going success of the Proms, the increased number of youth orchestras and choirs, the construction of new concert halls in such diverse centres as Belfast, Birmingham, Glasgow, Manchester, Nottingham and Northampton, and the almost continuous growth in the range of music available on CD, are evidence that public interest in orchestral music remains at a high level. Indeed, one year on from the opening of the Bridgewater Hall the Hallé Orchestra were able to report that the first year in their new home had seen the audience increase by 25 per cent. Research carried out by the Target Group Index shows that, so far from being in terminal decline, over the past decade the number of adults attending concerts has, taking one year with another, remained broadly constant, while for opera the number has actually increased, though the figures do not of course take account of changes in public taste, including an increasing audience for period instrument performances, or the growth in small-scale performances of opera.

Changes in public taste, as evidenced by the growing audience for period performances, provide a challenge to the older established orchestras to find ways of presenting music in ways that will stimulate the interest of new audiences, without alienating their long-standing supporters. Ernest Fleischmann's vision of a community or pool of musicians, who in addition to performing as a symphony orchestra participate in a wide range of musical activity, chamber ensembles of many kinds, jazz, and the teaching, in the widest sense, of both adults and children, is already a long way towards realisation, though as we move towards the twenty-first century the symphonic element of their work is likely to loom considerably larger than Fleischmann envisaged. Whether through involvement in education and other work in the community or, at a different level, participation in activities connected with fund raising, there is far greater contact between musicians and the audience than was the case a mere decade or so ago.

On the technological front, the digital revolution may well, by cable, satellite or conventional access, pipe music into every home on a far wider scale from anything yet experienced, but if professional sport is any guide, even saturation cover, such as that given to Wimbledon or the Open Golf Championship, so far from suppressing demand for the live experience, actually provides a stimulus. Just as the false prophets who feared that the birth of broadcasting would spell the demise of live performances were confounded, so too there is every reason to anticipate that the arts will benefit from new technical advances.

By 1996 London's orchestras were establishing more clearly defined areas of interest. This process began in 1984 with the LSO's move to the Barbican, continued in 1992 with the appointment of the London Philharmonic as the Festival Hall's first resident orchestra, to be taken a stage further when, as from the autumn of 1997, both the London Philharmonic and the Philharmonia were given status as resident orchestras. For its part the RPO is finding an independent niche, dividing its time between the Albert Hall, the Barbican and concerts in a multiplicity of provincial locations. For each orchestra there remains the on-going problem of identity, highlighted by the evidence of the Hoffmann report that audiences find it difficult to distinguish between them, to the point where there was even uncertainty on the part of some as to which orchestra it was that they had just been listening to.

Glyndebourne's 1996 repertoire included Handel's *Theodora*, with the Orchestra of the Age of Enlightenment in the pit, the London Philharmonic performing for the remaining operas, *Arabella, Cosi Fan Tutti, Ermione, Eugene Onegin* and a new production of *Lulu*, with the last-named brought to the Proms. Glyndebourne was also the venue for the opening event of the orchestra's autumn activities, a benefit concert in support of the London Philharmonic itself. This concert was only the second event of its kind to be staged at Glyndebourne, the London Philharmonic having given its services for an evening forming part of the fund-raising activity in connection with construction of the new opera house. Sir George Christie, who is numbered among the orchestra's Trustees, generously offered the new house for a fund-raising concert, and the evening was sponsored by the Ford Motor Company. Not much more than forty-eight hours before the concert was due to take place the advertised soloist, Cecilia Bartoli, became unwell, giving rise to one of those hair-raising rescue operations which shorten the life of orchestral managers. Cancellation could have been disastrous, but at all but the last moment the day was saved by Thomas Allen and Susan Graham. Despite minimum time for rehearsal – Miss Graham flew in from Amsterdam on the morning of the concert – a potential disaster was turned into a triumph, with the added bonus that the concert raised a six-figure sum for the orchestra's funds.

Serge Dorny's appointment as Artistic Director nominally ran from the beginning of August 1996. In practice he spent the early part of the year dividing his time between his responsibilities to the Flanders Festival and the activities of the London Philharmonic, some of the first fruits of which were announcements concerning future activities at home and abroad. In this country the orchestra negotiated a new partnership with the Congress Theatre, Eastbourne. Commencing in the autumn of 1996, the Eastbourne residency involves, in addition to concerts by both the London Philharmonic and its Youth Orchestra, a programme of education and community work arranged by the Education Department. For an orchestra which spends a significant part of each year performing in Sussex, there was much to be said for strengthening links with the community, performing for an audience drawn from within the county boundaries, rather than an audience which was largely drawn from further afield.

Touring was another area of activity to be brought under the microscope. The autumn of 1996 involved short visits to Germany, Vienna, Luxembourg, Italy and Spain. Concert performances of *Don Giovanni*, conducted by Solti, with a cast led by Bryn Terfel, were given to appreciative audiences in Cologne and Hannover before the opera was then brought to the South Bank, where Decca used the performances to tape the work for future release. Norrington took the players to Vienna for two concerts devoted to works by British composers, Britten, Elgar and Vaughan Williams, a repertoire far removed from that usually performed on tour, and an operatic concert in Luxembourg was the curtain-raiser to concerts conducted by Solti in Cagliari, Rome and Madrid. Further short visits to Spain, involving concerts in Madrid and Valencia, took place in January and February 1997, conducted by Pinchas Steinberg and Paavo Berglund. The patience of the players was sorely tried on one occasion when, following an early-morning flight from Gatwick to Madrid, they found that arrangements had been made for a concert the same evening by the National Orchestra and, because the National Orchestra was always given precedence, the starting time of their own concert had been put back to 10.30 p.m. However Spanish audiences are less bound by the clock; the concert was given to a full and appreciative house which, as Chairman Bob St J. Wright commented, 'had been warmed up first by a pretty good band'.

The changing circumstances of the 1990s pointed to a need for greater co-ordination of the orchestra's activities at home and overseas. The Channel Tunnel, and the increasing number of fast rail links within continental Europe, opened up exciting possibilities for residencies outside the shores of this country, comprising a series of short, concentrated visits arranged throughout the year. To provide a clearer focus for future touring activity, Van Walsum Management and Konzertdirektion Hans Ulrich Schmidt were appointed to represent the orchestra worldwide, one early result an announcement that as from 1998 the London Philharmonic would participate on a regular basis in the Vienna Easter Festival; Madrid was another city with which the orchestra was developing a continuing relationship. There are advantages to be derived from arrangements of this kind, including greater familiarity with the halls in which the orchestra plays and the opportunity of giving the same programme in a number of centres, spreading the cost of rehearsal over several performances, while staying in one city for several days reduces the strain placed on an orchestra by touring, the players benefitting from seeing something more of the city in which they are performing than the airport, the hotel and the concert hall, including the opportunity of familiarising themselves with the local restaurants.

Despite an improvement in the level of financial sponsorship, this came too late to affect the decision to restrict the number of concerts during 1996–97. Much of the year was built around music associated with 'Great Cities of the World', London, Vienna, Paris, Prague and St Petersburg, and despite a minimum of time for planning, Serge Dorny made his mark by arranging, in March 1997, a short series concentrating on the music of Haydn. In addition to a cycle of the *Paris* symphonies, under Norrington, the Queen Elizabeth Hall was the venue for two performances of *Orfeo et Euridice*, conducted by Frider Bernius. Less well-known than figures such as Ton Koopman or Sigiswald Kuijken, who made their name in this country thanks to the recording industry, Bernius, who has appeared at the Salzburg and Göttingen Handel Festivals conducting his own Stuttgart Barokorchester, is another of the expanding group of musicians who are re-examining performing style by the use of authentic instruments. Already at Glyndebourne, the wind players of the London Philharmonic had used authentic instruments for performances of *Le Clemenza de Tito*, conducted by Mark Elder. The Haydn series, involving the players in an area of the repertoire with which they were less familiar, took this experience a stage further.

In addition to the public performances, the Haydn Festival placed a special emphasis on education work. The foyer of the Queen Elizabeth Hall was the setting for two performances of the marionette opera *Philemon and Baucis*, conducted by Andrea Quinn; these involved members of the Youth Orchestra and the London Philharmonic Choir, soloists from the Trinity College of Music, and marionettes created by children from the Johanna Primary School. A second project took an ensemble drawn from the ranks of the orchestra to Hackney where, in a series of workshop rehearsals, the players worked with the Hackney Youth Orchestra, the project culminating in an early-evening performance, by the Youth Orchestra and an ensemble drawn from the London Philharmonic, of excerpts from one of Haydn's symphonies.

The International Series included two outstanding concerts under Bernard Haitink, concerts confirming this partnership as one which provides as near a guarantee of musical excellence as it is possible to find. Performances of Bruckner's Ninth Symphony and the Fourth Symphony of Shostakovitch, which from the orchestra's opening shrill scream seemed to probe ever more deeply the underlying despair pervading the whole work, produced a string of almost adulatory reviews, these concerts providing the clearest possible public statement that this was an orchestra supremely confident of its abilities, a view confirmed during Glyndebourne's 1997 season which, with as wide-ranging a repertoire as ever, saw the London Philharmonic performing for two new productions, *Le Compte Ory* and *Manon Lescaut*, as well as revivals of *The Marriage of Figaro, The Makropulos Case* and *Owen Wingrave*.

The summer of 1997 also marked the fiftieth anniversary of the formation of the London Philharmonic Choir, who for the past two years had been working under the direction of a new chorus master, Neville Creed, and for their Jubilee year the choir were graced by the patronage of HRH Princess Alexandra. Vaughan Williams' *Sea Symphony* was chosen as the principal work in the anniversary concert, given in the Royal Albert Hall under Vernon Handley, and if the dictates of economics had reduced the number of choral concerts promoted by the London Philharmonic itself, the choir was nevertheless leading a lively existence, engagements during the summer of 1997 including performances of Verdi's *Requiem* and *Messiah*, the latter given as part of the musical programme given in the open air at Hampton Court Palace.

The opening concert of 1997-98, given in the presence of the Duke of Kent and HRH Princess Alexandra, featured almost every aspect of the orchestra's work. The Youth Orchestra under their newly appointed conductor, the twenty-one-year-old Ilan Volkov, were entrusted with the year's opening music, two works by Mussorgsky, the Prelude to his Opera *Khovantschina*, with the Russian bass Sergei Alexashin as soloist in the *Songs and Dances of Death*. The London Philharmonic itself, supported by the London Philharmonic Choir and by London Voices, contributed the evening's major work, Beethoven's *Choral Symphony*. The Symphony was to have been conducted by Sir Georg Solti, whose death at the end of August dictated that this should be an evening of commemoration rather than one of celebration. Solti had whole-heartedly approved the idea of sharing the evening with the Youth Orchestra, and it was fully in keeping with his encouragement of musicians of the younger generation that the symphony was entrusted to a member of an emerging group of conductors, Joseph Swensen, the newly-appointed Principal Conductor of the Scottish Chamber Orchestra.

1998 would have marked the sixtieth anniversary of Georg Solti's first appearance with the London Philharmonic, conducting the Russian Ballet at Covent Garden, and in terms of longevity this almost certainly constituted an unparalleled association between conductor and orchestra. It may be that Solti will primarily be remembered for his interpretation of the great heights of the German repertoire, Beethoven, Bruckner, Strauss and Wagner. In his appreciation of the conductor, Bob St. John Wright drew attention to another aspect of his work:

'For me the opposite end of the musical spectrum holds the strongest memories. In his hands Mozart, particularly the operas *Don Giovanni* and *Figaro*, positively bubbled with his amazing unstoppable vitality and pulse; and a concert performance in the early 1980s of the last three symphonies still holds its place in my list of "greats"';

a verdict endorsed by bassoon player Michael Boyle, who wrote how:

'It was somehow unexpectedly the smaller-scale forces of Mozart or Haydn that brought out the best in him and the LPO. His acclaimed recordings of the Mozart da Ponte operas with international casts, the Haydn Symphonies in stunning Decca sound, perhaps display his work with the orchestra at its very best.'

By the autumn of 1997 the London Philharmonic had emerged from the traumas created by the Hoffmann enquiry and was on the road back to financial health. In the face of recent history an easy option would have been to play safe, designing conservative programmes unlikely to frighten an audience away. Such a policy will in the end lead to artistic stagnation and it is essential for the health of any orchestra that the repertoire is not allowed to stand still, and 1997–98 took the opposite tack, with wide-ranging and adventurous programmes, from the B minor Mass of Bach to a symphony by the contemporary Russian composer Galina Ustvolskaya. Serge Dorny was determined to break out of the confines imposed by the normal format of the symphony orchestra. Two programmes arranged for the early months of 1998 represented a considerable break with tradition, with a performance of Tippett's Oratorio *A Child of Our Time* preceded by gospel music sung by The London Adventist Choir, and a concert entitled 'Roots Classical Fusions', in which an hour of Indonesian gamelan music was linked to the *Turangalîla* Symphony of Messiaen, the two parts of the evening separated by an interval of an hour, the interval providing the audience with an opportunity of sampling a range of Indonesian food. In a further departure from the normal run of concert-giving, two evenings were given over to 'Silver Screen Classics', Carl Davis conducting the film scores for *Alexander Nevsky* and *Ben-Hur*, with the film projected onto a screen set up above the orchestra.

The featured composer of the year was Prokofiev, the four programmes of a Prokofiev Festival opening with the first of the two evenings devoted to films and their music, a showing of Eisenstein's *Alexander Nevsky*, for which Prokofiev had composed the music. The sound track had been edited in such a way that the music had been excised and, with orchestra dressed entirely in black, rather than formal evening dress, and the choir seated on either side of the screen, which was suspended in front of the Festival Hall organ, Carl Davis synchronised their performance to the appropriate points in the film, a marvel of timing that produced an enthusiastic response from a packed hall. The remaining concerts of the Festival featured a number of lesser-known works, including the ballet *Chout*, the performance of which was described in the *Guardian* as a 'tour-de-force' and the short opera *Maddelena*, while Vadim Repin, soloist in the two Violin Concertos, confirmed his status as one of the finest violinists of the younger generation. As had been the case twelve months previously the year was rounded off under the baton of Bernard Haitink, performances of Mahler's Fourth Symphony and Ravel's *Daphnis and Chloé*, given complete, providing a further demonstration of the rapport between the orchestra and their President.

It is inevitable that conductors loom large in the history of any orchestra. It has been the London Philharmonic's good fortune to have worked, throughout its life, with so high a proportion of the leading interpretative musicians of the day, from Beecham to Solti, taking in such distinguished names as Fürtwangler, Weingartner, de Sabata, van Beinum, Boult, Haitink and Tennstedt, an almost endless list. During the years leading up to the Second World War voices were sometimes raised complaining that the orchestra never played as well for other conductors as for Beecham himself, a criticism that was as much a tribute to Beecham as it was a criticism of the orchestra. It is possible to view the deaths of Klaus Tennstedt* and Sir Georg Solti as closing the door on an era in which the conductor was an all-powerful, dominating figure. Whether such icons of power are alien to the culture of the declining years of the twentieth century remains to be seen, but the reappearance of Christoph Eschenbach, with the promise of further concerts under his baton in future years, commitments made to the orchestra by Sir Georg Solti before he died, and the welcome return of Kurt Masur, re-establishing a relationship temporarily broken when Masur took on the conductorship of the New York Philharmonic Orchestra, were a further vote of confidence in the artistic quality of the London Philharmonic. In addition to concerts at which he was due to appear Masur unhesitatingly undertook to replace Solti, who was to have conducted the orchestra during the early part of 1998. With the names of several members of the younger generation, Mark Elder, Valery Gergiev, Paavo Jarvi, Alexander Lazerev and Mark Wigglesworth, appearing among the list of guest conductors, here was indication enough that the new century will find in its midst a rich vein of talent.

   Sir Thomas Beecham's intention in founding the London Philharmonic was to provide London with an orchestra which would be the equal of the great international ensembles of Berlin, New York and Vienna. In this he was outstandingly successful, and when Beecham turned his back on their affairs the orchestra found within its own ranks a succession of skilled administrators, Charles Gregory, Thomas Russell, Eric Bravington, Stephen Crabtree and many others, whose administrative qualities would have been outstanding in any walk of life, and who have bequeathed us an orchestra which stands in the very front rank. Sadly there remains an influential body of opinion which, while unhesitatingly according the Berlin Philharmonic, the New York Philharmonic and the Vienna Philharmonic the very highest status, regarding them as the touchstone by which others are to be judged, appears to have an inferiority complex about our own orchestras, giving no more than grudging acknowledgement and recognition of their high qualities. For those of us

---

*The death of Klaus Tennstedt on January 11 1998 was announced as this book reached an advanced state of preparation. The orchestra's concert on 4 February, conducted by his friend and colleague Kurt Masur, was dedicated to his memory and it was fitting that in addition to Schubert's *Unfinished* Symphony, the evening should include music by the composer with whose name Tennstedt became so closely associated, Gustav Mahler, a performance of *Das Lied von der Erde*, whose final *Abschied* was a poignant farewell to this much loved musician.

who live or work in or around London, it is our good fortune to have a great international orchestra sitting on our doorstep. It is an orchestra which from its long record of service, both to the audience, and to the community at large through its children's concerts and educational work, deserves continuing support.

APPENDIX A

Principal Conductors of the London Philharmonic Orchestra

1932–45   Sir Thomas Beecham (in absentia 1940–44)
1943–44   Anatole Fistoulari
1949–50   Eduard van Beinum
1950–57   Sir Adrian Boult
1959–60   William Steinberg
1962–66   John Pritchard
1967–79   Bernard Haitink
1979–83   Sir Georg Solti
1983–87   Klaus Tennstedt
1991–96   Franz Welser-Möst

Leaders of the London Philharmonic Orchestra

1932–36   Paul Beard
1936–39   David McCallum
1940–41   Thomas Matthews
1942–45   Jean Pougnet
1945–48   Andrew Cooper
1948–52   David Wise
1952   Andrew Cooper
1953–55   Joseph Shadwick
1957–63   Henry Datyner
1963–64   David McCallum
1964–76   Rodney Friend
1976–92   David Nolan
1992   Constantin Stoianov
1992–   Joakim Svenheden

APPENDIX B: OUT-OF-TOWN CONCERTS 1947–48 TO 1951–52

	(a)	(b)	(c)	(d)	(e)	(f)		(a)	(b)	(c)	(d)	(e)	(f)
Acton*	1	2	2	2	2	–474	Islington	–	1	1	–	–	
Bath	1	5	2	–	1	–134	Kingston	–	2	4	–	–	
Battersea	–	1	1	–	–		Leamington*	–	–	–	2	2	–260
Beckenham	–	2	2	–	–		Leeds	–	–	1	–	–	
Bedford*	1	3	2	2	1	–148	Leicester	2	1	3	2	–	
Bermondsey	1	2	1	–	–		Lewisham	6	6	6	6	6	–828
Bexhill	–	2	1	–	–		Lincoln	–	1	–	–	–	
Birmingham	1	1	1	1	–		Liverpool	–	1	–	2	3	–849
Blackburn	–	–	–	1	–		Llangollen*	–	1	–	2	1	–28
Boston	1	–	–	–	–		Luton*	2	1	1	1	4	–196
Bournemouth	–	–	–	–	2	+200	Malvern*	–	–	–	4	6	–468
Brighton	6	10	10	7	9	+162	Manchester	–	–	–	1	1	–180
Bristol*	4	10	2	–	3	+366	Middlesbrough	–	1	–	–	1	–269
Brixton*	–	–	2	4	–		Newcastle	1	1	2	1	1	–50
Cambridge*	–	–	1	1	4	–192	Newport	–	1	1	–	–	
Canterbury*	–	–	–	–	1	–73	Norwich	–	–	1	–	–	
Cardiff	–	2	–	–	–		Nottingham*	1	2	4	3	6	–910
Chatham	7	10	10	7	9	–1197	Oxford*	2	3	4	6	3	–555
Chelmsford*	–	–	–	1	2	–8	Reading	–	2	3	6	6	–942
Cheltenham	–	1	1	–	–		Rochester	–	–	–	1	2	–80
Coventry	1	1	2	3	5		St Pancras	–	2	–	3	3	–576
Croydon	1	6	5	10	5	+1610	Sheffield	–	–	–	1	1	–200
Dorking	2	5	2	–	1	–144	Slough	–	2	2	1	–	
Eastbourne*	–	–	–	7	7	+112	Southend	–	2	–	1	2	
East Ham	–	5	7	6	6	+516	Southampton*	3	2	3	4	6	–120
Edinburgh	2	–	–	2	2	+84	Stepney	–	2	–	–	–	
Enfield*	–	–	–	1	1	–91	Sutton*	–	2	2	2	2	–66
Epsom	1	–	–	–	–		Swansea*	–	8	7	6	6	–156
Exeter	–	–	–	–	1	–164	Swindon*	1	1	–	2	–	
Finsbury Park*	7	7	7	7	7	–476	Tooting	1	–	2	–	–	
Folkestone*	2	7	5	4	5	–155	Torquay*	–	–	–	–	1	–175
Glasgow	–	–	–	1	–		Walthamstow*	3	–	1	2	1	–23
Greenwich	–	1	–	1	–		Warrington	–	–	–	1	–	
Guildford	1	3	2	2	2	–268	Watford*	6	10	9	10	9	–225
Hackney*	6	5	4	3	4	–48	Wembley	6	8	–	–	–	
Hammersmith	–	3	–	–	–		West Ham	2	–	–	–	–	
Hanley	–	–	–	1	–		Willesden	–	–	–	1	–	
Harrogate	–	1	–	1	–		Wimbledon	7	7	5	6	1	–88
Harrow	–	–	2	1	–		Winchester	1	1	2	1	2	–430
Hastings	2	–	–	–	–		Wolverhampton	1	–	–	–	1	–94
High Wycombe	–	7	4	4	1	–165	Worcester	–	6	–	–	–	
Hornsey*	5	7	5	4	4	–472	York	2	1	1	–	3	–33
Hull	1	–	1	–	1	–211							
Ipswich*	–	3	4	3	3	+21	Net minimum deficit £10,022						

Column (a) shows the number of concerts in 1947–48 (b) 1948–49 (c) 1949–50 (d) 1950–51 (e) and 1951–52, and column (f) the deficit (–) or surplus (+) in 1951–52, assuming every seat in the house was sold for each concert, and after taking local authority grants into account.
* indicates that a grant was received from the local authority.

APPENDIX C: EDUCATION

A 'Kids' Concert' at the Royal Festival Hall is an experience far removed from that of the normal run of symphony concerts, with the level of enthusiasm and the decibel volume pitched considerably higher than that of an adult audience. Whereas the majority of adults take their seats in the last four or five minutes before the start of a concert, school parties begin to fill the hall up to half an hour beforehand. Concerts are billed to start at eleven o'clock, usually with a second performance timed at one, but to allow for latecomers, and those unfamiliar with the hall, there is a grace period before the players take the stage. At the outset the platform is lit by strong red spotlights and, mid-morning or not, the orchestra is kitted out in full evening dress, their entry the signal for frenzied applause. Once the concert gets under way there is a certain amount of whispering and associated shushing, but one instrument commands total silence, the harp.

Every concert is built round a theme. A typical programme, for an audience with an age range of up to nine or ten, given shortly before the 1996 Olympic Games, opened with Mozart's *Musical Joke*, used by the BBC as the theme music for show-jumping, and included music from the film *Chariots of Fire*, an Olympic song composed by Stephen Chadwick, and Mathias Bamert's *Olympics*, a showpiece for orchestra. Opening with an orchestral fanfare, a rondo theme is interrupted by episodes in which players compete to see who can play lowest, bassoon, double-bass or tuba; softest, flute, horn or triangle; or most beautifully, violin, oboe or xylophone, a simple way of introducing children to various instruments. It is obvious that the players enjoy this variation from the formality of the normal symphony concert. Entering into the spirit of the piece, the various sections, strings, woodwind, brass and percussion, encouraged the children to 'vote' for each winner, a highly vocal process. Many of the children bring their packed lunch with them, and after the morning concert is over, and as the early arrivals for the one o'clock concert begin to find their way upstairs, the hall is thronged with small groups sitting cross-legged to consume the contents of their lunchbox, to the possible bewilderment of casual visitors.

These concerts are designed for an audience which is not necessarily inherently musical and, with a high level of fun content, extend the children's range of experience, demonstrating that there is nothing forbidding about a symphony orchestra. The range of music, which is both enjoyable and comprehensible, crosses the barriers of classical, popular and ethnic music, extending the children's experience beyond the range of pop groups.

Children's concerts play a vital part in the work of trying to form the audience of tomorrow, but form only part of the education programme. The Education Department arranges training for teachers, provides schools with material containing suggestions for listening and creative work, linked to the concert attended by the children, and arranges workshops. These workshops take players into schools to work with teachers and children on practical music-making. Using an existing composition as a basis, the children are encouraged to compose their own pieces, which are then performed, some of those written in secondary schools by GCSE students brought to the Festival Hall. Schools taking part in creative projects are encouraged to develop stronger links with the orchestra through the Playerlink scheme. Led by a workshop leader, supported by a member of the orchestra, this involves a series of school-based workshops based on a theme chosen by the class teacher and related to some other area of their schoolwork. The workshops culminate in a concert in which the schools taking part in the scheme come together.

Participation is an important element of the programme. Sir Harrison Birtwistle has worked on projects linked to his own music as well as devising a series of participatory events based on the different sections of the orchestra. The 'Brass Blast' of 1995 involved over a hundred brass players, and the equally imaginatively titled 'Percussion Bash', which took place in 1996, was linked to a concert featuring the percussion department and including music by John Adams, Leonard Bernstein and Steve Reich before concluding with *Piece of Junk*, 'a work created for and by the London Philharmonic using infinite resources'. Two further events on similar lines, 'Stringstravaganza', and 'Whirlwind' were planned for future years.

More recently, the London Philharmonic's residency at Glyndebourne has involved the orchestra in collaboration with Glyndebourne Education, involving a range of activities, including projects for two Special Needs schools in South London, work with young prisoners detained at Lewes, and an opera project, based on Alban Berg's *Lulu*, with a group of music students in Lewes.

The orchestra's experience in this field has been put to good use overseas. Much of the goodwill generated during the tours of South Africa arose from a project given under the direction of Eugene Skeef, a South African musician now living and working in this country. The project included coaching – there is an enormous enthusiasm for music in the townships – children's concerts, visits to schools by players, and workshops. Franz Welser-Möst took a rehearsal of the Wits University String Orchestra, and Bob St J. Wright rehearsed a string orchestra, with an invited audience drawn from other black youth orchestras. One result of the orchestra's education work in South Africa has been an invitation, gladly accepted, to become patrons of the South African Youth Orchestra.

Work of this nature lacks the visibility of public concerts and is far from being self-funding. That it has been possible to develop so widely-based a programme is thanks to the generosity of sponsors, notably D P Mann Insurance and the State Street Bank. As an investment in the future, this must rank as money well spent.

APPENDIX D: SELECTED PERFORMANCES

Programmes are given at intervals of twenty years, showing the repertoire at different periods. The opening week of the 'Blitz' tour and the 'Historic' concerts given from 1957 to 1961 are also included. Choral concerts are with the London Philharmonic Choir except where shown otherwise.

1932–33 The Royal Philharmonic Society's 121st Season – Conductor Sir Thomas Beecham, except on 27 January

7 October Overture, Le Carnaval Romain (Berlioz) Symphony 38 (Mozart) Brigg Fair (Delius) Ein Heldenleben (Strauss)

20 October MYRA HESS Overture, Les Abercérages (Cherubini) Suite The Origin of Design (Handel-Beecham) Rondes de Printemps – Images No.3 (Debussy) Piano Concerto 24 (Mozart) Symphony 99 (Haydn)

10 November VLADIMIR HOROWITZ Overture, King Lear (Berlioz) Iberia – Images No.2 (Debussy) Piano Concerto 1 (Tchaikovsky) Symphony 3 (Mendelssohn)

24 November Macbeth (Strauss) Symphony 3 (Boccherini) Nocturne, Paris (Delius) Petrushka (Stravinsky)

16 December THEA PHILIPS, MURIEL BRUNSKILL, WALTER WIDDOP, WILLIAM PARSONS: THE PHILHARMONIC CHOIR Messiah (Handel)

27 January NICOLAI MALKO: JAN SMETERLIN Stenka Razine (Glazounov) Variations for string orchestra (Arensky) Piano Concerto – *First performance* (Szymanowski) Scheherazade (Rimsky-Korsakov)

9 February JELLY D'ARANYI, GASPAR CASSADO Variations on a Theme by Haydn, Double Concerto for violin and cello, Symphony 2 (Brahms)

23 February Overture, Les deux aveugles de Tolède (Mehul) In the Faery Hills (Bax) Symphony 8 (Beethoven) Symphonie Fantastique (Berlioz)

9 March ALBERT SAMMONS, LIONEL TERTIS Overture, William Tell (Rossini) Sinfonia concertante for violin and viola (Mozart) Symphony 2 (Tchaikovsky)

7 April Concerto grosso in G maj (Handel) Rondo Veneziano – *First UK performance, conducted by the Composer* (Pizzetti) Symphony 9 (Schubert)

1932–33 The Courtauld-Sargent Concerts (Conductor Dr Malcolm Sargent, except on 24, 25 and 27 April
October 10, 11, 13 THE PRO ARTE QUARTET Introduction and Allegro for Strings (Elgar) La Mer (Debussy) String Quartet Op 77 No. 1 (Haydn) Concerto for String Quartet and Orchestra – *First UK performance* (Martinu) Till Eulenspigel (Strauss)
November 14, 15, 17 NATHAN MILSTEIN Violin Concerto (Tchaikovsky) Symphony 6 (Sibelius) Violin Concerto (Brahms)
December 5, 6, 9 WILHELMINA SUGGIA, SAMUEL KUTCHNER, LEON GOOSSENS, JOHN ALEXANDER Theatre Overture (Kodaly) Cello Concerto (Haydn) Sinfonia concertante for violin, cello, oboe and bassoon (Haydn) Symphony 4 – *First performance* (Bax)
January 16, 17, 18 ALBERT SAMMONS, LIONEL TERTIS, ROY HENDERSON: AN UNNAMED CHOIR Symphony, Harold in Italy (Berlioz) Sinfonia concertante for violin and viola (Mozart) Belshazzar's Feast (Walton)
February 6, 7, 8 ALFRED CORTOT En Saga (Sibelius) Piano Concerto 2 (Chopin) Symphonic Variations (Franck) Symphony 4 (Brahms)
April 24, 25, 27 BRUNO WALTER: FLORENCE AUSTRAL Symphony 39 (Mozart) Closing scene – Götterdämmerung (Wagner) Symphony 3 (Beethoven)
'Blitz Tour' 1940 – Empire Theatre Glasgow 12–17 August
Conductors Dr Malcolm Sargent (Monday to Thursday and Saturday) and Basil Cameron (Friday)
Soloists Eileen Joyce (Piano Solos), Margaret Eaves (Soprano Solos) and Thomas Matthews
Monday First House and Tuesday Second House: Overture, Le Carnaval Romain (Berlioz), Londonderry Air (arr Grainger), Piano Solos, Romeo and Juliet Overture, William Tell (Rossini), Carmen Suite (Bizet), Soprano Solos, Tales From the Vienna Woods (Johann Strauss), Finlandia (Sibelius)
Monday Second House and Tuesday First House Overture, Morning, Noon and Night in Vienna (Suppe), Serenade from Hassan (Delius), Three pieces from The Damnation of Faust (Berlioz), Unfinished Sym. (Schubert), Peer Gynt Suite (Grieg), Soprano Solos, Overture Tannhäuser (Wagner)
Wednesday First House: Overture, Morning, Noon and Night in Vienna (Suppe), Piano Solos, New World Symphony (Dvorak), Nutcracker Suite (Tchaikovsky), Soprano Solos, March, Pomp and Circumstance 1 (Elgar)
Wednesday Second House: Overture, Semiramide (Rossini), Valse Triste (Sibelius), Soprano Solos, Poeme (Chausson), Overture, Tannhäuser (Wagner), Marche Militaire (Schubert), Piano Solos, Symphony 5 (Tchaikovsky)
Thursday First House: Overture, Zampa (Hérold), Three pieces from The Damnation of Faust, Soprano Solos, Waltz The Blue Danube (Strauss), Polovtsian Dances (Borodin), Barcarolle – The Tales of Hoffman (Offenbach), Piano Solos, Symphony 5 (Tchaikovsky)
Thursday Second House: Overture. The Barber of Seville (Rossini), Piano Solos, Symphony 5 (Beethoven) Barceuse and Praeludium (Jarnefelt), Dances from Henry VIII (Edward German), Soprano Solos, 1812 Overture (Tchaikovsky)

Friday First and Second House: Grand March from Tannhäuser (Wagner), Two Hungarian Dances (Brahms) Andante Cantabile (Tchaikovsky), Faust Ballet Music (Gounod), Piano Solos, Wine, Women and Song (Strauss), Bolero (Ravel), Rhapsody in Blue (Gershwin), Soprano Solos, On Hearing the First Cuckoo (Delius), The Three Bears (Coates), Finlandia (Sibelius)

Saturday First House: Overture, The Barber of Seville (Rossini), Piano Solos, Symphony 5 (Beethoven) Overture, William Tell (Rossini), Barceuse and Praeludium (Jarnefelt), Dances from Henry VIII (Edward German), Soprano Solos, 1812 Overture (Tchaikovsky)

Saturday Second House: Overture, Zampa (Hérold) Valse Triste (Sibelius), Soprano Solos, Nutcracker Suite (Tchaikovsky), The Blue Danube (Johann Strauss), Unfinished Symphony (Schubert), Piano Solos, Suite Peer Gynt (Grieg), Overture, Tannhäuser (Wagner)

1952–53: Royal Festival Hall (35 Concerts – *Concert promoted by the LCC)

23 September VICTOR DE SABATA Overture, The Magic Flute (Mozart) Symphony 4 (Tchaikovsky) Concerto a un altro giorno (Pizzetti) Suite Mother Goose (Ravel) Polovtsian Dances (Borodin)

6 October SIR ADRIAN BOULT: ALFRED KITCHIN Overture, Il Seraglio, Eine Kleine Nachtmusik (Mozart) Piano Concerto 2 (Rachmaninov) Overture, The Bartered Bride (Smetana) Enigma Variations (Elgar)

12 October (*Vaughan Williams Birthday Concert*) SIR ADRIAN BOULT: MARGARET RITCHIE, EMLYN WILLIAMS Song of Thanksgiving, Symphony 5, Flos Campi, Sons of Night (Vaughan Williams)

2 November SIR ADRIAN BOULT: CYRIL SMITH Overture, The Marriage of Figaro (Mozart) Symphony 94 (Haydn) Romeo and Juliet (Tchaikovsky) Piano Concerto 3 (Rachmaninov) Slavonic Dance 7 in C (Dvorak)

6 November BASIL CAMERON: MOURA LYMPANY Overture, Russlan and Ludmilla (Glinka) Tapiola (Sibelius) Piano Concerto (Grieg) Symphony 3 (Beethoven)

16 November NORMAN DEL MAR: DENIS MATTHEWS Symphony 4 (Mendelssohn) Piano Concerto 4 (Beethoven) Karelia Suite (Sibelius) Dream Pantomime – Hansel and Gretel (Humperdinck) Espana (Chabrier)

17 November SIR ADRIAN BOULT: ANDERSON TYRER Francesca da Rimini, Piano Concerto 1 (Tchaikovsky) Symphony 4(8) (Dvorak)

20 November SIR ADRIAN BOULT: JOAN CROSS, ANNE WOOD, RICHARD LEWIS, WILLIAM PARSONS Mass in D (Beethoven)

28 November SIR ADRIAN BOULT: DAME MYRA HESS Overture, Leonora 3, Piano Concerto 1 (Beethoven) Symphony 1 (Brahms)

1 December BASIL CAMERON: HALINA STEFANSKA Symphony 101 (Haydn) Piano Concerto 23 (Mozart) Prelude à l'après midi d'un faune (Debussy) Symphonic Variations (Franck) Les Preludes (Liszt)

2 December SIR ADRIAN BOULT: DAME MYRA HESS Symphony 5 (Schubert) Piano Concerto 2 (Beethoven) Siegfried Idyll, Overture, The Flying Dutchman (Wagner)

5 December SIR ADRIAN BOULT: DAME MYRA HESS Trumpet Tune and Air (Purcell) The Water Music (Handel-Baines) Piano Concerto 3 (Beethoven) Symphony 2 (7) (Dvorak)

9 December SIR ADRIAN BOULT: DAME MYRA HESS Academic Festival Overture (Brahms) Piano Concerto 4 (Beethoven) Introduction and Allegro for strings (Elgar) Symphony 2 – *First London performance* (Wordsworth)

11 December SIR ADRIAN BOULT: DAME MYRA HESS Overture, A Midsummer Night's Dream (Mendelssohn) Piano Concerto 5 (Beethoven) A Nottingham Symphony – *First London performance* (Alan Bush)

18 December FREDERICK JACKSON: ELSIE MORRISON, GLADYS RIPLEY, PETER PEARS, HERVEY ALAN Messiah (Handel)

19 December BASIL CAMERON: POUISHNOFF Overture The Pierrot of the Minute (Bantock) The Walk to the Paradise Garden (Delius) Piano Concerto 2 (Rachmaninov) Symphony 2 (Sibelius)

16 January SIR ADRIAN BOULT: JASCHA SPIVAKOVSKY Overture, Egmont (Beethoven) Piano Concerto 23 (Mozart) Overture, In the South (Elgar) Symphony 2 (Brahms)

*18 January SIR ADRIAN BOULT Overture Leonora 2 (Beethoven) Symphony 4 (Schumann) Symphony 9 (Schubert)

19 January BASIL CAMERON Polonaise and Waltz from Eugene Onegin (Tchaikovsky) Suite, Jeux d'Enfants (Bizet) Petrushka (Stravinsky) Coppelia Suite (Delibes) Ballet Music from Rosamunde (Schubert) Ballet Music, The Perfect Fool (Holst) Ballet Music, Le Cid (Massenet)

30 January GEORG SOLTI: RUDOLF FIRKUSNY Eine Kleine Nachtmusik (Mozart) Variations on a Theme by Haydn (Brahms) Piano Concerto 20 (Mozart) Symphony 4 (Brahms)

1 February SIR ADRIAN BOULT: MOURA LYMPANY Overture Cockaigne (Elgar) Piano Concerto 1 (Tchaikovsky) Symphony 5 (9) (Dvorak)

*4 February EDUARD VAN BEINUM Overture, Prometheus, Symphony 6 (Beethoven) Symphonie Fantastique (Berlioz)

10 February SIR ADRIAN BOULT: MOURA LYMPANY Overture, La Scala di Seta (Rossini) Le Rouet d'Omphale (Saint-Saens) Symphony 4 (Beethoven) Piano Concerto 3 (Rachmaninov) Overture in D min (Handel-Elgar)

16 February EDUARD VAN BEINUM: DENIS MATTHEWS Symphony 8, Piano Concerto 3, Symphony 7 (Beethoven)

20 February EDUARD VAN BEINUM: ANNE WOOD Tragic Overture, Alto Rhapsody (Brahms) Symphony 5 (Bruckner)

1 March EDUARD VAN BEINUM: CEINWEN ROWLANDS, ANNE WOOD, WILLIAM HERBERT, WILLIAM PARSONS Mass in D (Beethoven)

6 March SIR ADRIAN BOULT: ERIK CHISHOLM Overture Oberon (Weber) Music for His Majesty's Sackbuts and Cornets (Locke-Baines) Piano Concerto 2 – *First performance* (Erik Chisholm) Symphony 6 (Tchaikovsky)

13 March SIR ADRIAN BOULT Overture, Benvenuto Cellini (Berlioz) Symphony (Franck) Three Nocturnes (Debussy) Daphnis and Chloé Suite 2 (Ravel)

20 March WALTER SUSSKIND: CYRIL SMITH Overture, Prince Igor (Borodin) Classical Symphony (Prokofiev) Rhapsody on a Theme of Paganini (Rachmaninov) Symphony 4 (Tchaikovsky)

25 March SIR ADRIAN BOULT: STELL ANDERSON El Salón Mexico (Copland) Adagio for strings (Barber) Piano Concerto (Grieg) Symphony 2 (Sibelius)

4 April NORMAN DEL MAR: GWEN CATLEY Overture, Euryanthe (Weber) Bell Song from Lakmé (Delibes) Scheherazade (Rimsky- Korsakov) Doll Song from The Tales of Hoffman (Offenbach) Dances from The Three Cornered Hat (Falla)

6 April HANS SCHMIDT-ISSERSTEDT Overture, The Marriage of Figaro (Mozart) Symphony 8 (Schubert) Till Eulenspigel (Strauss) Symphony 1 (Brahms)

24 April SIR ADRIAN BOULT: CYRIL SMITH Academic Festival Overture, Piano Concerto 2 (Brahms) Enigma Variations (Elgar)

25 April JEAN MARTINON: GRETE SCHERZER Symphony 1 (Beethoven) Piano Concerto 2 (Rachmaninov) La Mer (Debussy) Bolero (Ravel)

27 April NORMAN DEL MAR: FRANK PHILLIPS Introduction and Bridal March from Le Coq d'Or (Rimsky-Korsakov) Peter and the Wolf (Prokofiev) Sabre Dance (Khatchaturyan) Symphony 5 (Tchaikovsky)

10 May SIR ADRIAN BOULT: PHYLLIS SELLICK Prelude Act 3 Lohengrin (Wagner) Italian Serenade (Wolf) Piano Concerto 1 (Tchaikovsky) Symphony 4 (Tchaikovsky)

25 May (*Coronation Concert*) SIR ADRIAN BOULT: DENIS MATTHEWS Street Corner Overture (Rawsthorne) The Banks of Green Willow (Butterworth) Piano Concerto 27 (Mozart) Symphony 2 (Elgar)

27 May (*Coronation Concert*) SIR ADRIAN BOULT: MYRA HESS, DENNIS NOBLE Festival Te Deum (Rubbra) Piano Concerto 3 (Beethoven) Belshazzar's Feast (Walton) – *conducted by the composer*

3 July VICTOR DE SABATA Overture Le Carnaval Romain (Berlioz) Symphony 39 (Mozart) La Valse (Ravel) Prelude and Liebestod from Tristan and Isolde (Wagner) Enigma Variations (Elgar)

January–May 1957: Royal Festival Hall – 'Music of a Century' (9 Concerts)

28 January 'Retreat from Wagner' CONSTANTIN SILVESTRI: JOYCE BARKER Closing scene from Götterdämmerung (Wagner) Three Nocturnes (Debussy) Le poème de l'extase (Scriabin) Symphony of Psalms (Stravinsky)

11 February 'Adventures in Tonality' HERMANN SCHERCHEN Academic Festival Overture (Brahms) Scherzo capriccioso (Dvorak) Philharmonic Concerto (Hindemith) Suite Provençale (Milhaud) Five Orchestral Pieces (Schoenberg)

25 February 'Strange Orchestras' HERMANN SCHERCHEN: HELEN WATTS, PHILLIPPE ENTREMONT Ionisation (Varèse) Piano Concerto (Jolivet) Suite The Firebird (Stravinsky) The Rio Grande (Lambert) Ballet mécanique (Antheil) Bolero (Ravel)

18 March 'Nostalgia' SIR ADRIAN BOULT CAMPOLI Two Elegiac Melodies (Grieg) Violin Concerto (Elgar) The Walk to the Paradise Garden (Delius) Symphony (Franck)

1 April 'Once Upon a Time' PAUL KLETZKI En Saga (Sibelius) Suite Mother Goose (Ravel) Till Eulenspigel (Strauss) Eventyr (Delius) Suite, Hary Janos (Kodaly)

15 April 'Voice and Verse' HANS SWAROWSKY: JENNIFER VYVYAN, PAMELA BOWDEN, WILLIAM HERBERT Das Lied von der Erde (Mahler) Spring Symphony (Britten)

29 April 'Primitive Strength' JANOS FERENCSIK: ERIC GREENE, OWEN BRANNIGAN A Night on the Bare Mountain (Mussorgsky) The Rite of Spring (Stravinsky) Sinfonietta (Janáček) Cantata Profana (Bartok)

13 May 'Humour' MASSIMO FRECCIA: ALDO CICCOLINI: ERIC BRAVINGTON Classical Symphony (Prokofiev) Concerto for Piano and Trumpet (Shostakovitch) Suite Pastorale (Chabrier) Concertino for Piano and Orchestra (Francaix) Symphony 2 (Malcolm Arnold)

27 May 'Signs and Portents' SIR ADRIAN BOULT March, Pomp and Circumstance 1 (Elgar) Ode to Death (Holst), Suite, Lulu (Berg) These Things Shall Be (John Ireland) Symphony 6 (Vaughan Williams)

1957–58: Royal Festival Hall – 'Grand Tour de la Musique' (8 Concerts)

25 November 'Hungary' JANOS FERENCSIK: BELA SIKI, WILLIAM HERBERT Festival Overture (Weiner) Symphony 5 (Lajtha) Piano Concerto No 3 (Bartok) Psalmus Hungaricus (Kodaly)

16 December 'Spain' ELEAZER DE CARVALHO: SEGOVIA Procesion del Rocio (Turina) Guitar Concerto (Ponce) Suite Don Quixote (Gerhard) Dances from The Three Cornered Hat (Falla)

3 February 'Russia' CONSTANTIN SILVESTRI: RUGGIERO RICCI Fireworks (Stravinsky) Violin Concerto 2 (Prokofiev) Dances from Gayenah (Khatchaturian) Symphony 10 (Shostakovitch)

24 February 'Germany' SIR ADRIAN BOULT: LEON GOOSSENS Overture, Simplicimuss the Simpleton (Hartmann) Oboe Concerto (Strauss) Variations on a Theme of Paganini (Blacher) Variations on a Theme of Mozart (Reger) Symphony, Mathis der Maler (Hindemith)

17 March 'France' MANUEL ROSENTHAL: GEORGE MALCOLM Ouverture de fête (Ibert) Rondes de Printemps – Images No 3 (Debussy) Concert Champêtre (Poulenc) Symphony 3 (Roussel) L'ascension (Messiaen) Suite 1, Daphnis and Chloé (Ravel)

14 April 'Scandinavia' THOMAS JENSEN: ANDOR FOLDES Swedish Rhapsody (Alfven) Piano Concerto (Saeverud) Symphony 6 (Sibelius) La cimetière marin (Valen) Symphony 5 (Nielsen)

5 May 'America' WILLIAM STEINBERG: IRIS LOVERIDGE An American in Paris (Gershwin) Piano Concerto (William Schuman) Symphony 3 (Roy Harris) Billy the Kid (Copland) Symphony 1 (Barber)

26 May 'England' SIR ADRIAN BOULT: DENIS MATTHEWS, MARGARET RITCHIE, JOHN CAMERON Overture, Portsmouth Point (Walton) On Hearing the First Cuckoo in Spring (Delius) Piano Concerto 1 (Rawsthorne) A Sea Symphony (Vaughan Williams)

1958–59: Royal Festival Hall – 'Music of the Twentieth Century' (7 Concerts)

30 September (1900–10) WILLIAM STEINBERG: EUGENIA ZARESKA, WALTER GEISSLER Overture, Cockaigne (Elgar) Six Orchestral Pieces (Webern) Das Lied von der Erde (Mahler)

11 November 1910–19 SIR ADRIAN BOULT: MINDRU KATZ Jeux – Poème Dansé (Debussy) Piano Concerto 1 (Prokofiev) The Planets (Holst)

9 December 1920–29 JAROSLAV KROMBHOLC: MONICA SINCLAIR, ROSINA RAISBECK, ALFRED ORDA, RAYMOND NILSSON La création du monde (Milhaud) Variations for Orchestra (Schoenberg) The Rio Grande (Constant Lambert) Glagolithic Mass (Janáček)

3 February 1930–39 WILLIAM STEINBERG: NORMA PROCTOR, HERVEY ALAN El Salon Mexico (Copland) Belshazzar's Feast (Walton) Cantata, Alexander Nevsky (Prokofiev)

3 March 1940–45 CONSTANTIN SILVESTRI: DAVID GALLIVER, BARRY TUCKWELL Overture, Street Corner (Rawsthorne) Serenade for Tenor, Horn and Strings (Britten) Symphony in 3 Movements (Stravinsky) Concerto for Orchestra (Bartok)

7 April 1946–49 SIR ADRIAN BOULT: EVELYN LEAR Overture, The Smoke (Malcolm Arnold) Concerto for seven wind instruments (Martin) Four Last Songs (Strauss) Symphony 6 (Vaughan Williams)

2 June 1950–59 WILLIAM STEINBERG: APRIL CANTELO, DAVID GALLIVER DENNIS DOWLING: THE JOHNNY DANKWORTH ORCHESTRA Pittsburgh Symphony (Hindemith) Lamentations of Jeremiah -Threni (Stravinsky) Concerto for Jazz Band and Symphony Orchestra (Lieberman) Improvisations for Jazz Band and Symphony Orchestra (Dankworth/Seiber)

1959–60: Royal Festival Hall – 'Music of the Twentieth Century' (7 Concerts)

29 September 'The Elements' WILLIAM STEINBERG Sea Interludes from Peter Grimes (Britten) Egdon Heath (Holst) La Mer (Debussy) Ritual Dances from A Midsummer Marriage (Tippett) Prometheus – Poem of Fire (Scriabin)

13 November 'The Philosopher' SIR ADRIAN BOULT: HEATHER HARPER, DIETRICH FISCHER-DIESKAU, RICHARD LEWIS, JOHN CAMERON, IAN WALLACE: THE AMBROSIAN SINGERS and THE LONDON PHILHARMONIC CHOIR Doktor Faust (Busoni)

8 December 'Personal Protest' JOHN PRITCHARD: ANNELIESE KUPPER, MONICA SINCLAIR, RICHARD LEWIS, FORBES ROBINSON Fragments from Wozzeck (Berg) A Child of our Time (Tippett)

26 January 'Humour' JAROSLAV KROMBHOLC: MARIA TAUBEROVA, JOHN WHITWORTH, JOHN HAUXVELL Overture, News of the Day (Hindemith) Suite Hary Janos (Kodaly) Carmina Burana (Orff)

23 February 'A Tale of Two Cities' SIR MALCOLM SARGENT Big Ben Variations (Ernest Toch) Overture Cockaigne (Elgar) Nocturne Paris (Delius) A London Symphony (Vaughan Williams)

26 April 'Primavera' JANOS FERENCSIK: JENNIFER VYVYAN, NORMA PROCTOR, MURRAY DICKIE The Rite of Spring (Stravinsky) Spring Symphony (Britten)

1 June 'Present Thoughts' WILLIAM STEINBERG: THE JOHNNY DANKWORTH ORCHESTRA Orchestral Variations (Copland) Sonata for 17 instruments (Maxwell Davies) Two pieces for Orchestra (Dallapiccola) Ebony Concerto (Stravinsky) Rendezvous (Salzedo/Lindup) Improvisations for Jazz Band and Symphony Orchestra (Dankworth/Seiber)

1960–61: Royal Festival Hall – 'Music of the Twentieth Century' (8 Concerts)

4 October JASCHA HORENSTEIN: ISAAC STERN Suite, Much Ado About Nothing (Korngold) Meditations (Gottfried von Einam) Violin Concerto (Berg) Fantasia concertante on a Theme by Corelli (Tippett) Chamber Symphony (Schoenberg)

8 November JOHN PRITCHARD: HEPHZIBAH MENUHIN Suite, From the House of the Dead (Janacek) Les offrandes oubliées (Messiaen) Piano Concerto 2 (Bartok) Symphony No 3 – *First performance, commissioned by the London Philharmonic Society* (Peter Racine Fricker)

13 December JAROSLAV KROMBHOLC: APRIL CANTELO, HELEN WATTS, RICHARD LEWIS, DUNCAN ROBERTSON, ALFRED HALLETT, DENNIS DOWLING, JOHN CAROL CASE, OWEN BRANNIGAN, MARIAN NOWAKOWSKI The Mystery of the Nativity (Frank Martin)

17 January SIR ADRIAN BOULT: YEHUDI MENUHIN Dance Concerto – Phalaphala – *First performance* (Priaulx Rainer) Violin Concerto (Elgar) A Colour Symphony (Bliss)

21 February COLIN DAVIS: DAVID OISTRAKH Variations for Orchestra (Schoenberg) Violin Concerto (Shostakovitch) Symphony in C (Stravinsky)

28 March SIR MALCOLM SARGENT: MAX ROSTAL, PAMELA BOWDEN, MARY WELLS, ALEXANDER YOUNG, RICHARD ATTENBOROUGH Fantasia concertante for violin and strings (Matyas Seiber) King David (Honegger)

2 May PIERRE MONTEUX Suite Protée (Milhaud) Symphony 3 (Pijper) Jeux – poème dansé (Debussy) Symphony, Mathis der Maler (Hindemith)

30 May JOHN PRITCHARD: SEGOVIA, ARDA MANDIKIAN, MARGARET LEIGHTON, GEORGE BAKER The Spell of May (Skalkottas) Guitar Concerto (Castelnuovo-Tedesco) Guitar Solos; Parade (Satie)

1972–73 – Fortieth Anniversary Season: Royal Festival Hall (30 Concerts – (*EEC Celebration concert))

28 September DANIEL BARENBOIM: PINCHAS ZUCKERMAN Overture, Euryanthe (Weber) Violin Concerto 1 (Mozart) Symphony 2 (Elgar)

4 October ALDO CECCATO: CHRISTOPH ESCHENBACH Classical Symphony (Prokofiev) Piano Concerto 5 (Beethoven) Symphony 1 (Shostakovitch)

19 October RAYMOND LEPPARD: PAUL TORTELIER Overture, Rosamunde (Schubert) Cello Concerto (Elgar) Suite The Rising of the Moon – *First performance* (Nicholas Maw) Enigma Variations (Elgar)
22 October EUGEN JOCHUM Symphonies 96, 97, 98 (Haydn)
26 October EUGEN JOCHUM: JOHN LILL, DOUGLAS WHITTAKER, MAURICE CHECKER Concerto da camera (Honegger) Piano Concerto 3, Symphony 7 (Beethoven)
31 October EDO DE WAART: ITZHAK PERLMAN Fanfare from La Péri (Dukas) Intégrales (Varèse) Violin Concerto (Sibelius) Symphony 6 (Dvorak)
5 November BERNARD HAITINK: IDA HAENDEL, HEATHER HARPER, ANNA REYNOLDS, GERALD ENGLISH, BENJAMIN LUXON Overture, Leonora 3 (Beethoven) Violin Concerto (Stravinsky) Requiem (Mozart)
19 November BERNARD HAITINK: JANET BAKER Aria Parto, parto – La Clemenza di Tito (Mozart) Wesendonck Songs (Wagner) Symphony 6 (Mahler)
23 November BERNARD HAITINK: ALFRED BRENDEL Lontano – *First London performance* (Ligeti) Piano Concerto 1, Totentanz (Liszt) Petrushka (Stravinsky)
28 November YEVGENI SVETLANOV: PETER KATIN, ALEXANDER VEDERNIKOV: STATE CHOIR OF THE USSR Prelude, Khovantschina (Mussorgsky) Piano Concerto 3 (Rachmaninov) Oratorio Pathétique (Svirdrov)
30 November YEVGENI SVETLANOV: DAVID OISTRAKH Symphony 21 (Miaskovsky) Violin Concerto 1 (Prokofiev) Symphony 2 (Borodin)
5 December JOSEF KRIPS: NATHAN MILSTEIN Symphony 2 (Searle) Violin Concerto (Brahms) Symphony 2 (Beethoven)
12 December KURT SANDERLING: LORIN HOLLANDER Concerto grosso Op 6 No 7 (Handel) Piano Concerto 2 (Rachmaninov) Symphony 4 (Brahms)
17 December KURT SANDERLING: JOHN OGDEN Suite 2 for small orchestra (Stravinsky) Piano Concerto 5 (Beethoven) Symphony 4 (Tchaikovsky)
8 January* BERNARD HAITINK: MARGARET PRICE, ROWLAND DAVIES Overture, In the South (Elgar) Arias and Duets from Il Seraglio (Mozart) Symphony 4 (Vaughan Williams)
22 January BERNARD HAITINK: ARTUR RUBINSTEIN Piano Concerto 2 (Chopin) Piano Concerto 2 (Saint-Saens) The Rite of Spring (Stravinsky)
25 January BERNARD HAITINK: VLADIMIR ASHKENAZY Piano Concerto 3 (Beethoven) Symphony 4 (Bruckner)
28 January BERNARD HAITINK: VLADIMIR ASHKENAZY Piano Concerto 20 (Mozart) Symphony 4 (Bruckner)
30 January EUGEN JOCHUM Symphonies 99, 100, 101 (Haydn)
15 February SIR GEORG SOLTI Symphony 5 (Schubert) Symphony 7 (Bruckner)
18 February SIR GEORG SOLTI: STEPHEN BISHOP Piano Concerto 24 (Mozart) Symphony 7 (Bruckner)
22 February SIR GEORG SOLTI: TATIANA TROYANOS, ANDRAS FARAGO Concerto for Orchestra, Bluebeard's Castle (Bartok)
27 February SIR GEORG SOLTI: JOSEPHINE VEASEY, STUART BURROWS, GWYNNE HOWELL, PAUL HUDSON: The Damnation of Faust (Berlioz)

3 April EDO DE WAART: JANET BAKER Sonata for Brass (Gabrieli) Washington's Birthday (Ives) Rückert Lieder (Mahler) Symphony 6 (Tchaikovsky)

8 April LOUIS FREMAUX/JOHN ALLDIS*: SHEILA ARMSTRONG, JOHN CAROL CASE, DAVID WARD Overture and Monologue from Act I The Flying Dutchman, Siegfried Idyll, Wotan's Farewell and Magic Fire Music (Wagner) Dona Nobis Pacem (Vaughan Williams)*

22 April JOSEF KRIPS: WALTER KLEIN Symphony 3 (Brahms) Piano Concerto 21 (Mozart) Till Eulenspigel (Strauss)

1 May ERICH LEINSDORF: PETER KATIN Symphony 3 (Mendelssohn) Piano Concerto 4 (Beethoven) Pictures from an Exhibition (Mussorgsky- Ravel)

4 May BERNARD HAITINK KYUNG-WHA CHUNG Concerto for Orchestra – *First performance* (Iain Hamilton) Violin Concerto (Tchaikovsky) Also Sprach Zarathustra (Strauss)

8 May BERNARD HAITINK: DANIEL BARENBOIM Academic Festival Overture, Piano Concerto 1, Symphony 1 (Brahms)

10 May JOSEF KRIPS: ILEANA CORTRUBAS, NORMA PROCTOR Symphony 8 (Schubert) Symphony 2 (Mahler)

1992–93: The International Series (40 Concerts)

17, 18 September FRANZ WELSER-MÖST MAURIZIO POLLINI Three Galaxies (Kuisma) Piano Concerto 4 (Beethoven) Symphony 2 (Schumann) Symphonies of wind instruments (Stravinsky) Prelude and Fugue for Strings (Britten) Suite The Love of Three Oranges (Prokofiev) *encore* – Overture, Die Fledermaus (Johann Strauss)

22, 23 September ZUBIN MEHTA: PINCHAS ZUKERMAN, SUMI JO, JOCHEN KOWALSKI, JEFFREY BLACK Six Pieces for orchestra (Webern) Violin Concerto 1 (Bruch) Carmina Burana (Orff)

7, 8 October JEREMY JACKMAN*/KLAUS TENNSTEDT : LUCIA POPP, ANN MURRAY, ANTHONY ROLF-JOHNSON, RENE PAPE Paraphrase on Mozart's Idomeneo (Robert Saxton)* Psalm 2, Warum toben die Heiden (Mendelssohn)* Symphony 9 (Beethoven)

13, 14 October KLAUS TENNSTEDT: NIGEL KENNEDY Violin Concerto (Beethoven) Symphony 1 (Brahms)

20 October FRANZ WELSER-MÖST: RADU LUPU String Sonata 3 (Rossini) Piano Concerto 1 (Brahms) Serenade for 13 Wind Instruments (Strauss) Suite, The Miraculous Mandarin (Bartok)

26 October FRANZ WELSER-MÖST: KYUNG-WHA CHUNG Stabat Mater in G min (Schubert) Violin Concerto 2 (Bruch) Symphony 5 (Sibelius)

17 November FRANZ WELSER-MÖST: NELSON GOERNER, ROBERT POWELL, JULIE WALTERS, BENJAMIN LUXON, CLAIRE and ANTOINETTE CANN, HELEN LEDERER, DAVID MELLOR, FRANK BRUNO, QUENTIN BLAKE, ZANDRA RHODES Toy Symphony (Leopold Mozart) Variations on a Nursery Song (Dohnanyi) The Carnival of the Animals (Saint-Saens) Revolting Rhymes – *First performance* (Paul Patterson)

28 November MARISS JANSONS: STEPHEN KOVACEVICH Overture, Oberon (Weber) Piano Concerto No 24 (Mozart) Ein Heldenleben (Strauss)

3 December BERNARD HAITINK: VICTORIA MULLOVA Violin Concerto 2, Concerto for Orchestra (Bartok)

7/8 December BERNARD HAITINK Symphony 39 (Mozart) Symphony 1 (Mahler)

14, 15 December FRANZ WELSER-MÖST: FELICITY LOTT, BERNADA FINK, FIONA JAMES, JOHN MARK AINSLEY Messiah (Handel)

26, 28 January FRANZ WELSER-MÖST: GITTI PIRNER Symphony 3 (Schubert) Burlesque (Strauss) Overture The Merry Wives of Windsor (Nicolai) Florentine March, Danube Legends Waltz (Fucik) Overture, Poet and Peasant (Suppe) Waltz, Artists Life, Overture, Die Fledermaus (Johann Strauss)

2 February FRANZ WELSER-MÖST: LYNNE DAWSON, WILLIAM KENDALL, SIMON KEENLYSIDE Offertory, Intende voci; Duet, Auguste jam coelestium; Offertory, Totus in corde; Mass in G (Schubert) The Firebird – complete (Stravinsky)

9, 11 February ROGER NORRINGTON: FELICITY LOTT, ANTHONY ROLF JOHNSON, JOHN TOMLINSON The Creation (Haydn)

16, 17 February ZUBIN MEHTA: ANDRAS SCHIFF Overture, Beatrice and Benedict (Berlioz) Piano Concerto 2 (Bartok) Symphonie Fantastique (Berlioz)

21 February ZUBIN MEHTA: MIDORI Overture, Le Carnaval Romain (Berlioz) Violin Concerto (Mendelssohn) Symphony 5 (Tchaikovsky)

18 March MARISS JANSONS: LIEF OVE ANDSNES Overture, The Italian Girl in Algiers (Rossini) Piano Concerto 3 (Rachmaninov) Symphony 9 (Dvorak)

21 March MARISS JANSONS: JARD VAN NES Verklarte Nacht (Schoenberg) Six Poems of Marina Tsvetayeva (Shostakovitch) Also Sprach Zarathustra (Strauss)

30 March FRANZ WELSER-MÖST: HILDEGARD BEHRENS Quartet 14 – Death and the Maiden (Schubert arr Mahler) Prelude and Liebestod from Tristan and Isolde (Wagner) Closing scene from Salome (Strauss)

6 April GENNADI ROZHDESTVENSKY: LYDIA MORDKOVITCH Horace victorieux (Honegger) Violin Concerto 1 (Shostakovitch) Scheherazade (Rimsky-Korsakov)

15 April FRANZ WELSER-MÖST: SERGEJ STADLER Violin Concerto (Schwertsik) Symphony 9 (Mahler)

20, 21 April FRANZ WELSER-MÖST: ANNE-SOPHIE MUTTER Spring Music (Nicholas Maw) Grand Duo (Schubert-Joachim) Violin Concerto (Sibelius)

27 April FRANZ WELSER-MÖST: H.K.GRUBER, DORIS SOFFEL, THOMAS SUNNEGÅRDH Frankenstein!! (H K Gruber) Das Lied von der Erde (Mahler)

6 May SIAN EDWARDS: EVELYN GLENNIE, CHRISTINA ORTIZ Suite 1, Wiener Chronik – Mazurka and Polka; Tree Songs – *first UK performance* (Schwertsik) Capriccio for Piano and Orchestra (Stravinsky) Waltz, Tales from the Vienna Woods (Johann Strauss) Rough Music (H K Gruber)

14, 15 May KLAUS TENNSTEDT Symphony 7 (Mahler)

19 May JACOV KREIZBERG: LUCY JEAL Romeo and Juliet, Violin Concerto, Symphony 4 (Tchaikovsky)
25/26 May BERNARD HAITINK: THE BORODIN STRING QUARTET Quartet 14 – Death and the Maiden, Symphony 9 (Schubert)
6 June FRANZ WELSER-MÖST: JUDITH HOWARTH, CHRISTINE CAIRNS, JOHN MARK AINSLEY, KURT AZESBURGER, MICHAEL GEORGE Symphony 1 (Shostakovitch) Mass in E flat (Schubert)

BIBLIOGRAPHY

Arts Council, *The Hoffman Report*, 1994
Arts Council, *Review of National Orchestra Provision*, London, 1994
Bensom, Tom and Parker, Maurice, *Sir Thomas Beecham: A Concert Calendar*, privately published
Boult, Sir Adrian, *My Own Trumpet*, London, 1973
Boult, Sir Adrian, *Boult on Music*, London, 1981
Cardus, Neville, *Sir Thomas Beecham*, London, 1961
Conway, Helen, *Sir John Pritchard*, London, 1993
Cox, David, *The Henry Wood Proms*, London, 1980
Elkin, Robert, *Queen's Hall*, London, 1944
Elkin, Robert, *Royal Philharmonic*, London, 1946
Erlich, Cyril, *First Philharmonic*, Oxford, 1995
Foss, Hubert and Goodwin, Noel, *London Symphony*, London, 1954
Geissmar, Dr Bertha, *The Baton and the Jackboot*, London, 1944
Gilbert, Martin, *The Second World War*, London, 1989
Hart, Philip, *Fritz Reiner*, Evanston, USA, 1994
Hill, Ralph (ed.), *Penguin Music Magazine*, London
Hill, Ralph (ed.), *Music 1950*, London 1951
Hill, Ralph (ed.), *Music 1951*, London, 1952
Jacobs, Arthur, *Henry J Wood: Maker of the Proms*, London, 1994
Kennedy, Michael, *The Hallé Tradition*, Manchester, 1960
Kennedy, Michael, *Sir Adrian Boult*, London, 1987
Kenyon, Nicholas, *The BBC Symphony Orchestra*, London, 1981
London Philharmonic Orchestra, *Yearbooks*
London Philharmonic Orchestra concert programmes
London Philharmonic Society, *Newsletters*
Middleton, Dorothy, *The Courtauld-Sargent Concerts*, privately published
Mundy, Simon, *Bernard Haitink*, London, 1987
Pearton, Maurice, *The LSO at 70*, London, 1974
Pettit, Stephen, *Philharmonia Orchestra*, London, 1985
Philharmonic Post, London, 1940–55

Railton, Ruth, *Daring to Excel*, London, 1992
Reid, Charles, *Sir Thomas Beecham*, London, 1962
Reid, Charles, *Sir Malcolm Sargent*, London, 1968
Reid, Charles, *Sir John Barbirolli,* London, 1971
Rosen, Carole, *The Goossens: A Musical Century*, London, 1993
Russell, Thomas, *Philharmonic*, London, 1942
Russell, Thomas, *Philharmonic Decade*, London, 1944
Russell, Thomas, *Philharmonic Project*, London, 1952
Sachs, Harvey, *Toscanini*, Philadelphia, USA, 1978
Shore, Bernard, *The Orchestra Speaks*, London, 1938
Sinclair, Andrew, *Arts and Cultures*, London, 1995
Stuart, Philip, *The London Philharmonic Orchestra – A Discography*, London, 1997
Wallace, Ian, *Promise Me You'll Sing Mud*, London, 1975
Wallace, Ian, *Nothing Quite Like It*, London, 1982
Wisden Cricketers' Almanack, London, 1941
Wisden Cricketers' Almanack, London, 1947
Wright, Donald (ed.), *Cardus on Music: A Centenary Collection*, London, 1988

INDEX

Adelphi Theatre, 55
Adeney, Richard, 49
Addison, Richard, 166
Aeolian Hall, 20
Albermarle, Countess of, 16
Albert Hall, Manchester, 56
Alexander, Mr A.V., 30
Alexandra, John, 6, 10, 25
Alexashin, Sergei, 234
Alexeev, Dmitri, 210
Allen, Peter, 131
Allen Thomas, 231
Alwyn, William, 148
Amis, John, 27, 47
Amy, Gilbert, 166
Ančerl, Karel, 136
Andrews, Bernard, 17
Andry, Peter, 154
Angeles, Victoria de los, 130
Anglo-French Festival (1940), 32–33
Ansermet, Ernest, 62, 68, 73, 77
Aprahmaian, Felix, 27, 42, 59, 61, 69
Argo Records, 154
Arnell, Richard, 102
Arnold, Malcolm, 49, 103
Arts Council, 69, 73, 75, 88, 115, 117–120, 122, 129, 145, 154–155, 157, 182, 187, 191, 195–197, 199, 201, 202, 205, 207, 208, 212, 216–219, 223, 224, 226, 227, 229
Arts Council/BBC Study of Orchestral Resources, 217, 224, 229
Ashkenazy, Vladimir, 145, 156, 175, 189, 219
Austin, Richard, 57
Australian Broadcasting Commission, 21, 30

Avery Fisher Hall, 209
Avison, John, 124

Bacardi Rum, 185
Bach Choir, 95, 143
Backhaus, Wilhelm, 123
Bagenal, Hope, 45
Baker, Janet, 141, 158, 181
Ballets Russe de Monte Carlo, (The Russian Ballet), 10, 15, 20, 21, 234
Barbican Centre, 183, 189, 190, 199, 204, 206, 220, 223, 230
Barbirolli, Sir John, 24, 30, 37, 47–48, 56–57, 65, 68, 86, 91, 114, 140
Barenboim, Daniel, 122, 146, 148, 149, 151, 153–154, 156, 158, 160, 162, 172, 175
Barlow, Stephen, 182
Bartoli, Cecilia, 231
Basil, Colonel de, 10
Battle for Music, 50
Battle, Kathleen, 210
Baudo, Serge, 193
Baylis, Donald, 3
Bean, T.E. (Ernest), 65, 87, 99, 125, 128
Beard, Paul, 10, 11, 15–17, 132
Beecham, Sir Thomas, 3–7, 9, 11, 14–22, 24, 27–32, 57–65, 68, 91, 94, 95, 102, 128, 177, 206, 210, 219, 235–236
Beecham Sunday Concerts, 10, 14, 42, 45
Beecham Symphony Orchestra, 3
Beer, Sydney, 26, 28, 54, 118
Beinum, Eduard van, 68, 73, 77–82, 84–91, 94, 101, 104, 110, 114, 116, 130, 167, 179, 236
Bell, Harriet, 208
Belle Vue Arena, Manchester, 56
Benjamin, George, 201

257

Bennett, Arnold, 15
Berglund, Paavo, 232
Berlin Philharmonic Orchestra, 17, 18, 64, 79, 149, 165, 219, 227, 236
Bernerd, Elliott, 188, 204, 210
Bernius, Frieder, 233
Bernet, Dietfried, 128
Bernstein, Leonard, 68
Benzi, Roberto, 128
Bevin, Ernest, 69
Biggs, E. Power, 116
Birtwistle, Sir Harrison, 215
Blech, Harry, 101
Blitz Tour, 37–39, 40, 59
Bloch, Ernest, 84–85
Blom, Eric, 77
Böhm, Karl, 190, 222
Bonnavia, Ferruccio, 37
Bonynge, Richard, 139
Boosey, William, 2
Boosey and Hawkes, 55, 87
Borsdorf, Adolph, 109
Boston Pops Orchestra, 55
Boston Symphony Orchestra, 89, 124, 163
Bottomley, Virginia, 228
Boult, Sir Adrian, 4–5, 20, 28, 30, 32–34, 39, 41, 46, 48, 50, 52, 57–59, 68, 72, 76, 84, 86, 88, 89, 91–94, 96, 97, 101, 102–104, 107–108, 111, 113–116, 119, 121, 122, 126, 128, 130, 131, 136, 139–143, 145, 146, 149, 153–154, 164, 166, 167, 176–177, 179, 181
Bournemouth Municipal and Symphony Orchestras, 1, 114, 96, 117
Boyle, Michael, 234
Boys, Councillor Walter, 98
Bradley, Francis, 10, 24, 25
Bradley, Richard, 145
Bradshaw, James, 10
Braithwaite, Warwick, 50, 57
Bravington, 106–109, 119, 122, 132, 150–155, 157, 161–164, 168–170, 172, 174, 175, 187, 236
Brendel, Alfred, 160
Bridgwater Hall, Manchester, 230
British Broadcasting Corporation (BBC), 2–4, 7, 10, 23, 49, 52, 70–71, 76, 78, 87, 91–92, 94, 95, 103, 114, 141, 171, 223
BBC Choral Society, 143
BBC National Orchestra of Wales, 172
BBC Northern Orchestra, 56, 172

BBC Salon Orchestra, 23, 24, 26, 49
BBC Scottish Symphony Orchestra, 171, 172
BBC Symphony Chorus, 182
BBC Symphony Orchestra, 4, 5, 11, 15, 20, 23, 47–49, 52, 55–59, 70, 71, 76, 86, 89, 91, 94, 99, 101, 102, 132, 138, 197, 217
BBC Welsh Orchestra, 104
British Council, 61, 115, 144, 147, 165
British Film Institute, 50
British National Opera Company, 25
British Rail, 160
British Transport Hotels, 160
Britten, Benjamin, 61, 63, 101, 102,
Brussels Philharmonic Society, 17
Buckingham Palace, 225
Buffalo Philharmonic Orchestra, 120
Burgos, Rafael Fruhbeck de, 130, 135
Burrows, Vincent, 59
Busch, Fritz, 14
Busch, Nicholas, 148, 159, 170, 186
Bychkov, Szymon, 193

Calder, Ronald, 220,
Cambridge Theatre, 47
Cameron, Alexander, 159
Cameron, Basil, 21, 28, 30, 32–34, 36, 39, 46, 48, 50, 53, 55, 57, 58, 62, 64, 67, 68, 76, 80, 88, 92, 94, 111, 116, 121, 123, 140
Campoli, Alfredo, 115
Cantelli, Guido, 66, 116
Canterbury Cathedral, 141
Cardus, Neville, 9, 11, 65, 86, 120
Carl Rosa Opera Company, 47
Carner, Mosco, 57, 101
Carnegie Hall, 145, 146, 209
Carnegie Trust, 51
Carpenter, James, 199
Carvalho, Santiago Sabino, 148
Catterall, Arthur, 48, 127
Casadesus, Robert, 123
Casals, Pablo, 128
CBS Records, 153
Ceccato, Aldo, 154
Celibidache, Sergiu, 68, 77, 79
Central Hall, Bristol, 52
Central Hall, Westminster, 2, 28, 51, 113
Chailly, Riccardo, 171, 173, 175, 182
Chandos Records, 194
Channing, Simon, 213, 220
Chappells, 2

258

Charles Barker Group, 175
Charles Russell and Company, 165
Cheltenham Festival, 62, 72, 73, 103
Cherkassky, Shura, 122, 145, 210
Chicago Symphony Orchestra, 147, 168, 170, 203
Choristers of The Abbey Church of St Albans, 209
Christie, Sir George, 220, 231
Christie, John (and Audrey) 8, 127, 182
Christie's Salerooms, 176
Christoff, Boris, 174, 186
Church Concerts, 110–112, 115, 118, 130
Churchill, Sir Winston, 30
City of Birmingham Symphony Orchestra, 2, 10, 24, 115, 117, 123
Clark, Edward, 33
Clark, Sir Kenneth, 107
Classics for Pleasure Concerts (see also Industrial Concerts), 111, 158, 161, 175, 186–190, 198, 202, 210, 211, 215, 220, 223,
Classics for Pleasure Records, 136, 153, 181
Cload, John, 145
Clothier, Michael, 161
Coates, Albert, 30, 62, 68
Cockerill, Winifred, 40
Cody, Maurice ('Bill'), 69, 80, 106
Cody, Rosalie, 156, 173, 192
Cohen, Louis, 68
Collins, Anthony, 6
Colston Hall, Bristol, 52
Columbia Record Company, 4
Commercial Union, 160, 161, 176, 187
Concertgebouw Orchestra, 13, 69, 73, 78, 80, 87, 138, 152, 153, 162, 171
Congress Theatre, Eastbourne, 135, 231
Conlon, James, 172, 175, 182, 184, 186
Cooper, Andrew, 67, 78, 104
Cooper, Joseph, 179
Corporation of London, 217, 223
Coulling, John, 119, 124,
Council for Music, Education and the Arts (CEMA), 51, 55
Courage Limited, 158, 175
Courtauld, Samuel, 12, 13, 14, 19, 28, 39
Courtauld, Mrs Samuel, 12, 13, 14
Courtauld-~Sargent Concerts, 6, 10, 12–14, 20, 28, 29, 39, 66
Cozens, John, 10

Crabtree, Stephen, 169, 170, 177, 185, 187, 236
Creed, Neville, 233
Cruft, John, 118
Cross, Joan, 55
Croydon Philharmonic Choir, 143
Cumberland, Alan, 148, 156, 185
Cundell, Edric, 39, 57, 62
Curzon, Clifford, 33, 175

Damrosch, Walter, 2
Dankworth, Johnny, and Orchestra, 130, 136
Dannett, George, 69
Datyner, Henry, 78, 119, 124, 131
Davies, Sir Peter Maxwell, 218
Davies, Sir Walford, 20
Davis, Andrew, 158, 162, 172, 194, 202, 210, 213, 221
Davis, Carl, 190, 235
Davis, Sir Colin, 111, 124, 130, 135, 138, 158, 219
Davis Theatre, Croydon, 28
Davison, Arthur, 119, 131, 158
Decca Records, 62, 92, 105, 112, 116, 125, 153, 232
Del Mar, Norman, 102, 116, 128
Dell, Sydney, 39
Departmnt of the Environment, 157
Derby Philharmonic Orchestra, 127
Derby String Orchestra, 127
Desderi, Claudio, 182
Désormière, Roger, 61, 68
Dillon, Maire, 208,
Dobson, Michael, 49
Dohnányi, Christoph von, 130, 139, 208
Dorati, Antal, 15, 135, 136, 139, 142
Dorny, Serge, 226, 231, 232, 235
Douglas, Keith, 42, 45, 48, 65
Douglas-Home, Sir Alec, 149
Downes, Geoff, 166
Downes, Edward, 145
Dresden State Orchestra, 11, 163
HRH The Duke of Kent, 186, 211, 225, 234
Dukes' Hall, Royal Academy of Music, 44
Dupré, Marcel, 68
Dutoit, Charles, 208

Eckersley, Roger, 3
Edinburgh Festival, 102, 134, 146, 148, 157, 159, 160, 162, 165, 189, 214
Elder, Mark, 233, 236

Elgar Society, 181
Electrical and Musical Industries (EMI), 62, 65, 66, 92, 105, 125, 128, 136, 153, 154, 158, 164, 194, 206, 209
Emerson Quartet, 212
Empire, Leicester Square, 191
Enesco, Georges, 77
English National Ballet, 205
Erlanger, Baron Frederick d', 12
Eschenbach, Christoph, 145, 172, 175, 182, 186, 189, 236
Esher, Rt Hon, The Viscount 12
Evans, Edwin, 15
Everest (Record Company), 105, 116

Fairfield Hall, Croydon, 129, 130, 141, 158
Family Concerts, 215
Ferencsik, János, 123
Ferrier, Kathleen, 89, 92, 105
Festival of Britain (1951), 100, 112
Fiedler, Arthur, 128
Fielding, Harold, 27
Figgures, Sir Frank, 164
Finsbury Park Empire, 45
Finsbury Park Open-Air Concerts, 71, 72, 95, 96, 111
Fischer, Annie, 122, 123
Fischer, Ivan, 213
Fischer-Dieskau, Dietrich, 158,
Fistoulari, Anatole, 15, 57, 58, 114, 115, 116
Fitelberg, Gregor, 68
Flesch, Carl, 25, 26
Flagstad, Kirsten, 75
Fleischamnn, Ernest, 226, 230
Fletcher, Elizabeth, 148
Ford Motor Company, 231
Foss, Hubert, 7
Fournier, Pierre, 68
Francescatti, Zino, 122
Freccia, Massimo, 116, 118, 128
Free Trade Hall, Manchester, 56
Fricsay, Ferenc, 126
Friend, Rodney, 131, 136, 145, 159, 160
'From Bach to Bartok', 113, 120
Furtwangler, Wilhelm, 3, 12, 17, 65, 66, 76, 77, 88, 116, 221, 236

Galliera, Alceo, 90, 116
Galway, James, 175
Garvin, Edward, 10
Gaubert, Phillipe, 33

Gavrilov, Andrei, 186
Gee, Leon, 213,
Gendron, Maurice, 68
Geissmar, Dr Berta, 12, 17–19, 21, 26, 27, 34, 37, 42, 44, 75, 84
Gergiev, Valery, 236
Ghandi, Mrs Indira, 128
Gielen, Michael, 215
Gilbert, Geoffrey, 17, 49
Glasspool, Wrayburn, 210
Glock, William, 125, 140, 202
Glover, Jane, 182 , 213
Glyndebourne Festival Opera, 8, 66, 127, 130, 132–134, 136, 140, 142, 149, 152–154, 156, 160–162, 166, 167, 182, 188, 200, 205, 210, 213, 220–221, 224, 231, 233
Goddard, Scott, 87
Godfrey, Sir Dan, 1–2
Goehr, Walter, 55, 57
Godlee, Philip, 65
Goodall, Reginald, 57
Goodman, Lord, 129, 146
Goodwin, Noel, 7
Goossens, Eugene, 11, 15,
Goossens, Leon, 10, 11, 23, 26, 127
Goossens, Marie, 10
Gowrie, Lord, 227
Graham, Susan, 231
Gramophone Company, 6, 10
'Grande Tour de la Musique', 121
Gray, Stephen, 119
Great Packington Church, 116
Greater London Council (GLC), 155, 157, 183, 195, 196
Greenfield, Edward, 148
Gregory, Charles, 24, 25, 30, 36, 39, 44, 57, 65, 67, 74, 75, 185, 236
Greyhound Buses, 185
Grierson, Ronald, 195, 196, 203, 204
Groves, Sir Charles, 111, 139, 154, 171, 193
Grumiaux, Arthur, 175
Gui, Vittorio, 133
Guilini, Carlo Maria, 146, 148, 154, 157–160, 165, 172, 173, 219

Haarlem Symphony Orchestra, 80
Hackney Youth Orchestra, 233
Haebler, Ingrid, 145
Haendel, Ida, 54, 149–150
Hadley, Patrick, 102

260

Haitink, Bernard, 128, 135–139, 142–149, 151–163, 166–167, 171, 172, 175, 179, 182, 186, 190, 191, 193, 194, 202, 208, 211, 215, 219, 221, 225, 233, 235, 236
Hallé, Sir Charles, 2
Hallé Orchestra (and Hallé Concert Society), 2, 3, 20, 21, 24, 26, 30, 39, 48, 51, 52, 56–57, 65–67, 70, 75, 86, 88, 96, 99, 103, 114, 117, 160, 201, 215
Hallgarten, House of, 175
Halstead, Horace, 26
Hambourg, Charles 32, 39, 54
Hampton Court Palace, 234
Handley, Vernon, 141, 181–182, 190, 233
Hanover Band, 225
Harris, Ronald, 148
Harrison, Julius, 14
Harty, Sir Hamilton, 2, 3, 29
Hawkes, William, 26
Haynes, Victor, 74
Hayward, Isaac, 97–99
Heger, Robert, 14
Henderson, Roy, 127
Henriot, Nicole, 61
Henry Wood Hall, 157, 170, 178
Henry Wood National Memorial Trust, 157
Henry Wood Promenade Concerts (The Proms), 2, 4, 13, 20, 23, 27, 28, 37, 39, 45, 48, 53, 58, 59, 70–71, , 76–78, 84, 91, 92, 100, 103, 114, 132, 139, 149, 159, 162, 180, 190, 206, 210, 214, 229
Herrod Atticus Open-Air Theatre, Athens, 213
Hess, Dame Myra, 27, 54, 110
Hess, Willy, 67, 78
Heward, Leslie, 14, 24, 39, 46, 88, 179
Hill, Ralph, 70, 71, 82
Hill, Robert, 148, 159
Hindemith, Paul, 13, 121
Hitler, Adolf, 18
His Master's Voice (HMV), 92
Hoffmann Committee, 218–220, 224, 235
Hoffmann, Judge Leonard, 218
Hoffnung, Gerard, 101
Holland, Francis, 97
Holland Gardens, Open-Air Concerts, 114
Hollreiser, Heinrich, 123–124
Holst, Henry, 46, 78
Holt, Harold, 6, 7, 14, 42, 44–46, 54–56, 119, 121–123, 126, 201
Hong Kong City Hall, 128

Hopkinson, Leonard, 17
Horenstein, Jascha, 126, 128, 130, 136, 137, 139, 146, 172
Howard, Frank, 10
Howard, Leslie, 30,
Howes, Frank, 10
Hunter, Ian, 122
Hunter, Pamela, 193
Hurst, George, 114, 115, 116
Hylton, Jack, 35–40, 45, 50, 55

Ibbs and Tillett, 119, 121, 126
Iliffe, Barrie, 144
Industrial Concerts (see also Classics for Pleasure), 111–112, 114, 118, 120, 122, 123, 130, 138, 142, 145, 148, 150, 158, 160
International Series, 187, 189, 193, 198, 200, 202, 210, 220
Iturbi, José, 86

Jackson, Frederick, 76, 82, 85, 128
Jackson, Gerald, 10, 17
Jacobs, Arthur, 53
Jacques Orchestra, 25
Jacques, Dr Reginald, 20, 39
Jameson, Sue, 173
Jansons, Mariss, 211, 215, 225, 226
Järvi, Neeme, 191
Järvi, Paavo, 236
Jarvis, Gerald, 145
Jayston, Michael, 193
Jenkins, Sir Gilmour, 122
Jochum, Eugen, 142, 145, 148, 149, 153, 156, 165, 172, 175
John Higham International Artists, 190
John Player & Sons, 165
Johnson, Walter J., 198
Joyce, Eileen, 34, 38, 50

Kamu, Okko, 191
Kanawa, Kiri Te, 162
Karajan, Herbert von, 66, 85, 116, 149, 219, 222
Kell, Reginald, 10, 17
Kempe, Rudolf, 219
Kempff, Wilhelm, 145
Kennedy, Nigel, 181, 211
Kenyon, Nicholas, 180
HM King George VI, 101
Kinsman, Tommy and his Orchestra, 102

Kirstenbosch Botanical Gardens, Cape Town, 222
Kisch, Royalton, 118
Kleiber, Erich, 14, 77, 82
Klemperer, Otto, 12, 13, 76, 116, 130, 140, 154, 219, 222
Kletzki, Paul, 114, 120, 126, 135
Knight, Wally, 40
Kogan, Leonid, 122
Kondrashin, Kirill, 126, 171, 172
Konwitschny, Franz, 123
Korda, Sir Alexander, 23,
Koussevitzky, Serge, 84, 90
Kovacevich, Stephen, 211
Kreisler, Fritz, 21
Krips, Josef, 66, 76, 86, 90, 114, 126, 128, 142, 146, 148, 149, 151, 156, 158, 172
Krombholc, Jaroslav, 123
Kubelik, Rafael, 66, 90,
Kubik, Gail, 110
Kuchmy, John, 50
Kuhn, Gustav, 173, 182
Kurtz, Efrem, 15, 127
Kyung-Wha Chung, 211

Lambert, Constant, 30, 50
Lambert and Butler, 175
Lambeth Council 224
Lawrence, Christopher, 226
Lawrence, Majorie, 68, 75
Lazarev, Alexander, 236
Lee, Jennie, 136
Leeds Empire Theatre, 39
Leeds Festival, 16
Leeuwin Estate, West Australia, 185, 189
Legge, Walter, 62, 66, 85, 128, 129
Leinsdorf, Erich, 68, 120, 146, 149, 158, 171
Leonard, Lawrence, 111
Leppard, Raymond, 154, 173, 175, 182
Leipzig Gewandhaus Orchestra, 163
Leon, Josephine St., 214
Levesley, Neil, 159
Lewisham Borough Council, 81
Leyton-Brown, Howard, 80, 88
Lill, John 149
Linz Bruckner Festival, 206, 208, 215
Litton, Andrew, 189, 193, 201
Liverpool Corporation, 23
Lloyd Webber, Julian, 174
Lloyds Bank, 175, 191

Lockier, Charles, 52
London Adventist Choir, 235
London Cello School, 44
London Coliseum, 28, 37, 45, 50, 61–62
London County Council (LCC), 51, 69, 73, 75, 77, 78, 81, 87–89, 94–99, 103, 108, 109–111, 117, 120, 122
London Festival Ballet, 114, 118, 130, 133, 164
London Mozart Players, 101
London Orchestral Concerts Board, 129, 148, 164, 195
London Philharmonic Arts Club, 47, 59
London Philharmonic Choir, 76, 117, 140, 141, 143, 146, 182, 193, 233, 234
London Philharmonic Concert Society Limited, 19
London Philharmonic Orchestra Limited, 74, 98
London Philharmonic Trust, and Trustees, 188, 204, 210, 220
LPO Council, 78–79, 107, 135, 188
LPO National Appeal Fund, 149
London Philharmonic Society, 122, 126, 130, 131, 134–135, 141, 157, 158
London Philharmonic Society (USA) Inc, 144, 147
London Philharmonic Youth Orchestra, 212, 231, 233, 234
London Regional Civil Defence Force Choir, 55
London Sinfonietta, 197
London Symphony Orchestra (LSO), 1, 3, 5–8, 11–14, 16, 24, 25, 27, 30, 42–44, 47, 52, 56–58, 61, 66, 70, 71, 75, 76, 78, 86, 94, 95, 101, 114, 131, 138, 143, 153, 154, 157, 164, 182, 183, 199, 203, 206, 217, 220, 224
London Voices, 191, 234
Long, Marguerite, 33
López-Cobos, Jesús, 172–176, 182, 186, 190
Los Angeles Philharmonic Orchestra, 226
Lott, Dame Felicity, 221
Lord, Roger, 80
Loss, Joe, 35
Loughran, James, 193, 201
Lovett, Samuel, 108, 119
Lucerne Festival, 210
Lupu, Radu, 175, 211
Lympany, Moura, 44, 54
Lyons, Sir Jack, 157

Lyrita Recorded Edition, 140, 148, 153

Maag, Peter, 176
Maazel, Lorin, 146, 154,
McArthur, Margaret, 55
McCallum, David, 16, 25, 26, 119
McCaw, John, 131
McDonagh, Terence, 49
McDonald, Gerald, 132, 154
McNichol, Richard, 176
Mackerras, Sir Charles, 162
Magee, Brian, 219
Magnani, Fausto, 32
Maguire, Hugh, 123,
Mahler, Anna, 57
Maksymiuk, Jerzy, 193
Malay Broadcasting Company, 49
Malcolm, George, 128
Malko, Nicolai, 79, 84–86, 88, 90
Malvern Festival, 92
Mandela, Nelson, 213
Marcou, David, 183, 186, 204, 213
Marks and Spencer, 158, 175
Mars Limited, 176
Martinon, Jean, 68, 77, 79, 83–86, 88, 94, 113, 116
Masur, Kurt, 193, 197, 198, 201, 206, 208, 210
Matthews, Thomas, 26, 38, 40, 49, 54, 67
Maxted, George, 108
Mayer, Sir Robert, 12, 19, 28, 39
McDonald's, 176
Mehta, Zubin, 154, 197, 206, 210, 211, 225
Mengelberg, Willem, 5, 11–13, 80, 167, 221
Menges, Herbert, 33, 113
Menuhin, Hephzibah, 122
Menuhin, Yehudi, 122, 123, 126, 130, 141–143
Metropolitan Opera House, New York, 68
Michael, Hermann, 128
Michie, Brian, 35
Miles, Maurice, 44, 111
Miller, Keith, 213
Miller International, 125
Mineapolis Orchestra, 67, 104
Mitropoulos, Dmitri, 78
Moiseiwitsch, Benno, 50, 54
Monteux, Pierre, 11, 126, 140, 179, 222
Moore, Alfred ('Tony'), 105, 106
Moore, Jerrold Northrop, 175
Morley, Reginald, 25, 49

Morley College Choir, 55
Morrison, Herbert, 69
Mozart Choir of Linz, 209
Mullova, Victoria, 211
Munich State Opera, 93
Münch, Charles, 61, 63, 68, 88, 126
'Music of a Century', 120, 121
'Music of the Twentieth Century', 122, 125
Musical Culture Limited, 26, 74,
Musical Manifesto, The, 34–36, 50, 62
Musicians Benevolent Fund, 138
Musicians Union, 52, 70, 86, 132, 157, 171, 220
Muti, Riccardo, 194
Mutter, Anne-Sophie, 175, 177, 212
Myun-Whun Chung, 201 221

Nagano, Kent, 198, 208,
National Association of Symphony Orchestras, 52
National Gallery, 21, 27, 42
National Lottery, 226, 228
National Philharmonic Orchestra, 54
National Theatre, 162
National Westminster Bank, 189, 202, 210, 220
National Youth Orchestra, 131
Neate, Kenneth, 81
Nehru, Jawaharlal, 128
Nettlefold, Mr F.J., 14, 28
New Era Concert Society, 87
New London Orchestra, 47
New Opera Chorus, 139
New Victoria Theatre, 130
New York Symphony Orchestra, 3
New York Philharmonic Orchestra, 30, 103, 160, 206, 236
Newman, Ernest, 9, 15, 189
Newman, Robert, 1
Newstone, Harry, 111, 123
Nikish, Artur, 221
Nixa Record Company, 112
Noble, John, 146
Nolan, David, 160, 177, 210
Norman, Jessye, 174
Norrington, Sir Roger, 197, 213, 215, 223, 225, 232
Norrköping Orchestra, 208, 210,
Norwich Festival, 16
Nottingham Music Club, 52

O'Dea, Thomas, 107–109, 117
Ogden, John, 136
Oistrakh, David, 148
Orchard Hall, Osaka, 209,
Orchestra of the Age of the Enlightenment, 201, 221, 231
Orchestra of Austrian Radio, 229
Orchestra of La Scala Milan, 32
Orchestral Employers Association, 86
Orchestre de Paris, 147
Ormandy, Eugene, 67
Orpheum Theatre, Golders Green, 46–47
Ostrowski, Avi, 185
Ousset, Cecile, 210

Palace des Beaux Arts, Brussels, 63
Palace Theatre, Manchester, 38
Palestine Symphony Orchestra, 120
Paray, Paul, 61
Pears, Peter, 55, 68
Parfitt, Harold, 119
Paris Conservatoire Orchestra, 63, 69, 73
Parker, Ted, 147
Peacock, Sir Alan, 145
Pears, Peter, 141
Pearton, Maurice, 7, 53
People's Palace, Mile End Road, 82
Pepper, Maurice, 108
Pešek, Libor, 221
Petain, Marshal, 33
Philharmonia Chorus, 129
Philharmonia Orchestra (and New Philharmonia), 62, 63, 66, 85, 87, 88, 91, 94, 99, 119, 125, 128–129, 131, 141, 146, 154–155, 157, 165, 166, 176, 183, 196–197, 199, 203, 204, 218–220, 223, 230
Philharmonic Choir, 76
Philharmonic Post, 28, 29, 35, 39, 54, 58, 71, 77, 80, 92, 93, 109
Phillips, Margot, 108
Philips Electrical, 153, 154, 158, 160
Pilgrim Trust, 27, 157
Pini, Anthony, 10, 11, 23
Pioneer High Fidelity, 175
Pitt, Percy, 3, 4
Pittsburg Symphony Orchestra, 119, 226
Player, John, 176
Pomeroy, Jay, 47
Pollini Maurizio, 175
Ponsonby, Robert, 202

Pope, Stanley, 94
Pougnet, Jean, 49–50, 67
Poulenc, Francis, 61
Pouishnoff, Lev, 54, 56
Powell, Lionel, 4, 5, 6, 7
Pretoria Arts Centre Trust (PACT), 213
Previn, André, 138, 153, 164, 171, 174
Priestley, J.B., 34, 50, 62, 78, 88, 98
Priestley, Brian, 139, 146
HRH Princess Anne, 189
HRH Princess Alexandra, 147, 234
Pritchard, John, 123, 127–132, 134, 135, 143–144, 146, 149–150, 152, 158, 166, 175, 179
Prudential Insurance Company, 201, 207

Queen Elizabeth Hall, 212, 215, 223, 224, 232, 233
Queen's Hall, 2, 4, 9, 13, 20, 26–28, 32, 34, 38, 40, 42–46, 50, 51, 62, 63, 83, 90, 175
Queen's Hall Orchestra, 1, 2, 25
Quinn, Andrea, 213, 233

Radio Luxemburg, 20
Raj Bhavan Open Air Theatre, Bombay, 128
Rankl, Karl, 68, 75
Rattle, Simon, 164, 189, 190, 194, 200, 207, 208
Rawson, Irmeli, 159
Raybould, Clarence, 101
Rees, C.B., 69
Reeves, Wynn, 21, 37, 67
Regal Cinema, Edmonton, 130
Reiner, Fritz, 113
Reith, Sir John, 3, 5
Repin, Vadim, 235
Ricci, Ruggiero, 123
Richter, Hans, 221
Richter, Karl, 158
Rickelman, Boris, 63
Ribbontrop, Joachim von, 18
Riddle, Frederick, 23, 106, 108, 109
Rignold, Hugo, 123–124
Ripley Choir, Bromley, 143
Ritterman, Dr Janet, 224
Rizzi, Carlo, 207
Rix, Sir Bernard Q.C., 199
Robert Mayer Children's Concerts, 10, 12, 14, 21
Robertson, James, 68
Robinson, Eric, 102

Robinson, Stanford, 76
Rodzinski, Artur, 206
Roll, Michael, 149
Ronald, Sir Landon, 3, 7
Rosenfeld, Ben, 170
Rosenfeld, Mrs Jackie, 170, 198
Rostal, Max, 25
Rostrapovitch, Mrsislav, 159, 160, 171, 172, 174, 175, 182
Royal Albert Hall, 4,12, 21, 45, 51, 55, 58, 60, 61, 63, 69, 73, 74, 76, 77, 79, 81–83, 85, 86, 89, 90, 92, 94, 95, 100, 101, 111, 112, 116, 118, 120, 123, 129, 130, 142, 186, 187, 207, 230, 233
Royal Albert Hall Orchestra 1, 7
Royal Ballet, 123
Royal Choral Society, 10, 14, 20, 43, 44, 54, 66, 73, 130
Royal College of Music, 6
Royal Festival Hall, 94–95, 99–101, 103, 104, 110–112, 116, 115, 118, 128–130, 133, 136, 138, 141, 142, 148, 156–158, 160–162, 164, 170, 176, 178, 180, 183, 186, 189–194, 200–202, 206–208, 213, 223, 224
Royal Liverpool Philharmonic Orchestra, 21, 23–24, 26, 49, 51, 52, 56, 67, 75, 78, 114, 117, 119, 123, 127, 160, 229
Royal Opera House Covent Garden 2, 10, 15, 17, 25, 34, 35, 62, 66, 73–75, 77, 79, 120, 127, 133, 167, 234
Royal Opera House Covent Garden, Orchestra of, 1, 104, 177
Royal Philharmonic Orchestra (RPO), 7, 65, 66, 87, 88, 91, 94, 102, 109, 128, 129, 132, 199, 203, 218–219, 223, 230
Royal Philharmonic Society, 1, 3–7, 9–11, 20, 21, 29, 39, 42, 44–46, 53, 54, 56, 64–66, 76, 87, 95, 122, 158, 161, 173, 174
Rozdestvensky, Gennadi, 202, 225
Rubinstein, Artur, 113, 123, 145, 149
Rugby School, 28
Russell, Dr Leslie, 78
Russell, Thomas, 18, 25, 27, 29, 32, 34–36, 39–42, 46, 50, 51, 57–59, 61, 65, 67, 71, 72, 75, 77, 78, 80, 91, 97–98, 100, 105–109, 150, 175, 185, 227, 236
Rycroft, Frank, 166

Sabata, Victor de, 68, 69, 71, 73, 76, 77, 83, 101, 116, 210, 236

Sachs, Harvey, 101
Sadlers Wells Opera (and Orchestra), 27, 104
Santa Cecilia Academy, Rome, 191
Salzburg Festival, 214
Sammons, Albert, 26
Sanderling, Kurt, 149, 172, 191, 194, 202
Sargent, Sir Malcolm, 6, 7, 10, 13, 14, 21, 24, 28–30, 32–34, 36, 38–40, 50, 57, 58, 66, 68, 72, 73, 88, 91, 94, 95, 101, 114, 123, 128, 130, 139
Sawallisch, Wolfgang, 116, 225
Scherchenn, Hermann, 120
Schmidt-Isserstedt, Hans, 114, 126, 146
Schoenberg, Harold, 55
Schuricht, Carl, 14, 77
Schmidt, Hans Ulrich, Konzertdirektion, 232
Scott, Charles Kennedy, 76
Scottish Chamber Orchestra, 234
Scottish National Orchestra, 2, 16, 24, 25, 52, 160
Schwartz, Rudolf, 90, 115
Scrowaczewski, Stanislav, 215
Seaman, Christopher, 131, 148
Segovia, 121
Sekers, Sir Nicholas, 135
Semkow, Jerzy, 142, 143
Serkin, Rudolf, 123
Seymour Hall, 86
Shadwick, Joseph, 104, 119, 131
Shaftesbury, The Earl of, 135, 145, 157, 170
Sharp Geoffrey, 88
Shawe-Taylor, Desmond, 120
Sherman, Alec, 57
Sheffield Festival, 16
Shelbourne, Philip, 168
Shirley-Quirk, John, 141
Shore, Bernard, 12
Shostakovitch, Maxim, 139
Sibelius, Jean, 84
Silvester, John, 26
Silvestri, Constantin, 120, 122, 130, 136, 139
Simonev, Yuri, 198, 207
Simpson, Robert, 142
Sinopoli, Guiseppi, 191
Skeef, Eugene, 214
Slatkin, Leonard, 192, 193, 200, 208
Smeterlin, Jan, 89
Smith, Hon. James, 35, 42, 122

Society of British Musicians, 32
Solomon, 54, 79,
Solti, Sir Georg, 15, 84, 90, 93, 136, 142, 146–149, 153, 154, 157, 160–163, 168, 169, 171–174, 177, 179, 182, 186, 190, 193, 198, 203, 219, 223, 231, 232, 234–236
South Bank Board and Centre, 183, 194–197, 199, 202–206, 211, 212, 215, 219, 223, 224
Stead, Francis, 24, 25
Stern, Isaac, 122, 175
Steinbach, Fritz, 221
Steinberg, Pinchas, 232
Steinberg, William, 119–121, 123–125, 179
Stephenson, Jean, 192
Stiedry, Fritz, 14
Stockholm Chamber Orchestra, 210
Stokowski, Leopold, 206,
Stoll Theatre, 63, 64, 69, 72, 74, 79
Strang, Dora, 42
Stratton, George, 10, 16, 17
Stravinsky, Igor, 13
Streatfeild, Simon, 106, 108
Stuttgart Barokorchester, 233
Sumi Jo, 222
Susskind, Walter, 163
Sutcliffe, Sidney, 80
Sutherland, Joan, 139
Svendheden, Joakim, 210
Svetlanov, Yevgeni, 130, 135–137, 139, 149, 182, 185, 186
Swan, Judith, 159, 184
Swansea Festival, 92
Swarowsky, Hans, 116
Swedish Radio Symphony Orchestra, 210
Swensen, Joseph, 234
Sydney Symphony Orchestra, 75
Symphony Hall, Osaka, 209
Szell, George, 14, 83, 120, 146
Szeryng, Henryk, 145

Turner, Eva, 54
Tauber, Richard, 35, 42, 45, 88
Tarjus, Blanchette, 68
Tate, Jeffrey, 202
Tausky, Vilem, 47, 57
Taylor, Charles, 44
Taylor, Donald, 50
Tennstedt, Klaus, 163, 171, 173–175, 177, 179–182, 184, 185, 189–192, 194, 197, 198, 200, 201, 203, 207, 208, 210–213, 215, 219, 221, 222, 225, 236
Terfel, Bryn, 232
Termikanov, Yuri, 185
Thaxted Parish Church, 110
Thebom, Blanche, 92
Thibaud, Jacques, 61
Thompson, Bryden, 194
Three Choirs Festival, 78
Tillett, Mrs Emmie, 119, 122
Tooley, Sir John, 202
Tippett, Sir Michael, 130
Toronto Symphony Orchestra, 163
Toscanini, Arturo, 20, 25, 69, 101, 179, 206, 221
Trinity School of Music, 233
Tureck, Rosalyn, 123
Tutu, Bishop Desmond, 222
Tyrell, Warwick, 222

Unger, Dr Heinz, 47, 57
Unsworth, Rowena, 187, 192

Valencia Orchestra, 87
Van Walsum Management, 232
Vanguard Record Company, 116
Variety Club of Great Britain, 149
Vaughan Williams, Dr Ralph, 16, 46, 102, 121
Vaughan Williams, Ursula, 116
Vengerov, Maxim, 210
Vered, Ilana, 160
Vienna Easter Festival 232
Vienna Philharmonic Orchestra, 64, 229, 236
Vienna Symphony Orchestram, 229
Vienna State Opera, 127
Vishnevskaya, Galina, 159, 160
Volkov, Ilan, 234
Vonk, Hans, 193

Waart, Edo de, 149
Walden, Lord Howard de 7, 8
Walker, Major Denzil, 119
Walker, Norman, 55
Walter, Bruno, 11, 13, 14, 20, 68, 73, 77, 88, 120, 140, 166, 179
Walton, Bernard, 17, 49, 131, 148
Walton, Richard, 174
Walton, Sir William, 102
Ward, Maurice, 26, 50

Watford Borough Council, 51, 88
Watkins, David, 148
Watson, Victor, 10, 23, 26, 49, 199
Watt, Laurence, 185
Webb, Gordon, 150
Webster, William 199
Weingartner, Felix, 11, 12, 21, 29, 221, 236
Weisgall, Hugo, 57
Weldon, George, 57, 111, 116
Welford, Ronald, 189
Weller, Walter, 189
Wells, H.G., 23
Welser-Möst, Franz, 190, 192, 193, 197, 206, 207, 209–211, 213–215, 221–223, 225–226
Welsh National Opera Chorale, 191
Weltman, Mayer, 184
Wetherall, Eric, 85, 87
Wigglesworth, Mark 236
Willan, John, 187, 188, 191, 196, 203, 205, 206, 213, 226
Williams, Averil, 166
Williams, Sir William, 107, 109
Wills, H.D & H.O., 135, 136, 158
Wilson, Sir Harold, 136
Wilson, John, 106
Wilson, Marie, 132, 182
Wilson, Sir Steuart, 92, 97
Winfield, Roger, 159, 165–166
Wise, David, 78, 104, 131
Wits University String Orchestra, 222
Wolff, Hugh, 175
Wood, Sir Henry, 1, 2, 4, 16, 20, 21, 28, 29, 32, 43, 45, 46, 48, 49, 53, 58, 59, 66, 68, 77, 88, 91
World Centre for Shakespeare Studies, 162,
World Record Club, 141
Wright, Bob St.J., 186, 220, 226, 232, 234
Wyck, Wilfred van, 118

Yi-Kwei Sze, 139
Yorkshire Symphony Orchestra, 75, 96, 117
Young, Lord, 223
Young, Patricia, 60
Youth and Music, 130
Yves St Laurent, 198

Zuckerman, Pinchas, 149
Zurich Opera, 226